MW00789311

The Cinema of Max Ophuls

FILM AND CULTURE SERIES   EDITED BY JOHN BELTON

TRB·

The Cinema of Max Ophuls

Magisterial Vision
and the Figure of Woman

SUSAN M. WHITE

COLUMBIA UNIVERSITY PRESS NEW YORK

Columbia University Press
New York   Chichester, West Sussex
Copyright © 1995 Columbia University Press
All rights reserved

Library of Congress Cataloging-in-Publication Data

White, Susan M.
    The cinema of Max Ophuls : magisterial vision and the figure of
woman/Susan M. White.
        p.   cm. − (Film and culture series)
    Filmography: p.
    Includes bibliographical references.
    ISBN 0−231−10112−0 (cl) : $59.50. − ISBN 0−231−10113−9 (pa) :
$18.50
        1. Ophuls, Max, 1902−1957—Criticism and interpretation.
        2. Women in motion pictures.   I. Title.   II. Series.
PN1998.3.064W5   1994
791.43'0233'092—dc20   94−30573
⊗   CIP

Casebound editions of Columbia University Press books are printed on
permanent and durable acid-free paper.

Printed in the United States of America

c 10 9 8 7 6 5 4 3 2 1

Contents

✦

$\mathscr{A}$cknowledgments

✦

So many people contributed to the writing of this book that I despair of naming them all. If you, reader, are among the unacknowledged, consider yourself warmly thanked (or accursed, as the case may be). I am very grateful to George Wilson, my dissertation advisor at the Johns Hopkins University, whose intellectual precision and great generosity offered a model that continues to challenge me, and to the other members of my committee, Neil Hertz and Richard Macksey, who are unsurpassed and unforgettable teachers and scholars. Also crucial to my years at Hopkins were Michael Fried, Ruth Leys, Mark Crispin Miller, Jeffrey Mehlman, and Emily Evans. To my fellow graduate students, Tomoyuki Satoh, Susan Z. Bernstein, Peter Fenves, and Jeff Wallen, I owe my love and eternal solidarity for your support, both intellectual and emotional. Thanks to Gayatri C. Spivak, whose courage is an inspiration. I must express my sincere gratitude to the members of the Society for Cinema Studies Dissertation Committee, Gorham Kindem, Alan Williams, and Linda Williams, who gave the 1987 SCS Dissertation Award to the embryonic version of this book. Thanks to the National Endowment for the Humanities, which granted me a Summer Stipend in 1988 for archival work in Europe, and to the Nederlands Filmmuseum, the Cinématheque Française, and the Filmmuseum der D.D.R. for their assistance in screening hard-to-find Ophuls films. Jean-François Catton, Jacques Aumont, and Anne Faisandier provided hospitality and suggestions that greatly advanced my research. Alan Williams and Lutz Bacher shared with me their wisdom, video tapes, photo collections, and archival materials beyond the most extravagant definition of collegiality. My colleagues and friends at the University of Arizona, especially my partner-in-crime Lynda Zwinger, Tenney Nathanson, Susan Aiken, Ed Dryden, Elizabeth Evans, Chris Kiesel, Peter Lehman, Barbara Kosta, and Mary Beth Haralovich have been invaluable in their moral, mental, and material support, as were William Paul, Rafia Zafar, Ira Konigsberg, Phillip Blumberg, Claudia Vera, Bonnie Hagerty, Margaret Goebel, Luann Musser, the outstanding staff of Film Projection Services, and the students in my 1992 Ophuls and von Sternberg class at the University of Michigan. Thanks to Hopkins' Joseph Marino and UA's Chris Johnson, whose computer knowledge saved my neck. Without Hilary Radner, my most faithful comrade, my interest in film would never have become a professional one. Patricia M. Woolf has been my guiding star. One sentence won't do to thank Michael Trosset, who has acted as my editor, cheerleader, and guide to the mysteries of cinema since I came to Tucson. Lee Van Demarr also provided valuable editorial help. I am grateful to Gaylyn Studlar, who shared her work on Ophuls with me when I most needed it, and to John Belton, Mary Ann Doane, Claudia Gorbman, and Ed Branigan for their encouragement. Virginia Wright Wexman provided my first opportunity to discuss Ophuls with other scholars at the 1986 SCS. Thanks to all those at Columbia University Press, including Jennifer Crewe, Adam Tibbs, and Ivon Katz (along with Roy Thomas, who could actually read my handwriting, not to mention my prose), who very efficiently helped me through the darkest hours of impending authorship. I want to thank my family: my beloved sisters, Cindy Smith and Theresa Beatty, and their families; my parents Frank and Cheryl White, and Robert and Thelma Sudderth (my mama), who have afforded me love, refuge, food, computers, money, humor, and patience over the years. Finally, thanks to Mimi, Mrs. Hugh L. (Jessie Cox) White, my grandmother, who taught me to love movies, and to whom this book is dedicated. Je vous respecte; je vous admire; je vous aime.

The Cinema of Max Ophuls

Introduction

What is man that the itinerary of his desire

creates such a text?

— GAYATRI SPIVAK,

"DISPLACEMENT AND

THE DISCOURSE OF WOMAN"[1]

Well I was trying to say that although Derrida was, in some ways, retracing the figure of woman, that's not identical with the project of feminism. And I was really talking about "global feminism," since that seems always to be on the agenda these days when one speaks in the West. It seems to me that if one's talking about the prime task, since there is no discursive continuity among women, the prime task is situational anti-sexism, and the recognition of the heterogeneity of the field, instead of positing some kind of woman's subject, women's figure, then you should start looking elsewhere in the globe. Psychoanalysis and counterpsychoanalysis can easily become the gift of capitalist imperialism to the cause of feminism.

— GAYATRI SPIVAK,

"THE PROBLEM OF CULTURAL

SELF-REPRESENTATION"[2]

◆

Opening Remarks: Max Ophuls in the Darkroom
of Feminist Criticism

Although they had long been admired for their polished workmanship, Max Ophuls' films did not become a cause célèbre until his last film, *Lola Montès* (1955), both scandalized and delighted its Parisian spectators with its exorbitant mise-en-scène and inflated budget. The emotional baggage brought by certain critics to that final and most intense wave of activity surrounding Ophuls' oeuvre was considerable. Not atypical of the tone of Ophuls' adherents is Claude Beylie's lamentation: "What filmmaker has been more ignored, more underestimated than Max Ophuls? What paltry and stubborn ostracism has, until recently, been practiced with respect to his work? . . . As for the historians of the screen, which one (up until the recent spectacular reinstatements) dared to situate him in his real place?"[3] The Ophuls mystique, born in the early 1950s in France during the director's final burst of cinematic creativity, was taken up by the *Cahiers du Cinéma* group, which granted Ophuls a special status among French directors (most of whom they of course execrated) and acknowledged him as one of the fathers of the New Wave.[4] According to Richard Roud, Ophuls' real "place" in cinema history is that of "beloved minor master."[5] As indicated in the title of this book, and echoed in Roud's comment, a sense of mastery, of the magisterial, emanates from the Ophuls text to become, as Freud's jargon would have it, "cathected" (*Besetzt*, charged with energy),[6] invested or occupied by those who would take up the Ophuls cause. This mastery is, however, menaced—diminished ("minor"). The fight to make a masterful artistic statement materialized in the "real" world many times in Ophuls' career: when he was forced to leave Germany just as his exquisite early film *Liebelei* (1932) was receiving plaudits; when Hollywood for six years proved impermeable to the émigré Ophuls' almost desperate need to direct; and not least when Ophuls' enormously expensive final film, failing to cover its production costs, was recut and almost destroyed as a work of art. In the last year of his life, Ophuls lived out a conflict that lay dormant in the subtexts of his films since he began to make them, a dialectic involving mastery and humiliation, profligate expenditure and ultimate sacrifice—all played out around the body, or rather, the image of a woman. It is this *gynocentric* dialectic that is examined in the pages below. Ophuls' works, in that they both typify and subvert the norms of European art cinema and the "classical" Hollywood film, offer unique insights into just how *woman* has acted as a figure for male and female pleasure and identification in the history of the cinema.[7]

During the past several years, "Ophuls"—the Ophuls text—has once again provided an arena for critical debate; but as we have moved away from auteur studies, emphasis has been placed by many critics currently reassessing his work less on proving its absolute quality, its fitness to be fixed in the cinematic firmament, than on asking what it means to use the female image or body as the locus for playing out the stakes of cinematic mastery.[8] This turn of events is ironic, in that the view of Ophuls as a director of women's films no doubt contributed to some of the critical underestimation of those films in the past.[9] In almost every appraisal of his work Ophuls has been characterized as a woman's director, that is, as both a director *of* women and as one whose films attract female spectators. In fact, Ophuls' films vary a great deal in subject matter and in ostensible address (they include comedies and tragedies, melodramas and swashbucklers). Still, even in the films (such as *De Mayerling à Sarajevo* or *The Exile*) where the plight of a woman is not the primary focus, Robin Wood is correct to point out that "one may feel an emotional gravitation to the female characters pulling against the scenario."[10] Richard Roud describes the gynocentric quality of Ophuls' cinema in these terms: "What are Ophuls' subjects? The simplest answer is: women. More specifically: women in love. Most often, women who are unhappily in love, or to whom love brings misfortune of one kind or another."[11] Beylie terms Ophuls' cinema a "'defense and illustration of the unhappy woman.'" In quotation marks in Beylie's text, these words function as a complex citation, not only of Du Bellay's *Défense et illustration de la langue française* but as a commonplace of thought about Ophuls. Beylie continues:

Indeed, he never glorifies the woman so much as after having precipitated her to the limits of degradation, driven her to despair (or to suicide), as though the depths of sorrow were for her the final stage of salvation here below. The farther she falls, the more her purity is revealed. . . . One may argue with this surprising moral (which was perhaps only the reverse side of an exacerbated Don Juanism), but who would contest the fact that Ophuls remains assuredly one of the most subtle portraitists of woman—of all women, whether they are honest women, tender shopgirls, streetwalkers, or even countesses—that the cinema has ever given us? (p. 6)

Is the woman's expression of desire only the flip side of "an exacerbated Don Juanism"—that is, modeled entirely on masculine desire? Is female desire finally different from male desire? These questions, so crucial to recent feminist film theory, are of paramount importance in Ophuls' works.

The woman's degradation and the suicidal despair noted by Beylie are sometimes expressed through the morbid examination of her "wounds." For example, Beylie waxes lyrical in his description of the protagonist of *Madame de . . .* (aka *The Earrings of Madame de . . .* and *The Diamond Earrings*) as she walks along the shores of an Italian lake, considering the painful fact of her dawning adulterous love. Beylie asks the reader (I will retain the emphatic French here), "Quel cinéaste aura jamais touché au si frémissant, au si écorché, au si saignant de la féminité?"[12] Although Beylie almost certainly is not conscious of the connotations of his choice of words, they nonetheless pin down a subtext of the film: his language might be taken to refer to the "bleeding" and "quivering" female sexual organ itself, perceived here as a sublime and mournful wound. Extrapolating from Beylie's reaction to *Madame de . . .* and from the subject matter of the films themselves, we may well find ourselves asking whether the woman's film, as Ophuls and other filmmakers have conceived it, is only a stage for the woman's ritual degradation, despair, and suicide, linked irrevocably to the wounded state of the female body and psyche.

To a certain extent, Ophuls' melodramatic depictions of that most wounded and degraded of all traditional feminine "types"—and Ophuls' favorite subject—the fallen woman (a figure traceable to the holy whore of ancient times),[13] reiterate the efforts of the nineteenth-century philanthropists who endeavored, according to Nina Auerbach, to "demythicize the fallen woman by making her victim rather than agent" of her fall.[14] The melodramatic and exemplary aspect of the fallen woman's situation is embodied in the "one constant element in the myth of the fallen woman, reaching back to the Old Testament and to Milton's epic recasting of it . . . the absolute transforming power of the fall" (p. 160). Such a view, consistently at work in Ophuls' films, runs counter to the more insistently feminist demythologizing of the fallen woman's state, in which she is seen as precisely *not* having irreversibly "ruined" herself. According to this alternative vision, also occasionally encountered in Ophuls' films, the prostitute is regarded as a "healthy adaptor, plagued by no special sense of sin, but turning to prostitution as a part-time job among others on the path to eventual marriage and respectability."[15] For example, borrowing a page from the ironic Maupassant, Ophuls occasionally blurs the borders placed around the liminal "bad" woman, presenting the bordello in *Le Plaisir* as part and parcel of nineteenth-century petty bourgeois life. Ophuls also sometimes depicts the woman's fall as a "fall up" (this is literally the case in *Lola Montès*). Even so, the fall will remain, for Ophuls, a transforming one, never completely demystified, serving always to sanctify the woman who has suffered its effects.

Still, although the nontranscendent and dedramatized view of the fallen woman is no doubt the more *empowering* one, the peculiar historical force of women whose "fall" gives rise to spiritual strength cannot be denied (Auerbach's example is Hawthorne's Hester Prynne). Thus, despite the fact that the Ophuls text is ultimately constrained to the notion that "a woman's fall is imagined as almost the only avenue through which she is allowed to grow" (p. 166), the magnitude (and explicitness) of that fall is striking. Like Lewis Carroll's Alice, Ophuls' Lola Montès, for example, is "a figure of simultaneous majesty and abasement in a world seemingly *created* by the catastrophe of her fall" (p. 167, emphasis added). Even as victim the woman is a creative force of impressive magnitude.

To answer a question posed above, although he does continue to call on the myths associated with the fallen woman's peculiar powers, Ophuls does not merely celebrate or mourn the sacred-beast status such a woman obtains. Instead, at their best, Ophuls' films make the sacralization of the scapegoated woman *itself* the object of cinematic inquiry. The interest of Ophuls' films lies, therefore, not simply in their exaltation of the woman-martyr but in their analytical approach to the process of marginalization of (the "bad" or amorous) woman and of other outcast members of society. In this way Ophuls to some extent breaks down what Auerbach calls the "social myth that aggrandizes the outcast" (p. 170). Rather than merely "appreciating" woman's martyrdom, or sanctifying her as a Prometheus or (as Catholic critics have argued) Christ figure, Ophuls' films reveal how women at every class level figure in the operation of fictionality, representation itself, and the process of exchange upon which patriarchal capitalism is based. Even those Ophul-

sian women who are not directly tied to the nefarious worlds of acting
and prostitution are drawn into a world where the processes of representation and exchange, as they relate to gender roles under patriarchy,
undermine the possibility of a middle-class heterosexual norm.[16]

Not surprisingly, then, recent reassessments of the films, at least
among feminist writers and ideologically oriented critics, have manifested a certain, not unwarranted, ambivalence about those films' position
with regard to the "dominant" ideologies of the West. In his description
of Ophuls' obsessive use of particular types of camera movements and
décors as a means of coming to terms with *la chose féminine* (as contrasted with Nagisa Oshima's supposedly more revolutionary mise-en-scène),
Stephen Heath articulates just such ambivalence:

That "Ophuls" is the name of a certain exasperation of the standard Hollywood
production of his time is no doubt the case, as it is too that that exasperation is
a veritable mannerism of vision, and of vision of the woman—with the masquerade become the very surface of the text, laid out, *exposed*: the masquerade of "the
woman" (the luxurious feminine of jewelry, furs, mirrors . . .), THE masquerade of the "woman in film," cinema's object, pursuit-and-goal (the ceaseless
enunciation of the ceaseless fascination of the ceaseless tracking of the woman
for the gaze, the look, of appropriation which, in its extreme in *Madame de . . .*,
is near itself to the impossibility known, half-seen). A Hollywood film, an Ophuls
film, *Letter from an Unknown Woman* is exemplary for the article, not typical, in its
demonstration of the relations sustained in cinema, as cinema, of woman and
look and narrative and scene.[17]

In this rather overwhelming passage, Heath is both *placing* Ophuls' film
about a woman's ultimate self-sacrifice for love within what he sees as the
fossilized ideological realm of "the standard Hollywood production" (or
what some have called the "classical Hollywood cinema"[18]) and at once
denying its typicality in that realm. Heath emphasizes the film's *ostensive*
function, its ability to serve as example, pointing to the very "relations"
(woman and look, narrative and scene) that, he believes, it finally sustains
through its formal characteristics.

Despite his effort to come up with an alternative mode of description,
Heath nonetheless seems to apply a binary logic to *Letter*, placing it within certain ideological boundaries separating Hollywood film from
"other," perhaps more enlightened cinemas. During the past decade,
feminist critics have begun to erode the either/or mentality that would

condemn all Hollywood and Hollywood-style film as automatically and irrevocably reactionary with regard to the representation of women.[19] But how far can we go in recuperating for the use of women(which women? where) what often seem to be traditional melodramas, such as Ophuls' early films (generally directed toward a mass audience), and "art films," as his late French films might be described?[20] After all, these films have been thought to present feminine desire as largely masochistic and the female body as prey to the male gaze. One does not have to go far, however, to see that both female masochism and the nature of the "gaze" are problematized in Ophuls' films. By bringing contemporary feminist theory into contact with more films by Ophuls than have previously been examined in that context, I push the limit for Ophuls' "recuperation" again and again, coming up with appropriately mixed results. It is no doubt already clear that there is a strain of old-world misogyny to be found in Ophuls' films. But there is also a serious and subtle probing, throughout the Ophuls oeuvre, of the consequences of that misogyny. In the final analysis I hope to have demonstrated that Ophuls' mise-en-scènes reveal an awareness of sociosexual mores that goes much farther than the "gallantry" toward woman ("la victime consentante du plaisir de l'homme")[21] with which his films are often credited.

Spiel im Kino: A Biographical Note

Maximilian Oppenheimer was born on May 6, 1902, in Saarbrücken, Germany, and died in Hamburg on March 26, 1957. In the fifty-five years of his life he directed more than two hundred plays, twenty-one feature-length films, several shorts, some operettas, and a number of radio plays.[22] He also wrote theater and film criticism, diverse literary sketches, a widely performed Christmas play (*Fips und Stips auf der Weltreise*), an anti-war song ("Murmeln"), and an autobiography, *Spiel im Dasein*.[23]

In 1919 Maximilian Oppenheimer defied the wishes of his family, well-to-do Jewish textile merchants and became an actor. At the same time, he changed his name to Max Ophüls, muting familial embarrassment about his profession (this name was chosen by his friend and mentor, director Fritz Holl, in amorous recollection of a Danish actress by that name). Until 1923 Ophuls had a mediocre success as an actor. At that time he was given the chance to direct a play at the Dortmund theater. This was the beginning of a brief but highly successful and extraordinarily active career as a theatrical director. Ophuls directed plays in a number of cities in Germany and Austria, including Berlin, Frankfurt, Breslau, and Vienna, where (in 1926) he was the youngest director ever to head the Vienna Burgtheater.[24] It was also in Vienna that Ophuls married Hilde Wall, a prominent member of the Burgtheater's troupe. Their son, Marcel Ophuls, born in 1927, is also a well-known film director.[25]

Max Ophuls' theatrical work drew on the most conservative traditions (as he describes the situation in Vienna in his autobiography) as well as on the radical theater in Lessing and Berlin and just about everything in between. While working at Berlin's Lessing Theater and writing radio plays in 1930, he became involved in Ufa (Universum-film-Aktiengesellschaft), the German national cinema industry, first as a dialogue director under Anatole Litvak, then as a film director himself. The most important film works from this period, both made in 1932, are adaptations of Smetana's *The Bartered Bride* and of Arthur Schnitzler's *Liebelei*, a play about a working-class girl's love for an army officer in turn-of-the-century Vienna. Soon after the latter film became a success in Germany, the burning of the Reichstag forced Ophuls and his family into exile in France.

In the ensuing years before the outbreak of World War II, Ophuls directed films in Italy, Holland, and France. He even visited the Soviet Union in 1936 at the invitation of government officials, who offered him a two-year contract to make films in the USSR. Ophuls refused the project, preferring to remain in France. The French films were the most numerous of the period (six feature-length and two short films), though *La Signora di Tutti* (Italy, 1934), which won the technical prize at the Venice Film Festival, is sometimes said to be his most innovative thirties film. *Yoshiwara* (1937) is generally considered to be Ophuls' worst film (even Ophuls himself agreed), and although *Werther* (1938) received favorable reviews, like the stylistically superior *Sans Lendemain* (1939), and *De Mayerling à Sarajevo* (1940), it too suffered from the unsettling effects of the war.[26]

Ophuls obtained French citizenship in 1938. His last prewar French film, *De Mayerling à Sarajevo*, was finished while he was on leave from the French army (where he served in an Algerian gunners' unit). During this period Ophuls made a number of anti-Nazi radio broadcasts, including his famous "good-night to Hitler."[27] At the end of the *drôle de guerre*, Ophuls fled to Switzerland. A version of *L'Ecole des Femmes* with Louis Jouvet was left unfinished as Ophuls once again escaped Nazi terrorism by flight, first into danger in Marseilles then (with the help of agent Paul

Kohner) to a recalcitrant Hollywood.[28] Here Ophuls waited six years to make a film. During that time he wrote (or dictated) his autobiography, a light-hearted account of his life to that point, and formed many film projects, several of which came to the brink of fruition. One nearly realized project was the film *Vendetta,* an adaptation of Prosper Mérimée's *Colomba,* assigned to Ophuls in 1946 by Preston Sturges (acting in an uncomfortable production tandem with Howard Hughes). Ophuls left the film after a few days, however, most likely because of artistic jealousy on Sturges's part. (The film was completed by Mel Ferrer.) Thanks to the intervention of director Robert Siodmak, an offer quickly ensued from Douglas Fairbanks, Jr. to direct a swashbuckler at Universal-International with Fairbanks as star (*The Exile,* 1947). Ophuls' reputation for being adept with melodramatic women's stories won him, in 1948, the direction of *Letter from an Unknown Woman* (also for Universal-International). He then went on to make *Caught* and *The Reckless Moment* for MGM and Columbia respectively in 1949. The screen credits for all of Ophuls' Hollywood films read "Opuls"!

Fall 1949 found Ophuls back in France under the auspices of Walter Wanger, working on a project to direct James Mason and Greta Garbo (who was to have returned to the screen from her retirement)[29] in an adaptation of Balzac's *La Duchesse de Langeais.* The project fell through, but Ophuls was able to direct four more films in France before his death. Among the writers and technicians for this last group of films were a number of people who had worked with Ophuls during his first production period in France. They included the writer Jacques Natanson, cinematographer Christian Matras, and decorator Jean d'Eaubonne.[30] *La Ronde* (1950) is Ophuls' second Schnitzler adaptation, while *Le Plaisir* (1952) is based on three stories by Guy de Maupassant, and *The Earrings of Madame de . . .* (1953) on a novella by Louise de Vilmorin.[31] Because *Le Plaisir* had gone over budget (production difficulties caused a hiatus in filming), the funds for *Madame de . . .* were more restricted. But the efficiency and economy with which Ophuls completed *Madame de . . .* seemed to indicate that he could again be trusted with an open-ended film budget. Thus he was given free reign by *Lola Montès*'s Franco-German production company, Gamma Films. Ophuls ended up spending 648 million old francs (an enormous sum at the time) on this, his only color and CinemaScope film. Despite the fact that it aroused considerable (often passionate) critical interest, *Lola Montès* was a commercial flop.

Ophuls is said never to have recovered from the assault on *Lola Montès* (including the murderous reediting job by Gamma Films, and rerelease under a different title). He went to Baden-Baden in 1956 to direct a radio play, and lectured in several German cities. In 1957 he directed a successful and visually opulent version of Beaumarchais's *Le Mariage de Figaro* in Hamburg (at the Schauspiel Theater), but was taken ill on the day of the premiere. He died three months later of a chronic heart ailment.[32]

Ophuls as Auteur

Oppenheimer, Ophüls, Ophuls, Opuls. The actor who changed his name to "spare" the feelings of his bourgeois family. The Jew who changed his name to one not German but Danish, a name fallen on by chance, a woman's name. The French citizen who stripped his name of the umlaut, disassociating it from anything German (or merely eliminating a redundancy of pronunciation in French).[33] Victim of American producers who further diminished his name by one letter, leaving it the jewel-like Opuls.[34] So someone rewrote, or history rewrote, a name that I and others have standardized as "Max Ophuls," in a transparently auteurist gesture, by means of which we have hoped to grasp a moving body of projects, textual remnants, films, many of which are known to us only as rumor (impossible to get hold of, or lost, as they are). So we report continuities, repetitions, and "themes" that appear over a span of time we have reconstructed, each to our own ends, but within the context of discursive trends of which we are often only half aware. One can see that the self-conscious scare quotes ("Ophuls") that Heath puts around this author's name bracket its graphic flotation as much as they call attention to the always problematic nature of auteur studies in film.[35]

As is implied by the term "mastery," used above to describe Ophuls' relation to his cinematic production, one can discern strong evidence of an authorial "presence" in many of his films. (The effects of the master's hand are presumably visible in "his" products.) During the course of this book, I often refer to Max Ophuls' representation of himself in his films (through what I will call "director-figures" or authorial surrogates, often only very loosely associated with the directorial function) and to other marks of his "enunciation."[36] And I also, more problematically, refer to the "text" of Ophuls' life as another way of showing how meaning is constructed in the films. Ophuls has often been called an ironic director because the obvious patterns of camera movements, repetitions of dialogue, and other details seem to imply a consciousness that invites us to distance ourselves from some events, pass judgment on particular characters, or reflect on an abstract "meaning" that is the result of intertextual references to other films, novels, or plays. Ironic doubling is strongly marked, for example, in *Letter from an Unknown Woman*'s train scenes, in which the echo of the words "two weeks" gives Lisa a premonition of impending loss. Danielle Darrieux's reading of Stendhal's *De l'amour* in *La Ronde* is a rich commentary on her state of mind, for those who know the work (and Ophuls' fondness of it). And how would we "understand" the duel scenes in *Letter from an Unknown Woman* and *Madame de . . .* if we knew nothing of *Liebelei*? (Differently, to say the least.) While himself remaining a fictional character, the enunciator Ophuls [37] will be posited in what follows as a locus of knowledge (he "knows," for example, that the image or the spectacle is potentially dangerous) and as a locus of ignorance or of unconscious knowledge (he does not necessarily "intend" to produce particular meanings but remains as the ostensible subject of that nonintention).

Acknowledging both the allure and the dangers involved in seeing cinema as "authored," critics including David Bordwell and George Wilson have commented that, even in the case of what I have called an "enunciative" cinema, there is "no good reason to identify the narrational process with a fictive narrator,"[38] and that "there are no grounds for recognizing in narrative film, a being, personlike or not, who fictionally offers our view of narrative events to us, although we are often tempted to do so."[39] However, as Wilson stresses, in the case of the Ophuls film (here, *Letter from an Unknown Woman*), "It is nevertheless a part of our deepest experience of *Letter* to feel, throughout its duration, that we are being shown its story through the guidance of a mind with whose strength and sympathy we seem to be acquainted."[40] Bordwell deals with this author-effect by referring to the phenomenon of "art cinema," a category more or less derived from the explicitly "authored" (mostly European) films of the fifties and sixties, in which "the consistency of an authorial signature across an oeuvre constitutes an economically exploitable trademark."[41] Certainly the exploitability of the Ophuls signature is, if anything, greater than ever before, if the spate of recent works on his films is a reliable indicator. (The exploitability of such a signature, of an authorial identity, is, interestingly, an explicit concern in many of Ophuls' films.) Bordwell's allusion to "art cinema" and to the phenomenon of the "institutional 'author'" highlights the political complexity of the notion of an authored cinema. Are the strongly marked authorial interventions of an Ophuls or a Hitchcock (whose mass-oriented films are generally not considered "art cinema") read by spectators as interruptions of Hollywood-style "naturalized" *histoire* (story, as opposed to *discours*, discourse),[42] jolting the spectator into a new awareness of what he or she is watching?[43] Or is the explicitly authorial voice in art cinema, which tends to foreground "author-as-narrator" figures, simply seen by the spectator (especially the American spectator) as allocating the film in question to an aesthetic realm ("highbrow culture") that cannot seriously engage with his or her viewing habits, perceived as it is as exterior to daily concerns?

As more sophisticated and intensive work is done on film spectatorship, especially on female and "minority" (not to mention Third World) spectatorship, it is becoming obvious that neither of these positions is absolutely right or wrong. We will see that in Ophuls' melodramas, which do not often take the license for self-exposure/self-expression taken in, say, the later French films, the marks of authorial enunciation (though muted) do complicate their relation to the genre. This increased complexity does not render the films "superior" to the run-of-the-mill woman's film, but does, I suggest, make available to professional critics and to "ordinary" spectators certain critiques of the process of representing women, especially women in middle-class environments. It is perhaps not too far-fetched to imagine that female spectators of the period came to a more critical understanding of the process of representing woman as a social and aesthetic entity by reading the contradictions between the ostensible position and desires of the filmic woman and the modes of her representation in the Ophuls film. In ferreting out those contradictions, I hope to be contributing to what Linda Williams has called "the most important task of feminist film criticism . . . that of locating the variety of different subject positions constructed by the text of the woman's film."[44] It is to be hoped that my textual/historical work will be followed up by specific research on the spectators of these films.

Ophuls' "directorial surrogates" are innumerable and serve many functions—ranging from the *meneur de jeu* figures in *Komedie om Geld* and *La Ronde* to the many scurrying directors of protocol, theatrical managers, agents, pimps, *entremetteurs*, impresarios, and so on in *The Bartered Bride*, *Liebelei*, *La Signora di Tutti*, *Yoshiwara*, *Sarajevo*, *Lola Montès*, and on down the line. Such figures were often included in both his theatrical and cinematic works, even when the text being adapted featured no such character.[45] Just how Ophuls' many authorial surrogates can be related to what Wilson calls the "implied film maker," much less to the "biographical" Ophuls and to attitudes that person may have held about women is, of course, sometimes no more than speculation. Although I do occasionally take license with the biographical Ophuls, attributing certain characteristics of his films to, for example, attitudes he may have held about being Jewish or about having lived in exile, the claims I make on this basis are specific and textually based. As Fredric Jameson puts it: "Where the older biographical criticism understood the author's life as a context, or as a cause, as that which could explain the text, the newer kind understands that 'life,' or rather its reconstruction, precisely as one further text in its turn, a text on the level with the other literary texts of the writer in question and susceptible of forming a larger corpus of study with them."[46]

Much of this book is concerned precisely with the notion of the construction of the individual in the Ophuls film, and just how the ideology of bourgeois individualism is conflated with the issue of female subject-formation in these films. What does it mean to be an individual? Are women individuals in the same way men are (or are not)? Any notion of "authorship" is necessarily affected by this inquiry. In summary, considering the antiauteurism that has taken over the academy in the wake of Derrida, Foucault, Barthes, Wollen et al., one might well ask just how a reinscription of the (male) author as "speaking subject" could serve any political or strategic purpose in a feminist reading of the films gathered under the rubric of that authorial name. This is certainly a question with which we must contend in our teaching practice, when showing "male-authored" films to our students in courses on feminist film theory. It is a question that has never been far from my mind in the writing of this book.

In her recent work on authorship in the cinema,[47] Kaja Silverman makes the case for refurbishing, to the ends of feminist criticism, a version of auteurism that may prove helpful in our assessment of the ideological stakes of analyzing male-authored texts. Silverman forges, in this context, what is perhaps a stronger link between the author "outside" the text and the various kinds of surrogates for that author within the text than Wilson or Bordwell might accept. She posits an author who is in some sense palpably "present" in the text (as body, as trace), whose relation to the author "outside" the text (the biographical author) is not effaced but continually interrogated, traced through "nodal points" where authorial desire may make itself known (recurrent scenes, places, actions traced across the authorial corpus—Ophuls' text is certainly fraught with such repetitions). Although the author's "secondary identification" with various characters who "stand in" for him in the film is certainly consistent with the dominant practice of sustaining male mastery by transcending corporeal limitations (something much rarer for women in cinema, tied as they are to their celluloid bodies), Silverman maintains that the "filmmaker's secondary identifications also depart from that paradigm altogether, and put in place a very different kind of authorial subjectivity—one which, for instance, is much more openly endangered and at risk" (p. 215).

The identity of this authorial subject "inevitably turns upon misrecognition" (asserting a coherency or integrity based on illusion). And his or her "voice" may be diminished, deprivileged, rendered ambiguous, even when, as in the case of both Hitchcock and Ophuls, the "authorial subjectivity is constructed through an identification with mastering vision" (p. 218). Silverman cites the occasions when, in a non-Hollywood context, filmmakers including Rainer Werner Fassbinder, Chantal Akerman, and others have made directorial appearances as weakened, sleazy, or confused characters "within" the text. Such appearances, she claims, act to *erode* rather than to reinforce their authority (for the female filmmaker, who has not long enjoyed such a privilege, this authority is constructed even as it erodes). So too might the "mastering vision" of Ophuls or Hitchcock be rendered problematic by the very fact of their subjecting themselves to the camera's gaze, even in the person of a surrogate if, as Silverman suggests, to be "inside" the film is always a position of lesser power than to remain "outside" in the world of production or as a mastering voice of God.[48] (In the case of Hitchcock's elaborately constructed screen persona—including in his television program—visibility may act to *mark* Hitchcock's "mastery": Silverman's claim may de dangerously formulaic.) Male filmmakers may also lose a certain authorial control of the text by including in their films "conflicting authorial systems," such as a strong (diegetic or nondiegetic) female voice, which is almost by definition not an authorial one in classical Hollywood cinema. And the dynamics of identification reconfigure what it means to be "in" the text. As Tania Modleski noted in her book on Hitchcock,[49] it is only through his work on Du Maurier's (reviled) text, *Rebecca*, that Hitchcock came to articulate one of his most important subjects: the "potential terror and loss of self involved *in* identification itself, especially identification with a woman."[50] In this masculine identification with the feminine, a certain female voice is valorized and perhaps even speaks "authorially." Is "mother," then, the author of Norman Bates's murders? Ventriloquism and projection have their complexities, to be sure: "mother" may be acting out revenge for her own violent death, the death of the "mother" in Hitchcock himself.

What, we may well ask, would be the status of the kind of feminine voice Silverman locates in certain male-authored films? For Silverman, and for the many feminist critics who have been analyzing film since the mid-1970s, the female voice exists even in Hollywood cinema "as one of its constitutent although generally submerged elements" (p. 211). We must read these films "transgressively," noting how even the ostensibly male-authored text permits (or *suffers*) an incursion of femininity either as an effect of its feminine *address* or as part of the authorial subject-effect itself. In the latter case, "femininity" emerges through the self-castration of the male author. In a culture that cannot read difference except as catastrophe, such male castration produces its "other," femininity, as artifice, as male projection. But like the author him/herself, a difference that is not simply projected or negated self continues to haunt the text. Paradoxically, our interrogation of the male author may serve to throw into disarray the very notion of authority that it would seem to support. Although it is certainly no place to locate an "authentic" or essential femininity (or even a femininity with which the female spectator may in fact identify), in Ophuls' as in Hitchcock's films the director's continual objectification or mise-en-scène of woman also involves a process of confrontation and identification that undermines the precepts of the directorial authority and gender stability.

Although Ophuls' women are not merely passive vehicles for projected male hostility or suffering, the preceding paragraphs make it clear that this form of projection nevertheless remains a crucial factor in the films. It is Gertrud Koch who has most emphatically stated that Ophuls himself identifies with woman—he "imagines himself in the female perspective" and "shows men's longing for the masks and mirrors of femaleness, for the grandiose feeling of female narcissism as the principle of a completely aesthetic form of life, broken by no reality principle in its romantic impulse."[51] As with Hitchcock, as Modleski sees him, "Ophuls'" own ambivalence about the masculine aggression toward and admiration of women that runs through his films can be read in a number of ways. It spells a narcissistic masculine identification with female suffering, a breakdown of the paternalistic auteur system—even as that system is being invoked. It also produces a site where female voices, if only those of female spectators or film analysts, as they read the evidence of masculinity's breakdown, can be heard.

Methodology and Contents

This book opens with a discussion of *The Bartered Bride* (1932) and closes with a chapter on *Lola Montès* (1955). In the intervening chapters I look closely at *Madame de . . .* (1953), *De Mayerling à Sarajevo* (1940), *Letter from an Unknown Woman* (1948), *La Signora di Tutti* (1934), and *Le Plaisir* (1952), and make lengthy asides to a number of Ophuls' other films. The films are not examined in chronological order. Instead, I have followed the logic of various theoretical concerns in ordering the material. For example, I use my discussion of *The Bartered Bride* to set up the various "economic" considerations pursued in greater depth in the next chapter, on *Madame de . . .* . A close reading of a film as superficially banal as *De Mayerling à Sarajevo* requires preparation, if it is to be convincing. Thus, at the risk of reading into *Sarajevo* the complexity of the stylistically less orthodox *Madame de . . .*, I discuss the earlier film only after having closely examined the latter film. Readers familiar with the Ophuls canon may be surprised that I do not write at greater length about some of the "major" films, such as *Liebelei*. I can only say that I selected for close study the films that present most strikingly a particular nexus of tropes surrounding (or producing) the figure of woman, although I have also aimed at "coverage" of the Ophuls canon by discussing in detail at least one film from each of his major periods of film production (German, American, early and late French periods). It is by reference to work in psychoanalytically oriented feminist film studies, to deconstruction, and to the various fields (such as structural anthropology, cultural studies, and Marxist economics) sustaining and questioning those practices that I have determined what constitutes "relevant" tropological systems.

Although the methodologies that I employ arise from diverse fields of study, each has proven useful in the process of forging questions about the intersection of the visual media with the cultural problem of femininity. I will not attempt, in this context, a general defense of the widespread use of psychoanalysis in feminist film criticism, though I take seriously Spivak's caveat about psychoanalysis, spelled out above in an epigraph taken from *The Post-Colonial Critic*. The advantages and the dangers of employing psychoanalytically derived categories in feminist scholarship have been widely debated.[52] Some of the dangers are obvious. If, for example, we accept the view that there is an essential, biologically based, psychological difference between men and women, profound changes may prove impossible, short of altering biology. And yet it is also to the advantage of the oppressed "other" that psychological difference (as contingent or fixed as its origins may be) be documented. Of course, biology itself is not directly reflected in human behavior: even if we were to "prove" that females are (to choose at random) less visually oriented than males, what may be done with this "knowledge" of biology is infinitely variable. (Gayatri Spivak has called for a "strategic essentialism" that would appeal to seemingly essential identities at certain political moments.)[53] Although a tendency toward hermeticism, essentialism, and ahistoricism (among other "isms") does plague psychoanalytic theory, its usefulness in describing the psychic structures sustaining the aesthetic realms of patriarchy is still unsurpassed—though, as Michel Foucault has observed, it may also serve to block other means of looking at social structures and historical evidence.

For those who are already familiar with the work of Laura Mulvey, Jacqueline Rose, Kaja Silverman, Mary Ann Doane, Gaylyn Studlar, Luce Irigaray, Tania Modleski, Judith Mayne, and the other psychoanalytically oriented theorists upon whose work I draw, my considerations of the problem of "the gaze," of Oedipal and pre-Oedipal phases, and of male defenses against female "castration" will be known territory. For those who are unfamiliar with this terminology, I have attempted to delineate my arguments as clearly as possible and to explain the meaning of any jargon I have (perhaps too readily) appropriated from the context of poststructuralist psychoanalytic studies. Like all the critics listed above, in making use of psychoanalysis as a means of understanding differences and similarities between male and female "visual pleasure" in cinema, I have struggled with the phallocentrism that is both documented and to some extent *furthered* by Freudian psychoanalysis. And like these critics, I challenge the bases of the first wave of psychoanalytic film criticism, which pessimistically relegated woman to the role of passive recipient of the aggressive male gaze and did not attempt to construct the subject of psychoanalysis *historically*, as I hope to do. I do this partly by looking at the ways in which women in Ophuls' films successfully combat their role as sexual spectacle, and partly by showing how Ophuls' films are, in response to the various historical circumstances under which they were made, already eroding the binary logic of, as Gaylyn Studlar puts it, "a system of visual pleasures constructed to gratify the unconscious desire of one gender at the expense of another."[54]

One

✦

Circulation and Scapegoating in *Lachende Erben* (*Happy Heirs*), *Die verkaufte Braut* (*The Bartered Bride*), and *Liebelei*

Women are exactly like the Jews, who by their financial power compensate for the oppression to which they're subjected. "Aha, you just want us to be merchants, do you? All right, then, it's as merchants that we'll lord it over you," say the Jews. "Aha, you just want us to be the objects of your sensuality, do you? All right, then it's as the objects of your sensuality that we'll enslave you," say women.

—LEO TOLSTOY, "THE KREUTZER SONATA"

What lies abstract in the Jewish religion, a contempt for theory, art, history, man as an end in himself, is the actual, conscious standpoint, the virtue of the money man. The species-relationship itself, the relationship of man to woman, etc., becomes an object of commerce! Woman is bartered.

—KARL MARX, "ON THE JEWISH QUESTION"

♦

Circulation and Subjectivity: The Go-Between

The most jaded truism about the cinema of Max Ophuls—that it is above all (and redundantly) a cinema of movement—is also profoundly true. One recalls the notoriously uninhibited motion of Ophuls' camera or the unbridled trajectories of *Le Plaisir*'s masked dancer. Ophuls' cinema is also, however, one of nonmovement, of a stillness that is both a form of captivity and a position of mesmerizing power: from the fixity of Louise de . . .'s entombed earrings to that of the caged and "savage" Lola Montès; from the threatening mannequins in the background of *Letter from an Unknown Woman* to the intimidating statues of the Emperor Franz Josef disrupting the amorous urges of the young Franz Ferdinand in *De Mayerling à Sarajevo*, and so on. The circle, dialectical synthesis of the moving and the fixed, is the place of the exchange of disease, of money, of women, and of images that go round and round on a painted background, on coins themselves,[1] on filmstock. In each of Ophuls' films, this dialectic is played out for different stakes, whether they be related to love, politics, Oedipal conflicts, or the struggle of various marginal social elements to come to the foreground of the representation, to attain some form of "subjectivity."[2]

Thus, despite its occasional technical imperfection, *The Bartered Bride* (1932), adapted from Smetana's Bohemian opera first performed in 1894, features many characteristics of Ophuls' "fluid" later style, including striking tracks, pans, tilts, and the carefully choreographed movement of figures.[3] A musical using spoken dialogue, interspersed with snatches of popular songs from Smetana's opera,[4] the film anticipates *Madame de . . .*'s preoccupation with the circulation of money, goods, and women and with the uneasy position of the middleman who facilitates or initiates exchanges.[5] Since this "middle man" will be a crucial character on Ophuls' stage, I will take a moment to examine his, or occasionally *her*, role. Often in Ophuls' cinema, these middlemen are more or less explicitly associated with the film director, as in *La Ronde*, where the *meneur de jeu* who brings the men and women together is also shown editing the film, or in *Madame de . . .*, where the jeweler keeps the story (and the film) going by buying and selling the protagonist's earrings.[6]

Ophuls' films both exalt and humiliate these "director-figures," middle-men, and the desiring women under their control, as is perhaps most readily apparent in the exaggerated ups and downs suffered by Lola Montès and represented/repeated in her circus trapeze act. The characters who serve both to "keep the circle turning" and, at strategic moments, to disrupt all circulation, share many of the functions of the scapegoat figures described by René Girard as victims of ritual violence.[7]

Women, we have noted, are most often the "victimized" figures in Ophuls' films, which are characterized by ritualistic repetition. We know, further, that Ophuls is a director who has been said to espouse the cause of women, even to identify, in hysterical fashion, with their plight.[8] An intense though intermittent and partially displaced *effect* of identification between the female protagonist and authorial (or *spectatorial*) vision is evident even in Ophuls' early films. For example, in *La Signora di Tutti* (1934) the camera reels sympathetically after the female protagonist has made herself dizzy by dancing in circles.[9] Later (in terms of the diegesis) the vaporous aura of the anesthetic gas administered to the dying protagonist invades the film's titles as their background. And yet, although the centrality of the female dilemma is not to be underestimated in this and other Ophuls films, the woman is only the most prominent of a constellation of character types whose common attribute is a tie to the process of circulation rather than to that of production.

The primacy of Ophuls' interest in problems of circulation and exchange is already clear in *The Bartered Bride*, where the woman's painful situation is part of a general reassessment of figures associated with the exchange process. Smetana's opera tells the story of Marie, daughter of indebted parents, who loves Hans but is forcibly betrothed to Wenzel, son of Micha, to whom they owe money. Marie's parents are the first to "barter" their daughter, to pay off their debt to Micha. The matchmaker, Kezal, arranges to buy off Hans with three hundred guldens obtained from Micha for arranging the marriage. Surprisingly, Hans accepts the money, promising only not to prevent a marriage between Marie and Micha's son. Of course, since this is light opera, Hans turns out to be Micha's eldest son by an earlier marriage and the legitimate heir to his fortune. He and Marie marry; Kezal and Wenzel are humiliated.

In Smetana's version of *The Bartered Bride*, Kezal the procurer is the female protagonist's enemy because he wants to marry her off to someone she does not love, and to make money doing so. At the end of the opera Kezal is chastised and ejected from the village, along with the complicitous stepmother. By contrast, Kezal is given surprisingly sympathetic treatment by Ophuls: "Kezal the procurer is, in Smetana, a bad lot with a bad character. In Ophuls he is the grease that keeps the cartwheels turning. He is not driven out, as in Smetana, but, with the group photograph he creates an ephemeral moment of harmony and peace."[10]

Ophuls (who was, as is the case with most of his films, coscreenwriter)[11] twists the plot, making Wenzel a charming if daffy character and Kezal the visual focus of much of the opera. Kezal is the great conciliator at the opera's end as well, and Hans both barters his bride and turns out *not* to be the heir to any fortune. Instead, he makes a deal with Wenzel, who wants to marry a circus performer, and the film ends with a double coupling in the "green world."

The "group photograph" at the end of the film features all the protagonists, brought together in an amiable final scene vastly different from that in the opera. Although it may seem, according to this description, that Ophuls is gutting Smetana's critique of bride bartering, this is not the case. Rather, Ophuls wants to place blame where it really belongs, rather than punishing the visual symbol of exchange—Kezal. Thus, in his exposé of the terrible destiny of a young girl forced to marry against her will, Ophuls does not follow Smetana's lead in treating the procurer as a scapegoat who symbolizes the alienating system of man's exchange of women, or Germany's inflationary economy in 1932, and who must be ejected to mitigate the results of that exchange. Both Wenzel, the simpleton, and Kezal, the procurer, are often at odds with the woman, as they occupy opposite positions on the wheel of social exchanges (emblematized first by a broken cartwheel, which opens the action of the film, and then by a wheel of fortune).[12] But the cruelty of this system will not be put on the heads of these two men in Ophuls' film.

As I have implied, it is not only sentimentality that drives Ophuls to give a more "humane" treatment of Wenzel and Kezal than does Smetana. Ophuls seems to want to avoid, short-circuit, or parody the sacrificial logic (the creation and ejection of scapegoats) manifest in Smetana's opera and in the other materials he directs and often adapts. He almost always espouses the cause of the one who promotes a frenzied circulation that does not precisely oppose, but, rather, *apes* the supposedly grounded and stable circulation of goods and money to be found in a patriarchal and capitalistic society. In this sense, the "performance" of this act of circulation is carnivalesque, as Bakhtin uses the term.[13] To cite Frieda Grafe once again:

[Ophuls] was not primarily interested in parents who barter their children like movable property. What interested him was the bourgeois Underground, the basis of bourgeois morality. In Ophuls' films it is forever threatened with being bankrupted by love, the unforeseeable element which destabilizes wealth. . . . The destruction of bourgeois concepts of property, of the smooth and consistent circulation of wealth is both total and subtle. Ophuls lifts the skirts of bourgeois morality . . . finding enormous fun in the process, enjoying dreadful puns and anything regarded as vulgar. (p. 56)

The love that would destabilize wealth is Marie's for Hans, as well as Wenzel's for Esmeralda the circus star, which is given less serious treatment in the opera than it is in the film. That the woman's love is allowed to take precedence over issues of primogeniture suggests the kind of "recombination, inversion, mockery, and degradation" of the established social order that has been associated with the Bakhtinian carnivalesque.[14] It is, therefore, essential to our reading that Hans, the humble postilion, does *not*, in Ophuls' film, turn out to be the legitimate older brother and heir, as he does in the opera. In this way Ophuls has turned the opera on its head.

Another curious displacement from the opera to the film, one not mentioned by Grafe, is that of the debt, said in the opera to be owed by Marie's parents to Wenzel's (and for which she is thus originally the bartering piece), but given a more "positive" narrative function in the film. In Ophuls' version, the three hundred guldens are made by the complicitous Hans and Wenzel to flow from the pocket of the matchmaker into that of the circus performers, after Kezal has given the money to Hans for the "sale" of his bride. The circus folk must render the money to the city hall, so that they may perform in the town. This indebtedness of the circus performers (who owe money from the previous year's performance—a detail absent from the opera) gives rise to an amusing scene featuring the Bavarian comedian/clown Karl Valentin as Brummer the circus director and Liesl Karlstadt (Valentin's real-life companion) as his wife, who argue nonsensically (and in dialect) with the mayor. In the film Marie's father (Krusinova, her only parent) is the substantial town mayor, rather than the indebted peasant who must, in the opera, sell his child to pay his debts. This parent is, therefore, not a debtor caught up in a system that exploits him—he is prosperous and willing to pay the matchmaker for his services. The film does not have the opera's melodramatic touch: the father "sells" his daughter because he wants to make the proper bourgeois alliance, not because he owes money. The daughter's exchangeability for money is thus not a product of feudal inequity but follows the logic of bourgeois exchange among equals— and produces laughter.

Smetana's *The Bartered Bride* seems to reflect a fundamental change that was taking place during the nineteenth century in Bohemia and elsewhere, regarding the emergence of the money form (versus barter) and the petty bourgeois "individual." Marriage for money, Georg Simmel has written, was an acceptable social institution in many "primitive groups": "The disparagement of personal dignity that nowadays arises in every marriage that is not based on personal affection—so that a sense of decency requires the concealment of economic motives—does not exist in simpler cultures. The reason for this development is that increasing individualization makes it increasingly contradictory and discreditable to enter into purely individual relationships for other than purely individual reasons."[15] In "bartering" his bride, Hans violates (perhaps recently created) social norms in more than one way, by seeming to prostitute his fiancée, by selling something that does not "belong" to him, and by revealing the economic motives of marriage as potentially comedic.

As mayor, Krusinova is the originator of the performers' debt. The matchmaker, who extracts money and facilitates exchanges involving uneasy equivalences between money, people, and representations, finds his double therefore in the mayor himself. Doubled or mirrored relations are iconically as well as thematically emphasized in *The Bartered Bride*. Occasionally this doubling is made explicit. In a spiel outside a photography booth, one of the circus performers describes the photograph as "a mirror image on paper," picking up in a metacinematic fashion the play on mirroring begun in the first sequence, as the circus rolls toward the town. In that scene circus director Brummer halts his wagon, gets out to observe the landscape, and gazes at himself in a small mirror. Later, Kezal catches on to Marie's new emotional state when he sees her, in a dramatic point-of-view shot taken by means of a mirror, kissing Hans outside her father's house. The "Indian"[16] carries around a full-sized replica of himself, which fascinates Wenzel. Wenzel's mother is shown combing her hair in a mirror when her son comes to ask to borrow three hundred guldens, and so forth. Each object and each individual is potentially split into its commodified other.

We can already observe that the money that is coldly paid to the girl's parents (indebted to Wenzel's father) as the bride price in the opera is given a more devious route in the film. Hans and Wenzel, set up as rivals in Smetana's work, here team up to get hold of money from Kezal. Kezal hopes to make considerably more through the match between Wenzel and Marie than he loses through his deal with Hans. (Wenzel's parents do give handfuls of money to Kezal when he reports that Hans has given up his bride. Kezal also later tries to extort three hundred more guldens from Krusinova.) According to the terms of their deal, Hans swears to Kezal that he will not prevent Marie from marrying Wenzel, instead (in a slight departure from the patrilinear theme of the opera) relying on Wenzel's attraction to Esmeralda to prevent this from occurring. As noted, Hans is paid the three hundred guldens, which he then passes along to Wenzel. The "idiot" uses the money to bail out the circus troupe and himself becomes a performer in their circus (as is also the case in the opera, but here with a much more satirical effect, since Smetana's circus folk are only using Wenzel to their own ends). Wenzel is finally coupled with Esmeralda, the daughter of the circus director, something only teasingly promised in the opera.[17] Love has deviated the course of monetary circulation, indeed, in a much more complex manner than in Smetana's opera, and much as it does in Ophuls' next film, *Lachende Erben.* And yet it is a "love" that does not serve to mystify the real relations between social groups.

We have observed that Ophuls' critique of the bourgeois economy takes an amusing detour through the domain of the spectacle, as the circus folk appropriate the money in the interest of their performance. In fact, for this very reason we might say that the circus folk are themselves presented with a measure of ambivalence, tied as they are to a nefarious kind of circulation (the bartering of women). Although they will be absolved at the end of the story, the circus performers do actually make use of the money for which Hans has sold his beloved: the circulation of something akin to blood money is in this way connected with performance, as well as with the director-like figure of Kezal. Woman, who is always already spectacle according to the norms of recent Western civilization, is linked to performers whose circus act spells out the topsy-turvy nature of the carnival world it embodies. However, as Mary Russo has observed, and as *The Bartered Bride* seems to imply, the world of carnivalesque spectacle does not unambivalently present the woman as empowered.[18]

Shifting to another aspect of the spectacle, the performance of Karl

Valentin (the circus director), a close associate of Brecht as well as of Ophuls, is an intriguing one. In his autobiography Ophuls reminisces fondly about the apparent collapsing of reality and the spectacle that took place in the mind of Valentin. For example, as soon as the circus tent was erected for the shooting of the film, Valentin took a pot of paint and inscribed on the canvas a statement to the effect that anyone who cut it would be "exposed to the rigor of the law."[19] The circus director is thus not associated only with the inversion of power structures. The role of this figure ranges, in fact, from the posture of the humiliated and indebted itinerant player to that of the arrogant *metteur en scène*, who puts Wenzel in a bear costume so that this middle-class son can be *baited*, an action rich in historical and social resonances. Wenzel's comical execution of the bear act is, however, quickly deflated when the real bear makes its appearance. *The Bartered Bride* is structurally symmetrical in that it begins with people chasing a pig and ends with a bear—the real one, which escapes during Wenzel's performance—chasing people.[20]

The playful humiliation of "the actor" Wenzel has strong affinities with the more horrifying representations of bear-baiting in Ingmar Bergman's films *Sawdust and Tinsel* (1953) and *The Seventh Seal* (1956). In the former, a circus troupe like the one in *The Bartered Bride* is subjected to various humiliations, just as the performers in Ophuls' film are obliged to pay in order to perform. In an interview with Marcel Ophuls, Max Ophuls called the circus "the foundation of our *métier*."[21] Its importance—and its ambivalent position in the modern world—are evident in Ophuls' works from beginning to end. Paisley Livingston comments on the circus performers in Bergman's film:

Outcasts, they are permitted only to camp at the boundary of a town where their role is to provide a sufficiently amusing spectacle at any cost. Even their right to perform is contested. They lack costumes, the external signs of a status which, although marginal, would at least assure them a place in the ring. They must borrow their costumes from the local theater, an institution granting its performers a role within the community. The theater director, although he displays his scorn for the pitiful troupe, acknowledges the fact that the actors and circus people belong to the "same contemptible pack." The two professions are the same, and as rivals, compete for the favor of the villagers, the actors risking their "vanity" and the circus performers their "lives."[22]

Livingston pinpoints elements of these scenes from Bergman which can be elucidated by reference to Girard's theories on ritual violence, and which in turn may influence our thinking on Ophuls. Actors and circus performers are engaged, in these films, in spectacles of humiliation which, according to Girard's notions, are modeled on rituals dating back to a remote past, a founding moment when a sacrificial victim was actually murdered by a group that commemorated the deed ever after through conventionalized performances. "Only when the conventions wear thin and collapse does drama suddenly return to the model as performance degenerates into a gruesome spectacle" (p. 60).[23] Like Ophuls, "Bergman condemns rituals in which a community attempts to resolve *its own* violence by directing it toward an individual unjustly accused of being its cause" (p. 62). *The Bartered Bride* deploys that convention whereby the actors/performers are given the ritual function of solving the community's ills—their intervention permits the proper outcome of the romantic intrigues and channels the scapegoating of the woman onto themselves (as they say to Krusinova, "Through our art your family relations will be put back to order"). The humiliation of the performers by a community seeking to channel its own violence is parodied, in that the bourgeois "heir" is (gently) made to perform the role of taunted victim. Thus the joyous spirit involved in turning social norms upside down is undercut by violence and humiliation, as it will be years later in *Lola Montès*. Ophul's staging of "foundational" violence is given historical specificity by its invocation of the tax through which the performers take on the role of (temporary) citizens.

Girard has claimed that all desire is an imitation of the rival's desire and therefore mimetic. By defusing the rivalry between Hans and Wenzel, Ophuls undermines the "mimetic rivalry" that sparks violence—a violence that is often the result of suppressing male-male desire. Even as we question the grounds of Girard's theory of mimetic rivalry, which is based on a rigid and universalized model of desire, we can acknowledge, as does Moi, that he is "furnishing an accurate description of [heterosexual] masculine desire under patriarchy."[24] This desire, mediated by real or imagined economic scarcity, seems inevitably to lead to scenes of scapegoating. Ophuls' comic solution to the problems of male competition for the same object (woman) is simply to have one of the rivals become caught up in a performance. Wenzel finds another object of desire in the circus and redirects the violence implicit to the situation of rivalry. That this solution is not always adequate becomes evident in Ophuls' later films, which often end in the mutual destruction of rivals.

Although Girard continually asserts that the victim of mimetic violence is arbitrary, he cannot, as Philippe Lacoue-Labarthe has demonstrated, maintain this claim.[25] Girard seeks the mythical moment of originary violence where the scapegoat is chosen more or less at random to end the outbreak of violence between "identical" rivals. But that originary moment cannot be found: the victim is historically connected to mimesis, to the reproduction of images. The scapegoating devolves on those who are producers and circulators of images—the poets in Plato, the women who are said to have been in almost every historical epoch the "privileged" objects of representation. In what would otherwise be violence among rivals, the circulators, those implicated in representation, come out as the scapegoats par excellence, the ones around whom a community (of men) finally coalesces. Insofar as women only have a value as *representation*—i.e., are exchangeable, circulated, always already displaced and, in this case, part of another family (the husband's)—they attract not only men but violence. Given the logic of sacrificial representation according to Girard, they are consequently thought to *incite* this violence. Far from being out of the picture, the image-object "woman" often takes the role assigned to the scapegoat as well. In Ophuls' films (and certainly at many other historical moments) the woman comes to manipulate that image herself, though her status as the object of male rivalry is never fully overcome—and new problems devolve upon her taking control of the image. Thus, the object of circulation and representation, as well as the individual seen as the primary circulator or representer (artist, go-between, Jew), can function as social scapegoats.

Freeze-frame: Laura Mulvey Redux

In *Madame de . . .*, *The Bartered Bride*, and elsewhere, the wild circulation of commodities and persons is halted by a frozen image—in the latter, the photograph taken by Kezal; in the former, a monument that entombs a pair of earrings below the statue of a saint at the end of the film. Individuals who act as emblems of the exchange process, but who are in fact marginal to the patriarchally grounded system of exchange, will ultimately struggle to call a halt to its movement, although this halting will often have the effect of fixing these individuals in uncomfortable postures, as when Lola Montès is poised precariously on a diving platform high above a water-filled tank.

The cycles of movement and halting in Ophuls' films achieve an effect similar to that described by Deleuze and Guattari in their elegy to capitalism run amok. These authors describe a painting by Richard Linder which depicts a "huge, pudgy, bloated boy working one of his little desiring machines, after having hooked it up to a vast technical social machine—which . . . is what even the very young child does." The text continues: "Producing, a product: a producing/product identity. It is this identity that constitutes a third term in the linear series: an enormous undifferentiated object. Everything stops dead for a moment, everything freezes in place—and then the whole process will begin all over again."[26]

In this deconstruction of the production-circulation dichotomy of classical economics, Deleuze and Guattari note a moment of blockage. Grafe identifies a similar blockage in *The Bartered Bride* as a reified instance of deviated circulation in the shape of the photo organized by Kezal and kept as a "souvenir." (The words "Fur Erinnerung" frame the photo in the last shot of the film.) This is not, however, the only photograph that figures in *The Bartered Bride*. Midway through the film, Hans and Marie take refuge in a photographer's booth at the fair,[27] but are interrupted in mid-photo by Wenzel's parents. The older couple, in hot pursuit of the erring pair, themselves stop in the studio: their images are (we gather) superimposed over the younger couple's image on the photographer's plate. Grafe notes that the female spieler emphasizes the "graphic" quality of the photo, as she calls out "photo-graphier-r-r-t" to the passing crowd. Thus, the image of the conservative, older couple is grafted onto that of the rebellious youths. At the end of the film the images have been disentangled, and clear representations of all the main characters, suitable for remembrance, are spread out before us.[28] Does the photograph serve merely to normalize the deviated flow of money and marriage alliances by fixing them in place? Yes, surely to some degree this must be true. And yet one wonders if the economy of the small village can ever really revert to the way things were. Ophuls has plugged his photographing machine into the social body and has extracted this third term, a film-object that freezes everything into place, recording it on celluloid. Ophuls' films, though they may be interpreted according to Oedipal schemas, also reframe the airtight worlds they depict, for which they are containers of sweet and painful recollection. They speak as well of a rhythmic energy which is that of a machine in motion, and of the breakdown of that machine in uncontrollable repetition, beyond souvenir, beyond pleasure, beyond subjecthood, beyond or outside the economic, taken up again in a "postmodern" economy in which images and soundbites recirculate in a global economy.

What does it mean to say, as I have throughout this chapter, that it is as an object of representation, an image, that the woman finds herself in the position of scapegoat? Some would say, as does Catherine Clément, that woman is punished for attempting to be something other than an image—and this is also true![29] Simply put, the circulation that characterizes the bourgeois economy is also caught up, by way of a nexus of metaphors, in an economy that is directorial, filmic, and feminine. This economy is not easily opposed to a masculine one. A *grounded* circulation, which uses woman as its bartering piece, is associated, as we have seen, with the limits imposed by patriarchal authority. However, both money and images can be drawn into forms of circulation that challenge this authority. In *The Bartered Bride*, "love" displaces and disrupts the circulation process, but it is a gentleman's agreement that determines how money and love are channeled; in Ophuls' later films the women themselves act to metamorphose their passive roles in this process.

In her early work on feminine desire and representation in cinema, Laura Mulvey conjectures that the woman who takes control of her cinematic destiny often does so by manipulating her own image, taking advantage of the potential that image has for fascinating and thus disarming the (male) spectator. According to Mulvey's foundational theory, it is the *still* image of woman that has the most disruptive potential, ironically enough, since it is as inactive object of the masculine gaze that women have also been deprived of subjectivity in cinema (both as spectator and as object of the camera's eye).[30]

Mulvey relates the still image of the woman to a halting of the narrative itself: "The presence of woman is an indispensable element of spectacle in the normal narrative film, yet her visual presence tends to work against the development of a story line, to freeze the flow of action in moments of erotic contemplation."[31] The movement of the narrative in classical Hollywood cinema ("the normal narrative film") reinforces the male ego by virtue of its placement of the masculine subject in the position of visual mastery dependent upon the spatial realism characterizing this cinema. Narrative movement ordinarily would, in addition, tell the story of how the bourgeois family is supposed to be under patriarchy.[32] The woman's image, by contrast, although it is appropriated by the man (director, photographer, and so on), belongs to the surface of the screen, across which it is deployed as a lure for the male gaze, and as the locus of both identification and desire for the female spectator. But even though it is man who has deployed the woman's image for his own erotic or financial gain, according to Mulvey's theory, the very immobilizing power of the (still) female form forces the man to come to terms once again with the castration crisis he had experienced early in the process of Oedipalization.

Mulvey's fundamental argument, feverishly debated among feminist theorists, discarded by some, holds that the woman's image, so troubling to the male spectator, may be treated in one of two ways by the possessor of the filmic apparatus. Both of these "treatments" can be traced in Ophuls' films. As the familiar litany goes, the woman is either *investigated* by the narrative—through surrogate (male) spectator, narrator, and director-figures—and is found guilty or lacking (as in, among countless other films, Hitchcock's 1964 *Marnie*, in which Sean Connery discovers that Tippi Hedren is a thief—and frigid) or else she is set up as a fetish object, which functions to reassure the threatened male subject.[33] The gauze-lensed, heavily costumed, in-excess-of-Hollywood production, such as Josef von Sternberg's filmic treatment of Marlene Dietrich's body, is a well-known medium for this kind of fetishizing capture of the woman.[34] For Mulvey there is an ironic empowerment of woman in this very brandishing of the (fetishized) feminine image, even if it is the man who does the brandishing. The woman's body is brought forth as a *threat* to male intactness, a threat the woman would take advantage of in order to construct her own space within the narrative, halting it, breaking it up, disrupting its unity. This argument, difficult to follow when one thinks of the film medium as completely controlled by oppressive masculinity (how, in that case, would women have any influence at all on the medium?), becomes more interesting when discussing the woman's film (not to mention films *by* women)—and thus at least half of Ophuls' work. In these films the *female* spectator's desire to maintain the narcissistic predominance of her own projected image is supported by her (indirect) commercial control over these films. It is, of course, also possible to read the mesmerizing potential of the female image as a product not of female intentionality but of male fantasy—or paranoia.

The radical reading of the fetishized woman as potentially empowering for women is a milestone in feminist film theory, but the theory lacks flexibility, most importantly because it is fundamentally a male construct, based on masculine fears concerning the female body. This puts the female spectator in an awkward situation, as has been amply documented by recent film scholarship. But the woman's demonstrably strong narcissistic investment in the still image (delineated by Doane, Mulvey, and others) is not simply *opposed* to her "entrapment" by the aggressively used moving image. Rather, in Ophuls' films, movement is often associated with an attempt to break out of the confining still image and is thus not necessarily linked to the telling of a man's tale. The still image (or any emphasis on the represented person *as* represented— defined and framed by their representation by another) is always potentially an emblem of the oppressive fixing of the individual in the sexual role that defines his or her place in the society or the work of art in question. Immobility is as much an emblem of death as it is one of feminine power, as William Guérin notes in his comments on the last images of *Caught*: "Prisoner of the frame, literally crushed by the angle of the shot, Leonora seems to be definitively sworn to immobility, thus to death."[35]

The still image that captures and fixes its subject is often, in Ophuls' films, the product of patriarchal desire: King Ludwig wishes to (and does) have Lola Montès's portrait painted, and to take as long as he can in doing it, so that she is effectively immobilized; the protagonist of *Caught*, Leonora Ames, is alienated as a series of still press photos when she gives herself in marriage to the mentally deranged millionaire; the young model in *Le Plaisir* is drawn into a cycle of ever-increasing violence as her lover paints her portrait over and over again. But Ophuls' calibration of motion and stillness (circulation and freeze-frame in *The Bartered Bride*) to different moments of desire's trajectory will prove difficult to categorize: in *Lola Montès*, the still figure of the woman (Lola rips open her dress to show her body to the king) and the moving "figures" of the dance (Lola is a professional dancer) both serve to captivate her audience.

Guérin has noted in Ophuls' films a pattern involving the "straight line" and the "arabesque," the former associated with death and the paternal order (again, the duel is the ultimate incarnation of this kind of movement), the latter with woman and with the "baroque" surface of the Ophulsian image. It is along this sinuous surface that the eye is constantly moving, but it is a form that can also be associated with entrapment and death, as the arabesque becomes more and more tightly controlled.[36] Nor, of course, is narrative "movement" always in support of male ego-structures. It is true that the superfluous woman is sent away in several of Ophuls' films along a straight line (often railroad tracks).

However, it is also the case that in her moments of daring self-expression Lola Montès rides her horse or runs in the direction of her desire along a "straight line."[37] So, too, is Marie's desire born at the end of the squealing pig's linear trajectory—but Marie is static.

Just as movement is ambiguously cathected for the woman in Ophuls' films, the *danger* (both moral and psychic) involved in the attempt to approximate an image (the still image) is never far from the surface of Ophuls' films. This is not only because mimeticism—the imitation of images—is almost always depicted as morally suspect (although this is the case in *Caught* and in *Madame de . . . .* These films' heroines are reluctant to give up the fur coats that help create the images of the women they believe they should be, and then are forced, to their great unhappiness, to remain). This danger also springs from "Ophuls'" apparent belief that images themselves, particularly those associated with sexuality and inflationary circulation, are intrinsically productive of violence. (In *La Signora di Tutti, Letter from an Unknown Woman,* and elsewhere, Ophuls uses the soundtrack as a "positive" counterpoint to the treacherous image track.)

In *The Bartered Bride* the appropriation of the photographic images of the characters (during the photography sessions) is a playful gesture, not yet ripe with the portent felt in the later films. Still, in halting the narrative as they do, Kezal and the photographer are performing an ambiguous action. Do they represent the system that exists by appropriating and selling the woman's image at a profit? (Although all the characters are in the final "souvenir photo" that Kezal organizes, it is only the young woman who has been endangered by his economic activities.) Or are they allies of the woman who has deviated the flow of money and images? In Ophuls' later films, the figures of performance (here, the circus folk), who sell themselves to the crowd, are more and more conflated in function with the role of the woman, until we end, in *Lola Montès*, with a courtesan as circus star. And like Marie in *The Bartered Bride*, Lola will also be bound to an oppressive contractual relationship, of the sort omnipresent in Ophuls' films. Lola is offered a contract for her circus performances; Marie's father signs a contract for his daughter's marriage.

Although Mulvey's original argument has been critiqued to within an inch of its life, it nevertheless points to patterns of movement and non-movement in classical narrative cinema that certainly recur in Ophuls' cinema. We have already noted that female characters in these films often attempt to appropriate their own sexualized images as a means of controlling their fate. The still image of the woman brandished by the man as an attempt to reassure himself of his own mastery most assuredly rebounds to bring him horror. This is the case, for example, in *Le Plaisir*, where the artist who becomes more and more obsessed with painting his mistress (both taking control of and *selling* her image) is himself destroyed in the bargain. The feminine investment in the still image of her own body must be read against the background of her struggle to keep moving. In *The Bartered Bride*, for example, the woman must *flee* with her chosen lover before their images are fixed on the photographer's plate. In these films movement can be *movement forward* associated with both the woman's aggressive, "masculine" sexuality and with a personal freedom that is most often doomed (as in the sleigh ride in *Liebelei*, repeated as pure movement without the protagonists present on camera at the end of the film).[38] Movement can be *circular*, both entrapping and entrancing—in entertainment or in love (Lola's circus, or the ball scenes in several Ophuls films, where the oblivious lovers dance in circles). Movement can also be *vertical*—either exultant or suicidal: the female protagonist's initial fall from her skis in 1931's *Die Verliebte Firma* (The Company in Love), which brings her to the attention of the film company that hires her, and the prurient ascent of the camera in front of *Le Plaisir*'s Maison Tellier; or the suicide leap following a vertical ascent, as is found in *Liebelei*, *Le Plaisir*, and *Lola Montès*.[39]

Femininity, Jewishness, Authorship

The director-figures who seem to control the movement of the plot are in Ophuls' films almost always male and, like the jeweler in *Madame de . . .*, *The Bartered Bride*'s Kezal, or the brothel owner in *Yoshiwara*, they seem to be divided in allegiance between the "masculine" world of honor, stability, and grounded values and the "feminine" world of half-truths, vacillation, and ill-gotten gains. They are torn between a frenzied movement that torments the woman (but by means of which she might break free), or the stillness that is her self-inflicted death (as the printing presses halt their unnerving racket on the image of Gaby Doriot's face at the end of *La Signora di Tutti*), and the honorable discharge of their duties in the male-dominated society.

What is the force behind this association between the "feminine," directorship, and inflationary exchange? This question, which lies at the heart of Ophuls' directorial sensibility, can be answered only by working through the body of Ophuls' films and placing them within their historical context. Although the most pointed instance of such an association will be found in *Madame de . . .*, throughout Ophuls' works the woman who produces only repetitive and prevaricating stories, like the jeweler who only accumulates the profits of an artificially inflated exchange value, or the filmmaker who creates only obsessively repetitive works that concentrate on selling the woman's image—all are included with the prostitute and (covertly) the Jew in the "scandalous" group representing the realm of exchange divorced from that of production. The power and historical precedent of this series of associations can be traced through media other than the cinematic. In an article on George Eliot, Catherine Gallagher describes certain attitudes about exchange value that became prevalent during the second half of the nineteenth century:

A marketplace not directly bound to production, a commodity value wildly incommensurate with the value of labor embodied in the commodity, is, according to just about everyone, a bad thing. And as this economic discourse finds more popular expressions . . . one detects a growing hostility towards groups that seem to represent a realm of exchange divorced from production: for example, traders in general but especially costermongers in works like Mayhew's *London Labour and the London Poor*, prostitutes in the works of Mayhew, Acton, W. R. Greg and others, and the Jews in the works of almost everybody.[40]

The association of Jews with the pernicious effects of the realm of exchange is only alluded to in Ophuls' adaptation of Sabina's libretto for *The Bartered Bride*, which makes no mention of Jews. The allusion is, however, a striking one, consisting of an ironic reference to the Rothschild bank (seat of an enormous Jewish fortune that had great influence on European financial markets), which slips into the film as an amusing side-issue.[41] Driven from his country a year after making this film by a political movement that was founded on the image of the Jew as a dangerous and parasitical circulator of money, Ophuls seems already in this film to be developing a complex and perceptive counterargument to the metaphors that would describe the middlemen of capitalism as parasites, and women as dangerous, derivative, and interchangeable chattel.[42]

However the role of the Jew has been read in light of the history of the capitalist economy, or that of the matchmaker in the historically foundational exchange of women, or that of the actor in the history of drama, Ophuls seems to be linking these figures in a strangely meaningful dance. All are scapegoats for the negative effects of those interlocking systems of exchange because, perhaps unconsciously, *they reveal the mechanisms that make such systems work*. And these exchange artists, as we might label them, are also often a potential point of departure for protests against the configurations of power that sustain the systems in which they work. Thus the three hundred guldens are circulated through the hands of the "strangers"—the circus performers—before they can act to correct the course of desire among the village inhabitants.

Love Makes the World Stop

According to the vision of the world available to us through *La Ronde*, all members of the (in this case Viennese) society are involved in the processes of circulation.[43] Individuals who promote social exchanges reveal the mechanisms of those exchanges by increasing their frequency or by tying them together in an ideal unity never achieved on the "free market," where a connection might be missed. Nothing is left to chance, or, rather, chance is fragmented by the use of melodramatic predestination and explicit authorial intervention. This answers for the agonizing atmosphere of the closed "Viennese" circuit (Ophuls' prototype of the controlled European society) as well as for its beauty as formal system. The ineluctably important issue is not so much that there *is* circulation or fixation of images, capital, jewelry, but rather *how* this movement is controlled, who (other than "fate") has the right to call a halt or to start a cycle.

The movement of the narrative is "masculine," as Mulvey uses the term, only if it is legitimated by the patriarch's name and guaranteed ("grounded"), in an economic sense, by productive labor—labor that would not merely be the recirculation of the same objects or simulacra for higher and higher profits. It is evident that bourgeois logic attempts to cover its own tracks, to repress or marginalize the processes of circulating capital and reaping profit, which are of course the very basis for bourgeois capitalist society. Thus, as we have observed, a characteristic of "bourgeois" narrative is that the intermediary role of the bourgeoisie (managers, shop owners, and so on) in the economic system is often symbolically or actually displaced onto marginal figures such as the Jew or the prostitute or the actor in an attempt to mitigate the *malaise* evoked by the selling of commodities for profit.[44] There can also be a digressive narrative movement that is radically destabilizing, disseminating the meanings that would ground the sense of the tale: "With Ophuls there is neither a main actor, a star, nor a theme. No single subject is allowed to parade itself as one. The main points are minor points. Digression is everything—anything to break up a subject or the impression of an exhaustive, rounded work of art."[45]

Still, Ophuls' narratives do not all recount disruptions of bourgeois life. Grafe's statement that in Ophuls' films *love* represents a challenge to staid bourgeois morality and interrupts the normal flow of the exchanges (of women) underpinning bourgeois society is only partly valid. Grafe's treatment of the topic anticipates a discussion by Gertrud Koch that takes a different perspective.[46] Despite Grafe's striking description, "love" is not a one-sided term, serving only anarchic functions. Using her readings of *Liebelei* and *La Ronde* as points of departure, Koch argues that Ophuls' films reflect a valorization of emotion, a romantic protest against the rigid social mores of the closed cultural entities he chooses to depict. Love serves, in this case, to "re-Oedipalize" the flow of energy (in Deleuze's and Guattari's terms), to reintegrate moments of social revolt into familial structures.

We might extrapolate from Koch's discussion and say that, despite Grafe's claim, a protest carried out through love is not essentially anti-bourgeois. Romanticism's advocacy of immediacy (instant and true love despite social barriers) might be said to reproduce bourgeois false consciousness, to dictate that individuals are free agents unbound by social and economic constraints—capable therefore of *unmediated* relationships. However, *The Bartered Bride* shows less tolerance for bourgeois norms about love than does *Liebelei* (1932), made soon after it.[47] In its exposure of the structure of the mediated exchanges that constitute familial life, *The Bartered Bride* does use love as a disruptive force, precisely because it is the woman's operatic desire that not only prevails (this happens even in so hallowed a middle-class/peasant narrative as Smetana's opera) but also redirects the flow of money and alliance. *The Bartered Bride* anticipates Ophuls' later films, where the bourgeois romantic hero (or the aristocrat caught up by the nostalgia for bourgeois life seen in *Liebelei* and elsewhere) has become an object of suspicion to the director.

In his later films Ophuls concentrates distinctly on the representation of situations and emotions (primarily involving female characters) that cannot be completely recuperated into standard narrative practices. Films such as *Liebelei* or the (supposedly) narratively "conventional" films of his first French period have often been seen as falling short of the irony of the later, overtly analytical works. We have already seen, however, that even in Ophuls' early cinematic works the issue of woman's exchangeability is sometimes bluntly considered, without benefit of distracting secondary elaboration. Ophuls' film career begins and ends with the thematization of women's movements in this process of exchange, from which they occasionally try to break free, and in which, as we have noted, women act not alone but *politically* as figures of condensation and displacement.

Inheritance, Patriarchy, and Lachende Erben (Happy Heirs)

The "thematization" of women's movements is imbricated from the start of Ophuls' cinematic career with issues related to representation, monetary exchange, and the status of patriarchal authority. *Lachende Erben* (1932), made just after *Die verkaufte Braut* (*The Bartered Bride*),[48] focuses lightheartedly on the question as to whether a young man is worthy to inherit his uncle's wine empire, and despite its lack of cinematic distinction, it provides an entry into this set of issues. Curiously, this film reinstates the plot device discarded from *The Bartered Bride:* the young man with whom the young woman falls in love *does*, in *Lachende Erben*, turn out to be the legitimate heir to a fortune, unbeknownst to her. But the film also exercises a number of rather overdetermined double binds and displacements with regard to this scenario of legitimation. For example, young Peter Frank (the heir) can only prove himself worthy of inheriting his uncle's estate by violating the explicit terms of Herr Bockelmann's will.[49] This will prescribes a month of abstinence from alcohol before Peter can inherit. Bockelmann also enjoins Peter to bring the company's rivalry with his greatest competitor, Stumm, to a "good ending," an ambiguous command that constitutes the tongue-in-cheek Oedipal puzzle dominating the film's genealogy, as we will see.

In a complex double movement, Peter both obeys and defies his uncle's imperative to constrain his desire to drink and his free will in marrying. He refuses his inheritance for the sake of a woman he meets *by accident* on a train as he returns home for his uncle's funeral. Thus he seems to choose her freely, not realizing that she is the very woman des-tined to him by his uncle—the daughter of rival winemaker Stumm. When, to her dismay, she finds at the end of the film that Peter is the heir to Bockelmann's estate, indeed the son of her father's rival, he defiant-ly drinks wine, disinheriting himself and proving his disinterest in money. (As Peter "Frank" the young man is not obviously the Bockel-mann heir—clearly Peter's relation to his uncle is through his mother—matrilinear if not matriarchal.) Later Peter discovers, in the codicil to the will, that his uncle had stipulated that the inheritance could be passed along *only* if Peter does disobey the wine-drinking clause (show-ing himself to be a true lover of wine). The will of the patriarch dictates that Peter must choose wine over money: in fact he chooses "love" over money. Thus, even as he attempts to defy the Oedipal interdiction, he obeys its imperative, follows his own desire, and takes his allotted place on the family tree. At the heart of this comedy lies the fantasy that the violation of the law will lead to unimperiled enjoyment of what was for-bidden, a variation on the Oedipal drama, in which the subject falls more utterly under the effects of the law when he has violated it.[50]

On the part of the young woman (Gina), there is also an Oedipal drama in play—one that will become more explicit in *La Signora di Tutti, Komedie om Geld*, and *Lola Montès*. Her beloved widowed father "Robby" has begun to court a new wife, as she finds out by reading his appoint-ment calendar. Her romance with the young man whom she believes to be only the advertising chief for Bockelmann serves as a distraction from her unhappiness at her father's display of interest in another woman. As in *The Bartered Bride*, the young woman is aware that her father wants only to arrange a "proper" marriage for his daughter and has in this case attempted to "buy" her a husband by offering to sell land cheaply to the less prosperous Bockelmann, with the implied agreement that the sale will lead to the children's marriage.[51] Although *Lachende Erben* seems to be a faded negative of *The Bartered Bride* (in that the young man is to be the one bartered), both films actually emphasize the *woman's* defiant desire. Gina does not want to be simply the means of joining two wine firms. But where *The Bartered Bride* amusingly derails notions of legitima-cy and filiation, *Lachende Erben* features a heroine who marries the very man who will profit her father and fortune. The un-Ophulsian propriety of this happy ending is mitigated only by a redefinition of patriarchal authority. Bockelmann, the (dead) paternal figure is, ironically, invest-ed with a bon vivant's tolerance for the young man's urges—while the dour relatives, who want to turn the winery into a mineral water factory and (paradoxically) seek to thwart Peter's attempt at sobriety, represent de-authorized patriarchal rigidity.

Spivak has cautioned against "idealist" analogies between the subject and the commodity, the emergence of the money-form and that of the "phallus as transcendental signifier."[52] These issues are considered more carefully later, in my discussions of *Komedie om Geld*, *Madame de . . .*, *The Reckless Moment*, and other films dealing with the question of money and its relation to woman. For what concerns *Happy Heirs* and *The Bartered Bride*, one might note that Spivak herself constructs an analogy between the monetary and the psychological realms in the case of systems of inheritance: "Inheritance in the male line by way of patronymic legitimacy, indirectly sustaining the complex lines of class formation, is, for example, an area where the case of the money-form, and that of the ego-form in the dialectic of the phallus, support each other and lend the subject the attributes of class- and gender-identity."[53] Both films under discussion trouble the terms of patronymic legitimacy and its relation to the money-form though rather differently, as we have seen.[54]

Class Consciousness, Fathers, and Fallen Women in Liebelei

Turning to another aspect of familial patterns in Ophuls' films, the daughter who remains alone with her indulgent father is a topos not only in *Lachende Erben* but also in (among others) *Liebelei* (1932). This was Ophuls' most successful German film, the last he made before his forcible exile, and one of his most visually arresting. Although Ophuls does not use in it the many crane shots, long tracking shots, and "extended vertical shots" that will characterize his later style, as Robert Chamblee observes, "the sensibility which was to create those shots is abundantly present."[55] The exploration of vertical space is extensive (especially in the opening sequence at the opera house) and is further emphasized by the dramatic importance given to "the fall" later in the film. Scenes in *Liebelei* are quoted almost verbatim in later Ophuls films, particularly in *Letter from an Unknown Woman*, which shares its Viennese setting, and in *Madame de . . .*, which it resembles in plot. Indeed, *Liebelei* contains many of what Silverman calls the "nodal points" organizing Ophuls' authorial corpus, "fantasmatic" scenes expressing "Ophuls' " filmic desire.[56]

Many complaints have been made about Ophuls' alteration of Schnitzler's pessimistic play. Similar charges were lodged against Ophuls' adaptation (*Werther*, 1938) of Goethe's *Sorrows of Young Werther*, in which Lotte reciprocates Werther's love for her (famously unrequited in the novel). In Schnitzler's *Liebelei* the young reserve officer Fritz Lobheimer promises eternal love to a working-class girl, Christine Weiring, only to die in a duel over another woman. Correctly sensing that she has been used as a sexual convenience, Christine commits suicide. In Ophuls' version of the tale, Fritz does die in the duel over another woman, but we are given to understand that his love for Christine is nonetheless sincere and pure. This sentimentalization of Schnitzler's play is no doubt indicative of Ophuls' general tendency to "positivize feelings," in Koch's words, and underwrites Ophuls' conflicted urge to "stick to the emphatic construction of the bourgeois individual."[57]

Koch finds evidence of this ideological structure at the most discrete level of Ophuls' cinema. She describes *Liebelei*'s "aesthetic transposition of the positivizing of feelings that follow the diagonals of shots" as a device peculiar to Ophuls: characters who have the emotional upper hand, especially if their actions are guided by love, are characterized by a dominant gaze that moves along a diagonal path (p. 320). Koch notes this phenomenon in scenes including the one where Fritz's friend Theo begs their commandant to stop the impending duel between Fritz and the Baron, husband of Fritz's mistress. Theo declares that to protest the duel he will sacrifice his military career and go to live (in "gentle" colonialism, one assumes) on a coffee plantation in Brazil. The gaze of the commandant, who refuses to do as Theo wishes, is dominated by that of the young officer, standing higher on the image axis. Koch finds in this scene a *romanticizing* of bourgeois notions about "not wasting" life: the pragmatic, liberal bourgeois Theo Kaiser (who is pragmatic about his love with his *süsses Mädel*,[58] Mizzi, as well) is romanticized through his gesture of love for his friend. We will see that a larger view of Theo's role in the film—one that is not bound by the dynamics of the gaze in this particular scene, may indicate that he is not so unambiguously "life enhancing" as both Koch and Chamblee claim.

As is the case with much Hollywood cinema, which tends to sentimentalize, Ophuls' presentation of Fritz's love for Christine is a product of an allegiance to bourgeois mores. The attitudes subtending the film cohabit strangely with the antibourgeois undercurrent we observed in *The Bartered Bride*. Fritz turns away from his love for a jaded and very demanding Baroness (Olga Tschekowa, an older woman, to boot) to his fresh love for a young girl, the daughter of a kindly musician. As we can see from his facial expression, from his inhalation of the hallowed air when the lieutenant enters the humble home of the musician and his daughter, Ophuls' Fritz is attracted to the comforts of this petty bourgeois home. His rejection of the Baroness is also a rejection of upper-class values, an ironic turn toward the small pleasures of canned music (to which he dances with Christine in a bistro) versus the live music to which he dances the same waltz with the Baroness. Only a fade to black separates the two scenes, underscoring both their similarities and differences.[59] This "continuity" achieved via the waltz is one of Ophuls' signature ("nodal") moments. Both scenes are shot using elements that will form part of Ophuls' stylistic repertory. The scene in the cafe is beautifully blocked, so that the small space, with its mirrors, tables, and door arches, is used to its full expressive capacity. The relative coziness of this scene also contrasts nicely with the physically more spacious (though psychologically more claustrophobic) scene at the Baroness's home.

Like the girls' fathers in *The Bartered Bride* and *Lachende Erben*, Christine's father ("Weyring" in the film; "Weiring" in the play) only wants what's "best" for her. Though he proves too weak to help her, his wishes for her future are not tainted with the patriarchal urge to control the direction of her desire—indeed, he tells a rather long story to Christine's stuffy suitor, a fellow musician (not unlike the stuffy young military suitor in *Letter from an Unknown Woman*—a film in which the more *dashing* male love interest is a musician), about having thwarted his sister's passion through his overprotection. Herr Weyring states emphatically that this is something he will not do to his daughter. But the emphasis on *lack* of direction in the film is a cover for a profound anxiety about what it means to direct lives, and what it means to let female desire and/or the working of chance intervene.

Coziness and claustrophobia, freedom and rigidity: the permutations of these qualities are carefully mapped onto the world of object and representation and find many modes of expression in these films. In *Liebelei*, as in *Lachende Erben*, the rigid symbol of paternal interdiction is a displaced one. In this case the man who fills that role is not a father but a husband, the Baron von Eggersdorf. He is the first of a series of nobles and military men in Ophuls' films who, often most unwillingly, play the role of the castrating father. (In *The Bartered Bride* it is not so much paternal "interdiction" as the father's sale of his daughter in the marketplace of alliance that is deflected onto another figure, Kezal, the matchmak-

er.) Chamblee claims that Ophuls' transposition of Schnitzler's play
(Ophuls was cowriter on the film) from civil to military life is a reflection
of Ophuls' "searing denouncement of the perniciousness which auto-
cratic militarism produces within a society" (p. 43). And it is certainly the
case that the rigidity of the military mindset is conflated here for the first
but not the last time in Ophuls' works with the most oppressive elements
of masculinity.[60] The sterility, hierarchality, and death-dealing qualities
of the military stand in contrast to the simplicity and "life enhancing"
(Chamblee) qualities of petty bourgeois life. Chamblee further postulates that Ophuls "remained scrupulously faithful to the spirit of Schnitzler's play" in his redefinition of the play in military terms, in that the
social criticism made by the Ophuls film, though displaced, is in its way
as rigorous as that made by Schnitzler. It is true that the class issues have
been to some extent muted: the virginal middle-class girl is not simply
used and tossed aside by the upper-class officer—instead he really does
love her. The critique of class society is strictly from a bourgeois perspective, but Ophuls' film takes on a military color since it is a lieutenant
who holds the firmly bourgeois belief in the superiority of hearth and
home. The bourgeoisie stands in opposition to both the aristocracy and
military protocol. The deadly element in the Ophuls film is not class
inequity per se, but an almost abstract notion of hierarchy in conjunction with oppressive masculine "honor."[61] Thus, in moving from *The
Bartered Bride* to *Liebelei* we can discern the basic constellation of Ophuls'
ambivalent treatment of the middle classes, depicted as both the only
place where social freedom can abide and as the final link in a chain of
social hypocrisy. Koch's reading of the power of the *moral* gaze in *Liebelei*
is indicative of the plurality of effects the gaze can produce in Ophuls'
films. The (phallic) male gaze is nevertheless also operative in *Liebelei*, if
only as a placemarker for a supperanuated system.

It is already obvious from earlier remarks that music plays an important role in *Liebelei*. Through music and the notion of "theatricality" as
manifested in the film, we can trace the film's deconstruction of its own
moral dichotomies. Although by this time Ophuls had already made two
"musicals" (*Die verliebte Firma* and *Die verkaufte Braut*), this is the first of
his films in which music takes on something like the complex thematic
significance it will have in his later films. The film begins with an opera
performance (Mozart's *Abduction from the Seraglio*, not mentioned in
Schnitzler's play) which brings together all the principals: Fritz and
Theo in the orchestra seats, Mizzi and Christine in the balcony, the

Emperor as an unseen seer (whose role as counterspectacle is reiterated in *De Mayerling à Sarajevo*), Herr Weyring as an unseen cellist in the orchestra pit, and the Baron (who balefully notes Fritz's departure, to see the Baroness, soon after the opera begins) in a box seat. Also present in this scene is a "director-figure," whose type recurs in many of Ophuls' films—the stage manager—who peers out at the audience through the eye sockets of a mask of tragedy figured on the curtain, and anxiously coordinates the temporal elements of the performance. (This "director" plays another important role in tying together the various characters in the film: he uses a pneumatic device to speak to the porter,[62] who is talking to the Baroness, who has called to see what time the opera will end, so she can know when to expect her husband.) The first scene's arrangement of the main figurants at the opera presents visually the class consciousness supposedly absent from the film: the characters are rigidly hierarchized in order of class by their seats in the opera house. As in *Die verliebte Firma*, the action in *Liebelei* begins on a fall. The girls drop their opera glasses while trying to get a better look at the Emperor; the glasses fall on Theo's hat, knocking it to the floor, as Fritz grins with amusement. The commandant, occupying a box seat with his wife, notes the violation of protocol. We will see in *Lola Montès*, as well, that being higher up does not necessarily mean being at the top of the social hierarchy (although it will *also* mean that): Lola's rise in social status is at one point signaled by a descent from the cheap upper chambers of a hotel down to the more expensive first-floor rooms. In *Liebelei*, the girls in the upper balcony overstep another symbolic boundary from their position above the aristocracy. Their possession and dispossession of the enormous pair of binoculars—the mark of their visual mastery—is what triggers the opening of the film's action, as though through their desiring gaze the first domino of a carefully set-up game is knocked down.[63]

The stunning opera sequence is only the start of the film's meditation on women, performance, the gaze, and social hierarchy. Another theatrical moment added, like the opera, to the film features shy Christine as a performer—an early sister of the bold exhibitionist Lola Montès. Like Lola, Christine goes to an audition at a pivotal moment in the film's plot.[64] Christine sings both demurely and passionately for the elderly men watching and listening to her performance. The most moving song, at the juncture where the camera moves from a long shot to a medium shot of the young woman, thus from the auditioners' to "our" point of view, is about a brother and sister relationship. The song provides a

bridge to a parallel scene, bringing forth the dark overtones that performance will take in Ophuls' later films. Crosscutting indicates that the
audition is going on more or less simultaneously with the duel in which
Fritz is killed. According to Chamblee, the "life enhancing" characters in
the film (Herr Weyring, Christine, and Theo) are musicians, who stand
in opposition to the deadly seriousness of military and aristocratic hierarchy.[65] But in fact, each of the musical moments in the film is a prelude
to disaster. Weyring is interrupted at a rehearsal to go to Christine, who
is about to commit suicide. Theo, a rather parodic musician, pounds out
a tune on the piano under Mizzi's orders as she goes, dressed in Theo's
regimentals, to open the door to his flat and admit the Baron. As is the
case in both *Letter from an Unknown Woman* and *Le Plaisir*—and perhaps
even in *Caught* and *Lola Montès*—a stagy piano performance is linked not
so much with "life enhancement" as with sexual obsession, failed masquerade, and death. When Mizzi opens the door in her carnivalesque
disguise, we find that the Baron has come to challenge Fritz to a duel.
Theo and Mizzi, the soldier and the shopgirl,[66] have actively orchestrated a romance between Christine and Fritz that will throw the latter off
his guard, perhaps indirectly killing them both.

Like the scene where Mizzi parades in uniform, the opening sequence
at the opera house indicates the potential breakdown of the military-the-
ater opposition so often found in Ophuls' later films. Such a breakdown
throws into relief both the theatricality of the military and the deadly
consequences of directing the actions of others in a play one has con-
cocted.[67] A brief ceremony in the Emperor's box announces his arrival
(which the film spectator does not see). A group of officers enters the
box and parts symmetrically, forming two lines to flank the Emperor. No
sooner has this taken place, however, than Mizzi (gasping "Der Kaiser!")
drops the glasses that, by knocking off Theo's hat, will tie together the
threads of the narrative. The two women crouch in embarrassment as
the entire audience turns around to gaze at their sovereign—and, quite
by chance, simultaneously at the adjacent balcony behind whose railing
the girls have concealed themselves. All eyes seem to be upon the offend-
ing women when, in fact, the opera spectators are looking at the Emper-
or, the supreme commander, the young women's "opposite" in gender,
social status, and military affiliation. Or *are* the people looking at him?
By dropping the glasses the girls break the "hierarchy" of locked gazes.
Since the film audience does not see the Emperor, Mizzi and Christine
in some sense replace him, or at least prove (almost) capable of sustain-

ing the gaze he must support and return. But, of course, this is not necessarily a position of power: they have turned quickly from privileged
spectators—even shopgirls may look at a king—to embarrassed performers.[68] As Patrice Petro observes:

The high percentage of women in early film audiences was in fact perceived as
an alarming social phenomenon, one which confirmed the breakdown of traditional values elsewhere evidenced by the declining birthrate, the rising marriage
age, and the influx of women into the industrial labor force. The presence of a
female audience, in other words, not only represented a threat to traditional divisions between public and private, cultural and domestic spheres; it represented
a threat to the maintenance of social legitimacy, to the distinctions preserving
traditionally defined male and female gender roles and responsibilities.[69]

The opera was not so much a "mass cultural" event as cinema was in
Germany during this period, but the emphasis on female spectatorship
here can perhaps be read as a reflection on the female cinema audience,
on women's avid—and dangerous—consumption of the visual spectacle
of cinema. This period costume drama, in which theatrical spectatorship
around the turn of the century, and cinema spectatorship through
1932, are intertwined, provides a place for the return of the look upon
the female spectator. From spectator the woman is resituated as the
more "proper" (though still dangerous) spectacle. And although the
Emperor seems more than equipped to demonstrate his power even *as*
spectacle, later films show how vulnerable he, too, can be. In *De Mayerling à Sarajevo*, *The Exile*, and *Lola Montès*, the suffering monarchs are
curiously feminized through their contact with women of lower social
rank, and through their obligatory performance of their kingship—perhaps even in their role as *spectators* of the women they desire.[70] In *Liebelei*
the stage manager seems to coordinate this complex performance, from
the vantage point of his gaze through the mask of tragedy (out of whose
"eye" the camera moves at the beginning of the scene). This stage manager's preoccupation with time, which parallels that of the erring
Baroness, also points to the dialectic between (unstable) theatrical time
and (fixed) cinematic time.

Liebelei ends with Christine's leap (implied, but not actually depicted)
from the window of Fritz's flat, after she finds out about the sad circumstances of her lover's death. Her father realizes what she is about to do
and runs after her, but too late. The sentimental and sacrificed daugh-

ter of a grieving father is a locus classicus made familiar to American readers in the melodramatic fiction of Stowe and Dickens. This "Protestant Pietà," as Leslie Fiedler has termed "the white-clad daughter, dying or dead, in the arms of the old man, tearful papa or grandfather or (in America) the woolly-haired slave,"[71] is strongly marked as an affective force in *Liebelei*, although, like the leap, it is invisible. The film's last shot is a lingering look at the snowy fields through which the young lovers had earlier driven a sleigh as they swore eternal love to each other. So too will Ophuls endeavor to draw a mantle of snow-white purity around the fallen woman in his later films, a gesture that feminist readers of the films must certainly call into question—and one that Ophuls himself sullies through repetition.

One of the most poignant scenes in *Liebelei* involves not the innocent Christine but the guilty Baroness, who is sent away on a train by her brother-in-law just before the duel. When the Baroness attempts to take the hand of her brother-in-law through the train's open window, he refuses it. Of course, there is dramatic irony in this indifferent representation of forcible exile in a film made just before its director left the country under constrained circumstances. Perhaps in filming this scene Ophuls recalled another, earlier expulsion that had taken place—his own exit from Vienna years before when the administrators of the Burgtheater began to feel that its director should not be a Jew.[72] One wonders if his depiction of the harried stage manager in the wings of the theater at the Vienna Opera is somehow inflected by that earlier experience. This "revelation of the inner gears" of the theatrical performance (a gesture that Jane Feuer terms "Brechtian")[73] depicts the theatrical action as inexorable, fixed to an exigent temporality, one that controls the actions of the "director" as well as those of the characters, whom he links via his "tragic" vision through the mask. A subtler connection may be forged between the relatively minor characters, the stage director and the Baroness, both driven by time. This connection may have influenced Ophuls' later depictions of the woman exiled by train. The farewell scene at the train station certainly becomes one of Ophuls' most striking topoi, and after *Liebelei* attention and sympathy will be focused on the characters involved in such departures. The adulteress who is exiled and marginalized from the action of the film in *Liebelei* reappears as the central character in *Madame de . . .*, in which the issues of legitimation/legitimacy, oppressive patriarchy, performance, and the expulsion of scapegoats that we have observed in early films by Ophuls emerge fully blown.

Two

✦

The Economy of the Feminine in *Madame de . . .*

*A coat as such no more expresses value than does the
first piece of linen we come across. This proves only that,
within its value-relation to the linen, the coat signifies
more than it does outside it, just as some men count for
more when inside a gold-braided uniform than they do
otherwise.*

—KARL MARX, CAPITAL, VOL. 1

*Opera is not forbidden to women. That is true. Women
are its jewels, you say, the ornament indispensable for
every festival. No prima donna, no opera. But the role
of jewel, a decorative object, is not the deciding role; and
on the opera stage women perpetually sing their eternal
undoing.*

—CATHERINE CLÉMENT,
OPERA, OR THE UNDOING OF WOMEN[1]

Is this thy soft Family Love
Thy cruel Patriarchal pride
Planting thy Family alone,
Destroying all the World beside.
And he who make his law a curse
By his own law shall surely die.

—WILLIAM BLAKE[2]

Still Unpaid

In Dickens's *Little Dorrit* (1857), the evils of industrial society are writ in large letters. The burden of mismanaged capitalism lies heaviest on the shoulders of the small man and woman, the debtors who populate the prison where Little Dorrit, the most luminously innocent of Dickens's characters, is born into debt. Filial Dorrit privately pardons her debtor-father a thousand times over for his shameful state, while she maintains, throughout most of the novel, an unimpeachable sense of honor concerning the irreducibility of debt itself. Even if the debt that drove her father into prison is a result of his having been cheated (which it in fact is), *he remains responsible for it*. Dorrit's only moment of relaxed virtue is when she doubts this (ironic?) tenet of Dickens's moral code, when she cries out in a single anguished instant that the debt should be forgotten, absolved. Her suitor, the sympathetic Clennam, is horrified by this taint, this "speck of prison atmosphere" upon her.[3]

Thus, Dickens the social critic does not cross the line of demarcation that would take him out of the ideological realm of the capitalist system he criticizes. *A debt is not to be forgiven.* Dorrit's *womanish* and dishonorable misunderstanding of the absolute nature of the debt can be pardoned because it stems from her *womanly* pity for her father, a pity that cannot be shared by the society because it would destroy the "honorable" basis of participating in the capitalist society. In Ophuls' work, as in much European and American literature and cinema of the nineteenth and twentieth centuries, the debt is often specifically attached to the crisis of masculinity: to be a man is to pay one's debts. The woman, on the other hand, who is "insufficiently Oedipalized," as psychoanalytic theory would put it, exists in a state of unresolvable debt. Such a woman is *tainted* by debt, and yet it is not really hers to repay: the debt is neither so radical nor so amendable as is the man's. The woman is never obligated to break free from her mother,[4] from her family, from dependency on the man, as is her brother—who otherwise is no man at all—and yet the woman is living on borrowed time. The source of woman's social "indebtedness" is, oddly, her refusal to undergo the loss man must suffer in the resolution of the Oedipal complex. According to Freud's revolutionary formulation, the girl holds on to her mother, merely *adding* the longing for father, and then for her husband. Brother, on the other hand, must turn away from mother and from the immediate gratification of his senses or else lose the most sensitive organ of all. Somehow, as Kaja Silverman wryly observes in *The Acoustic Mirror*, man's *fear* of loss is displaced onto woman: *she* is lacking, castrated, less than honorable in making good her losses, paying her debts—although, strangely, she is also characterized as never giving up anything. Woman's *real* losses—that of her mother as primary object of desire, of her own sense of intactness when society tells her that by definition she is not enough—are acknowledged by Freud only belatedly.[5] Somehow Freud's description of female loss does not take on the *grandeur* of the male Oedipal sacrifice (as can be observed in *Little Dorrit* as well). Still, Dorrit is tainted by her father's loss: his social "castration" is projected onto her, as Silverman describes male loss in general. Psychoanalysis and the culture from which it arose thus oscillate between viewing woman as castrated and as narcissistically whole. Dickens at least raises the woman's dilemma in the tragic proceedings.

As is indicated above, one must map the connections between economic concepts such as debt, production, and circulation in Ophuls' films in order to provide the groundwork for analysis of contrasting representations of the men and women who must undergo loss within Ophuls' distinctive characterization of the cinematic image. In studying these interconnections, I also examine the influence of the nineteenth-century realist literary tradition on Ophuls' sometimes only marginally realistic films.[6] This chapter works primarily to show how the woman in *Madame de . . .* (1953) is situated as the object of exchange between men, and elucidates how this economy functions through its marginalization of those "unproductive" members, like coquettish women, who are associated with debt, inflation, and specularity. It ends with a discussion of Ophuls' 1936 Dutch film *Komedie om Geld* (*Trouble with Money*), a late film of his French productions of the thirties, *Sans Lendemain* (1939), and his 1949 "film noir" *The Reckless Moment*, in the context of speculation, debt, and spectacle.

The Earrings and Narrative Movement

Madame de . . . represents a powerful instance of Ophuls' radical reading of the woman's social role. The film begins by overcoming what seems to be a narrative impasse—there was, according to the opening inscription, almost no story at all:

Madame de . . . was a very elegant, very brilliant, very celebrated woman. She seemed destined to have a pleasant [pretty] life without problems. It is probable that nothing would have happened without this jewel.[7]

These two beginning inserts, written in a flourishing hand, act as the authorial "voice" otherwise absent from this film. In its lack of an overt director-figure, "author," or *meneur de jeu*, *Madame de . . .* more closely resembles Ophuls' American films than the other, self-conscious, works from his second production period in France. *The Exile* (1947), Ophuls' first American film, also begins and ends with writing (historical plaques both commemorating and creating the events of the narrative), which is partly obscured by a shadow falling across the bottom of the initial plaque. *Madame de . . .* is peculiar in that the initial ellipsis of the title, signaled by the three suspension marks standing in for the syntactic "future" of the story, is never filled in. We never discover the surname of Louise de . . . (as the film's final shot emphasizes for the last time). No closure of the film is possible: it is merely cut off, as the name on the plaque in this last shot is cut off. And the mystery of this name, whose *particule* ("de") seems to lend it an obscure social power, is associated from the start with the "central" object of the narrative—the jewels or, more precisely, the earrings of Madame de . . . .

The relationship between narration and the earrings' movements is made clear by this insert: it is the earrings rather than psychological motivation that will provide the impetus of the intrigue, just as a lost lottery ticket motivates the action in René Clair's *Le Million* (1931), and a missing sum of money is pivotal in *Komedie om Geld*.[8] "Madame de . . . seemed destined to a life without problems"—this is the way many authors have translated "une vie sans histoire."[9] Literally, however, this woman has led a life "without history" or "without a story." The jewels cleave in twain the otherwise undifferentiated life of a young married woman, making possible the beginning of the tale. Later in the film, when the Baron has given the jewels back to Louise by concealing them in some flowers, she comments, upon catching sight of them: "En voilà une histoire!" which could be translated as either "Here's a story!" or "Here's trouble!" And when the jeweler sees that Louise has reported as stolen the earrings she sold back to him, he remarks that "Cette histoire de vol [this story of a theft] est inadmissible." Such stories are impermissible. The jeweler himself will rewrite this chapter by selling the earrings back to her husband, M. André de . . ., the General (a military general in the film, though not in the novella).

That the earrings seem to control the lives of the men and women in the film reverses the more usual character psychology based on interiority or character development. This antipsychological bias can be seen in most of Ophuls' films, where social structures and representational concerns sometimes seem to outweigh psychic inwardness. As both theatrical and cinematic director, Ophuls often adapted modernist works, such as those by Stefan Zweig and Arthur Schnitzler, which themselves tend to empty out questions of personality. Robert Chamblee has observed, however, that it would be an exaggeration to claim that the characters in *Madame de . . .* are completely without the earmarks of the rounded literary character: "It is of vital importance to note . . . that while the actors may be used compositionally, they are always psychologically individuated through the acting."[10] Indeed, the tension between the impersonality of their social roles and the brilliant acting of Danielle Darrieux (Madame de . . ., or Louise), Charles Boyer (the General, or André), and Vittorio de Sica (Baron Donati) serves to *individuate* the characters more than in perhaps any other film by Ophuls. Like Gertrud Koch, Chamblee notes that "character relations are frequently articulated by spatial coordinates in Ophuls' films."[11] Mary Ann Doane demonstrates just as forcibly, however, that the repetitious quality of the mise-en-scène and the dialogue in *Madame de . . .* acts to frustrate the spectator's expectations concerning character development, as do the numerous other systematic blockages of the "desire for narrative" in the film.

The operative word in this debate is, perhaps, *tension.* The often-cited direction by Ophuls to Danielle Darrieux that she must use her charm, beauty, and intelligence to "incarnate a void" in playing this part indicates that the film plays on the spectators' tendency to read character depth into the performance of a fine actress, while such depth may be an illusion.[12] Ophuls foregrounds the act of performing as well as the situation of beholding the performances in the film. To see the point of the film as the *achievement* of personality depth through suffering (overcoming the shallowness of vanity, the tendency to *perform* rather than to feel) is to ignore the film's complex play with the instability of both "character" and narrative, especially when the character involved is markedly feminine.

The jewels in *Madame de . . .* are exchanged for money. In separating them from their surroundings by means of the first scene's opening shot, this paradigmatic (substitutable) quality is emphasized. In this scene, the "themes" of absence, of detachability, and of representation or demarcation (by means of the frame) are also metonymically linked to the place of the woman put into circulation by the film's titles. The camera pans across an elaborately cluttered dressing room as a young woman in medium shot (whose face is not shown) searches through her possessions while she sings and speaks aloud to herself. This panning shot begins, however, with a close-up of the jewels themselves, a pattern to be followed regularly throughout much of the film, where opening shots of scenes detail the jewels or objects associated with them. In this scene, Louise looks into her drawer, considers, and then passes over the earrings, her hand trembling as though she hesitates to touch the contents of the jewelry box. The song she sings, interspersed with words spoken half-audibly, is peculiar. This tune will become the theme of the film, repeated most often in conjunction with appearances of the earrings.

[*She looks at the earrings and speaks*] The problem is that he gave them to me the day after we got married. . . . [*Singing, as she opens the closet*] I won't get 20,000 francs for all this. [*Speaks*] Oh, no. I absolutely refuse to be separated [separate myself] from my furs. [*She takes a hat down from the closet*] In these cases one must dress simply. [*She sits at her vanity table to fix her hat, and we see her face for the first time in a small oval mirror on the table. She then picks up a diamond necklace, a cross, and some emeralds.*] I'd rather throw this river [of jewels] into the water than to be separated [separate myself] from it.

The initial scene of the film thus creates a "blank" enunciative space where the woman's point of view is followed, though displaced, but in which she is not seen seeing until her face is reflected in the mirror. This occurs only after we have been shown the repertory of finery that is to play such an important role in the film. The woman becomes, in a sense, merely a supplement to her own sartorial excess.[13] Louise refuses to *se séparer* from her necklace or from her furs for money, although, as we are to learn later, she needs this money desperately. The refusal may be read to demonstrate Louise's initial psychological investment in her finery: she refuses to be deprived of her cherished female accoutrements, of that which, indeed, will prove to constitute her as subject. "My cross? Oh, no, I adore it," Louise remarks with unconscious irony as she considers whether to sell her cross. Religion, whose increasing importance in the film has been read as another sign of growth in Louise's subjective depth, is in fact associated with the ornamental and is repeatedly linked to her jewel fetish during the course of the film. There is, of course, one item Louise values less than she values the others: the pair of heart-shaped diamond earrings seen in the first shot of the film and already given narrative centrality. In making her selection of what jewel to sell, Louise is torn between the use and exchange values of her possessions. Louise's presentation as one of the objects on her table (we see her reflection from the table) also indicates her "doubled" nature as commodity. Such use values, "as material, carry—support or transport—the possibility of being deported or transferred elsewhere!"[14] Thus begins the movement of the commodity-fetish in the film.

The Plot

A brief summary of *Madame de . . .*'s rather convoluted plot may be helpful at this point. The heart-shaped diamond earrings which, as we have seen, act as the narrative vehicle for this film's events, are sold by Louise de . . .,[15] a giddy and narcissistic (though charming) woman, in order to pay certain unnamed debts, amounting to twenty thousand francs. Louise de Vilmorin's novella describes these debts as the result of Madame de . . .'s habitual lying to her husband about the amount of money she spends.[16] The earrings are sold to the jeweler, M. Rémy, who had sold them to her husband, M. de . . . (the General), to give to his bride on the day after their marriage.

After selling the earrings, Louise pretends to lose them at the opera. They are reported as stolen by the manager of the opera house, and the story appears in the newspapers. Shocked and worried that he will be implicated in a scurrilous affair, the jeweler approaches the General, tells him the truth about the earrings, and sells them back to him. The husband then gives them to his mistress, Lola, who is on her way to Constantinople. She soon loses them by gambling at the roulette wheel. An Italian diplomat, Baron Fabrizio Donati, buys them from a jeweler in Constantinople (South America, according to Vilmorin) and returns with them to Paris, where he meets Madame de . . . . The pair falls in love and Donati gives Louise the earrings, which she first takes with her on a trip to the Italian lakes (where she struggles unsuccessfully against her love for Donati). Louise later wears the earrings after pretending to find them in her glove drawer, not realizing that her husband has been told of her earlier sale. Neither does she tell Donati that she had once owned the earrings. The General surmises that the earrings are a gift from Donati, becomes angry and, taking them from his wife, returns them to the diplomat, who also sells them back to M. Rémy. Donati is so disgusted with his lover for having lied to him about the origins of the earrings that he breaks off their romance. She begins to pine away. The General then buys the earrings once more and coerces Louise into giving them as a gift to his niece, who has just given birth to a son. The niece sells the earrings back to M. Rémy when her husband has financial difficulties; the jeweler approaches M. de . . . for their "usual transaction" (the latter's purchase of the jewels), but the General angrily refuses. Mme de . . . finally sells all her possessions to buy the earrings, which have become quite valuable after all this reselling. The General, outraged by his wife's obsession and Donati's "stupidity," challenges the diplomat to a duel. Although he no longer loves Louise, the Baron accepts, knowing that to do so is "a veritable suicide." Louise, rushing to the site of the duel with Nanny, dies of heart failure when her lover is shot, offscreen. The final sequence of the film shows the church where Louise had previously prayed to the statue of her saint. Her earrings are now enshrined here, labeled with a plaque stating that they are the "gift of Madame de . . . [the rest of the plaque is obscured]."

Coincidence and Fiction

As Alan Williams has commented, this film is unusual not simply because there is a "clearly identifiable object of value" guiding the narrative, nor because it is an *object* rather than a human being that is of such central importance to the movement of the plot, but because of the "comparatively great number of transfers of a single object and that this manipulation is so *evidently regular*."[17] Both Williams and Doane insist upon the ironic intrusiveness of the film's repetitions. This intrusiveness "works against the transparency of narrative," according to Doane, who concentrates upon the "dialogical" aspect of Ophuls' film text.[18] Such a dialogical text brings to the foreground the artifices of storytelling. The characters themselves do not notice the patterns of movement that are so obvious to the spectator. André de . . . does not, for example, realize that he is repeating his wife's words when he says of the Baron Donati that "les nouvelles sont excellentes"—that his health has not been endangered by his recent fall from a horse.[19] Often the characters' lack of control of the film's events, the ascendancy of the narrative function itself, is named chance (*le hasard*) or fate (*le destin*) in *Madame de . . . .* In the absence of an overt director-figure, such as the one in *La Ronde*, one way in which the functioning of the narrative is foregrounded is in the unlikeliness of the coincidences that keep the earrings moving. Doane particularly emphasizes this point:

Now, in the aesthetic work, coincidence which is too strong or too visible becomes contrivance. It is "unnatural" and thus reduces the credibility of the constructed world, its *currency*—when we say "I don't buy that" we are also saying "I don't believe it." Through its convoluted structure, the text, like Madame de with her lies and fainting spells, invites disbelief—which suggests that the film is *about* the credibility of stories. It refuses to sell itself to the spectator under the traditional terms of fictional exchange—it establishes another kind of economy. (pp. 229–30)

Doane's linkage of "currency" and "spectatorial belief" in the narrative gets to the crux of the film.[20]

We should note that at one point in the film, when the earrings make an especially unlikely appearance, André remarks to the astonished M. Rémy that "chance [*le hasard*] is completely natural." Perhaps he means that this is the case within the confines of the narrative.[21] He is not naive about women, or about narratives either. In calling attention to its own status as fiction, and to Louise as a creator of fictions, the film operates a "curious *mise en abyme* structure"[22] because Madame de . . . is the character who tells misleading stories. It is when (the more naive) Donati finds out that Louise has lied about the earrings that he abandons his love for her. She is, as Doane puts it, "linked with the trait of deception." "The trait is, in fact, ideologically determined as a 'feminine' one. *But the film tends to de-sexualize deception as well as fickleness and infidelity, by assuming them as characteristic traits of its own narration*" (pp. 254–55, emphasis added).

One wonders why Doane backs away here from the specifically feminine association "ideologically" attached to the notions of deception and fickleness.[23] The film is not "feminized," however, by an *unreliable* narrative, one that presents events that are later shown to be false. This would mean that the fiction has the possibility of telling a truth, even though the narration might momentarily be false or unreliable. *Madame de . . .* is, rather, a frustrating narrative that emphasizes its *overall* lack of relation to the referent by exaggerating certain cinematic conventions, leading us to see the cinema narrative and woman as inveterate liars, rather than seeing the trait of lying as desexualized. The "Maupassant" figure in *Le Plaisir* puts it succinctly: "Women lie without knowing it, without wanting to, without understanding." Problems arise only if we want to believe that the story is *real*, as Donati wishes to believe that Louise's tales about her life are real. Thus the film stresses instead the more general problem of the suspension of disbelief in a fictional tale.[24] Louise's lies are intimately connected with the question of our relationship to narration, but her deception is not subsumed to the workings of the fiction: it is, rather, the model for its fictionality. The fact, as Alan Williams has pointed out, that Fabrizio Donati *fell in love with a lie* (p. 118), is indicative of the erotic centrality of the woman's relation to fiction. "Je ne vous aime pas" ("I do not love you") is Louise's perpetual refrain of love to Fabrizio, first pronounced when she is about to leave for Italy in order to escape her growing passion for the diplomat. It is clear to the spectator and to Donati that she means the opposite of what she is saying. We want the obvious lie to conceal a truth.

It is the woman's link with the deceptive capacity of the narrative that gives force and coherence to *Madame de . . . .* Louise's habit of deception is spelled out in an early scene of the film. After giving the earrings to his mistress in secret, André returns home for the evening. In an intricately shot scene, he manages to extract an indirect apology from Louise for having deceived him. The apology is not made for lying: it has another referent entirely: the "*loss*"—or sale—of the earrings. This little problem of reference does not, however, seem to bother the General: he knows very well that she is lying, but accepts her apology anyway. Like many bored Ophulsian married couples, M. and Mme de . . . sleep separately, and in this scene are occupying their respective bedrooms.

> GENERAL: [*Stands in front of mirror, tweezing his eyebrows, then goes to his bed. Calls out to his wife*] Are you sleeping?
>
> LOUISE: No, I'm too nervous about those jewels.
>
> GENERAL: You can just tell everyone that you have found them again [instead of allowing the servants et al. to be suspected of theft].

LOUISE: Pardon me for my clumsiness.

GENERAL: What?

LOUISE: [*Loudly and emphatically*] I said, pardon me. I didn't know you were hard of hearing.

GENERAL: All of us in the artillery are a bit deaf.

André accepts the woman's problematic relationship to the truth—as long as she asks his pardon, and as long as she recognizes that she is in his debt.[25] Later, when Louise uses the earrings to signify her love for Donati, the General will be less lenient in allowing unorthodox or ambiguous reference to obtain. He will then want the earrings to have one meaning—a kind of exchange value that *he* determines.

The earrings, through their coincidental returns, are linked to various powerful intersubjective undercurrents in the film, including the return of a rejected "uncanny" aspect of female sexuality, associated with chance and with destiny through the figure of the old nanny who reads cards.[26] Nanny's "doubling" of Louise by means of costume at the end of the film underscores this uncanny quality of the feminine, in that Nanny herself is given repeatedly to be a superstitious character.[27] A reading of the film according to Girardian principles would hold that the earrings attract Donati because, although he never saw them on Lola, they are already invested with the desire of another (man). And from André's position the earrings do signify such a *directed* desire. However, such a reading may be a way of repressing that which is uncanny in the woman herself, since in it she becomes merely the intermediary for the desire of another man. The "Girardian" reading tendered above would repress that which is uncanny in the woman herself, since according to such a reading the woman becomes merely the intermediary for the desire of another man. Donati may be drawn to the jewels because they have been cast off or forcibly taken from the woman, without specific reference to any masculine presence, as the socially manufactured symbol of her " lack."

Authorship, Femininity, Production

In the novella from which the film was adapted, the principal characters have no given names: they are known only as the ambassador, Monsieur, and Madame de — (a blank space is left at the end of the name, rather than the ellipses found in the film). In the film the names have become Fabrizio Donati (which is perhaps a reference to Stendhal's Fabrizio del Dongo in *The Charterhouse of Parma*), Louise, and André de . . . .[28] Like her novelist namesake (Louise de Vilmorin), Louise de . . . fabricates stories that must be acted out by others. Near the beginning of the film, for example, she sends her husband from opera box to carriage to opera box on a search for the earrings that she knows to be pointless because their "loss" is her fiction. To give this coquettish and prevaricating Louise the same first name as her maker, her own author, underscores the disturbing connotations surrounding any feminine production that is not that of children (disturbing enough in themselves). And yet, a coquette is not always punished; a woman who weaves fictions may find a place in society, if a somewhat scandalous one. Donati, we have noted, will fall in love with Louise's lie, "Je ne vous aime pas." Only when the woman attempts to live her scandal as truth, to appropriate, to really possess that which was loaned to her, will the scandal become a catastrophe. When Donati discerns her lie about the origin of the earrings, when he is confronted by the patriarch's insistence that Louise is marked by lack, he abandons his love for her.

Catherine Gallagher has described the scandalous effect of a woman attempting to write, to invent her own fictions. "Both the woman artist and the prostitute," she writes, "are established in the sphere of exchange that excludes 'natural' generation and substitutes for it an exhiliratingly dangerous love affair with a multitude."[29] Since Ophuls has given her the name of the novella's author, Louise shares the author's unstable but exciting position with respect to the multitude. The woman's effort to control her own life manifests itself in *Madame de . . .* as a specifically economic activity. She wishes to participate in the marketplace with the men around her, but is never on equal footing. The circulation of the earrings in the film produces gains for certain individuals (notably for the jeweler, who profits "parasitically" from the circulation of the object). M. Rémy sells the earrings to the General several times and, when the earrings have become so value-laden that they consume the worth of all that Louise owns, ends up completely stripping her of her possessions. We may see this as a parable of Louise's having learned to value love over material objects. It is equally plausible to read it as the impoverishment or "castration" of the once narcissistic woman, who at first does not recognize the value of the phallus/earrings—but finally loses everything to prove their worth. Or is this ending merely the result of the woman's attempt to participate equally in the sphere of exchange? Once again we find ourselves moving between psychic and material spheres. In this context, concerning the woman's role in the various economies we are discussing, Doane remarks that

Michèle Le Doeuff has, quite legitimately, warned us about the metaphorical use of the term "economy" in contemporary theory—the resort to phrases such as "libidinal economy," "textual economy," "classical economy," "general economy"—a usage which absolves the theorist from a confrontation with the economy "proper" insofar as it refers to such things as prices, exchanges, markets. However, the injunction negates the profound connections between the different economies, a connection which is, perhaps, most visible in the cinema. The economy of the text, its regulation of spectatorial investments and drives, is linked to the economy of tie-ins, the logic of the subject's relation to the economy—her status as consumer of goods and consumer of discourses.[30]

When we say that the woman is attempting to participate equally in "the sphere of exchange," we must remember that that economic text is written in more than one register, not least in the one involving the exchange of goods, in which woman herself is both commodity and consumer.[31]

The pursuit of the earrings is the site where the telling of a story coincides with that metaphor of an empty or groundless "productivity" run amok. Gallagher details the historical climate of the late nineteenth century that created the metaphor of female authorship as whoredom, and finds evidence that, in her writings on "bad women novelists," George Eliot forged a new version of this metaphor as a means of countering that other, more predominant one, where writing is a quintessentially masculine activity, and where the penis is equated with the pen (46). Eliot's metaphor substitutes instead the notion that women, in writing, do not really "produce" but only repeat formulas and phrases that have already been written by others. Inflammatory repetition that would masquerade as original production can only be lies or exciting and immoral half-truths. Although Eliot's attitude toward "scribbling women" is clearly disparaging, the metaphor of lying repetition serves to wrest the pen away from the male writer, thus enabling Eliot's own writing—as well as the prevarications of Louise, caught in the midst of narrative repetition.

Spectacle, Debt, and Scandal

Louise's commitment to the sphere of exchange does not involve only the earrings but has to do with both money itself and other items. We have observed that she is in debt at the beginning of the film and for that reason sells her jewels. Hurriedly drinking her morning coffee while gazing up at her husband's portrait, Louise goes to M. Rémy's shop. The pattern involving contract,[32] object, and representation is repeated in a short scene inserted between Louise's leaving her home and her arrival at the jewelry shop—a scene whose importance is redoubled by its repetition at the climax of the film. Entering a church and approaching the altar where the statue of her patron saint is displayed,[33] she walks brusquely to the altar, kneels, and prays:

> LOUISE: Be good to me, my little saint. I won't forget you, whether he accepts or doesn't accept. So be it.

Louise then moves over to where an old woman is selling votive candles. The candle-vendor loudly asks for "quatre sous," as Louise chooses a candle. Thus a contract with the saint—one in which the woman accepts the will of the "divine" other as part of the contract—is sealed by a monetary exchange (although the amount of money involved is negligible, and the saint is represented by a raucous old woman).[34] During this clearly perfunctory visit to the church, a young officer (the only other person present in this scene except for the old woman) openly stares at her, then lowers his head—as though realizing that such looking is what got him into trouble in the first place. By contrast, in the last moments of the film when an anguished Louise enters the church to make a more serious deal with the saint—Donati's life in exchange for the earrings—there is no ironic witness to the transaction. If Louise has arrived at a more "authentic" emotional state at this point in the film, this is expressed in terms of her no longer presenting herself to another's vision. The young officer's shame also prefigures the unhappy consequences, for a number of the film's characters, of looking at the coquette.[35]

As is indicated by this early scene with the young officer and by Louise's later flirtation with her numerous suitors (ironically endured by her husband), the woman's relationship to the crowd, omnipresent in Ophuls' films from *Die verliebte Firma* (1931) onward, is spelled out largely as a visual one, in which Louise the coquette is continually displayed (usually, though not always, for the benefit of more than one person) as the object of a spectacle. She publicly performs her role as a flirt at the ball where she is first introduced to Donati and where she "tortures" the young Englishman who is in love with her (by allowing him to hope for more), while Donati and her husband look on. After the Baron is metonymically linked to Louise by dancing with her at numerous balls, he too will become an object of public attention and commentary, just as Fritz and the Baron's wife (in *Liebelei*) excite obscene remarks by the officers when they dance together too often. When, earlier in the film, Louise's suitors crowd around her on a stairway (one of the more than fifty shots of stairways for which the film is famous), two of the men are singled out and we overhear their plan to dine with Louise at the "Café Anglais." The General, however, vetoes this suggestion, remarking to Louise that "your suitors flatter me less than they annoy me. Individually [*isolément*], each one of them is boring, but as a group, they are unbearable."[36]

Louise's coquettish rapport with the longing masses is, even now, wearing on her husband. But André's remark masks his fear of the even greater danger of her being singled out by the eyes of *one* man. At the jeweler's shop, when she first appears, the young assistant (the jeweler's son) is reprimanded for looking "too long" at the lovely client. Indeed, Louise says to the jeweler himself, who stares at her when she proposes to sell the earrings, "Ce n'est pas moi qu'il faut regarder" ("It isn't *me* you should look at"). Like many of Ophuls' heroines, Louise must develop a strategy to deflect the perils often implicit to occupying the position of the object of the spectacle, curiously conflated with the woman's problematic situation as the source of the fiction and as rival to the explicit or implicit director-figure.

That to be the object of the spectacle is a dangerous, or at least a *painful,* position is shown when, near the end of the film, as Louise suffers the humiliation of rejection, André theatrically opens the curtains to flood her face with light. This gesture recalls that of a director who turns the lights upon a star he is filming. Louise's response is to cry out in pain, as Nanny runs across the room to close the curtains. When Louise finds that she has fallen in love with the Baron, she puts it in specifically visual—and passive—terms: "I only want to be looked at by you." At one of the balls frequented by Donati and Louise while André is away on maneuvers, a scrawny admiral's wife remarks that the pair meets in public because "they can't see one another elsewhere" (imply-ing, perhaps, that their very visibility is in question outside the public arena). The absurdity of the admiral's wife's "look" ironizes that of the lovers—although Louise has, of course, *denied* her own look in this scene. For the woman to look first, to look desiringly, renders her unwor-thy of love. And yet the female spectator is inscribed emphatically—though unglamorously—in this scene.[37]

We can see that as he falls in love with Louise, Fabrizio begins to act as a specular object. He is also *addicted* to the act of looking. This becomes clear in the famous montage sequence of balls, joined by dis-solves, where ever-shrinking amounts of time pass between the moments when the potential lovers meet. The addictive nature of looking is indi-cated by Donati's repeated pattern of words ("two weeks without *seeing* you; . . . two days without seeing you; . . . twenty-four hours without see-ing you"), which become more and more ardent as time goes by.[38] And when Louise faints at the hunt because she fears that Donati has been hurt, her humiliation is framed in this way: "I have made myself into a spectacle. I want to leave" (Je me suis *donnée* [given myself] en specta-cle). Interestingly, this fainting occurs when Louise is shown to *look* through a pair of field glasses at her lover. This is an instance of her being "punished"—as are the two young women in *Liebelei*—for attempt-ing to appropriate vision. Or is it that the woman's desiring look is lethal, as is implied in *Letter from an Unknown Woman,* and as is the case in Niblo's *Blood and Sand* (1922), where the woman literally "gores" the man with her look?[39]

We might also recall that being the object of vision is associated with thievery in the opera house where Louise "loses" her earrings.[40] In the adjoining opera box where André is searching for the "lost" earrings, an angry man confronts him, saying he has been looking too long at his wife and thus must suspect her of the theft. André's witty response to this is to say that the man is paying the price for marrying a beautiful woman. Of course men stare at beautiful women. André has often seen this gen-tleman looking at Louise—and *not* because he suspected her of a theft. Is it the case, however, that a man's eyes are attracted to a woman because of some quality she has *stolen* or that she wishes to steal, perhaps from the man himself?[41]

The dialectics of the spectacle are, in fact, very complex in *Madame de* . . . . As long as Louise is admired by the multitude and uses the earrings given to her by her husband as a jewel befitting the social ornament that she is, she is safe from his wrath. Only when her sense of indebtedness overcomes her, when she tries to put the earrings into circulation as an exchange value, does she reveal the nature of the system in which she moves.[42] Only when she wants to remove herself from the eyes of the multitude, to be looked at by only *one* person (not her husband)—and perhaps to return that look—is her indebtedness within the marriage relationship made apparent.[43] In both the novella by Vilmorin and in the film, Louise is deeply in debt almost from the very start of her marriage. The earrings, given to her on the day *after* her wedding, are, technically, given in exchange for her virginity or for an alliance with her family, and thus her possession. But the marriage contract, like almost all the many contracts depicted by Ophuls, is not a contract between equal parties. For the use of the man's name, for the protection afforded by his position, the woman is shown to be hopelessly in debt. The earrings begin as an emblem of that debt.[44]

Nor is Louise de . . . fully able to use the name of the man who has married her. The name is both referred to and veiled; it is elided, hidden by napkins, carried away on the wind. At one point Louise goes to the customs house in order to pick up some imported items for a friend ("I had to give a little money and a signature in order to reclaim them"). But because she has no name of her own and must—perpetually, problematically—use that of another, by definition she can only forge "her" signature.[45] The payment of a fee is here juxtaposed with the signing of a document, and with the start of Louise's relationship with Donati. Later in the film, when she has gone to Italy, she will refuse him her signature—will refuse to respond to his letters at all, although she does write him. She tears up her letters and they dissolve into snowflakes outside her train compartment window. This unsuccessful attempt to bury her passion and his is troped as "illegitimate" writing, and sinks into the deep, cold snow.

For Doane, the deletion of Madame de . . .'s surname exercises a function similar to the concealment of names in, for example, the epistolary novel. "The title of the film thus alerts the spectator to the fact that the story involves a scandal and it manifests a certain delicacy in concealing the name of the agent of the scandalous actions."[46] But as is the case with the problem of "fictionality," Doane shifts the emphasis from the woman, whose name is concealed to "avoid scandal," to the workings of the text itself. "Yet, the question of agency immediately becomes problematic with the prologue's claim that there would be no story, hence no scandal, if not for the earrings. Blame is displaced to an inanimate object, the accessory in a lady's wardrobe and, furthermore, the mechanism of the narrative. The scandal is generated by the textual work; it does not pre-exist that work to be represented."[47] By insisting upon the scandalous effects of the textual work itself (an idea that is certainly supported by the opening titles of the film), Doane overlooks the play with names that we have discussed above: in naming the protagonist after her author (she has no first name in the novella), the screenwriters are, on the contrary, *producing* a scandalous reading of the text. Giving the protagonist the author's first name implies, among other things, that the tale is autobiographical. The woman author is not permitted self-concealment: her "truth" will be exposed, the veil lifted.[48]

The Name of the Father

Louise is not the only one who has problems with the "paternal" name. André de . . . has no patronymic himself. A preliminary response to this would be to say that no one "has" the name of the father, just as no one possesses the phallus. The emphasis falls, however, on the *woman's* lack of the name/penis/phallus. This is the case on a general cultural level in European societies, and distinctly true of this film. The woman is not, however, the only one in a difficult psychological situation in this film. Louise's underlying belief in—and resentment of—her husband's role as the representative of the phallus (her bitter glance at the portrait suspended commandingly above her as she drinks her coffee) is shown in no uncertain terms to be oppressive to him. One of the key elements of this film is the complexity of the husband's role, as enacted by Charles Boyer. *Madame de . . .*, of all Ophuls' films, is the one that most stringently attempts to demonstrate the contradictions involved in occupying the position of the patriarch. Appearing first in a painting and later linked with Napoleon, who is also depicted in a painting, André himself complains that he does not like the "personnage" that Louise has made of him, although he has made an effort to resemble it, in order not to displease her.

It is worth noting that Louise de Vilmorin does not depict André as a military man. Ophuls and his screenwriters made that and a number of other changes.[49] In almost all of Ophuls' films an effete, monocled, and uniformed military officer plays an important, frequently a sinister,

role. And this figure often oscillates between carrying out his patriarchal task and performing directorial functions (though these often
coincide). André's citation of Napoleon puts emphasis upon his role as
a strategist in the film: "Napoleon was only wrong twice in his life. At
Waterloo and when he said that in love the only victory lies in flight.
One must face [*braver*] the adversary." André speaks these words just as
Louise, sadly reclining in her room, begins to realize her love for
Donati. The General shows, at this point, sympathy for his wife's suffering and does not think she should flee her "enemy." Louise will later
face Donati, but it will not turn out as her husband had hoped. Just as
Napoleon was wrong at Waterloo, André is wrong in this case—and
when it begins to be a question of *patrimony*, of acceptable upper-class
behavior, he changes his tactics.

Donati finally gives Louise the earrings after they have been out of circulation for the longest period in the film—while the two of them fall in
love. As the exchange is being made (unbeknownst to Louise), the two
are standing in front of the large painting of Waterloo in Louise's glass-
enclosed parlor. Embarrassed by her love and by her impending departure for Italy, for which Donati reproaches her, Louise looks at the painting and, like an awkward schoolgirl speaking her piece, cites Victor
Hugo's poem, "L'Expiation": "Waterloo, Waterloo, mournful plain."
They speak of the participants in the battle, then the scene becomes
more tender. A servant (Julien—a reference to Julien Sorel?) walks by
with a lamp as the couple begins to embrace, reminding them of their
potential visibility through the glass walls of the parlor. Just as in *Liebelei*,
there is the danger of the lovers being caught by the husband in his own
home (although Louise and Fabrizio have only a brief embrace with
which to reproach themselves). Donati now tells Louise of the "folie" he
has committed by sending her the earrings hidden in some roses. Louise
runs up to look at them and puts them on lovingly, as Nanny watches.[50]
Meanwhile, the General returns home and decides his strategy: gently
chiding Donati for not having warned him of the visit, André sends him
to the door with Louise. At this moment, half-closing the door (which
now stands as a vertical barrier between them), she whispers, "Je ne vous
aime pas." To which Donati answers, "Revenez" ("Return"). Negation is
answered by repetition.

Although the battleground is one laid out between the two lovers,
André has certainly stepped in as one of the antagonists. The General
has won the skirmish, but he will lose the war of emotions. Donati, the

diplomat, fails in his professional role and is drawn into action. The duel (which the General engineers in order, once again, to make his wife an *object* rather than a subject of the conflict) will be provoked, at the end of the film, when André insists that Donati considers military men "superfluous." It is interesting that Louise receives the earrings as a *gift* from Donati, one given her behind her back, as it were: she is outside the circuit of exchange at this moment—it really is one "between men," as later scenes indicate.

> ANDRE: You claimed that the army and consequently the generals composing it are useless.
>
> FABRIZIO: I remember it in other terms.
>
> ANDRE: How?
>
> FABRIZIO: I said that if the diplomats did their work better there would be fewer soldiers [*militaires*].
>
> ANDRE: So you find me excessive [*de trop*].
>
> FABRIZIO: Take it as you like.

As this dispute becomes a challenge to a duel, another man at the gentlemen's club, where the scene takes place, is horrified that the men should fight for "professional" reasons. Insofar as the two men's roles are at least partially determined by their status as military and as nonmilitary men, it is true that the reasons for the duel are professional ones.

The ambivalence Ophuls shows here and elsewhere toward the military man is reminiscent of that of Erich von Stroheim (toward the characters most often played in his films by himself), and ties into class conflicts drawn from the use of nineteenth-century melodramatic themes in the early cinema. Ophuls again complicates the use of such figures, so that it would be hard to say if these scenes are examples of Ophuls' "antimilitarism." For these men the uniform is the ultimate form of virile display, and the uniformed man, in the position of the patriarch, wields all the power that can be wielded from the top of the hierarchy—an excess of power, indeed. The General is eager to show that he sits at the top of the hierarchy of virility: he is amused, for example, when the noise of the new cannon being fired outside his office window frightens the less "manly" jeweler. Even the soldiers under the command of the General have no respect for this representative of the circulation-process: "Oh, don't bother to salute; it's only a merchant," they remark as he drives by in his carriage.[51] The military man in this way attempts to set up ironclad dichotomies between his own hierarchically based masculinity, and the operations of capitalism and theatricality, dichotomies that must ultimately break down. André himself, for example, both enters into trade with the jeweler and becomes a specular object entrapped by the very emblems of his power, unhappy with that *personnage* he is forced to approximate. The position of the patriarch is ultimately shown to be as "empty" as the coquette's. Silverman describes the dilemma of masculinity in Lacanian terms:

The attributes of the Symbolic are infinitely relocatable, and exist purely at the level of signification. The distance between the phallus and the penis cannot be bridged; the latter is cut off from the former, relegated to the domain of inadequacy [cf. Lorena Bobbitt]. But because the inadequacy of the male subject must never be acknowledged, our culture attempts at every point to blur the distinction between that subject and the Symbolic; to foster the belief that the penis is the phallus, and that the gaze of the male subject coincides with the Gaze of the Other. This *méconnaissance* can only be sustained through the female subject, whose castration and guilt, endlessly perpetuated through displacement, thus becomes the topics of a compulsive restatement.[52]

Ophuls' cinema both "acknowledges the inadequacy of the male subject" and permits its men to make use of their ability to approximate the phallus, to bridge the distance between penis and phallus. Throughout *Madame de . . .* André oscillates back and forth between a certain enslavement to the "direction" of others—particularly that of his wife—and calling in the debts that are due him, directing the behavior of others.

Louise attempts, blindly, to direct her husband and others by means of the earrings. But as has been noted, the earrings have come into her possession only at the cost of a great debt. She cannot control them. Nor, indeed, can André, although he attempts at crucial junctures to exercise control as a prerogative due to him. The question of the debt recurs immediately in a brief scene that takes place while André searches the carriage for the lost earrings. A man approaches him and asks, ironically, "What are you doing on all fours [*à quatre pattes*]?" André turns the irony on his interlocutor: "I'm looking for the 15,000 francs that you have returned to me—because you *have* repaid them, haven't you?" The other man's composure crumbles, and he shrinks away declaring that it is only a matter of "seconds" before the debt will be settled. André is not reluctant to invoke his authority if he is threatened, but this authority is ultimately ineffectual in dealing with the recalcitrant underlings occupying the liminal spaces of the film. André's authority is manifested "directorially" when, upon his return home to continue looking for the earrings, the General orders the servants to appear before him. As is often the case in Ophuls' films, the minor, supporting actors grumble when ordered to play their parts. One woman argues as she climbs the elegant staircase that she was "hired to do the cooking, not to look for the earrings."[53] The musicians don't like to perform, either; at the end of the ball sequence, when Louise and Fabrizio are left dancing alone into the wee hours (another signature scene for Ophuls), the musicians engage in class protest, insisting that "baron or no baron," they are going home. Thus, on a minute level, the directorial function is mocked by those who must make the film work. In this film, directing is often shown to be not so much a question of masculine control as one of *lack* of control: he is resisted by his characters, and his actions are ineffective or actually backfire. On a more literal level, the musicians' comments represent Ophuls' frequent shifts to the ironic point of view of the working class, the producers of the commodities exchanged, in this film, among the higher classes.

The jeweler is, of course, the film's most amusingly unconscious agent of chance. Without realizing the implications of his actions, he constantly puts the earrings back into play when it seems that they might rest elsewhere. It is made clear that the jeweler is also strongly linked to the directorial function when, at the shop, he repeatedly orders his son to bring him things: "the earrings . . . ; my hat . . . ; my cane."[54] It is not merely, one should say, that Ophuls feels guilty for ordering people about and therefore manifests an ambivalent attitude toward directing. Rather, there is a paradox at the heart of the Ophulsian film aesthetic: the direction of films and of human beings is an act of self-sacrifice on the part of the director, and yet it involves a necessarily false assumption of identity, in the form of the representation of characters, who are tormented by being in the spotlight or on the market. André does not wish wholeheartedly to shine the inquisitor's light on his wife. In one of the most tender scenes of the film, when the General begins to sense that his wife is really in trouble, he goes from room to room *closing* the shutters and curtains (the camera is situated outside the windows and pans with the General's movements, as does the camera in "Le Modèle," one of the three sketches comprising *Le Plaisir*). As he does this we can hear him saying to Louise: "I respect you, I admire you [then, in a quieter voice, which she does not hear], I love you." This touching testimony is accompanied by his attempt to block out the camera's eye from the scene, just as the door blocks Louise's and Fabrizio's gazes as they first speak of their love. André's dilemma is that he can only express his love in the form of an oppressive gift that serves to place the woman in an unequal relationship.

Neither do women have clear access to directorial functions. Just as telling a story is equivalent, for the woman, to telling a lie (she has no relationship to the truth, which is grounded in masculine authority), a woman's directing becomes a manipulation that rebounds to destroy her. At best, directing is empty repetition, at worst it is torture. And yet it is only in this seemingly empty and painful reproduction of artifice and ritualized behavior that one can come to understand what structures our experience as social beings. By exacerbating them, the director tests the rituals of behavior as they are mediated by auditory and visual experience.

Women, Production, Instability

In associating the problem of film direction with the earrings' accumulation of exchange value (for they do become more and more expensive, and it is the jeweler who profits), Ophuls accomplishes several things. First, we can see how intertwined is the relationship between the jeweler and the female protagonist. On the one hand, the relationship is structurally an antagonistic one—Louise must perform her fainting act to get what she wants. By the end of the film it has become impossible to distinguish the performance from "real" illness. Louise will die of the act she has been putting on. The jeweler operates behind Louise's back on several occasions, finally absorbing all her money and possessions. And yet there is a certain homology between M. Rémy,[55] the jeweler, and Louise de . . . . As we saw in chapter 1, both the woman and the merchant are linked to the circuit of exchange, rather than to that of production. Of course, Louise's role differs completely from that of the male characters in the film in that she is *herself* an object of exchange, rather than an equal trading partner. I will now define in greater detail how it is that the woman is able to take the role she does within the economy of this plot.

Gallagher notes that "the process of exchange, of circulation, are distinguished from those of production by all [classical] political econo-
mists." The sphere of production is generally "identified as the source of
value, the source of real wealth" (p. 42). Women have been associated
with the sphere of exchange rather than with that of production since
ancient times—as items of exchange, as a type of currency, as a commodity. Only by completing the transaction of exchange—that is, by taking on the role of wife—can woman leave the sphere of exchange and
become a "producer." (Just having a baby won't do it. Out of wedlock the
child is only part of a wild proliferation.) According, once again, to an
ancient association that has persisted, to a large extent, into the twentieth century, the prostitute (like the female writer) never manages this
transition.

Like money, the prostitute, Aristotle is the first to tell us, is incapable of natural
procreation. For all of her sexual activity, indeed because of all of her sexual
activity, she is unable to bring new substances, children, into the world. Her
womb, Aristotle says, is too slippery. And yet she is a source of proliferation. What
multiplies through her, though, is not a substance but a sign: money. Prostitution, then, like usury, is a metaphor for one of the ancient models of linguistic
production: the unnatural multiplication of interchangeable signs. (p. 41)

Gallagher's choice of words in this passage indicates the strength of the
emphasis traditionally put upon production as morally distinct from circulation.[56] Louise's relationship to the problem of the accumulation of
profits and thus to the earrings themselves is articulated in terms of both
use value and of exchange value in the film. As a childish "coquette," she
does not produce value but merely accumulates profits—for others—by
generating a debt that puts the earrings in motion, as well as by remaining, as they say, "in circulation" among the men of her acquaintance.

Dishonesty, thievery, instability, fickleness—these are all attributes of
the woman who defies the double-edged marriage contract that, on the
one hand, is meant to stabilize her and, on the other, serves to give her
the power of the narcissistic woman over her husband as one of many
suitors. André's subjugation to the narcissistic woman is made clear in
the ballroom scene where he describes to Donati his wife's ability to torture those who love her. Woman's tormenting "instability" can be characterized in a number of ways. Her sexuality, in Freudian terms, con-

demns her to a kind of movement which may never be completed, which she may be unable or indeed refuse to accomplish. This is the (imaginary) movement from the clitoris to the vagina as primary erogenous zone. The pure pleasure provided by the (supposedly phallic) clitoris is separate from the question of reproduction and from the relationship to the masculine sexual organ implied by the vagina's receptivity. If the prostitute uses her vagina to achieve a certain kind of exchange value that is not in the sphere of production, the clitoris has, rather, a use value, as do the earrings for Louise when she buys them back for the last time and no longer wears them but keeps them for her own private pleasure.[57] I might add here that woman is also obliged to perform another kind of movement not necessary to the man: this is the transition from the mother as primary love object to the father, and later to other men, as he will fulfill her desire to have the phallus found lacking in the mother. The "exacerbated Don Juanism," the movement from object to object, previously referred to (citing Beylie) in the introduction, may indeed be more fundamentally feminine than masculine. Don Juan as a figure of male anxiety about feminine mobility?

If the theory of movement from clitoris to vagina is a masculinist one (the primacy of the "receptive" vagina at the expense of the more sensitive clitoris), it nonetheless does not come without some expense on the part of the masculinist (not always male) theorist. The "man" pays for this reassuring theory with precisely that queasy sense that the woman is greasily mobile. A similar no-win situation prevails in the case of the logic of fetishism. Freudian fetishism involves a perpetual movement of oscillation in which the (male) spectator goes back and forth between, on the one hand, the belief in (the already fictitious, never "real") phallus of the mother, because her castration would be unbearable to him, and, on the other hand, the knowledge that she has no penis/phallus. That oscillation finally fixes itself on a still image, a reconstruction, as has been mentioned, of the last thing seen before the future fetishist's eye fell on the place where the maternal phallus was found to be lacking.

The instability of feminine sexuality is thought to be most unnerving for men. The fetish is itself an attempt to *stop the movement of meaning*, although this attempt will always, by definition, be a failure (since the fetishist will continue to oscillate). A more radical way of interpreting the fetish object—one that might be applicable to this film—has been discussed by Sarah Kofman and Jacques Derrida. Kofman emphasizes both the "back and forth" oscillating movement that is necessarily the mode of apprehending the fetish, as well as the lack of a revealed "truth" in the fetishistic oscillation. When the man (boy) discovers that the phallic quality he has attributed to the mother is a "lie," he is only uncovering the lie foisted off on the woman—that the "truth" of her castration is itself a fiction. Woman's truth is that she is castrated, while castration itself is fictional.[58] I will return to this discussion below, in my consideration of the Deleuzian "masochistic contract," seen by some feminist theorists as one means of grappling with the problem of "feminine castration."[59]

For women, productivity is often synonymous with the "natural" productivity involved in procreation, in giving birth to a child (although this too has sometimes been undercut by attributing to the man alone the "creation" of the child, while the woman is seen as a mere incubator).[60] Louise de . . . is conspicuously childless: indeed, she is *confronted* later in the film with her "lack" of an infant, a lack whose stereotyped meaning she fiercely resists. Wishing to halt the movement of the earrings by grounding them in a legitimate form of exchange from whence he can draw profit, the General presents them, in Louise's name, to his niece, who has just given birth to a son. The General's conduct may reflect motivations similar to those at work in a scene in *Daniel Deronda*, where Daniel forbids Gwendolen to exchange for money the necklace she has lost by playing at the roulette wheel and which he has retrieved for her. This is a gesture, as Gallagher puts it, of the "valorization of genealogy over exchange: the father orders the daughter to vacate the marketplace and remain dependent on his legacy alone" (p. 50).[61] As they enter the young mother's chambers, André expresses the hope that the earrings will soon lose meaning altogether for Louise, assuring her that they can become like "bits of broken glass"—worthless. From enjoying Louise's role as the narcissistic woman, the General has come to desire her castration, her recognition that the jewels she wears (when she wears them according to her own desire and outside the patriarch's purview) are without any value whatsoever. At this moment André is exercising to the greatest degree what I have called his patriarchal and directorial authority: his reason for making Louise give the earrings to the niece is "to keep them in the family." Louise vows never to forgive him. This is, indeed, the point of no return for their marriage. It is now evident that the only appropriate exchange for the earrings would be the production of a child, "un beau garçon," like that of the niece who has obligingly provided the family with a male heir.

Her relatives assume, in this scene, that Louise is weeping because she, too, wants a child. But this is not at all the case. She hardly even looks at the baby. She wants the *earrings*, which have by this point in the film become associated with a narcissistic sense of self that may not even be connected to her "object" love for Donati.[62] Louise's desire to possess something does not necessarily mean that she wishes to produce a child, who would be the father's possession, marked with the paternal name.

Doublings and Returns

We may come to understand something more about how Louise functions as a "nonproductive" coquette with respect to the other characters in the film by examining some of the repetitions and symmetries in the film's mise-en-scène and editing that set up its psychological atmosphere. The ambivalence felt by the General toward his wife is underscored by the doubling of Louise's coquettish traits in the form of the courtesan Lola. An avowed playgirl, and a more prototypical example of the circulating female commodity than is Louise (in that this playgirl cannot be halted even momentarily by marriage), Lola is off to the gaming tables of Constantinople. In a bantering conversation that takes place in the train compartment before her departure (echoing in a somewhat perverse manner that between young Stefan and his mother in *Letter from an Unknown Woman*), André reproaches his mistress for leaving him. She retorts that it is *he* who is leaving *her*, since one way of leaving a woman is to allow her to leave.[63]

These concerns—the wordplay about who is leaving whom—are taken up at length in *Lola Montès*, particularly in the sequence between Lola (it is surely no coincidence that the names are the same) and Liszt. Who is enslaved to whom? Relational contracts are often ambiguous in these films. There is also a question about the meaning of the act of writing in this scene, which will be repeated in another way by Louise and Donati, though almost wordlessly. André asks Lola to send her address so that he may write her; she answers that he would not write anyway. He replies that there will probably be someone there whom the letters would disturb (that is, a new lover). Lola pouts, replying, "I hope so," then smiles. Often, in Ophuls' films, the prominently placed communication devices are instrumental in the destruction of the characters, or else they are simply ineffective or blocked. In any case, they are never neutral: in this film writing is continually made to represent the unnaturalness and incomprehensibility of desire, as when Donati must look up in the dictionary the word "desiderio" while writing to Louise. Writing, in words or images, proves to be an abortive or opaque mode of communication, a device of desire's deferral, prefiguring the death of love, and death itself.

The departure scene just described forms a pendant with another important scene in the train station. Together they produce one of the most outstanding cases of uncannily revealing symmetry in the film. In the conversation that takes place between Lola and her lover, the contradictory position of the General (with respect to his own use of "patriarchal" power) is made clear. He comments to Lola that "one doesn't do what one wants in life." "Particularly when one is a general," she adds. A second later, however, the General describes how he has punished a lieutenant who disobeyed orders. After impulsively giving the earrings to Lola, André looks at the number of the train compartment—thirteen. He then insists that Lola bet on the number thirteen when she arrives at the casino, in this way attempting to control an element of her economic future. When Lola disembarks from her voyage, she pauses on a ramp to say good-bye to her admirers (as Louise stands on a staircase to do the same thing), among them an Englishman reminiscent of the English swain who insisted that Louise was torturing him. The courtesan and the Parisian lady are thus treated as doubles in more than one way. The wild expenditure and proliferation of value that have been associated with Louise is even more exaggerated in the case of Lola, who will gamble away all her possessions immediately—while it takes Louise the length of the entire film to lose her possessions by gambling on love.[64] Gambling in a casino is the most extreme form of nonproductive, inflationary exchange in the film, and it is, as we have seen, distinctly associated with the figure of a high-class prostitute.

There are several lingering close-ups on the number thirteen during the sequence in Constantinople, which, of course, repeat the close-ups on the train compartment's number. This repetition of the number thirteen might be described as the peculiar meeting place of an act of volition (the General *tells* her to play the number—the repetition is not inadvertent) and an involuntary repetition (the return of the earrings) that borders on the uncanny. Indeed, the number thirteen is itself a rather uncanny number. In this sequence it signals an effort on the part of the General to repress something disturbing about the women he loves. The General sends the earrings away with Lola in an attempt to banish the frivolity, the "étourderie,"[65] the lies, the deception that he has found in his wife. Donati, as a kind of double of the General, will be the vehicle of the return of the repressed (an "involuntary" result of the General's act). And, as in the Freudian uncanny, which functions through repression and return, there is something familiar about Donati. The General knows him, even if we, at first, do not.

Although Donati turns up again and again for Louise before she really knows who he is, he is nonetheless familiar to her, too, as her description of his clothing at the customs house makes clear. ("You were wearing cufflinks shaped like horse's heads and your eyes were brown then, just like they are now," she says, when their carriages happen to collide, though she pretends not to have noticed him at the customs house). In Freud's description of the uncanny, it is that very thing which is most familiar, most *heimlich*, that suddenly seems to us *unheimlich*, strange and unfamiliar. This is the functioning of the unconscious, that which is most our own, in some sense, but which is inaccessible to us except as slips of the tongue or *actes manqués*, such as Louise's carriage colliding with that of the man who will be her undoing, or the General's bad advice, his insistence that Lola bet on a particular number. It is the failure of André's conscious plan that will insure the return of the earrings in the possession of Donati.

We might note, parenthetically, that Freud's most cherished example of the uncanny occurs on a train:

I was sitting alone in my *wagon-lit* compartment when a more than usually violent jolt of the train swung back the door of the adjoining washing-cabinet, and an elderly gentleman in a dressing gown and a travelling cap came in. I assumed that in leaving the washing-cabinet, which lay between the two compartments, he had taken the wrong direction and come into my compartment by mistake. Jumping up with the intention of putting him right, I at once realized to my dismay that the intruder was nothing but my own reflection in the looking-glass on the open door. I can still recollect that I thoroughly disliked his appearance.

Instead, therefore, of being *frightened* by our 'doubles', both Mach and I simply failed to recognize them as such. Is it not possible, though, that our dislike of them was a vestigial trace of the archaic reaction which feels the double to be something uncanny?[66]

This example of the uncanny is related both to the "inner compulsion to repeat" (evident, as we have seen, in *Madame de . . .*) and to doubling in its avatar as a reassurance against death and castration, and, finally, as the "uncanny harbinger of death" explicitly associated with the double in Ophuls' films.[67] That which is *other* in ourselves is almost by definition productive of horror. The contrivances of a cinematic plot, such as the fact that André and Fabrizio happen to know one another, are the way in which unconscious motivations may be spelled out on the surface of the cinematic text. What I earlier called "the ascendancy of the narrative function," speaking of the role of coincidence in the film, can thus be likened to the functioning of the unconscious. In this interaction between the two men, who seem to understand one another so well (as Donati puts it, upon being challenged to defend his honor, "Nous allons certainement nous comprendre"—"We will surely understand one another"), André's mistrust of woman, perhaps even his desire to destroy the woman, is presented in the guise of the giver of gifts, first as himself and then as his double, Donati.

The gift of the earrings, like the gifts described by anthropologist Marcel Mauss, is one that seems to insure the indebtedness, the impoverishment of he or she who receives it. Indeed, the General's niece says she must sell the earrings to prevent her husband from going bankrupt. The phrase is ambiguous, as though it were *because* of the earrings that he is in danger of this taking place. The risk of permanent indebtedness seems to be particularly acute, in modern Western society, if the recipient is a woman. In the transactions involving the earrings, Donati is little more than intermediary, a "third term," as Mauss describes such characters.[68] The gift constitutes an irrevocable and dangerous link between giver and recipient. We might also remark that the General knows that the giving of gifts is dangerous. When, for example, the jeweler states that he thought he was rendering a service to the General and to his wife by buying back the earrings, André replies that when *he* renders a service, he tries to "make sure that it is not returned." He does not want to be repaid (to have "himself" return as "other"), but wishes, rather, to reserve the right to remind others of their debt. He goes so far as to insist that the jeweler bill him for the very time he has spent bargaining about the earrings. Later in the film, the train sequence is repeated, using similar camera movements and framing, only this time it is Louise rather than Lola who will go on a voyage. Unbeknownst to her husband, she is taking the earrings with her. Thus, what the General had done consciously earlier in the film—sending the earrings away—is now repeated unconsciously. The earrings will, nonetheless, return as they did before, and Louise will pursue her fatal love affair with the Baron.

Let us return briefly to the Baron Donati. There is some irony in the fact that an actual director, Vittorio de Sica, plays a role that is so destructive to the heroine, and is then killed at the end of the film. The Baron's first name seems to be etymologically related to making or manufacturing; the last name is morphologically reminiscent of the French and talian words meaning "gift" and "to give" (*le don, donare*). "Donati" is he who has given them or those things that were given. If Fabrizio Donati is a disappointing character, and if this film is structurally more intriguing than is *Liebelei*, this is because Ophuls' later films tend to underscore the impossibility of determining the "truth" of woman and the imbecility of thinking that one has found this truth in "castration." In the oscillating movement of the fetishist, Donati is both fascinated and appalled by Louise's lies, yet he loses his love for her because of her lying. Donati wishes to promote the belief that the phallic earrings come from the woman's side of the family (Louise "plans" to tell her husband, she says to Donati, that the earrings were given to her by an aunt who never speaks to the General), that they originate in the woman (they are "as though made for" Louise, he remarks). When he discovers that this lie is also a lie meant *for himself*,[69] that the earrings/phallus have a paternal origin (made for her *by the husband/father*), Donati lapses into self-pitying disappointment in the "castrated" woman whose relationship to the process of inheritance and exchange is alarmingly mobile. We have observed that in *Liebelei* the young man becomes disgusted with the noblewoman he loves and turns to the more fascinating, pure, and innocent young opera singer. In trying to make the younger woman embody both the purity required of a melodramatic heroine and the alluring fascination of the star, while splitting off the function of the "disillusioning" castrated/castrating woman, Ophuls gives *Liebelei* a kind of melodramatic closure not found in *Madame de . . . .*

A Lady's Jewels

At one point in the film, in what seems at first to be a throwaway line, the General comments, rather sarcastically, that the Baron rides as well as a

D'Artagnan. Like Fabrizio del Dongo, D'Artagnan is a young naive: he is the "fourth musketeer" in Dumas père's novel *The Three Musketeers* (1844). Numerous connections are discernible between *Madame de . . .* and *The Three Musketeers*. Both narratives concern the disappearance of a lady's jewels under compromising circumstances. In *The Three Musketeers*, the queen gives her lover two diamond studs from a necklace that had been a birthday gift from her husband, the king. "When objects unduly change place," writes Ora Avni in an article on Dumas' novel, "the wheels of narrative begin to turn."[70] Thus, as in *Madame de . . .*, the jewels are first metonymically linked to the husband and to the marriage contract, binding the woman under patriarchal law, and then linked to the woman's desire for liberty from that contract. Donati resembles both the lover (Buckingham) and the emissary of the diamonds (D'Artagnan). The difference between the two stories is also apparent. In *The Three Musketeers* the king never becomes aware of the transgression of his law. The law is subverted, but the king remains a figurehead, untouched. Avni points out that there is a similarity between the blindness of this king and that of the king in Poe's story "The Purloined Letter," as Lacan describes it.[71] In that story a compromising letter is stolen from the queen, in the very presence of the king, who notices nothing. According to Lacan, the letter *must* return to its point of origin (to the queen), leaving the law intact, the position of the patriarch unaffected. Such is the law of the Lacanian signifier. The earrings would also represent a certain "truth in sufferance," that is, in movement. That "truth," woman's lack of the phallus and the man's problematic possession of it, is found in the contract that opposes the masochistic one to be discussed below—the marital contract based on patriarchal supremacy. This contract "reappropriates symbolically," as Derrida puts it, the detached phallus for both partners:

As soon as truth is determined as adequation (to an original contract: the acquittal of a debt) and as unveiling (of the lack which gives rise to the contracting of the contract in order to reappropriate symbolically what has been detached), the master value is indeed that of propriation, hence of proximity, presence and preserving: the very same provided by the idealizing effect of speech.[72]

Avni argues that, in *The Three Musketeers*, the law has been subverted by the instability of an object whose meaning, once the emblem of legitimacy, has changed during the course of the novel. The human subjects *are* determined by the itinerary of the object-signifier, but for Avni this itinerary is not predetermined. Who knows where they will stop?[73]

In *Madame de . . .* the patriarch is not blind. He attempts to embody the law, showing at every instance the painful impossibility of remaining adequate to that law. The tragedy for André is that he can only represent his desire, his love, as he eloquently declares, closing the curtains as though it were something that does not bear our examination, through a gift that is fundamentally oppressive to the woman. Louise is, at one point, in a position of blindness (Lacan's *autruiche*, unaware of her situation with respect to the intersubjectivity she inhabits), not knowing how much the others know of her lies and believing wrongly in her mastery of the game. When she recovers from this state of blindness, her interest in the jewels has been irrevocably separated from that of her husband.

The doubleness of the earrings will be maintained in the film, reflected, as implied above, in the three pairs of doubles at the duel scene. The women have been dressed more and more alike as the film progresses; Nanny splits off from the younger woman, perhaps as the representative of the superstitious, the *unheimlich* aspect of Louise's feminine nature. Donati and André are also dressed similarly and bring along their doubles as their seconds in the duel: the ambassador now coalesces the doubts of the General about the nature of woman, and so André will attempt to destroy Fabrizio. Unlike the letter in Poe's story, which, although it may speak of the queen's love, will be prevented from besmirching the patriarchal law, the earrings will come publicly to represent something about Louise's desire. The end of the film shows us that, like that of the French queen's diamonds, the meaning of an object can change, can be partly controlled by the woman, although only at the cost of her life. Her agency, like the surplus value of the commodity as Marx describes it, is ghostly.[74] Let us compare, briefly, the end of Vilmorin's novella with the film's ending.

Last Words

In the final scene of Louise de Vilmorin's novel, the protagonist is dying. She calls to her side the ambassador who, having withdrawn his affection, is inadvertently killing her. Alas, by the time he arrives, Mme de is no longer able to recognize him. M. de , initially unwilling to admit the ambassador to his wife's presence, now stands with him by her bed and the two men watch her expire. The dead woman's open hand discloses the diamond earrings she had been clutching.

The ambassador and M. de exchanged a look: "She is dead, take this heart that she is giving to you," says M. de to the ambassador, "the other one belongs to her, I will take care [dispose] of it."

The ambassador took the heart that Mme de was holding out to him. He kissed the dead woman's hand, then abruptly left the bedroom and had himself driven to the jeweler's shop.

"Seal this heart to a golden chain," he said, "and seal this chain to my neck. I don't want to wait."

An instant later he was returning home, giving orders, having his bags packed, sending wires and leaving the city.

In the meantime, M. de placed the other heart on his wife's heart, then he called the nurse and the bedroom was soon filled with a sound of skirts and of mournful cries. The dinner candles glowed with a funereal light. M. de had his tailor summoned and, without telling him the reason, ordered mourning clothes.[75]

Thus, at the end of the novel the husband disposes of the earrings. Of course, he unites the lovers in a romantic gesture, but it is he who chooses to do so. The two men signify their grief by ornamenting their bodies and Louise's. The earrings are no longer uncannily paired but have found, separately, their final resting place. M. de takes on mourning garb in order to signify his loss. A tragic love story has become, in the end, a duel of wills between the ambassador and the social butterfly, a duel ending in her death and his banishment. The husband in black remains on the scene, still an anchor of domestic life and presumably reflecting on the follies of love. The violence implicit to the kind of desire experienced by the characters in the novel falls back, as it so often does in fiction, on the head of the woman.[76]

Toward the end of the film version of *Madame de . . .*, Louise, now dressed in dark clothes and almost purged of her earlier "vanity," pays a visit to Donati in his office in order to dissuade him from fighting the duel. A flash of her former specular self shows forth when she declares that she is "no longer pretty" and therefore not worthy to be fought over.

"More than ever," her lover responds, inspiring a smile of rapture on Louise's face. This smile immediately falls as she realizes that she has relapsed into the same trap that doomed all of the film's protagonists. "I'm incorrigible," she murmurs. She then admits that her old habits of lying and frivolity, qualities of the woman she once was, now constitute the unhappiness of the woman she has become. The music swells as Louise cries out that Donati should not fight for her since he no longer loves her: "Because you *don't* love me anymore . . . ?" She gasps and, as he remains silent, her head falls. "It is suicide," she says. Donati replies, "Perhaps."

A short and elegantly shot scene follows, in which André practices shooting at a human-shaped target. The precision of his shooting indicates to us that Donati is indeed doomed to die. After André fires, hitting the small heart drawn on the mannequin, there is a pull-back to a close-up of a monocled man (in a striking three-quarter profile pose) who declares that the opponent is "un homme mort." This dapper man, who was also present in the hunt scene, is the distilled incarnation of André's deadly, upper-class aggression. In the last scene of this film, as in *Liebelei*, a pair runs toward the duel scene, which is not shown at all in the latter film and is shown only briefly in the former. The pair rushing to the duel consists, in *Liebelei*, of a man and a woman (Theo and Mizzi). In *Madame de . . .* the couples consist of identically dressed men (fighting the duel) and women (running up a hill to find the men). They are divided by sex in the later film, and will not be reunited. Heterosexual love, sanctioned in death by Vilmorin's novel (and by Theo and Mizzi at the end of *Liebelei*), seems to have reached an impasse at the end of *Madame de . . .* .

I have alluded several times to a tension in the film concerning, to put it rather vaguely, the attitude of the film's implied narrator or filmmaker toward Louise. Her remark that she is "incorrigible" can be read (as it is tentatively read above) as a momentary relapse into coquettery. To believe that Louise has, in this scene, finally stripped herself of the vanity that would be morally fatal to her if she were a character in, for example, a novel by Stendhal, does not tell the whole story.[77] Nonetheless, on one level, the woman has been castigated by the events of the film for her frivolity, for her willingness to present herself with a certain theatrical quality, an air that indicates or points to both the fictitiousness and the self-awareness that goes along with the personality of the giddy woman-performer. There is an implication that presenting oneself purely as a spectacle for another's eyes, though perhaps in its way "charming," is ultimately reprehensible. In order to assume moral stature, Louise must turn away from exterior concerns to more spiritual ones, which would seem to proclaim a certain *inwardness* of her being.

An important study by Michael Fried[78] traces the way in which obvious self-awareness on the part of an actor or of a figure in a painting became, during the eighteenth century, psychologically unacceptable to the beholders or audiences of those works of art. The situation of the actor was described by Diderot and others as a complex, even paradoxical one, because although the actor could not *seem* to be self-aware, he or she must maintain an absolute and *actual* self-awareness in order to achieve the desired effects.[79] We can hardly doubt that Ophuls is to some degree serious in presenting Louise's transformation as a spiritual odyssey toward a more authentic (less theatrical) self, perhaps as a response to this strong cultural prejudice described by Fried as prevalent in eighteenth- and nineteenth-century Europe.[80] This kind of character development runs contrary to the modernist tendency toward self-conscious characters who constantly refer to their own status as fictional entities and thereby implicate their beholders in this fiction, often eliciting extreme discomfort or boredom on the part of these beholders, who do not wish to be aggressively engaged by the spectacle. Although the *characters* only intermittently show this form of self-consciousness in *Madame de . . .*, we have seen that the narrative itself seems to do so.

At the end of the film our voyeuristic relationship to Louise is curtailed—she no longer demands to be looked at.[81] For Ophuls this "self-consciousness," which Louise attempts to combat as a "moral" problem, can also entail a serious commitment to both the inevitability and the desirability of a certain theatrical self-presentation, especially on the part of women. What, after all, *is* a coquette except a woman who is aware of the (positive) effect she is having on her audience? (She also seeks, we might add, to enhance that effect.)[82] Ophuls' final *sanctioning* of such behavior is not merely condescending infatuation with female coyness but is a recognition of the necessity of assumption of self as role in the public and private arenas, as well as the privilege of the woman to wear her femininity as an armor. This self-expression can, as we have seen, become extremely painful, and that must, of necessity, draw the spectator into a difficult erotic relationship with the spectacle, especially, as we have seen, if that spectator is herself a woman.

In the context of surface and display, Alan Williams links Ophuls to a certain "union of opposites" to be observed in the French *moraliste* tradition, as in the works of Pascal and La Rochefoucauld: "Nos vertus ne sont que nos vices déguisés."[83] As André remarks to Louise, "Our marriage is in our image: it is only superficially superficial." Authenticity is not really *opposed* to artifice in Ophuls' films, but rather the former is an instance of the latter.

Masochism and Spectatorship

At the end of the film, the earrings have been encased with a plaque stating that they are the gift of Madame de . . . . Let us remember that earlier in the film Louise had made a deal—a contract, if you will—with her saint and had sealed it with a candle costing *quatre sous*. In Vilmorin's novella there is no mention of a statue. The association between a statue and a secondary contractual relation points to a structure that subtends this and other films by Ophuls. What is this secondary contract? An indication of its role can be found in Ophuls' obsessive images of snowy countrysides where women are photographed wrapped in furs or looking out at the snow, as in his systematic contrasting of the moving and the fixed image and, most importantly, in his emphasis upon the contract as the binding relationship between men and women. Contracts are an explicit theme in *La Signora di Tutti, De Mayerling à Sarajevo, Lola Montès*, and elsewhere and are implicitly present in many of Ophuls' other films. They are often eventually or immediately oppressive for the Ophulsian woman, as is the marriage contract.[84] Many of the recurrent scenes and concerns in Ophuls' cinema are strongly reminiscent of images and themes to be found in a novel that became an important diagnostic tool for Freud and later for Deleuze and others. This novel is Sacher-Masoch's *Venus in Furs* (1870).[85]

Louise's earlier role as a torturer of men, her insistence, in the first scene of the film, that she not be separated from the furs that form a part of her sexual identity, and this link in Ophuls' work between the frozen image (statue or painting) and the sexual domination of or *by* the spectator of that image all serve to underline the rapport between the masochistic text and Ophuls' cinema.[86] It is, above all, the *rejection of the father figure* that most closely ties Ophuls' cinema to the masochistic text. Just as, in Stendhal's works, the father is spurned by the protagonist, who forms a union with the maternal figure that is sustained out of the reach of oppressive paternal power, so the patriarchal function is put into question by some of the contractual systems in films by Ophuls.[87] The program at the heart of contractual and aesthetic masochism is precisely the subversion of paternal law by means of the newly imposed rule of a certain mother figure, whom Deleuze terms the "oral mother." He defines masochism in the strictest sense as

a story that relates how the superego was destroyed and by whom, and what was the sequel to this destruction. Sometimes the story is misunderstood and one is led to think that the superego triumphs at the very point when it is dying. . . . The masochist . . . introduces himself into this age-old story by means of a very specific act, the instrument of which is the modern contract; with the most curious consequences, for he abjures the father's likeness and the sexuality which it confers, and at the same time challenges the father image as the repressive authority which is constitutive of the superego. In opposition to the institutional superego he now establishes the contractual partnership between the ego and the oral mother. (pp. 111–12)

The masochistic aesthetic emphasizes *formalism* (p. 95), a concern that echoes throughout Ophuls' cinema, specifically in its emphasis on "storytelling" and on ritualistic repetition (both evident in *Madame de . . .*).

It is risky to speak of masochism in the context of the so-called woman's film, made with reference to the genre conventions that are associated with female spectatorship. Often these are love stories with female protagonists, as one could describe *Madame de . . . .* Associating masochism with this genre seems, to some critics, to reiterate the stereotype of woman's supposed penchant for suffering. In describing this *particular* masochistic structure, I am, however, not primarily speaking of female pleasure in seeing pain inflicted on women with whom they would identify. Rather, I am concerned with the means described by Deleuze of rejecting the male's superior claim to the phallus and all that it represents, a psychic formation Silverman also discerns in Freudian masochism.[88] Although I will claim that he does not foreclose the function of the phallus itself, the Deleuzian masochist is said to deny maternal castration through a fetishistic use of the image. In the process of undermining the superego, the representative of the paternal superego may seem still to have the power to judge, to condemn—but in fact it is dead, "displayed like a hide or a trophy." Such is the uniformed, menacing male's display as a *trophy*, seen again and again as a figure in Ophuls' cinema. The framed portrait of the military man in full regalia that Louise confronts before her transgressive selling of the jewels, like the moment in *Letter from an Unknown Woman* when the General poses beneath his crossed swords, blatantly depicts the vengeful potential of the paternal superego. The portrait intimidates the young woman who stands before it, but—and here is its double function—the portrait also represents the reduction of the man to his quintessential role as a place-holder for a force he can never wholly embody.

The General plays a double role, as one of the many men "masochis-tically" enslaved to Louise and as the paternal figure who is mocked, denied, and undermined. So too does the marriage contract double as a contract that oppresses Louise and as a masochistic contract that insures her domination as the fetishized "oral" mother. This oral mother is a pre-Oedipal, authoritative, and powerful figure whose relationship with the child predates the paternal interdiction and whose authority is, accord-ing to Gaylyn Studlar, therefore completely unrelated to the castration complex. Studlar acknowledges that, since fetishism is based on dis-avowal, it is usually associated with the denial of the mother's castration, but insists that fetishism can be, more primordially, an assurance against the loss of the mother herself. Even the passage through the castration complex is, according to this view, not enough to obliterate the child's awe for the mother: "Chasseguet-Smirgel goes so far as to suggest that the contempt for women Freud believed as an inevitable male reaction to the perception of female 'castration' is actually a pathological response to maternal power."[89]

Studlar's examples drawn from the cinema of von Sternberg are illu-minating and follow closely the Deleuzian schema for the etiology of masochism. In *The Devil Is a Woman* (1935), for example, Don Pasquale's enjoyment lies in the telling of his story of masochistic enslavement to the woman (a pleasure initially denied but made obvious as the film progresses). He finally allows himself to be killed in a duel for the love of Concha Perez, in order to satisfy her desire for another man, just as Fabrizio Donati will allow himself to be shot "for Louise" at the end of *Madame de . . . .* The advantage to Deleuze's description of masochism is that it does not deny the importance of the mother figure. Freud, on the other hand, claims that the punitive male (in these cases, the man who fights the duel) is actually the more significant figure and that the woman is only present to disguise the homosexual implications of the pleasure felt by the masochist when he is being punished.[90] Rather, maternal power *in itself* persists, although it is my opinion that this may be bane or blessing since maternal power recollected from infancy may lead to fear of and violence against women later in life.

This film may, however, be read only up to a certain point as a male masochist's tale of the triumph of the mother (if Donati is identified as the primary masochistic figure in *Madame de . . .*) . Although André is shown to have a number of masochistic traits, it is the relationship between Donati and Louise that is formulated most consistently as a fetishistic and masochistic one. Louise herself also worships at the shrine of an exacting woman—her saint. If her relationship to that woman can be described as masochistic (entailing pain, renunciation, an ever-stricter contract, and so on), then it is possible to consider the masochistic ideal to have been fulfilled in *Madame de . . .* from an unexpected purview, and, indeed, from a strictly feminine one. But Ophuls' films evince only a wavering faith in the (male) masochistic scenario, in that there exists the continual possibility that masochism, which works best in suspense and at a distance, will break down when the woman comes too close and the workings of the castration complex are revived.[91] In fact, this seems to me to be one of the main problems with the celebration of the pre-Oedipal that can be seen in many feminists' works. The earlier phase must inevitably be read through the Oedipal, although there has also been an attempt to revive Freud's notion of the *negative Oedipus* as a means of constructing a more positive form of female identification with the mother.[92] Thus, although the function of irony can be overemphasized in Ophuls' films, one might describe as ironic the filmmaker's attitude toward the masochist's suspension of disbelief. Deleuzian masochism may be a problematic place whence to figure female power, but in its possibility of providing an ideal mother figure with whom to *identify*, as well as to hold in awe, the theory serves to flesh out Silverman's valuable discussion of the political importance of the "negative Oedipus."[93]

Believe in Me

Two scenes from the film underscore the fragility of the masochist's fetishistic beliefs. The first is the sequence when Louise is away on her trip to Italy, where she wanders alone and preoccupied with her budding love, and receives letters from Donati which she does not answer. Donati's love is most intense at this point, although its distant quality is made clear by his need to look up the word "desire" in his dictionary when he is writing one of these letters to Louise. Caught up in waiting for Louise to return, he neglects the duties of his office and wanders aimlessly, carrying with him in his portfolio a flower that Louise has sent him, rather than attending to the "masculine" affairs of his diplomatic position. Donati's union with Louise is marked, then, by a feminization that is put into relief by his encounters with André, who seems to be in a particularly manly state of mind—wearing his epaulets and pointing to Donati's flower when it accidentally drops. This scene might tempt one to reinstate the Freudian notion that the masochistic bond with the woman disguises a homosexual desire for the father figure. Such a reading seems particularly apt since the meeting occurs in a scene where a large number of officials are gathered to celebrate a union, likened to a marriage, between Italy (Donati's country) and France (André's). One might interpret Donati's solemnity at this moment to a sense of guilt at defiling the sacrament of (Louise's) marriage. This could also be a symbolic wedding "at a distance" with Louise. But there is yet the possibility that this is a symbolic marriage with André himself, with Donati standing in as the bride (with flowers). Because the boy's pre-Oedipal attachment with the mother can never be completely reinstated, the earlier attachment is to some degree being read through his desiring relation to the father. The father figure's authority is continually questioned, but it is never entirely eliminated.[94] The situation is a dangerous one for women, who move from being the object of a masochist's worship to the denigrated, postcastration "mother" in an economy in which male homoeroticism must be denied.

A further illustration of the paternal function's participation in the masochistic schema can be found in the ballroom scene where the General issues a displaced castration threat, forcing Donati to acknowledge that the woman does not have the right to the earrings. "Let the woman's lack be a warning to you," he seems to tell Donati when he calls him into the masculine domain of the smoking parlor, after having taken the earrings from Louise. And as in Freud's description of the etiology of the castration complex in the boy child, the male experiences the sight of the female genitals as a look at a castrated penis only under the influence of the threat of castration. It is in the next scene that Donati becomes furious with Louise's "lies" about the origins of the earrings, after he has been threatened by her husband.

To summarize, the problem of belief in *Madame de . . .* is one that is directly tied to the problem of believing (in) a woman. This belief or nonbelief in the woman offers a model for belief in the narrative itself. To reiterate: we learn something we have "always known," that stories—including the "story" of feminine castration—*are always fictional.* When Louise lies, she claims the right to possess the maternal phallus—both to *have* and *identify with* the mother, according to Silverman's discussion of the negative Oedipal complex. Donati believes he has found the truth in Louise's "castration." The (male) fetishist, and the cinematic spectator, also "know" that Louise is lying, that her "phallus" is not real—as he or she knows that the film image is a not a slice of reality. In order to "enjoy" the woman or the film, this knowledge must be set aside or concealed—although, on the other hand, it is possible that female spectators see the signs of the revival of the positive relationship to the mother that Louise seems to experience.

Such radical inquiries into the question of belief (*la croyance*) are the subject of a well-known essay by the French psychoanalyst Octave Mannoni: "Je sais bien, mais quand même . . ." ("I know, but just the same. . .").[95] An excellent example of the coexistence of a belief with its opposite can be seen when Louise packs to leave on her trip to the Italian lakes, as Nanny tells her fortune with a pack of playing cards. At first Louise is impatient with the too obvious or seemingly absurd predictions made by Nanny: "You are going to take a voyage; you are going to have trouble with your husband." But when Nanny puts down a card and gasps, Louise's interest is aroused. Now the old woman predicts "a great love, shared." Louise is dumbfounded and at this moment clearly believes in the prediction, perhaps saying to herself, "I know that reading the future with cards is nonsense, but I believe this prediction all the same." Our attraction to the narrative is structured as a disavowal—the erotic force comes from the woman's denial of reality, which we can adopt as our own.

Donati's naive belief in Louise offers us a model for our own (spectatorial) belief in her extraordinary (phallic? maternal?) qualities. As Mannoni points out, the existence of a naive believer who permits us simultaneously to mock and to retain the remnants of beliefs we have "overcome" is a common literary device, related to the adult need to convince children to believe in various mythical figures so that the adult can hold on to some portion of that belief ("Let's go see Santa Claus"). And yet we can see very clearly that Donati's belief in the "phallic" woman rests upon the knowledge of her castration: to take an example from the film rather literally—he only pursues her at the customs house because he

"knows" that she no longer has the earrings that she "formerly" possessed (before the subject's awareness of castration). Louise's attitude
toward superstition and her behavior toward her patron saint at the end
of the film (associated, as we have seen, with the maternal register) are
indicative of the woman's ability to adopt fetishistic practices, both the
"pre-Oedipal" variety, which emphasize the replacement of the lost
mother, and the Oedipalized scenario involving the maternal phallus.
But like the man, the woman also experiences fetishism as a vacillation
that sometimes collapses in upon itself. At the end of the film Louise will
give the earrings to the saint, repeating Donati's earlier attempt to
"return the phallus to the mother (who never lost it)." In doing so, she
reproduces the fetish that has been annihilated (for Donati) earlier in
the film. Fetishism is inscribed at a higher level, indeed: "I know that the
fetishized woman has been shown to be castrated, but I will believe in
her just the same." This (ironic) view of the fetish does not prevent the
film's ending from being solemn, touching, and quite sincere. It may
also be possible to read this gesture in another way, as Louise's final
repayment—or even her utter disavowal—of the debt that plagued her
at the beginning of the film.

Maternal Contract

At the end of the film, the wrath of the patriarch seems to have pre-
vailed. The lover is killed, the woman dies of sorrow. And yet, in her contract with the saint, in this monumentalizing of the female figure even
within the institutional context of the Church, Louise has attained a
measure of triumph. The saint has failed to hold up her end of the bargain, in that she has not saved Donati's life,[96] but with her dying gesture
Louise is able to pass on the debt that had seemed to ruin her; she is able
to make a gift of it, to inscribe it with the only name she has. However,
only by turning to an *institutional* framework is she able to do so. This
creation of a personal religion may support the masochist's supposed
eschewal of institutions for the sake of the spontaneously generated contract that would create the law. Louise's contractual relationships with
men have proven to be deeply flawed—the marriage contract was always
unequal; the husband's agreement to allow his wife to make him suffer
was only temporary; Donati's loving idealization (an agreement signed
at the customs house and sealed with the earrings) could not withstand

his disillusionment. Louise must then turn back to her own earlier commitment to the woman's image, investing that image with the "ghost" of her own value.

The ending of the film certainly *gestures* toward the reinstatement of the woman untouched by the castration complex. This turn to a feminized institution as the resting-site of the woman's debt may be the only vision available to Ophuls of the woman empowered, since the men depicted in this film seem even less able to believe in the phallic/pre-Oedipal mother figure than is the woman.[97] Although a more profound critique of patriarchy's positioning of woman as perpetual debtor would involve an absolute refusal to assume that debt, this essentialist construction of a feminine subjectivity that can pass along its debt may be a necessary moment in the creation of a sexuality that has deconstructed dichotomy. Still, the lack is not erased: Madame de . . . is still marked with the sign of the ellipsis on the plaque at the end of the film.

There is, in fact, a paradoxical feeling about the last scene of the film, which can be described without reference to psychoanalytic terminology, but to which I have referred in terms of Mannoni's "je sais bien" configuration. The paradox is that we know Louise is bad, a liar, flirtatious, "empty," but is she not also a tremendous and memorable woman? That the man—preoccupied, perhaps, with his male rival/beloved—is somehow not quite able to see this is important. The ambiguity of the monument—an entrapment or an arresting and thereby powerful tableau of the phallic woman—is contained in this phrase on the plaque. Is it Madame de . . . who is "donnée," given in effigy to the institution? Or is Madame de . . . the subject of the act of giving? Alan Williams interprets the ending of the film to mean that Louise has been raised in effigy by a man and has finally been fixed with the name of a man: "The Place of the Mother has been invaded by the Name of the Father."[98] Perhaps we should instead reiterate that the place of the mother still remains nameless—though not for long.

This remnant of ambiguity with respect to sexual politics is characteristic of Ophuls' cinema. The film presents no solution to the pain and injustice evident in representations of sexual difference. Indeed, as Catherine Stimpson has written, "A male writer [or filmmaker] may speak of, for, to and from the feminine. He cannot speak, except fictively, of, for, to and from the female. This inability hardly has the dignity of a tragic fact, but it does have the grittiness of a simple fact."[99] We might add that an adequate definition of what it might mean to speak "from the *female*" can only be achieved contingently, contextually, and historically. In *Madame de . . .* Ophuls reformulates both ironically and, one might say, sentimentally, the functioning of sexual difference with respect to the cinematic image, within the context of the female French citizen's slow accession to full legal rights under the law. And always in the background, to be read in the discourse on commodity exchange, is the issue of the marginality of the Jewish citizens of France when the discourses of nationalism on the part of the Left and the Right had historical bases in anti-Semitism.[100]

Thievery, Credit, and Blackmail

Ophuls' only Dutch film, *Komedie om Geld* (1936), his penultimate French film of the thirties, *Sans Lendemain* (1939), and his American "film noir," *The Reckless Moment* (1949), each discussed in this section, approach the question of circulation and spectacle from diverse perspectives, preparing the way for *Madame de . . .*'s virtual dissertation on the topic. The link between money and the role of woman is indirect but solid in *Komedie*, which is Ophuls' most obviously "Brechtian" film. In his last Hollywood film, *The Reckless Moment*, made for producer Walter Wanger at Columbia Pictures, the issue of femininity is directly linked to the problem of money and credit. In any event, *Komedie om Geld*, *Sans Lendemain*, and *The Reckless Moment*, his most commercially successful American film, have plots that revolve around "money's congruence with those who are marginal,"[101] and push the problem of credit to its farthest limit.

Komedie om Geld was an extremely influential film in Holland, introducing new techniques and helping to revitalize the ailing Dutch film industry.[102] The film is based on an original story by Ophuls and centers on a number of characteristic Ophulsian preoccupations. It is, for example, the first of his films to feature an overt master of ceremonies, or director-figure,[103] here standing before a revolving wheel, as he tells the story of bank clerk Brand's loss and recovery of £50,000 sterling. Like *Madame de . . .* this film focuses on a loss that is ultimately fictional, but that becomes embroiled in matters of *credit* and *credibility*.

It begins with a swindle: "the old dog trick." Ferdinand, Brand's brother-in-law, sells his dog to a gullible couple, then whistles for it to return to him, apparently an habitual means of making money. Ferdinand takes refuge with Brand, who is fishing, and thus escapes detection by the police. However, Brand's superior learns of the escapade and forces Brand to sign a paper advising him to have no more contact with his brother-in-law. Ferdinand intercepts a small boy who is stealing apples and sends him to make some honest money, by delivering a note to Brand at the bank. While he's there, the hungry boy watches a bureaucrat eat his lunch, then lock the remaining food in his desk. Brand is meanwhile picking up the £50,000 at the cashier. He wonders aloud how much this would be in guilders. A montage sequence alternates between Brand and the boy, who runs from the bank. (A flashback late in the film reveals that, in his search for the food, the boy had cut a hole in the delivery bag Brand used to transport the money from the Continent Bank to the Neptune Bank.) Meanwhile, Brand discovers the note saying Ferdinand's dog is being taken away because the dog tax wasn't paid. Brand lectures his brother-in-law on honesty, but agrees to loan him twenty guilders. (During this conversation, as we later discover, the £50,000 fall from the bag into a cellar, unbeknownst to the two men, who stand arguing on a bridge.) When the money is found missing, Brand is fired from his job (for "giving the bank a bad reputation"), and tries unsuccessfully to find another. His daughter, Willy, is dismissed from her job as an exercise instructor, then refused a job as a governess because of her father's suspected (but unproven) theft.

Ferdinand tries to comfort Brand by saying, "Don't worry. . . . I've been in debt for years. The important thing is that you continue to have credit." But credit soon runs short: a montage sequence using complex voice-overs shows various merchants dictating letters citing Brand's lack of payment. Brand manages to get a job in a bowling alley but overhears one of the patrons saying he has refused Willy the governess job (which she had pretended to land) because she's an embezzler's daughter. The sound of a bowling ball (coupled with a startling image of the ball rolling toward the camera) segues into the sound of Brand returning home. He writes a suicide note to his daughter. During a fade to black (in one of the film's many amusing cinematic tricks), a male voice says: "I would like to ask you to join me in a moment of silence to honor the deceased." A fade-in shows a board meeting. Is Brand dead? No, it's Dr. Rinkemaus, a member of the International Financial Institute's executive board. A discussion ensues concerning the institute's many debts: "Good banks don't want to deal with us anymore." This scene is crosscut with that of Brand attempting to kill himself with gas. An employee of the firm is dispatched to get the "man suspected of having the money." Brand is rescued from his gas-filled room (he had turned on a gas chandelier without lighting it—a chandelier that reappears, with a note of black humor, on the master of ceremonies' stage set). Brand is then made director of this firm, which seeks to finance low-income housing. The president appeals to Brand's "leadership" qualities—when in fact it's assumed that Brand has the £50,000 and can thus guarantee the solvency of the company.

Although Brand denies having any money, the head of the firm insists that he is actually concerned not with money per se but with *credit*: "People are supposed to think that there is money, so when they ask, one can answer with good conscience 'yes.'" Brand agrees to serve as director of the firm and busies himself with a model community (the "New Life"), whose design he alters, as he circles around the model town, according to populist sentiment ("To every man his own little piece of land") and personal quirks ("No gas: it has bad associations for me"). Meanwhile we discover that the company officials are simply allowing Brand to "play" at being director. Trouble erupts as carnival music intrudes into Brand's office from outside. Interestingly, the music involves the defeat of the Spanish Armada, whose "silver ships" are spoken of in specifically economic terms.[104] Following a 360-degree shot around Brand, who raves about the music, Ferdinand (who has been hired as a doorman) goes outside to pay off the organ grinder.

Willy has her own agenda. A series of vacation scenes follow the progress of her love affair with a German gas station attendant. In their palatial home Willy and Brand argue over her love affair. (Brand seems, among other things, to object to the young man being German!) Disgusted with their new way of life and Brand's deception about the money, Willy runs away with her boyfriend, staying (platonically) with him at Ferdinand's house. (As in *Lachende Erben*, a dog is used to help guard the hero/heroine's virtue.) Brand, who has been pressured to use cheaper brick in his housing units, resigns from his post after having nightmares about Willy and his job. But Moorman (his boss) will only allow Brand to leave if the money (the now virtually fictional £50,000) remains at IFI. It seems that loans have been taken out against the phantom sum. Ferdinand agrees to help Brand. They begin by getting completely drunk and sending the bill to Moorman. They then return to the bridge where they had stood arguing earlier in the film, and while reenacting the scene Ferdinand falls through a grid into a cellar—where the dog finds the money as his master is being rescued. Still drunk, Brand taunts Moorman with the money, on his way to the Neptune Bank: "It's over with director Brand and back to courier Brand." Moorman calls home to have his things packed so he can escape to Lisbon. A complex series of events—including the refusal on the part of the Neptune Bank to have the money repaid since the insurance company has already done so—leads to Brand's being sentenced to one year in prison for embezzlement. The master of ceremonies intervenes with the flashback showing Brand's innocence and with the boy who will bring the film to a "happy end" by appearing with Brand's friends in his defense. The last scene of the film takes place in the emcee's "fantasyland." Brand is fishing—he's again become a citizen "satisfied with a fishing rod." The film's theme song about money is given a new moral: "Money which is mute, which straightens what's bent, which is worshiped, which he desired until it taught him to despise it . . ."

Marc Shell has noted that "credit, or belief, involves the very ground of aesthetic experience, and the same medium that seems to confer belief in fiduciary money (bank notes) and in scriptural money (created by the process of bookkeeping) also seems to confer it in literature."[105] In my reading of *Madame de . . .* I noted a similar process linking belief in the cinematic image to belief in woman as "economic" entity. *Komedie om Geld*, a film marked by the anxieties of pre–World War II Europe's inflationary economies, places its protagonist in a state of involuntary indebtedness. Paradoxically, Brand's loss of the money also puts him in the position of guarantor of credit for the International Financial Institute: he becomes a potential cornucopia of credit through the financiers' suspension of disbelief. Shell points to a fundamental mistrust of bank notes and of credit money as the "extreme form of paper money."[106] Nonetheless, although the lost money first acts, like the earrings in *Madame de . . .*, to absorb Brand's resources (as is shown in the montage scene of his debts), it later takes on a kind of ideal status, providing him with an inflated value. Like Louise de . . ., Brand becomes a kind of "blank check." Not surprisingly, it is Brand's daughter who suffers from the deception inherent in the situation. Interestingly, she turns for help to Ferdinand, the author of the dog trick involving an even more overt financial malpractice than Brand's. Ferdinand and the dog redeem themselves by recovering the money, while the flashback structure of the film "fills in" the information lost to the spectator concerning the money's fate. Still, although the film ends on a note of cau-

tion regarding the circulating medium of money and its shadowy representations, it is money itself that has taught Brand to "despise it," as the
song says. The artifice of the medium of cinema, both embodied and
ironically commented upon by the master of ceremonies, intervenes to
save the day. As in *The Bartered Bride, Madame de . . .*, and so forth, the
larger institutions of society project their own *groundlessness* upon a circulating nexus of scapegoats. *Komedie*'s underlying populist sentiments
(noted by Barry Salt) regarding the importance of solid housing for the
masses represent an attempt to find a ground in a substantial referent—
home sweet home, a sound investment. Thus, again, Ophuls attempts to
have it both ways. His narrative produces sympathy for the Ferdinands of
the world, who live by credit and sleight of hand ("Not an eighteen-carat
guy," as one character in the film puts it). However, it also invokes the
politically ambiguous but fundamentally bourgeois credo of the home-
owning citizen as the ground of society.

The grounding of bourgeois society in the "maternal sacrifice" that
becomes literally financial can be observed in both *The Reckless Moment*
and, in a very different context, *Sans Lendemain*, Ophuls' first film with
actress Edwige Feuillère, a rather hot French star of the late 1930s.
Eugen Schüfftan also photographed this film, and of all Ophuls' thirties
films this one fits best, both thematically and visually, into the aesthetics
of French Poetic Realism.[107] *Sans Lendemain* combines the issues raised
by woman's self-presentation as an erotic being in films from *La Signora
di Tutti* to *Divine, Letter from an Unknown Woman, Madame de . . .*, and *Lola
Montès*, with the specifically economic problems (the falling due of a
debt) found in *Komedie om Geld, The Reckless Moment*, and *Madame de . . .*
again. *Sans Lendemain* (literally, "no tomorrow") is virtually a mirror
image of *The Reckless Moment*, though they are a decade and a continent
apart. In *Sans Lendemain* Evelyne, a once-respectable woman who has
been reduced to dancing in a sleazy nightclub, once again meets the
man—Georges—whom she had loved and lost years before (cf. *Letter
from an Unknown Woman*). When the film opens, Evelyne is working in
"La Sirène," an ironic name for this unwilling siren's place of employ-
ment. Her devoted friend and impresario (read "pimp") Henry guides
her in her decisions. However, we learn that prior to this Evelyne had
been courted by a young Canadian medical student (Georges Rigaud).
But her underworld husband (whom she had been made to marry when
she was very young) had reappeared and blackmailed her into leaving
Georges. The gangster-husband was later killed, leaving her with a son.

As her life crumbled, she began to work as a dancer in joints around town, finally descending to nude shows. When Evelyne encounters Georges once again, in the film's "present," she is determined that the now respectable doctor will never know what she has become. She borrows money from an old associate of her husband, who believes that she is setting the doctor up for a fall. Interest on the loan is put at 70 percent of anything she takes: in fact the interest will be paid with her life. With the help of Henri, Evelyne sets up a luxurious apartment and pretends to be the respectable woman she still superficially resembles. Georges, of course, falls in love with her once again, and she decides to send her child away with him, promising to join them in Canada later. Instead, rather than sully Georges' memory of her, or be forced to work in even sleazier shows, she jumps into the Seine.

Idealization of a lost bourgeois respectability runs high in this film, a collaborative adaptation by Ophuls, Hans Jacobi, and André-Paul Antoine, a frequent coworker whose play formed the basis of *La Tendre Ennemie* (1936). This formerly middle-class woman has fallen into gangsters' hands and longs to regain her former station. As noted above, this mirrors the topos of *The Reckless Moment*. In that film, the female protagonist's "forbidden love" is actually a gangster who longs for home and respectability. But both women are forced to lose their loves for the sake of debts they cannot pay. Rather than killing herself, Lucia Harper (Joan Bennett) throws a man's body into the water (in the style of a film noir heroine) and is then buried alive (melodrama-style) in her family. Evelyne, on the other hand, joins her sisters in Ophuls' films in their leaps into the void.

Robert Lang has correctly described *The Reckless Moment* as a critique of the patriarchal family.[108] Like *Mildred Pierce* (1945), this film lies at the juncture of several genres, notably the family melodrama and film noir, both of which it exemplifies in visual and thematic terms. Barry Salt sees the film as an "original combination of at least two sub-genres, namely the 'lady in a jam' type of thriller, and the 'mother coping in husband's absence' domestic drama."[109] William Paul notes that Ophuls' American films are unusual in his career in that they might all be characterized as genre works, while his French films cannot.[110] *The Reckless Moment* tells the story of a woman, Lucia Harper, who is left in charge of her family while her husband Tom is away on business in Berlin. The worlds of noir and melodrama divide, for most of the film, between the "island suburb" of Balboa,[111] which is orderly and sunny, and the dark world of the city, to which she must travel to meet the man blackmailing her daughter. Between those two worlds is the confined space of the family car (like one of Ophuls' carriages) she uses while driving back and forth, and while ferrying across the water to and from the mainland.

The opening scene of the film features a montage sequence depicting the bay and the suburb it surrounds. A male voice-over describing the setting and what is about to unfold lends a noirish atmosphere even to this brightly lit series of shots. Interestingly, this voice-over disappears, never to return, much as does the omniscient narrator in Flaubert's *Madame Bovary*. Joan Bennett, as Lucia, is a concerned mother rather than a film noir heroine, though the dark glasses she wears early in the film both figure her emotional "blindness,"[112] and prefigure the way she will be drawn into the chaotic world of the film noir villains. Her entrapment within the extended family is immediately thrown into relief as her son David (David Blair) calls after her car, "Mother, where are you going?" She is unable to answer him—and thus begins the double life she will lead throughout the rest of the film. Lucia's daughter Bea (Geraldine Brooks) has fallen in love with a slick ladies' man, "ex-art dealer" Ted Darby (Shepperd Strudwick), whom she met while taking art classes in the city. Taking advantage of Tom Harper's absence, Darby attempts to force Lucia to pay him to stop seeing Bea. He has arranged a meeting in an empty and darkly lit hotel bar for this purpose. Lucia refuses to pay him and returns home across the water to confront her daughter over the love affair. At one point, as mother and daughter argue in Bea's bedroom over Darby and over Lucia's now-regretted decision to allow Bea to go to art school, half the frame is obscured by an easel holding one of Bea's paintings. The other half frames Bea herself. The content of the painting is obscured: more important is the mere fact of representation. As an artist, Bea holds the potential to turn the tables on the woman's traditional role as object rather than subject of representation, just as Lucia is (reluctantly) reversing the gender roles in the family hierarchy. However, Bea's excursus into the world of art has only served to objectify her the more emphatically. She is even not loved by Ted Darby but is the object of his blackmail, and in this way forces her mother to take the role—that of protective "patriarch"—which will underscore her inadequacy even as she succeeds in keeping her family together.

The film noir world invades the suburbs as Darby visits Bea by night, in a secret rendezvous in the boathouse. As Lucia sits at her desk writing and tearing up an anguished plea for help to her husband, Bea confronts and accidentally kills Darby in the boathouse (like several of Ophuls' female protagonists, Darby's injury is the result of a fall). Unaware of what she has done, Bea returns to bed, leaving the body to be discovered by her mother the next morning. Here Lucia commits one of the "reckless" actions described by Lang as resulting from her attempts to be the man of the house.[113] In an act that is doubly illegitimate (both illegal and gender transgressive), Lucia takes the body out into the bay and dumps it, appropriately, along with the boat's anchor (the instrument of Darby's death, when he fell through the handrail to the sand below after Bea had struck him). Raising issues alluded to by the editors of *Framework*, Mary Ann Doane remarks that

motherhood is delineated as the repression of desire (Mrs. Harper's strict regulation of her daughter's sex life) and the body (she is constantly telling her son to put on more clothes—"Pull up your socks," "Put on a shirt," etc.). An inordinate amount of film time is spent on a scene in which Mrs. Harper laboriously and in silence (there is no music on the soundtrack, only the sound of lapping waves) drags Darby's body down the beach to the boat in order to take it away and conceal it—in what is basically a literalization of the "maternal function" of hiding (or repressing) the body. A mother's instinct to protect the fully legalized institution of the family is, interestingly enough, itself outside the law.[114]

As though in response to Lucia's anchorless state, there soon appears another blackmailer, Donnelly (James Mason), an "Irish racketeer."[115] Darby, it seems, had given Bea's love letters to the sinister Nagel (Roy Roberts), Donnelly's partner, as (of course) collateral for a loan. With Darby's death already discovered by the police, the letters now implicate Bea in an apparent murder. Again a split frame indicates conflict: when Donnelly initially comes to the house to demand $5,000 for Bea's letters, he stands outside in the shadows, while the family inside the well-lit house sits down for dinner, framed by the windowpane before which Donnelly stands:

The two worlds—the world of the *film noir*, and the world of the family melodrama—are thus represented in background and foreground within the same frame. The one is paranoid, involving men, money, perverse sexuality, and sadistic power imbalances. The other is concerned with what is right and what is wrong, and with the prohibition and interdiction which keeps bourgeois morality in balance.[116]

The two worlds, as Lang also observes, have completely distinct styles, each typical of the genre it seems to represent. As another "good bad man" Donnelly embodies both the threat of the film noir world, and the vulnerability of the substitute "man of the house." He seems to represent something about Lucia's repressed sexuality, and yet he assumes what is almost a maternal role toward her, fretting over her smoking too much, helping her shop at the drugstore, and pitying her when she has trouble coming up with the money.[117] Lucia is certainly a woman in distress, and Donnelly will move slowly from antagonist to admirer to imitator of her maternal heroism. Like the director-figures in earlier Ophuls films, and like the ex–art dealer whom he syntagmatically replaces, Donnelly is linked to the nefarious world of unproductive circulation. Lucia reproaches him, noting that her son David had worked hard to save $40 the summer before, hard work being something that Donnelly would know little about. In the drugstore, Donnelly buys Lucia some filters for her cigarettes, in a double-edged gesture that seems to invest her with phallic power as it places him in the concerned maternal role.

It is in the economic realm that Lucia's inexperience as head of the household is most telling. Lang notes that the crucial melodramatic theme "of the woman's lack of access to economic power . . . is rendered here with unusual explicitness."[118] In a scene echoing the openings of *Madame de . . .* and *Caught* (1949), Lucia dons her mink coat to visit a loan company. A cut followed by a tracking shot reveals her as she descends the bank's stairway (one of two emphasized in the film) to go down to the safety deposit boxes below, accompanied by a bank official in the act of telling her that she must have her husband's signature for such a sizable loan—to which she meekly acquiesces. Next she is shown ascending a dark staircase to the rather shady Coastways Loan Company, where she sits in a glass-enclosed booth that further emphasizes her isolation. She fumbles the request for money (not knowing whether she wants to "make" or "get" a loan—a symptomatic confusion) and is completely thrown when asked what she might offer as collateral. Like Lola in *Madame de . . .*, she is framed by bars in the next scene as she sells her jewelry to a pawnbroker located in a seedy part of Los Angeles. Lucia is trapped in a masculine sphere in which she has little to barter, and where her children serve only to impoverish her further. Moreover, the film is set at Christmastime, traditionally one of economic distress and domestic crisis that can be contained only with difficulty. Lucia does attempt to maintain control, including financial control. She frets over expenses, enjoins Sybil, her African-American housekeeper (Frances Williams), to cut down on the meat bill, and when David asks for a dollar she rapidly demands, "What for?"—passing along the question asked her by the disapproving older woman at the loan company.[119] It has often been noted that Lucia's main activity regarding her son is to continually remind him that he needs to put on his shirt, his shoes, and so forth ("For once," she exclaims, "I'd like to see you fully dressed!"). David's parody of dangerous masculinity forms a pendant with the foolishness of the doddering father-in-law (Henry O'Neill), who from time to time half-heartedly offers his help to Lucia. Between these two paragons of masculinity stands the absent Tom: we are led to wonder whether Tom himself can anchor the family only at a distance. The greatest strength in the film seems to rest with Sybil, a silent, watchful figure, much like the valet in *Letter from an Unknown Woman*. Robert Lang has aptly called Sybil the "moral center of the story."[120] Like the "good" director or fellow actor, Sybil often throws the frantic Lucia her cues, intuiting her troubles and helping her to prevent the situation from deteriorating completely. One can only regret that African-American actors were almost without exception given such caretaking roles. In Ophuls' films we have seen, in any case, that suffering alongside the heroine is hardly a passive activity but entails its own complications and active decisions.

When the wrong man is arrested, Lucia "confesses" Darby's murder to Donnelly, who does not believe her. Refusing his half of the (unforthcoming) blackmail money, Donnelly then fights with and kills Nagel in the Harpers' boathouse, and finally crashes his car. Interestingly, the climactic scene in the noirishly lit boathouse anticipates Donnelly's ultimate shift of blame to himself. As Nagel threatens her, Lucia is standing in front of an empty picture frame, where Donnelly will position himself moments later during the fight with Nagel. Thus the "frame," with all its burden of representation and culpability, falls upon Donnelly, who confesses to the police before he dies that *he* murdered Darby. Donnelly's car crash is reminiscent of the final scenes of *Madame de . . .* in a number of respects. Having thwarted Lucia's attempt to tend his wounds, he slips away with Nagel's body in his own car. Lucia follows in her car with Sybil (who declares at this point that she "like[s] Mr. Donnelly"—thus stamping him with the melodramatic seal of approval), arriving at the scene of the car crash only after it has occurred, much as Louise and Nanny arrive too late at the duel between André and Fabrizio. The final scene of both films depicts the real or emotional death of the female protagonists: here, Lucia weeps over Donnelly as he gives her the incriminating letters before he dies. And as at the end of *La Signora di Tutti*, a telephone call (one of many in *The Reckless Moment*) helps to restore a semblance of paternal leadership and familial order. Just after she returns home, Lucia is called downstairs to the telephone to answer a call from Tom in Berlin (curiously, there is never a reverse shot of Tom in the film; Lucia might still be speaking to Donnelly . . .). Pulling herself together, Lucia walks down the staircase that has been the locus of many family crises, emphasized by low-angle shots and the dark shadows of the rails cast upon the walls. During this final scene

no shadows of the balustrade fall on her, but she is placed now quite literally behind its bars, in a tableau that visualizes Donnelly's perception that she is a "prisoner." The narrative is concluded with a seal of traditional order—reference to the Christmas tree, in a vapid conversation that overdetermines the sterility and emptiness of the family structure that Lucia has labored so hard to protect.[121]

In this conversation Lucia hands the reins of the family back over to her husband, who did not even realize that she had ever held them, and who inspires no confidence that he will do a better job than she.

Three

✦

Directorial Protocol and the Failed Sacrifice
in *De Mayerling à Sarajevo*

> *The act of regicide is the exact equivalent, vis-à-vis the*
> *polis, of the act of patricide vis-à-vis the family. In both*
> *cases the criminal strikes at the most fundamental,*
> *essential and inviolable distinctions within the group.*
> *He becomes, literally, the slayer of distinctions.*
> —René Girard, *Violence and the Sacred*

◆

Mimetic Violence and Political Change

From Mayerling to Sarajevo: from the suicide of ill-starred, high-born lovers to the assassination of a couple about to stand at the head of an empire. A past to which protocol forbids any allusion. A death in two moments: the periodicity of ritual sacrifice. *De Mayerling à Sarajevo* (1940) is a film about the perils of directorship, failed sacrifice, and the allure of the bourgeois mode of life the in turn-of-the-century Austro-Hungarian Empire. Focusing on a male monarch, the film examines the relinquishing of masculinity, and the mimetic dangers of femininity to be found in almost all of Ophuls' works. The film's atmosphere of crisis corresponds with the political trauma breaking out across Europe in 1939, when the film was made.

Much of the violence in *Sarajevo* originates with a particular character who, like John the valet in *Letter from an Unknown Woman* or the General in *Madame de . . .*, acts as a stand-in for the film's director. In *Sarajevo* the character who "directs" the film's events functions more overtly than do most such Ophulsian figures to maintain an oppressive social and aesthetic hierarchy. In this case, the rigid structure of imperial protocol under the Hapsburg empire is the real villain of the piece. If *Sarajevo* strikes the viewer as more naive than the usual Ophuls product, it may be because Prince Montenuovo (Aimé Clariond) is more a *negative* than an ambiguous character, representing in an almost allegorical fashion the forces of mimetic violence. To some degree, the very bare-boned naïveté of the film makes it useful for those interested in Ophuls' cinema.[1]

De Mayerling à Sarajevo shares with the later French films (such as *La Ronde*, whose setting is also Vienna) a number of important technicians and writers, including the musician Oscar Straus, the decorator Jean d'Eaubonne, the scriptwriter Jacques Natanson, and others. Although the "mobile *mise en scène*"[2] characterizing Ophuls' style is less elaborate than in the later films (or even in some of the earlier ones—compare *Sarajevo*'s eighteen tracking shots to *La Signora di Tutti*'s fifty-nine),[3] there is considerable stylistic resemblance between this and the films of the 1940s and 1950s. The layered look of the foregrounds, with obstacles like gates, doorways, and gauze between the camera and the characters is unmistakably Ophulsian.[4] Crane and tracking shots on stairways, outside windows, and so forth are less involved than they will become but are nonetheless distinctive.[5]

In Mayerling, Austria, on January 30, 1889, the Crown Prince Rudolf and his mistress committed suicide.[6] A popular French film was made about this incident—Anatole Litvak's *Mayerling* (1936). As Richard Roud comments, Ophuls' *Sarajevo* was "presumably an attempt to cash in on and repeat the great success" of the earlier film.[7] His last film before leaving for the United States via Switzerland, *Sarajevo* was completed hastily and only after Ophuls had been drafted into the French army. He was granted a leave to finish it in December 1939.[8] Both the reference to the earlier couple's death and the fatality implied by the film's title (the "inevitable" progression from suicide to assassination) indicate this film's debt to the earlier one. Despite what some critics have said, the intertextual play does not detract from Ophuls' film, but lends a dimension to *De Mayerling à Sarajevo* that fits the idiosyncrasy of Ophuls' film corpus. This work is considerably more than a cashing-in on another film's popularity, although there are a number of (obviously intentional) superficial resemblances between them.

The doubling of a double death is also familiar to us from Ophuls' emphasis on the repetitious and contagious qualities of death. In these films people almost always die in pairs, though scarcely ever on-screen. In this case, the film's pair is matched with a couple that ceased to exist long before the beginning of the story, a couple whose death has been hushed up, "repressed," by the royal family. The repercussions of the death of Rudolf and Maria Vetsera at Mayerling will only be fully comprehended *en après coup*, in a deferred manner, when the First World War begins, after the assassination of Franz Ferdinand and his wife.[9]

De Mayerling à Sarajevo differs from the Ophuls works analyzed up to this point in that the film's protagonist is a man. However, as in *The Exile* (1947), throughout *Sarajevo* one can sense a pull toward the leading lady—Ophuls was certainly tempted to treat *her* story at the expense of his.[10] But Ophuls was also interested in the dilemmas confronting the royal male. In both *The Exile* and *Sarajevo* the heir apparent fulfills some of the functions undertaken by female characters in the other films.[11] This is not to say that femininity has no specificity in the films and is entirely a matter of position and role-playing (although that is partly the case). Much of what the young Archduke suffers in *Sarajevo* comes from his association with the woman who is to be his wife: femininity is also contiguity, proximity. The situation is further complicated in this film by the resurgence of the dichotomies between military and middle-class values, between theatricality and bourgeois authenticity. The Archduke Franz Ferdinand must play the roles of military commander, royal scapegoat, object of a national spectacle, and middle-class family man.

Sarajevo raises a number of the "mimetic" concerns discernible in Ophuls' other works, including a preoccupation with imitation, with the production of images, and with role-playing, all of which often lead to some form of violence. And as is often the case in Ophuls' films, *Sarajevo* reaches an impasse concerning the possibility of political change. Here, once again, Girard's views on desire, sacrifice, and violence may be of explanatory value: "Two desires converging on the same object are bound to clash. Thus, mimesis coupled with desire leads automatically to conflict. . . . The mimetic aspects of desire must correspond to a primary impulse of most living creatures, exacerbated in man to the point where only cultural constraints can channel it in constructive directions."[12] In *Sarajevo* both the rivalry among potential heirs to the throne and the "violent unanimity" of the people acting against the "sacred" scapegoat (the king) accrue causal power—triggering World War I and even (according to the film's epilogue) World War II. For Girard social cohesion is always a product of such outbursts of violent unanimity as the rising up of the Serbian and Bosnian people against Franz Ferdinand—and the mimetic function that leads to conflict is basic to human psychology. My interest in his theory is more textually than psychologically based: as a film text, *Sarajevo* follows the pattern of contagious violence that Girard discerns throughout the history of Western literature and elsewhere.

Given by the plot of *De Mayerling à Sarajevo* to be caused by the perfidy of an evil official (Montenuovo, the "head of protocol"), the wider context of the film demonstrates that the sacrificial nature of the protagonists' deaths is a product of the position held by Franz Ferdinand—as a head of state—and of his refusal to embody the rigid rules of etiquette laid down by that position. The film tells the story of young Franz Ferdinand's boredom and loneliness in his role as heir apparent and of his resentment of the manipulations of the imperial bureaucracy. Franz Ferdinand takes his place in the pantheon of alienated male characters in Ophuls' films, including André de . . ., who despises his "role," and Smith Ohlrig (Robert Ryan) in *Caught* (1949), who finds it impossible to assume the patriarch's mantle and falls ill instead, like Louise de . . ., of a heart attack brought on by strong emotions. Franz Ferdinand's permissive ideas concerning Slav nationalism, which were greatly exaggerated for the purposes of the film, and his marriage to a woman from the lower reaches of Czech nobility, alienate him from the imperialistic program of the Austro-Hungarian monarchy. To a certain extent he might be seen, along with Smith Ohlrig, Lola's ringmaster, and others, to belong to that group of men, as described by Kaja Silverman,[13] obliged or actually willing to "give up" his phallic privilege.

It is crucial to note that the critique of the institution of monarchy attributed by the film to Franz Ferdinand is for the most part a fiction by Ophuls and his writers. Although he advocated a kind of federalism, within the context of "The conservative tenets of his house,"[14] and refused the ironclad etiquette inherited from the Spanish Hapsburgs (mostly because it meant constant humiliation for his wife), Franz Ferdinand was no democrat. Indeed the principle of legitimism was of great importance to him. These are typical of his remarks on the eve of World War I: "A full concord with Russia [*Dreikaiserbundnis*], the maintenance of peace, and the strengthening of the monarchical principle—this is my life's ideal, for which I shall be enthusiastic and shall work with all my strength."[15]

Further, when Franz Ferdinand's youngest brother, Karl Friedrich, married a commoner (Berta Czuber, the daughter of a university professor), the aristocratic Franz was so annoyed that he refused to see his brother again. Egalitarianism was obviously neither the goal nor the impetus of Franz Ferdinand's marriage, although the film would have us think so.[16] Robert A. Kann has written that "The most conspicuous trait in the archduke's character, or, rather, in the general reaction to his personality, was his extreme unpopularity in every stratum of society."[17] Although there is a commercial reason for creating a more conventionally sympathetic (i.e., middle-class and good-hearted) protagonist than was the bigoted and staunchly (even fanatically) Catholic heir apparent,[18] there are other tensions that produce this deformation of the political character and beliefs of Franz Ferdinand. The context provided by Ophuls' oeuvre makes it clear that Ophuls has a particular interest in exaggerating the heir apparent's doubts about the place of the monarch.

As in *The Exile*, the man's refusal to adapt to the norms of a hierarchy, to *represent* that hierarchy, is expressed in terms of a relationship to a woman "inappropriate" to the rank of her lover. And like Lola Montès, Sophie Chotek (Edwige Feuillère) will be able to approach the monarch only by means of a breach of etiquette—a transgression, as it were, that seems to promise the ruler the possibility of escaping from the laws he must embody. She frees him from social constraints only to expose him to the generative violence that seeks, in these films, to use the king either as an entrapped figurehead of order or as a scapegoat for social upheaval.[19] The monarch is shown in all these films to be a particular type of placeholder, one who can only occupy his position by means of an enormous (in this case—absolute) personal cost. Although it is an earlier film, *Sarajevo* articulates this "feminization" of the monarch much more intricately than does *The Exile*. Franz Ferdinand's feminization is bound, as in *Madame de . . .*, to contractual law (in *Lola Montès* the contract is virtually that of prostitute to client) and to a highly elaborate use of the symbols of hierarchy and physical position (composition, arrangement), conflated in the figure of the uniform and in the statues shown in the films.

The situation of the royal personage resembles that of the woman in Ophuls' films, in that neither is really an "individual," except in the most painful and problematic way. In considering the work of Schnitzler, Sidney Bolkosky has pointed to a "Viennese" pattern also evident in Ophuls' cinema: "Misogyny in Vienna was not simply hatred of women. It disallowed female individuation, forcing women to be children, lustful prostitutes, or morbidly depressed nonentities."[20] Because he must act primarily as the representative of power and authority to his people, the monarch has, like these women, lost any claim to individual rights, which are recuperated and labeled in *Sarajevo* as *bourgeois* rights. Both opposed to and symmetrical with the bourgeois mode of individuation is the sacrificial model, referred to above, in which the individual is singled out only to act as a social scapegoat. We will see how this is spelled out quite explicitly in this film.

Not surprisingly, the overtly *political* lesson Ophuls seems to draw in this film is layered and displaced. The power of the film lies in its ruthlessly humorous interrogation of the art of film-directing as it relates to the depiction of social hierarchy and the differential representation of men and women, and in its depiction of those who are exiled or expelled—or marginalized even as subjects of the empire. The "political" thus enters the frame from a different angle than one might have anticipated from such a subject. One of the most pressing "political" concerns in the film is whether individualism itself is either possible or desirable. The emergence of the individual is agonizing—and has other negative consequences as well. But unless this emergence takes place, the characters exist as if already dead, caught in the lifeless cycle of social interaction. The ideal balance of the bourgeois individual neatly articulated within a functioning and enlightened social body can only be grasped in retrospect, situated in a utopian elsewhere. And we have already observed that the problem becomes even more complex when the subject of that individuation is female.

As Ophuls' cinema matures, it manifests an increasing irony toward "bourgeois" solutions to violence, as it becomes more evident that they cannot solve social problems without *hypocritically* instituting forms of ritual victimization that are ugly (or, rather, *homely*, in both senses of the word) and lacking in the austere splendor of the aristocratic ceremonies of sacrifice. There persists nonetheless the strong pull toward this bourgeois utopia and a nostalgia for its makeshift answers to the problems of desire (mimetic and violent) and social control. For this reason, those critics who speak of Ophuls as "undermining" his own text, as though he would negate the sentiments aroused by the bourgeois plight, are incorrect, for the case is much more complex. In *Sarajevo* the "bourgeois solution" is advanced with apparent sincerity. And yet, a residue of doubt about the bourgeoisie remains.

De Mayerling à Sarajevo reverses the topos of the "family romance," defined by Freud as the child's fantasy that of belonging to a family superior to its own—a fantasy played out in such films as *Letter from an Unknown Woman* and *Caught*.[21] In those films the young women fantasize about becoming aristocratic but maintain a strong though not altogether conscious investment in the erotic potential of the middle-class couple. In *Sarajevo* the royal couple struggles to achieve a bourgeois existence rather than submitting to the straitjacketed life of the royal family. Such an exaltation of the bourgeoisie at the expense of the upper classes is typical of the melodrama as Peter Brooks and others have described it. To put it simply, since the genre arose after the French Revolution as a battle cry of that newly empowered class, in melodrama the bourgeois way of life necessarily proves superior to all others.

Paternal Authority Cast in Stone

Several scenes illustrative of the rather abstract issues raised above will now be discussed in some detail. The first involves Sophie's second meeting with Franz, during which they fall in love. In a previous scene, the

Czech countess had been chosen to give a welcoming speech to the Archduke, who, fatigued from his travels around the empire, had yawned and glanced continually at his watch. Offended, Sophie had rushed away from the podium, back to the humble home of her father, who was very much frightened when Sophie was subsequently called away to an audience with Franz Ferdinand.

The motif of the watch is established as a structuring device for the following several sequences of the film. A dissolve to black opens the next scene in a close-up on the dark coat worn by Sophie's father. He is walking away from the camera toward the seated Sophie. (Shots in the film often begin with characters moving toward or away from the camera.) A number of shots taken from various angles are alternated, emphasizing the bourgeois *Gemütlichkeit* of the little room, with a clock ticking away in the background. The Count insists that his daughter apologize to the Archduke; indeed, he fears that she has ruined herself through her imprudence. She pouts, neither accepting nor refusing to apologize. He repeats over and over again: "Scandal; it's a scandal!"[22] Very soon the doorbell rings and we cut to the peasant servant in the front foyer, where a soldier demands the Countess's attendance on the Archduke. A dissolve to a long shot shows that she has been taken to a kind of park (quite a stagy one), with benches, lamp posts, and a large statue of Franz Josef in the background. Chairs are placed in the foreground; the soldier takes Sophie by them as they go toward the place where she is to meet the Archduke. There is then the first of the near point-of-view shots from the *statue* to Sophie, returned by Sophie as she gazes back at it. A number of shot–reverse shot series link Sophie's vision to that of the statue, or, rather, oppose them in a dynamic of looks. A cut to Franz Ferdinand in a light uniform displaces the shot of the statue, but it continues to be visible on the edge of the frame throughout most of their interview.

Sophie Chotek presents the grievances of the Czech people to the Archduke as the pair stand some fifteen feet from the statue. She says that she is not interested in "politics"—that would not be comely in a young woman, we are to suppose—but he encourages her to admit that she despises the Hapsburgs. "You are of a rare frankness," Franz tells her, when she informs him that the Czech people are oppressed in his name. The couple then moves closer to the statue and they sit down on a bench, where the statue can be seen behind and between them. Franz asks the guard not to disturb them as they continue their political discussion. A dissolve takes us back to Sophie's father, who awaits her anxiously. He turns to look at the clock behind him (in the same small parlor), which now reads 1:45. A cut to the statue "looking" at the young couple links the benign old man with the more oppressive paternal presence of the Emperor's statue. A pan to the bench shows the Countess and the Archduke still in earnest discussion, a discussion that has obviously become a courtship. "It's late," she says. He checks the time: "It's four o'clock." "Oh, I have to go!" She rises to leave, and they continue speaking as they walk toward the statue. Sophie describes her duty as the mistress of her father's house, and they gaze up at the statue—"Between us, he's very ugly," comments Franz Ferdinand. "He's dreadful" is her reply. The Archduke complains of being continually obliged to dedicate statues like it in various places where it is not a welcome sight. They sit down again on a bench, this one closer to the statue. He sighs over his lonely life: "The moments that I have just spent near you tonight are the best I have had for a long time." A crane shot to the statue emphasizes its vacant stare at the heir apparent; a dissolve back to the parlor of the Choteks ends the scene.

This scene between Sophie and Franz is reminiscent of any number of trysts taking place on park benches and lit by lamplight in Ophuls' cinema. Anxious waiting is also often a part of the scenario: in *La Signora di Tutti* the trysting couple is called in from the garden, and the heroine cools her heels in the parlor as her suitor's mother confers with him about her morals. The young woman's nervous looks at the clock punctuate the scene. There are also structural resemblances between *Sarajevo*'s first pairing of the lovers and the scene in *Madame de . . .* where Fabrizio Donati and Louise meet in the library in front of a painting of the battle of Waterloo, which serves as the representation of her absent husband, that film's "patriarch." Even more striking is the similarity to the scene in *Lola Montès* where the king interviews Lola *in the wings of the theater* after seeing her perform. Not only is the setting similar in mood and also late at night, after the performance, but in both cases the quality of the woman's performance is in question; in both cases she has surpassed her role as a sovereign's subject by an act of audacity. Paternal authority is dispersed over the rigid figure of the imperial statue and the timorous, petty-noble-as-bourgeois, who sets up the problem of time as a measure of patriarchal control (a problem that becomes more clear in subsequent scenes). Sophie and Franz find themselves in the double bind of recognizing the "ugliness" of the paternal role embodied in the Emperor's statue and simultaneously realizing that this figurehead is necessary both as a social anchor and, for Franz, as the condition for the possibility of his sexuality. Sophie's desire for Franz to play the imperial role is only vaguely articulated as an *aggressive* desire, through which she might "capture" him as a sexual object, a pattern made more evident in Ophuls' representation of women in the later films. Rather, the woman in this film asks that her husband occupy contradictory roles—he must be both phallic (imperial) and castrated (enslaved to the woman), and, finally, comfortably middle-class. The situation is somewhat different in *The Exile*, in which the woman does not know who her royal lover really is. Still, although that film plays on the woman's naive and true love for her unknown hero, it is clear that his desirability springs from the very qualities that define him as royal.

The end of this sequence exemplifies the adulation of the bourgeois way of life discussed above. Although he is a count (part of the petty nobility), the presentation of Sophie's father emphasizes the modesty of the family's circumstances. The room in which we see the father is a small one, the servant is a peasant, and so on. The setting is, in fact, similar to the parlor of the Weiring home in *Liebelei*, where the young nobleman Fritz stops in for a breath of the simple values of the petit-bourgeois family. The alternation between statue, couple, and father is, for all the lightness of touch that reigns in this sequence, heavily coded in terms of the Ophuls opus. Surveillance, patriarchal authority, and the passage of time are familiar motifs that continue to structure the film in overlapping segments.

A dissolve shows Sophie's return home, where she finds her father asleep in the parlor, where the early morning light throws latticework shadows on the wall, as in a later "familial" scene in Maria Theresa's chambers. Sophie wakes her father to say that the Archduke had apologized *to her* (rather than she to him) and that he had been "charming." Interestingly, the woman throws the transgression in the camp of the man: in this way he (willingly) falls under her sway. The father is pleased: "The affair will have no consequences (*suite*)." In thinking that the "affaire" is without consequences, Sophie's father is wrong, of course. As though to demonstrate his fallibility, there is now a fade to black, then a detail shot of a dossier on a table in Prince Montenuovo's office. Montenuovo asks one of his aides for this dossier, which turns out to be that of Sophie Chotek. The Prince looks at a photograph of the Countess (malevolently taking possession of her image in his role as director-figure) and comments on her beauty. *Surveillance* thus continues in a new form (after the stony surveillance of the couple by the statue), one that is specifically associated with the Prince.

Of Burghers and Brides

Sophie's affair with the Archduke is eventually found out because, appropriately enough, of his carelessness with a watch containing the Countess's photograph. Montenuovo then offers Sophie the position of official courtesan, going so far as to proffer a restrictive contract to that effect. She rebelliously refuses, in the manner of Lola Montès and her ringmaster in their first scene together. Because Sophie is not of high enough rank for a legitimate marriage with the Archduke, and because the pair persists in publicly proclaiming their affection, a morganatic marriage is proposed as a solution. A series of dissolves takes us to a montage of contracts and documents in preparation for the morganatic marriage of Sophie and Franz Ferdinand. Another dissolve shows a circle of inkwells and several pairs of hands engaged in writing, in filling out the contract and its copies. As in *La Signora di Tutti*, a circle of men gather around a table to determine the destiny of another man.[23] An old man reads the contract aloud in the background: the Archduke is to renounce for himself, for his wife, for their descendants, and so forth, all the hereditary privileges of the Hapsburgs. The phone rings, interrupting the reader, who announces that the Archduke has refused the morganatic contract.[24] The tool of evasion is not a train (as elsewhere in the film) but a ship, as the Archduke links his fate to that of the Countess. The morganatic contract (in this instance) is the formalization of the woman's inability to signify within the patriarchal system of heredity and, for Franz Ferdinand, it will be the declaration of his contamination by the woman: he will also lose the ability to bring children into the royal line, to confer his name upon them. Franz cannot yet accept this verdict. The couple resorts to the strategy described above in this chapter as a "return" to the bourgeois mode of life. The Archduke's fantasy is superficially opposed to that of Lisa Berndle in *Letter from an Unknown Woman*, where the woman's humble background is, at least on the most obvious level of the film, pushed aside. "To share the woman's fate" is, in these early films of Max Ophuls, to share the lower social status of the films' heroines. Later films will often more explicitly involve the woman's rejection of the fate dealt her by society—through her "narcissistic" withdrawal into love. To share the woman's fate also means to reject the meaning of "castration" within the patriarchal system. Later scenes demonstrate how Franz's marriage involves a feminization, a castration in the eyes of Law which he will endeavor to declare invalid.

The following scene indicates, first, how spectatorship works in conjunction with the problem of royal duty and, second, how the bourgeois family romance intervenes repeatedly into this aristocratic setting. There is a dissolve to a moving ship, then a cut to its interior. Franz and Sophie have evidently run away after refusing the terms of the morganatic marriage and are now taking tea together on the ship, seated in front of a window that looks out over the deck. They have adopted the name "Mayer" (just as Franz Ferdinand's real-life brother adopted the even more revealing name "Burg" when he married beneath him—thus retaining a bit of his "Hapsburg" identity, while becoming a "burgher"), and are attempting to begin a humble, middle-class existence. The servants (including the coachman-valet Janachek, played by Aimos) are having trouble remembering to address the Archduke as "Mr. Mayer."[25] But even from the supposedly isolated confines of the ship, the couple cannot be protected from a fateful vision. Their tea is interrupted when the sounds of a trumpet and of bells ringing bring them out onto the deck, where they can observe, first through Franz's opera glasses and then, conveniently (though improbably), with the naked eye, the oppression of the Croatian populus by the soldiers of the Austro-Hungarian Empire. Although he avoided attending a performance at the opera, Franz is a horrified (but protected) witness to the deeds of "his" troops. The glasses provide the link between this scene and another at the opera, where the Emperor's opera glasses are prominently displayed on the ledge of the imperial box. Even now Franz Ferdinand acts as the old man's eyes, though we might also think that it is only Franz's status as "bourgeois" that gives him this privileged vision of social reality. The martial laws and the new curfew are read aloud to the crowd: a soldier dictates their fate in the name of the Emperor. Meanwhile, Sophie and Franz speak of the "hatred, violence, and blood" that are the tools of the empire. After a number of shot/reverse shots between the noble couple and the spectacle before them, the crowd revolts and a man is killed by the soldiers, then carried off by his weeping relations. Sophie finally urges Franz to "accept [the position as heir to the throne]; it's your duty."

This permutation of what I have referred to as the "bourgeois family romance," after Freud, is inflected here with the logic of the sacrifice, similar to that described by Girard. The suffering of the innocent Croatians is conflated with the marginal status of the aristocratic scapegoat, and yet it is a middle-class couple that observes the scene outside. The structure of the film is in this way highly complex: Ophuls has managed to make this ultra-aristocratic story into a bourgeois drama. Once again there is an effect of textual *folding.* In the middle of the film Franz has aspired to the status of the unencumbered middle-class citizen. Thus, it is only retrospectively that this is a reversal of the family romance: the upper-class couple will later remember that it was once "middle-class." For what concerns the *prospective* view of the film, from this point on, the Freudian logic of the family romance obtains. A bourgeois man, Mr. Mayer, will have repressed his class origins to become an archduke. The transition to the aristocratic is, of course, via the spectacle of violence produced in the realm of representation observed by the bourgeois individual. Because of the recollection embodied in the name "Mayer," its ominous echoing of the repressed "sacrifice" at Mayerling, this harking back to bourgeois simplicity is always associated with the corrupt system that has destroyed the previous heir, and with the uncanny effects of repetition. And it is, of course, from the perspective of the bourgeois Mayer that the spectacle of victimization, which seems to require a *conscious* scapegoat, in the person of the Archduke as a substitute for the suffering Slavs, can be played out.

For Sophie Chotek the fall into the pseudobourgeois state does not change her situation in the world as markedly as it does that of Franz. She has, as we have seen more than once, been associated with a more or less middle-class ethos, although such a characterization is hardly apt, historically speaking. Franz has taken on something of the status of his wife: it is Sophie who will insist, after they see the cruel death of the Slav from their vantage point on the ship, that Franz return to stem the flow of blood, in the name of "duty." Sophie does what another woman, Franz's mother, Maria Theresa, was unable to do: she speaks the Law, inciting the man to his God-given task. His return to the royal house is, therefore, in a way determined by the will of the woman. But can the woman who speaks the Law really provide an alternative to the institutions erected by patriarchy?

A dissolve reveals a close-up of the morganatic contract, a document of "renunciation" which is read aloud by Franz Ferdinand (offscreen). He recognizes that his marriage is "not according to the rule" and that he must renounce, in particular, the possibility that his heirs will one day rule the empire. Sophie will sustain even fewer rights and privileges. There is then a dissolve *through* Sophie's wedding veil, as she moves forward to look at herself and Franz, behind her, in the mirror. Shrieking with laughter, she mocks (imitates) the language of the contract that ties Franz to her, just as the copiers of the contract had also imitated or ventriloquized the voice of the Archduke as they were writing. "I renounce . . ." says Sophie, listing the unpleasant duties and people that go with the frequentation of the Archduke's family. He laughs with her. Dressed in her white gown, facing the mirror, Sophie has become the object of both her own and the man's gaze, but it is her voice that speaks the last word. To their contract, she counters with her own version of the contract of marriage. The scene also signals the discomfort and fascination that the woman is conditioned to experience when confronted with her own mirrored image, as occurs, notably, in the beginning of *Caught* and twice in *La Signora di Tutti.* The camera in this scene seems to suffer from something like the "hystericization" that Doane discerns in the wild panoramic movements in *Caught.*[26] Like the woman, the camera peers *through* the veil. The woman's laughter, her proximity to the mirror, her mocking tone, all establish her precedence with respect to the man in this scene from *Sarajevo.* She is estranged from herself by means of the document that now regulates her as a partner in a marriage that limits her range of action and, visually, by the garment that veils the camera and puts her in the specular position of the bride, she who is looked at (in the mirror by both herself and Franz). Already "castrated" (or, according to the terms of the masochistic contract, *phallic* herself), the woman can mock the formalization of the renunciation that is so painful to the man. The narrative is disturbed here by the strident feminine voice that attempts to use to her own advantage the contract that is a declaration of her insufficiency. The episode suggests that the woman weakens the man in that the forced acceptance of the morganatic contract is a curb to Franz Ferdinand's ability to produce royal children. But there is also the implication that she offers him an alternative source of power, a means of casting doubt on the validity of the laws that would regulate his existence. The marriage contract both hems in the woman and invests her with tremendous power over her husband and other men, a power with which they can identify in the interest of undercutting the oppressiveness of the patriarchal system. Dressed in the garments of a perilous rite of passage, from virgin to matron,[27] Sophie lends Franz Ferdinand the force of her "feminine" irreverence toward the institution that has formulated the contract. The Archduke is thus able to *make use* of what Freud termed the "woman's hostile bitterness against the man" incited by the narcissistic loss entailed in the loss of virginity.[28] Her righteous anger forms the base from which Franz Ferdinand will counter the traditions that deprive him of individual freedom.

Gender Disturbances and Recalibrations

The disturbance in gender-identity that troubles this film is made more apparent in the next scene, which takes place in a billiard hall where one of the royal servants and a number of townsmen are at play. A variety of cuts frames the different characters in this scene of a type found frequently in Ophuls' films, one where the lower-class characters are given a chance to speak their piece. Janachek, the Archduke's raucous-voiced valet, is particularly talkative as he plays billiards (cf. *Madame de . . .*) and discusses the imperial ball that his master and mistress are to attend that evening. Sophie, now the Duchess of Hohenberg, is an object of special concern. The humiliation that she must undergo because of her morganatic marriage seems to strike a peculiar chord with these middle-to-lower-class characters. One man, for example, chimes in: "You know, as a woman, I never would have accepted that." The servant answers that he knows the marriage is for the best. The other man repeats, "Well, if I were the Duchess—" and the servant retorts, "Ah, there's no risk of *that*." Another man complains that there was no ball, no parade for the marriage. The servant replies, "That's the fault of commerce. I, too, am expecting [*j'attends*] a child—a son who looks like me [*me ressemble*]. He will succeed me in my business, which will be named 'Oppenheim and Son'" (an obvious reference to Ophuls' abandonment of his family name and business!).[29] The men then praise the politics of the Archduke, his idea of "The United States of Austria," and hope that he will be allowed to remain active. The valet must now leave instead of completing his billiard match. But before going he suffers what might be called a case of hysterical identification with his masters:

> SERVANT: It's not a Thursday like the others. Today we're trying on the uniform for the great court ball.

MAN: Are you going?

SERVANT: *We* are going.

MAN: And she—is she invited?

SERVANT: Naturally—we won't leave the Duchess at home. She'll be officially presented for the first time tonight.

The "feminization" to which we have referred is clearly deflected onto this group of men who seek to identify with the desires and interests of the Duchess. The servant is going to the ball with the Archduke (although they will, of course, take along the Duchess). One of the men even declares that he is going to have a baby! This child is, however, part of a patrilinear process: he will take up the business of the father. A form of hermaphrodism is humorously offered as the solution to the contradictions involved in the society's self-reproduction.

Sarajevo is worth watching if only for the ensuing ball scene, whose economy in arranging intensely invested elements ("nodal scenes," as Silverman describes them), from the Ophuls canon is admirable. A dissolve from the closing door of the billiard hall to the large inner palace doors as they open provides an ironic version of the graphic matches and matches on movement seen earlier in the film. A series of high-angle shots shows the grand staircase of the Imperial Palace that was roped off in the first scene of the film. The early roping-off of the staircase might be seen as prophetic in that it anticipates the symbolic blockage found in this scene. The Archduke and the Duchess are shown from behind, climbing the steps with slow dignity. Franz is now wearing the dress uniform that was missing in his first appearance at the palace: in this he is *obeying* the Emperor, as well as imitating him: this is the double bind presented by the model-obstacle as described throughout Girard's works: to obey one's model is to imitate and therefore to compete with him. "Like father, like son . . . ." As the couple ascends, a medium shot from the middle of the stairway reveals that they are met by one of Montenuovo's lackeys, who informs them that only members of the imperial family may use the stairway. The Duchess, it seems, must use the "small staircase." Franz attempts to intervene, but Sophie (whose lip trembles in close-up, a standard Edwige Feuillère acting device) insists on facing this final humiliation. She turns to walk down the stairs, her long white gown trailing behind her. Franz looks after his wife and then, shouting

"Present sabers," follows her. He kisses her hand and they leave together, as an unseen audience bursts into applause. There is a dissolve onto a balcony, where assembled nobles applaud Franz Ferdinand's action (his *acte*).

As has been said many times, the stairway is something of a testing ground for Ophuls' characters. It is always a site for traumas, especially traumas concerning the control of the gaze, sexual domination, and death (as when the mother in *La Signora di Tutti* tumbles down a staircase in her wheelchair, or when the model in *Le Plaisir* and Christine in *Liebelei* use them as jumping points for suicide attempts, or when Lisa spies on her lover in *Letter*, and so on). The staircase is always a place where looking and being looked at take on a problematic quality. Sophie's humiliation, a social one, might also be regarded as a sexual humiliation, if we are to follow the line of thought broached with respect to the "feminization" of Franz Ferdinand. Of course, women may use the grand staircase, but only if they are participating correctly in the patriarchal system of the Hapsburgs. Franz Ferdinand has violated the monarchy's peculiar system of alliances (which is not exogamy as we know it, but closer to incest since he was to have married his cousin) and has married, for love, a woman of inferior endowments. Montenuovo senses the potential for political crisis in this *mésalliance* and uses protocol to ward off the possibility of violent consequences. Now Montenuovo is telling Sophie that she must use the "small" staircase; she cannot borrow the phallic proportions of the imperial patriarch but is reduced to her "real" state (castrated—or clitoral, since the clitoris is, generally speaking, smaller than the penis). Franz sizes up the situation at a glance and, at his wife's insistence, does not support her pretense to the big one. Rather, he *follows* her (subsumed under her status) but, apotropaically, commands the presentation of sabers as they leave. This phallic display, for the benefit of the woman, is roundly applauded by the noble crowd. The sound of their applause comes as a surprise—we didn't know they were watching. Surveillance is again revealed retrospectively; the meaning of the scene is altered by our belated awareness of it as spectacle. The Archduke and his wife have, for the moment, turned the spectacle of victimization to their own advantage. But Sophie will now be obliged to live isolated from the court life of the regime, as Franz continues his forced travels throughout the empire. It is when he, accompanied by Sophie, is forced to visit Bosnia during a period of political unrest, that the assassination takes place.

They Shoot Countesses, Don't They?

To close, a word on "female directorship," maternity, and the image in *Sarajevo*. Early in the film, Maria Theresa, taken with Sophie's beauty and her love for Franz Ferdinand, sends the young woman to live with the Archduchess Isabelle. Isabelle's daughters are Sophie's "rivals" for the hand of Franz Ferdinand, although the latter's interest in the Countess is a closely guarded secret. A decisive scene in this misbegotten family romance opens with a fade to black, then to a high-angle long shot of a group of girls on a lawn as they pose for a photograph. The Archduke Franz Ferdinand is among them. The next shot establishes this as the point of view of Sophie Chotek, as she closes the window out of which she had been looking.[30] At the other side of the room, Isabelle is looking out a window symmetrical to the one mentioned above. She shuts the curtains, clearly irritated with Sophie for gazing out the window. "Don't you have anything else to do?" The Archduke Salvator, Isabelle's husband, enters the room and chats with Sophie about his cheese-making. Isabelle reproaches her husband for not being concerned with his "descendants [*descendance*]": he doesn't care which of his daughters, if any, marries the Archduke. Here is a man who has abdicated from the masculine privilege and responsibility of determining inheritance (as will Franz Ferdinand, though reluctantly). Isabelle then calls Sophie back to the window. Sophie, who has not finished arranging the table, joins Isabelle at the window with exaggerated patience. "Which one of them [the girls] does he prefer?" the Archduchess asks the Countess. Outdoors, the photographer is having problems composing the shot because there is an uneven number of women. "What is wrong?" shouts Isabelle out the window. Another cut outdoors shows the daughters calling to Sophie to come sit in the picture "for symmetry." Sophie is ordered outside. Although Isabelle seems to be in a spectatorial position, she is actually calling the shots. The nervous photographer is at last able to arrange the group satisfactorily, placing the girls around the Countess and the Archduke. In a point-of-view shot through the camera lens, we see the group upside-down, traversed by cross-hairs: "It's splendid," states the photographer. He runs over for a final stab at arranging and then looks again into the camera, but the shot cannot be taken because the sun has disappeared. The girls run away, and he sits on the ground dejected. At this point the photograph of the amorous couple simply will not take. Maria Theresa has placed Sophie in the hands of a mother who is willing to embody the

Law, to arrange, to *direct*.[31] Isabelle is literally directing a scene to be photographed, although she does so from a distance (and the photograph is
a failure). The maternal solicitude to be observed in Maria Theresa's
scene with Sophie (in which she shows a photo to the latter) has become
the interference of a harsh mother involved in the (abortive) *making* of
a photograph. Even, therefore, at the most superficial level of the film,
the act of directing is regarded with suspicion. Like many of Ophuls'
female director-figures, Isabelle is intimidating and emasculating. Her
husband is left to rather pitiful pleasures. Are these women, then, being
mocked for their assertiveness? There may be such a remnant of stereotypical sexism in this film—but one could just as well say that this and
other films by Ophuls share with the cinema of that era the difficulty of
articulating feminine aggression while his films simultaneously operate,
as we know, out of a fundamental sense of malaise about directing itself.

The paternal figure is given to be rather a silly one in this scene. He
is concerned with the delights of food (his cheeses) rather than with the
problems of alliance and inheritance, which he explicitly leaves to his
wife. The behavior of this Archduke, with his domestic concerns, tends
to connect him with what we are terming the "bourgeois" aspect of this
film, with its attention to the comforts of home. Some of the film's
implicit critique of the bourgeoisie, which on the whole it views favorably, is reflected in the difficulty of reconciling the masculine with the
bourgeois. Nonetheless, Salvator is certainly given as a more sympathetic character than his wife. Although this film's critique of the very concept of patriarchal lineage is more ambiguous than is the case in *Madame
de . . .*, this scene does seem, to some extent, to continue the kind of questioning of the importance of inheritance or heritage we observed in *The
Bartered Bride*. *Sarajevo* later contradicts itself on this point by indicating
that the strictures of the morganatic contract—specifically those concerning lineage—are tragic ones. While Ophuls finds appealing the
depiction of the *insult* offered by the patriarch through the morganatic
contract, the resulting indirect defense of patrilinearity goes to some
extent against the grain of the other films.

Sarajevo also reaches an impasse concerning the nature of feminine
desire. The patriarch, we have seen, is presented as both the only possible
incarnation of masculinity and as completely undesirable. Sophie, like
The Exile's Katia, can only love the outlaw son (the heir), but to remain
with her that son must adhere to the rule of the feminizing contract. Does
the woman represent the possibility of a new kind of regime, by under-

mining the phallic order (as in the bridal scene), or is she merely castrating? Is Sophie's "desire" for the boy in Maria Theresa's photograph equivalent to the stultifying capture of the man as a royal statue or a sacrificial lamb? Surely not, but there is some hint here of the danger presented by desire itself, though Sophie's gentler wish to captivate or to capture is drowned in the problems of social cohesion and mass conflict. Perhaps once again, the ending of the film is best read through the lens of Deleuzian masochism: the Archduke surrenders to the powerful "mother" and willingly suffers death so that the "father" within him may be destroyed. Ophuls seems undecided, though passionately so, about this series of questions posed by the film. In chapter 4, many of the same problems will be approached from a more directly psychoanalytic perspective, which will be brought to bear upon a film that represents, in many respects, the pinnacle of Ophuls' thought on the problems of sexual difference as it relates to the cinematic image—and to the soundtrack.

Returning for a moment to the political context of *Sarajevo*, I will remind the reader that Ophuls became a French citizen in 1938. The work of Marcel Ophuls has also reminded us that anti-Semitism was on the rise in France throughout the 1930s. This anti-Semitism quickly penetrated the French film industry. (The German film company Tobis Klangfilm dismissed its Jewish personnel in France in 1935.[32]) Critics including Lucien Rebatet called for the persecution of the "organized band of invaders" who were "coloniz[ing]" the French film industry.[33] Christopher Faulkner comments that

the Jew is the figure of heterogeneity, that the Jew *figures* heterogeneity, both in the real and in writing. . . . "Jewish" becomes an omnibus adjective of opprobrium that can designate a person, place, attitude, condition, idea, situation, politics, behavior, etc., as in Chaplin, Hollywood, pacifism, decadent, . . . etc.: "capitalisme juif," "juiverie hollywoodienne," . . . etc. In Rebatet's writing the word "Jew" is not merely a serviceable epithet of scorn or abuse; it is the floating signifier of Otherness which formulates the division between the same and different, inside and outside, French and non-French. (p. 145)

Certainly Ophuls was aware of and deeply affected by the atmosphere reigning within France's film industry and taking over France itself throughout this period. The decision of the Archduke to return to his duties and to travel into dangerous territory knowing that this spelled his doom must have been psychologically—as well as practically—difficult for Ophuls to film. I hope to have shown in this chapter that Ophuls' response to the political situation is not limited in his French films of the 1930s to the conflicted paean to democracy found in *Sarajevo*. Ophuls continues, rather, to develop his vision of the process of scapegoating those who, as "floating signifiers," are associated with the processes of circulation and representation already begun in his early German films. Thus, despite their "cold efficiency and taste for virtuosity as an end to itself," and their "stand[ing] for a cinema that was both romantic and coldly calculating, and one preoccupied with failure, with repetition and return, with closed circles and unresolved conflicts," as Thomas Elsaesser describes the work of German exiles in France during the thirties, Ophuls' films inscribe themselves into the French cinema history of the period in a profoundly political way. Clearly I must disagree with Elsaesser's assessment that

there was little in [the exiles'] work that could be called "autobiographical" in a strict sense, which is why an auteurist-thematic approach to their films yields disappointing returns. It was not social realism or political commitment they were after, and one looks in vain for topical references.

As will be seen in my discussion of some of Ophuls' other films of the 1930s in later chapters, "political commitment" and "topical references" may be defined in more than one way.[34]

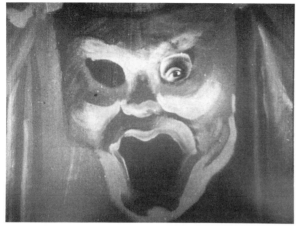

1. The stage manager peers out of the mask of comedy in *Liebelei*'s opera scene.

2. "I swear that I love you for all eternity." Fritz (Wolfgang Liebeneiner) and Christine (Magda Schneider).

3. Mizzi (Luise Ullrich) and Theo (Willy Eichberger) combine music, the military, and crossdressing.

4. The Baroness (Olga Tchechowa) is sent
away by her brother-in-law (Paul Otto): the first
Ophulsian woman to be banished by train.

5. Theo protests the duel to hiscommanding officer.
Note their separation by "rigid" symbols of the military.

6. Christine's father (Paul Hörbiger) asks permission
of his "deaf" conductor to go to his suicidal daughter.

7. Christine leaps from the window to her death.

8. Point-of-view shot from the perspective of the Emperor's statue as it stands watch over the courtship of Sophie Chotek and the Archduke Franz Ferdinand (John Lodge).

9. The Archduke is called to duty by the shocking sight of the Emperor's troops oppressing the people.

10. After the morganatic marriage, Sophie is humiliated by Prince Montenuovo's order that she must use the "minor" staircase.

11. A sinister shot of the monocled Prince Montenuovo (Aimé Clariond).

12. Lisa Berndle (Joan Fontaine) lines up with the boys in *Letter from an Unknown Woman.*

13. Lisa looks down the staircase to surprise. . .

14. . . . . her mother (Mady Christians) and her stepfather-to-be (Howard Freeman) in a sexual pose.

15. Lisa spies from the staircase as Stefan Brand (Louis Jourdan) brings a giddy beauty home with him.

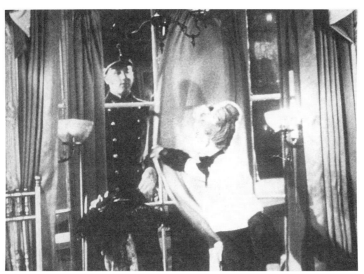

16. Lisa closes the curtains on the soldiers admiring her beauty through the window.

17. Lisa gazes adoringly at Stefan in *Letter from an Unknown Woman.*

18. Theatrically framed by curtains, Lisa and Stefan take their "imaginary train ride."

19. During their evening at the Prater, Lisa sees her "knight in shining armor" behind glass . . .

20. . . . . and Stefan is doubled by a wax figure of Schubert.

21. One of the Prater's cynical female musicians takes a lusty bite of a frankfurter as she watches Lisa and Stefan dance.

22. The camera takes the position formerly occupied by Lisa as the latter takes the same path as her predecessors into Stefan's apartment.

23. Stefan, who has "captured" Lisa in the small mirror in front of her, comes to tell her he must leave for Milan.

24. Stefan looks at a photo that the dying woman had sent him in which Lisa and Stefan, Jr. (Leo P. Pessin) also take an "imaginary voyage."

25. Lisa, dressed in a "masculine" suit, buys white roses to take to Stefan. Her hat resembles that of the old man selling the flowers.

26. Stefan remembers Lisa in a montage of images, ending on this dissolve that melds their faces into one.

27. John (Art Smith) "signs" the letter for Lisa.

28. Stefan's final vision of Lisa, whose superimposed image slowly dissolves.

29. Scene still from *Caught* (this part of the film directed by John Berry): Leonora (Barbara Bel Geddes) pays for her classes at the Dorothy Day charm school.

30. Leonora attempts to choose between her rich husband, Smith Ohlrig (Robert Ryan), and the "man with the cloth coat," Dr. Larry Quinada (James Mason), toward whom the composition is weighted.

31. Louise de. . . (Danielle Darrieux) purchases a votive candle for "her saint" near the beginning of *Madame de . . ..*

32. Louise confesses her debt to the jeweller, Mr. Rémy (Jean Debucourt).

33. Mr. Rémy's advantage in an early resale of the earrings is indicated by his position in center frame and General de . . .'s (Charles Boyer) bowed head.

34. Louise de . . . spies Donati from afar in *Madame de* . . . .

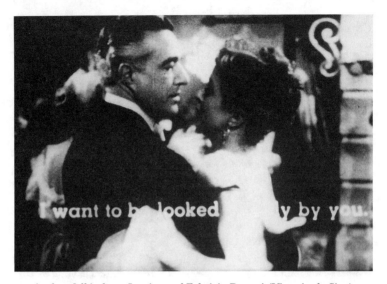

35. As they fall in love, Louise and Fabrizio Donati (Vittorio de Sica) dance more and more frequently, and aspire toward a monogamy of vision: "I only want to be looked at by you."

36. The General torments his unhappy wife by insisting that they go to the theater: once more the theater and the military are conjoined.

37. Forced to give the earrings to her husband's niece, Louise is unable
to admire the younger woman's new baby.

38. The earrings in their final resting place at the foot of
Louise's saint: "Don de Madame de."

39. In an early scene of Lola Montès, Lola (Martine Carol), Ivan Desny (Lt. James), Lola's mother (Lise Delamare), and the Baron's secretary (Jean Galland) discuss Lola's "sale" to the gouty Baron. The layered composition and the discussion of Lola's portrait emphasize the issue of representation.

40. The masking of the shot contrasts with Lola's unmasking, as she bares herself for Louis I of Bavaria.

41. The canted angle indicates the Ringmaster's (Peter Ustinov) unbalance in Lola's presence, even as he orders her to still her movements.

42. Lola poses as the "Venus in Furs," while Ludwig (Anton Walbrook) and the painter (Werner Finck) conspire to keep her pleasantly trapped in Bavaria.

43. Posed beside the giant ear, the king refuses his duty as "magisterial" voyeur and auditor.

44. Valet number 12 duns the Ringmaster for payment before bringing him a whiskey.

45. In turn, the Ringmaster sells access to Lola's body for one dollar.

our

✦

Aggressivity, Image, and Sound
in *Letter from an Unknown Woman*

> *"They played Beethoven's 'Kreutzer Sonata.' Do you*
> *know its first movement, the presto? You know it?" he*
> *burst out. "Ah! It's a fearful thing, that sonata. Espe-*
> *cially that movement. And music in general's a fearful*
> *thing. What is it? I don't know. What is music? What*
> *does it do to us? And why does it do to us what it does?"*
>
> —LEO TOLSTOY, "THE KREUTZER SONATA"

♦

Star Stares on Stairs

Letter from an Unknown Woman (1948) reaches its climax when, after ten years of separation, Lisa Berndle (Joan Fontaine) catches sight of her lover, Stefan Brand (Louis Jourdan), at a performance of *Die Zauberflöte*. The moment's structure of watching, of imbricated looks, is complex. Taking a position that is, in the Hollywood cinema, often given to be a masculine one, in that it gives her a particular kind of visual power, Lisa stands on the grand staircase of the Vienna Opera House. The "camera's rhythmically gliding fluidity" adds to the sense that Lisa's steps are indeed, as she says, measured by fate.[1] She pauses as she overhears Stefan's name whispered by a group of people gazing down to the main hall below, while a footman announces the "second act," not only of the opera but of Lisa's fatal love story.[2]

LADY: Look, isn't that Stefan Brand?

FIRST GENTLEMAN: He returned last week.

SECOND GENTLEMAN: A concert tour?

LADY: A pleasure trip, most likely.

SECOND GENTLEMAN: The way he's burning himself up it's a wonder he's still alive. Ten years ago, he showed great promise. . . . Too bad. With that talent he could have been a great pianist.

FIRST GENTLEMAN: Perhaps talent is not enough.

LADY: Perhaps he has *too many* talents.[3]

As Lisa moves forward toward the banister, we adopt the group's vision while they watch Stefan climb up the other side of the double staircase and overtake two young women, whose hands he suavely kisses. A medium close-up of Lisa establishes this shot retrospectively as her point of view. Although Lisa's look at Stefan is loving and "womanly"—that is (depending on which critic one reads), a look that tends to *collapse space*, to diffuse its power in identification, or one that simply brings a woman's knowledge with it, it is also a look that diminishes Stefan, who appears tiny and pathetic as he is observed unawares. Lisa seems distressed by the power of her gaze to accomplish this diminution of her idol.

Johann Stauffer (Marcel Journet), heavy with military gold braid, has walked ahead of Lisa, but now turns to look at his obviously chagrined wife. A latecomer in terms of the narrative, Stauffer becomes one of its most important observers. His point of view is notably espoused by the camera when, near the end of the film, he sees Lisa enter Stefan's apartment for her final, painful meeting with him. When, in those last scenes of the film, Stauffer begins to watch the activities of his wife and her erstwhile lover, the surreptitious spying that has been a major moving force of the film's events takes on the destructive potential that seemed often to be latent in the "loving" voyeurism and passionate eavesdropping of the other characters, especially Lisa.

In this scene at the opera, Stefan Brand, who has for so many years been the object of Lisa's adoring aural and visual drives, becomes at last the butt of public derision. Popular acclaim has turned to popular ridicule, to Lisa's manifest horror. And yet, as Alan Williams has pointed out,[4] this destruction of the man (the plot indicates that Stefan will die in a duel at the hands of Lisa's husband) is at least partly Lisa's responsibility. This casting of Lisa in the role of "femme fatale" takes place not because of "Ophuls"'authorial agency's ambivalent attitude toward her (which is Williams's claim), or because the filmmaker is "confused," but, I argue, because of the nature of the Ophulsian cinematic image as it is inflected by sexual difference. That is to say, at issue is not the woman's wickedness and consequent ability to bring harm to those near her (as may be the case in *La Signora di Tutti*). Rather, sexual distinctions themselves, as they are fixed into representations on the screen, dissolved into various patterns of desire, and fixed again in repetitions of historical moments, bring about the (pleasurable) destruction of those characters in Max Ophuls' films who fall prey to the power of the image—and cannot be delivered by sound.

The Plot

Letter from an Unknown Woman is a riveting cinematic expression of female suffering for love, and perhaps because of that has attracted a great deal of critical attention. If that love is masochistic, then the film is a tribute to the heroism of female masochism, through which Lisa manages to have her own way in the guise of submitting to another. The film alters significantly the terms of the Stefan Zweig novella from which it was adapted by Howard Koch, John Houseman, and Ophuls (the most significant changes are discussed below). The film was one of the last U.S. productions Koch worked on, since he was soon after blacklisted by Hollywood during the McCarthy era.[5] Koch was responsible for Ophuls' involvement in the project. When producer John Houseman invited Koch to "dramatize" Zweig's *Letter from an Unknown Woman,* the latter immediately thought of Ophuls, a personal friend. "Fortunately, Houseman had seen *Liebelei"*[6] and managed to persuade William Dozier, vice president of finances and president of Rampart Production Company, and his wife, Universal star Joan Fontaine, that this "foreign director" could put over the sentimental story with restraint. *Letter* was the first of Ophuls' two films for Universal-International, under whose aegis Rampart was working. Koch details Ophuls' intense involvement in reworking the script, stamping it with his directorial concerns. In addition, another Hollywood exile, Franz ("Frank") Planer, who had photographed *Liebelei,* was available to shoot *Letter.* With his help Ophuls came closer to perfecting the cinematic style that had eluded his effort in the French films of the 1930s, although, as Lutz Bacher has documented, Ophuls "mobile long-take" style was somewhat inhibited by *Letter*'s producers. Many difficult compromises were struck during both shooting and postproduction.[7] Universal's executives (especially Dozier) had high hopes for the film, but a misbegotten ad campaign pitching it as a passionate love story helped to sink it.[8] After it fizzled out in the United States (contributing to the poor mental and physical state of its director, who had a strong emotional investment in the film, according to Bacher), the British critical community discovered it, and it had decent runs in Great Britain and on the Continent. Not surprisingly, the film had a respectable television career—no doubt many women isolated in their homes during the conformist early 1950s (when the film was popular on television) took comfort in *Letter*'s peculiar championing of female desire. The film's version of Zweig's novella is as follows:

Stefan Brand (Louis Jourdan), a Viennese musician and man-about-town, returns home one night after having been challenged to a duel. His friends say they will come for him at five A.M., but Stefan responds with jokes, and the would-be seconds express doubt that he will be there when they return. After he enters his apartment, Stefan's manservant John (Art Smith) hands him a letter, which he begins to read, leading to a flashback narrative that comprises most of the film.

The flashback tells the tale of Lisa Berndle (Joan Fontaine, also providing frequent voice-over narration as the letter is "read"), the fifteen-year-old daughter of a respectable Viennese widow in reduced circumstances. Lisa falls in love with the new tenant of her building, Stefan Brand, a concert pianist, though he hardly notices her. Her adolescence is spent watching and listening to her idol from afar, as he leads the carefree life of a handsome and popular piano prodigy. Soon, however, Lisa's mother (Mady Christians) remarries, and Lisa is obliged to move to Linz, a garrison town, where her stepfather (Howard Freeman) is a military tailor. At eighteen she is courted by a young officer (John Good). Defying her parents, she refuses his proposal and returns to Vienna. In Vienna she divides her time between her work as a model and her obsessive observation of Stefan's movements. One day, however, he notices her on the street, not recognizing her as the little girl he once knew, but as a beautiful and mysterious woman only too willing to be seduced.

They spend an evening and a night together, and plan to meet again, but Stefan is called away to play at La Scala before these plans come to fruition. Despite his promises, he never contacts her again. Although Lisa bears his child (Leo B. Pessin), she does not attempt to speak to Stefan, wanting to be the only woman (she later tells him) who "asked you for nothing." Years pass, and Lisa finally marries (for "convenience") Johann Stauffer (Marcel Journet), a wealthy general. One night, when the couple is at the opera, Lisa again encounters Stefan. Vaguely sensing her significance to him, Stefan pursues Lisa, who says little and leaves with her angry husband. In a rapid sequence of events, Lisa decides to leave Johann and throw herself at Stefan's feet, but once again her lover does not remember her. She goes to her son, who soon dies of typhus. She, too, is dying of the disease even as she writes the letter. As Stefan finishes reading it, the flashback and the frame narratives meet. The duel he now chooses to fight is with Johann Stauffer. Smiling, he bids adieu to his vision of Lisa as a child, and goes willingly to his death.

Paranoia and Audio/Visual Duality

In describing the mechanisms of paranoia in Hitchcock's *The Birds* (1963) and *North by Northwest* (1959), Jacqueline Rose outlines the way in which paranoia enters into the specificity of the latter's filmic discourse:

What then is the cinematic code which dominates the segment in which the aggression of a false imposition of identity is objectified into assault? The segment is structured according to the basic opposition of shot and counter-shot which sustains a dialectic of vision (the look) alternating between the observing subject and the object of his vision. The code occults the position of the camera by setting up an opposition between two terms: the observer and the observed. The opposition is however a lure *in its very structure*. Firstly, the camera has to identify not only with the subject (Thornhill) in order to show what he sees, but also with the object of vision in order to show the subject. The series can therefore only be structured by a partial activation of the potentially aggressive reversal of its system. . . . The opposition shot/counter-shot therefore contains its own principle of instability prior to the moment of its activation.[9]

Rose describes here the "false imposition of identity" Roger Thornhill (Cary Grant) is subjected to in *North by Northwest*. A series of significant coincidences forces Thornhill to take on the name and follow the itinerary of a nonexistent government agent (much as Lisa must submit herself to another's "will"), and thus expose himself to attack from the various objects under observation. Rose's remarks pertain to the film's notorious sequence in which the retaliatory object is a crop-dusting plane controlled by an enemy agent. In an attempt to define the power of such aggressive "returns" of the human gaze, Rose delineates the regressive structures that partially constitute the spectator's response to the "dreamlike" structure of classical cinema. The "regressive" aspect of the cinematic experience, as described by Metz, Kuntzel, Eberwein, and others, is grounded in what Lacan has conceptualized as the imaginary dialectic. To reiterate earlier remarks, the imaginary phase is a specular phase, "a predominantly visual register," as Rose puts it (p. 101), during which the ego is formed as a kind of misrecognition (described by Lacan as a false sensation of wholeness modeled on the integrity of the self reflected in the mirror). This moment is accompanied by an aggressive rivalry toward the other who is determining the desire and integrity of that self. "Paranoia," writes Rose, "is latent to the reversibility of the ego's self-alienation," and "will also be discharged where the stability of the system is threatened" (p. 88). This "externalization," the split into self and other, can be related to the polarization of sexual difference itself, which becomes caught up in the earliest aggressive impulses of the ego, partly because of its custom of objectification. The disruption that has its source and/or model in sexual difference is often stabilized, in Hollywood films, by the formation of the marital couple, as in *North by Northwest*, or by the incapacitation of one of the poles of difference—or both. In *The Birds*, as is often the case in the cinema, it is the woman (*objet extraordinaire*) who is incapacitated. So too in *Letter*, the polarization between observer and observed (although it does not necessarily involve the animation of an inert object) will reveal a lethal potential. The woman's problematic status as subject of the gaze—and her dawning ability to objectify the man—activates this potential, unleashing violence as the binaries of male-female, subject-object, heterosexual-homosexual and so on, are broken down.

Although the dualism implied by Rose's description has itself been "under attack," and rightly so, by recent feminist criticism, *Letter* never entirely escapes its thrall—despite the best efforts of Ophuls himself.[10] Indeed, the difficulty of transcending the dualisms of self-other, male-female, looker–looked at is the overriding concern of the film's "symbolic structures." In both this chapter and the next, we will see that Ophuls has, since his earliest films, used music as a means of suturing these troubling differences. As Catherine Clément observes, music has often served similar purposes, always problematically: "At stake is the question of why we in Western culture wish, on the one hand, to deny that music has social meaning and, on the other, to ascribe to it transcendental significance."[11] *Letter* is the most striking instance—perhaps the culmination—of this ambitious ambivalence about music in Ophuls' films (is it "socially" grounded, or transcendent?). In any event, as we shall see, Ophuls' aesthetic philosophy attempts to place music's functions distinctly in opposition to those of the dangerous visual realm. *Letter from an Unknown Woman* shows us both the poignancy and the futility of such an attempt, and permits the mapping of music's movement from supplement to deconstructor of the visual.

In the context of *Letter*'s visual realm, the aggressive potential of the gaze ultimately redounds upon the two protagonists. The observer-observed polarity takes the form of the apparent opposition between the framing narrative—Stefan's reading of the letter—and the action of the story unfolding in the flashback narrated by Lisa but imagined (imaged) by Stefan and an invisible authorial agent.[12] Brand, who could never "see" Lisa while she lived, is privileged after her death with an ideal vision of her life through the device of the letter. It is only then that Lisa's role as his double will become clear to him, "unfolding," as Walter Benjamin's words suggest, "the views of himself under which he has encountered himself without being aware of it."[13] Stanley Cavell has made a number of remarks pertaining to the peculiar character of Stefan's final perception of Lisa. Drawing on Freud's description of the 'uncanny,' Cavell places particular emphasis on the moment when Stefan finishes the letter and then covers his eyes with the "outstretched fingers of both hands in a melodramatic gesture of horror and exhaustion"—when the letter unleashes "an assault of images" from earlier moments of the film.[14] Cavell asks how these visually innocuous scenes should induce such strong feelings in their beholder. Appropriately, he links this horror with the various difficulties Stefan has in acknowledging Lisa—in recognizing the subjectivity of the other—a process made even more problematic in the dynamics of desiring and looking in the cinema. Cavell also invokes in this context Freud's notion that "the finding of an object is in fact the refinding of it."[15] For Cavell, *Letter from an Unknown Woman* founds a genre related to the "comedies of remarriage" he describes in *Pursuits of Happiness.* These cinematic comedies also involve a "rediscovery" of a marital partner (or its equivalent).[16] Such rediscoveries must be brought about by the elimination or domestication of "male villainy" (maleness itself, interestingly enough, being defined by villainy) and by the woman's "establish[ing] her right to existence in the form of a metamorphosis . . , apart from or beyond the satisfaction by marriage . . . and with the presence of her mother and of her children."[17] *Letter from an Unknown Woman,* Cavell notes, "emphasizes, by failure, fantasies of metamorphosis and fantasies of perfect communication and of the transcendence of marriage."[18] My so far more Lacanian description of the problems of recognition, communication, and transcendence of gender roles differs from Cavell's mainly in its less optimistic expectations ("the most secure conjugal happiness") of the cinematic moment when men and women, men and men, women and women lock eyes (or voice and ears) and lose (or find) themselves in one another. The perception of the other's "subjectivity"—especially when that "other" is a woman who must "establish her right to exist"—is made difficult or impossible when the projected image of that other seems to imply an aggressive opposition—or *return*—of the kind described by Rose. Oedipus and Nathaniel, E. T. A. Hoffmann's protagonist in "The Sandman," put out their eyes (or are threatened with it) instead of covering them, on perceiving the villainy of their maleness and, for Nathaniel, the horrifying lifelessness of their women.[19] The beautiful image of the object of desire presents a double danger—effectively, a double bind. Danger is perceived in representation itself (particularly *gendered* representation, as earlier chapters have demonstrated), and in its potential transformation into resisting subjectivity. In *Letter* the "return" of Lisa's lovely image is the more powerful because Stefan does not seem to be able to *see* her at all during most of the film—neither as *dangerous* image nor as potential subject—exhibiting a form of blindness virtually unique to the "bad good men" of melodrama. It is, however, finally Lisa's *voice* that makes the most uncanny return to Stefan's apartment, though in a deferred, less *immediate* medium than was his music for her.

Capture, Visibility, and Lack

In *Letter* Stefan's ideal (and absent) point of view is tacitly attributed to the agency of an "author," traceable in the film through various well-documented enunciative gestures. The authorial placeholder in the film is the mute valet, John, who "knew all along" who Lisa was, and who ultimately signs the letter for her.[20] The mute valet, as third term (i.e., between the observer and the observed), takes on something of the role of the birds in Hitchcock's film, in his interception and reversal of the protagonists' looks—but John goes farther in that he also lends subjectivity to Lisa. Indeed, it is he who gives Brand the letter that sends him to his death. Lisa is an author in her own right (displacing the authorial function found in the novella, as we shall see), although she is barred from the signing of her tale. Lisa's inability to sign results literally from her death, but figuratively from her being a woman, and therefore not the traditional arbiter of her own tale, as well as from the letter's role as part of a larger interrogation of circularity and deferral in the film. This can only take place if Lisa's subject status (in Stefan's eyes) is itself deferred until the last moments of the film.

Throughout most of *Letter* (within the framed story), Lisa "sees," "hears," and *narrates* Brand. She supposedly is not privileged to witness the images her narrative induces, and thus does not perceive its gentle ironies at her expense. This issue is complicated by the fact that her ocular point of view, as well as what Bordwell and Thompson call her "range of knowledge," is, in fact, often espoused.[21] This almost frightening ability to show Brand to himself (*his own* image also uncannily returning with aggressive impact) does, however, give Lisa some visual control. Within the diegesis itself she succeeds in taking possession of Stefan's image through her son, who resembles him in name, physical appearance, and musical talent. (Like his father, young Stefan may also have "too many" talents to live, as the child's most extensive scene implies.) In Zweig's novella the young woman speaks of the older Stefan's "glance intended to attract and trap [women],"[22] which he gives indiscriminately, even unseeingly, but which makes the protagonist his "dog-like" devotee just the same. From worshiping male "freedom," the nameless young woman terminates Stefan's wandering by having his child: "Now, at last, I had captured you."[23] The novella emphasizes the physical intermingling of genetic material: the woman literally takes a part of the man, as well as duplicating him. In the film this aspect of the story has been entrusted to visual (and aural) effects.

What is Lisa's relationship to her own visibility? Vision takes a decisive role in the etiology of Lisa's love for Stefan, but not before hearing has laid the groundwork. Another often-analyzed scene in the film features the teenage Lisa sitting on a swing below Stefan's windows, out of which Liszt's "Sospiro" pours. Obviously physically aroused by the music (though she is only half aware of this), Lisa toys with the ropes and looks anxiously at the window when Stefan begins to have trouble with the piece. Marie, a rather vulgar playmate, is (as George Wilson puts it) "taking a lusty bite from a piece of cake she is eating"[24] (like many of Ophuls' "sexpots," she is voracious in her appetite for food). Marie is engrossed in a description of one of her admirers, "the bonny one with the long nose and the yellow hair. . . . I'm going to have to do something about that boy if he doesn't keep his hands to himself!" "At this remark," Wilson notes, "there is an immediate cut to an insert of Brand playing the piano in his room and then to a shot of *his hands* as they powerfully strike the keys."[25] The romantic quality of Lisa's dawning passion is being "ironically" compared to that of her more earthy companion. The visual disadvantage permitting this irony at Lisa's expense is made more explicit as the scene continues. Frustrated by his performance, Stefan ceases to play and exits from the building. As he leaves, Lisa opens the front door for him, and she and Brand exchange looks as she stands behind the glass panes of the building's front door. She declares, via the letter, that from that moment on she was in love with him. A sexual tension that was already mounting through Lisa's aural pleasure reaches the crisis point as the first visual interaction takes place between the man and the girl. Framed by the glass door that she is holding open for him, Lisa smiles shyly (but ardently) as Stefan thanks her for this service. But only at the end of the film will Brand in fact *see* Lisa, when he halluci-nates the girl behind the glass door as he leaves his building to fight the duel with Stauffer. Stefan's desire for Lisa can, it seems, only come as the product of a repetition. In contrast, Lisa seems to experience this first encounter as an immediate source of both humiliation and desire. The girlfriend who witnesses Lisa's flirtation with the handsome neighbor tauntingly accuses her of blushing, which Lisa acknowledges in the voice-over. From this moment Lisa will devote her life to pursuing Brand, but in a peculiarly roundabout way that is, she claims, occasioned by a (perhaps theatrical) recognition of inadequacy on her part—reflected in the need to blush. She has seen Stefan, knows that she is without him, and wants immediately to have him, to hold his image in her hand and feel herself bathed in his music.

Yet to say that she wants the man is not quite accurate. The little girl cannot have direct access to the particular sexual power that is associat-ed with the man and emblematized, in the film, by his role as a per-former, a concert pianist. For Lisa, he is out of the realm of ordinary mortals. Lisa seems to be the one "framed" behind glass in this scene, but in fact his gaze is blocked by the pane between them. Like the flash-back structure separating them through most of the film, the pane of glass is not transparent, but mediated by the cultural conditions of mas-culinity and femininity. Here again, however, the "virile display" bears a close relation to the feminine. This is especially so in *Letter* when the dis-play begins literally to collapse around Stefan's ears. From one point of view, *Letter from an Unknown Woman* tells the tale of the detour in Lisa's sexual development as she attempts to identify herself with the (phallic) prowess of the urbane pianist, while steering clear of the deadly conse-quences that follow upon being locked in the gaze of the other. This is indeed what would occur if she, too, were a naive performer of her sex-ual role. Instead she carries out a tactical avoidance in the guise of masochistic "waiting" to be acknowledged.[26] Ophuls' cinema continual-ly shows us that the visual field of the other is a place of extreme danger. This danger persists in homosexual as well as heterosexual desiring looks, even as the former break down the terms of gender "opposition." *Letter* can easily be read as a depiction of "impossible" (same sex) love, in which the stakes of "captivation" are very high. Certain strategies must be devised to deflect the "castrating" or captivating potential of the gaze. These strategies are most often only temporarily successful, and often provide pleasure only through the medium of pain.

In stating Lisa's case as one in which she feels "inadequate" vis-à-vis Stefan, I make overt reference to Freud's description of the prototypical little girl's recognition of her own "castration." Upon sighting the little boy's "obviously" superior (that is, larger) sexual organ, a sequence of thoughts is said by Freud to take place in the female child's mind: "She makes her judgment and her decision in a flash. She has seen it and knows that she is without it and wants to have it."[27] Of course, this "immediate" recognition is (as usual) only triggered by the man's gaze: his look determines Lisa's sense—or pretense—of inadequacy.

Transvestism and Masquerade

Lisa's strategic response to her own "lack" is, therefore, overdetermined. Upon discovering her love for this man—that is, having become aware that she is lacking—Lisa takes definitive measures. A brief montage sequence shows how she sets out "quite deliberately" to prepare herself for him. She irons her clothes, for example, so that Stefan will not be ashamed of her untidy appearance. According to the logic that defines woman (or gay man) as "castrated," the shame is Lisa's own; the attention to clothing is the first of the strategies, referred to above, that serve to deflect the harmful gaze of the other. In this brief series of vignettes, connected by dissolves,[28] the girl is next shown reading about the lives of the great musicians, as well as attending a dance class, and riding in a streetcar. These scenes are particularly notable: Lisa's "preparation" for her loved one is already double-edged. Naturalized by the transition from early to late adolescence, Lisa's acquisition of the secondary sexual characteristics of womanhood are explicitly given as a kind of masquerade, as a learning process that can be more or less successful, and that has a certain measure of arbitrariness about it. She chooses femininity as a means of achieving her desire. Let us also note that, in reading about the musicians, Lisa could as easily be described as *imitating* Stefan as preparing herself to be his companion.

In the scene of the dance class, as well, several elements of the mise-en-scène reveal conflicts concerning sexual identity at work. These conflicts might be said, in the terms set up by Joan Riviere and elaborated upon by Mary Ann Doane and others,[29] to take the form of a vacillation between "transvestism" and the less easily recuperable "masquerade of the feminine" in the film. In the dance sequence, Lisa is practicing with the elderly dance instructor in a small antechamber separated by a glass partition from a double line of boys and girls, who are stiffly walking through the figure of the dance. Lisa's difficulty in integrating herself into the normal (if peculiarly ritualized) practices of heterosexual involvement is underscored by her initial separation from the other youngsters and by her slight disruption of their organized interaction when she tries to seek a partner among them. (One may certainly recognize this scene as virtually an explicit reference to the difficulty of growing up gay.) The accomplishment of this attempt is not depicted: that is, we do not see Lisa dancing with a little boy, as do all the other little girls.[30] She dances with the dancing master (an older man) and then alone. The extent of Lisa's intractability in the arena of courtship will be brought to the surface in the scenes in Linz.[31]

The dance scene prefigures Lisa's dances with Stefan later in the film when she is, again, dancing both with an older man and, in a sense, alone. Interestingly, while she practices with the dance instructor Lisa is standing on the side of the room where the *boys* are lined up. This detail reinforces the already established confusion in the positioning of Lisa with respect to gender. It is strategically necessary for her to acquire the allurements of the feminine, but she must place herself in the role of the "male" if she is to carry it through. This role is itself not safe from the violence implicit to the workings of the image: the mimetic explosion that takes place at the end of the film, where doubles of the main characters appear in force, has as the central object of representation the *male* figure.[32] At the heart of this film is Lisa's attempt to wear her sexuality as a toreador wears his cape: its detachability is the most important quality. This is true both of her *transvestism* and of her relationship to the "masquerade" of the feminine:

The masquerade, in flaunting femininity, holds it at a distance. Womanliness is a mask which can be worn or removed. The masquerade's resistance to patriarchal positioning would therefore lie in its denial of the production of femininity as closeness, as presence-to-itself, as, precisely, imagistic. The transvestite adopts the sexuality of the other—the woman becomes a man in order to attain the necessary distance from the image. Masquerade, on the other hand, involves a realignment of femininity, the recovery, or more accurately, simulation, of the missing gap or distance. To masquerade is to manufacture a lack in the form of a distance between oneself and one's image. If, as Moustafa Safouan points out, "to wish to include in oneself as an object the cause of the desire of the other is a formula for the structure of hysteria," then the masquerade is anti-hysterical.[33]

Doane's description of woman's need to *deny* "femininity as closeness" must be understood not as a denial of the possibility of experiencing emotion or identification with regard to the image of women in cinema, but as a means of establishing other options for women within the structure of patriarchal spectatorship. Lisa *deliberately* sets out to "feminize" herself for Stefan, on the model of the lovely women who visit him. Thus she abolishes the so-called inevitable connection of "immediacy" (lack of distance, perspective) to female sexuality, that is, to the woman's sexual perception of herself. (It is my belief that women also learn to objectify—and to look desiringly—at other women in a way that does not imply identification.) In Ophuls' cinema, being bound to the attributes that produce sexual allurement can be fatal to the characters—both male and female. Indeed, in these films both men and women use the tactics of transvestism and masquerade in order to express desire (the "masculine" position) and to avoid being fixed to the (fetishized "feminine"— or "castrated" masculine) sexual identity they are performing.

Consequently, masquerade might be described as the taking on of feminine characteristics, that is, of both secondary sexual traits, and a particular way of attracting and deflecting the gaze of the other. The masquerade demonstrates woman's distance from her sexuality and hints at man's *closeness* to, or unconsciousness of, his. The position of the object of the spectacle, usually occupied by the woman as a "fetish" of sorts, is not contingent upon the characteristics of one gender or the other: he or she who fails to recognize the contingency of sexual identity is at a great disadvantage.

The question of how fetishism functions in the cinematic apparatus and its narrative traditions has, as we have noted, been brought most prominently into debate by Laura Mulvey. Mulvey describes how the body of woman has been used as fetish object in the classical cinema, showing how woman as image (paradoxically, as "virile display"), whose fascinating qualities lie in her phallic promise, protects man from the implications of "castration." As previously indicated, Mulvey follows Freud in seeing woman-as-fetish as a double-edged phenomenon, conveying both reassurance and threat to the male spectator. Similarly, Lacan has pointed to how the masculine "parade" of virility, through which man attempts to approximate the phallic function, may come dangerously close to the feminine masquerade, backfiring as irreversibly as does the feminine masquerade, and in this way fixing the male into an "overidentification" with the male function, with the image of his sexuality.

As we saw in the analysis of *Madame de . . .*, the problem of belief seems to be the vital one in the play of fetishism, transvestism, and masquerade. The belief that one is in possession of or in the place of the phallus, that the source of one's allure is real, or even the continued belief by spectators in the reality of the fetish, seems to put the performer of sexuality into the grave danger we have discussed concerning the fixed image. Indeed, the very belief in the possibility of an intact phallic function—the belief that anyone possesses the phallus, or the attempt to foist such a belief off on others—is fatal. If the General, Lisa's husband, seems to be the only adult in this film, it is because he is the only character who, in acting the phallic, no longer believes it is possible to possess it. Masquerade is described from the point of view of the female subject: it is her knowledge of the construction of her sexuality that is important. Fetishism and transvestism both rely on the belief of the spectator in the exciting possibility that woman is in possession of the male organ or—according to a Deleuzian masochistic scenario—that the woman has a privileged relationship to the pre-Oedipal "uncastrated" oral mother. The epistemic state of the object of vision is more or less irrelevant in these instances. In a homosexual context, the danger lies in both the reproduction of the phallic system, and the attempt to move *outside* it, or to dissolve it from within. The *shattering* quality of gay and lesbian love lies in its destabilization of a gender system that by definition wreaks violence on the desired other (the homosexual, the "woman"). Ophuls pushed (as we will see) for greater homosexual "visibility" in this film, but was discouraged from doing so.

The Persecuting Gaze and the Sound of Music

Because she is a child, Lisa is barred from attending Stefan's concerts by herself (and her mother's inhibiting presence is obviously not desired). She makes up for this inability to see her beloved in the flesh with a mediated experience. Riding on the open back section of a streetcar, she listens to the conversations of people who have just been to Brand's concert, and mischievously steals the program notes from the pocket of a large and sober-looking gentleman. This scene is echoed when little Stefan, Lisa's son, later wants his mother to bring him an opera program. Lisa's belief in Brand's superiority, expressed by her worship of his image, borrowed from the pocket of the patriarch, will be disillusioned when that image is ultimately shown to be a hollow one. The image, one might add, is valuable here only as it is metonymically linked to the vanished musical performance. Her fascination with and necessary distance from the desired object are caught by the nature of the photographic image as well as by the notes that drift away. It is apparent that the position of the fetishist is available even to Lisa, and that the man may be a fetish-object, a stolen or borrowed appendage momentarily appropriated from the stern father figure. (Studlar observes that Stefan's possessions "become part of the strongly fetishistic component in her attraction to him," p. 43.) The possibility exists that the woman may be disappointed in the man when she recognizes that although he is in possession of the male sexual organs he does not, of course, have the phallus itself. Although she avoids the fetishizing of her own body, she will place Stefan in that role and will eventually permit him to do the same to her, running the risk, when she finally decides to close the distance between them, of destroying the frail thread of belief that feeds their love. At a distance she can remain a "woman" for him, rather than a desiring female subject or a man who reflects his own homoeroticism back to him.

At night Lisa passes "the happiest hours of [her] life" listening to Stefan play, unknowingly, "just for" her. No longer able to remain in bed while she can hear the music wafting into her room, the girl rises and slips past her mother, who is seated behind the parlor's glass doors playing solitaire. The potentially persecuting gaze of the mother is averted,[34] as Lisa has apparently devised a system for sneaking past her, by hiding in the shadows of the door frame. The doors are made of glass, which highlights the possibility of the mother looking through them to see the girl, but which also serves to frame the mother as a kind of *tableau vivant* of the lonely middle-aged widow. The glass door acts as the emblem of a fragile but definitive separation—Lisa rejects both the solitude and the bourgeois expectations of her mother, a woman given to be looked at in her genteel but threadbare circumstances (not sentimentalized as are Christine's in *Liebelei*). As Bacher notes, "A strong sense of spatial separation is created by the multiple planes of the setting: Action in close shot in the foreground plane, middle ground action with the mother framed by the window panes, and the far distance again separated by frames, those of the windows to the exterior, which, like the foreground, is in darkness." (2:415)Once again, the transparency of glass reveals *blindness.*

Despite this carefully constructed distancing, Lisa's mother retains the power to censure her daughter's behavior by a shrewd, though not visionary gaze (as opposed to the visual powers later attributed to Lisa's father). The travails of Frau Berndle seem to be of no interest to the girl. Indeed, the reference to the "persecutory" potential of the mother's look may seem to be exaggerated, on the evidence of the older woman's subdued presence in the film, but the few interactions that take place between mother and daughter are quite striking. Indeed, the very muting of the role of the mother, juxtaposed with other elements indirectly pointing to the workings of a maternal function in the film, should (according to Freud's "dream logic") indicate that Lisa's relationship to her mother is crucial to the effect of the film. The mother's role in the constitution of the subject, especially the female subject, is easy to underestimate, hidden as it is "under" the investment in the father and in men.[35] Ambivalence toward this mother is part of what energizes "the aggressive potential of the gaze" and the consequent instability of the classical film system, which tends to draw its energy from the regressive impulse of the imaginary, finding "symbolic" resolutions only with some difficulty. I have linked this regression to the paranoia associated with the formation of the ego. The mutual looking of mother and daughter draws upon that energy and reinforces the sense that Stefan's music may provide a less "persecutory" medium, one longed for and remembered by Lisa as "maternal." Or, as Tania Modleski puts it, Stefan is associated with the "pre-Oedipal" father, the father who stands in opposition to the stiff patriarchs inhabiting Ophuls' films.[36] Thus, Stefan's musical ability, which both constitutes him as a "man" and curiously unmans him, draws Lisa intensely. To cite Rose, once again:

Paranoia could be said to be latent to the structure of cinematic specularity in itself, in that it represents the radical alterity of signification (the subject isspoken from elsewhere). To suggest this is to challenge the idea of the spectator's subsumption into an imaginary totality and to point to the potential splitting of that totality within the moment of its own constitution. For the woman, the alterity of signification is the locus from which she is spoken as excluded and also from which she is *taken* as picture—the image representing the moment of freezing of her sexuality. (p. 89)

Rose alludes here to an essay by Freud,[37] in which a young woman externalizes her sexual feelings, creating the fantasy of being secretly photographed. Rose notes that "for the woman it is the infantile image of the mother which lies behind the delusion of persecution even where the persecutor is apparently a male" (p. 103). Paranoia, at least in Freud's first outline of its operation, is generated by a repressed homosexuality. Lisa's spying on Stefan, in this case, could be seen as a version, a displacement of her wish to spy on the sexual activities of her mother, in whom she has a strong erotic investment that also expresses itself as identification. (Note that the "paranoid structure" of the film includes the fact that Lisa *is* being spoken from elsewhere, paradoxically, by herself.) Lisa's relationship to her mother is partly responsible for the disruption of the former's heterosexual development, despite the fact that the latter seems to foster Lisa's maturation by finding (unexciting) young men for her. But this scenario obtains only if we assume that the goal of maturation is—heterosexuality. Lisa's rejection of male suitors may also be read as mature *homosexual* desire, with Stefan as its "feminized" object. This conjecture concerning the role of the mother, which becomes even more emphatic from a Deleuzian perspective, is borne out by the next scenes of the film.

Significantly, in the transom scene Lisa can often only listen to rather than see her beloved.[38] Whether the decision to avoid depicting Lisa's "look" resulted from shooting constraints or not, the elegance, rhythm, and musically directed timing of the transom scene indicates that much consideration was given to its choreography. Indeed, according to Bacher, the scene where Lisa listens at the transom grows from the brief description in the shooting script to a "complex fifty-five second set-up (shot with the Woodlin crane), a lateral traveling left which combines with an axial traveling in/vertical traveling up in order to both fluidly follow her climb up to look through the [curtained] transom and to express her pleasure with Stefan's music" (2:421). The reason for this complex reworking of the scene's "previsualization" was probably a mixture of contingency and deliberate decision. Perhaps it would not have "looked well" for a young girl to spy in this way on a man (the way Norman Bates is shown to be an explicit voyeur in *Psycho*): instead the more "feminine" aural bath is substituted for Lisa's gaze. The filmmakers seem continually to mediate, even frustrate, Lisa's visual perception of Stefan, first (as is also the case in the novella) by delaying her initial view of him, then, later by impeding her view in various ways. And as Lisa does come to "see" and visually possess Stefan more definitively, her disillusionment grows.

Lisa makes an apparently banal remark later in the film, which emphasizes just how much she hears—and how much more Ophuls' heroines hear than do his "ordinary" characters. "Sometimes," she says to Stefan, "I felt when you were playing that . . . that you hadn't quite found—I don't know what it is—what you're looking for." Like John, Lisa can "hear" even if she cannot speak her truth during the course of the framed narrative. The "sonorous envelope" in which Lisa surrounds herself,[39] and which provides her "happiest hours," links Stefan with what Michel Chion has called the "uterine night," the voice of the mother sensed by the prenatal child enclosed within it. Stefan's elusive, permeating notes stand in contrast to the flat, intrusive accents of the mother—but also stand in for them. Thus, the role of the "good mother," as well as that of pre-Oedipal father, is occupied by Stefan. Not surprisingly, Chion describes that voice as "ambivalent," even "horrifying," and as an "umbilical net" that "invokes a cobweb." It is perhaps Lisa's real mother's voice that, like her gaze, seems bent upon trapping the girl, while it is Stefan's music that actually performs the mother's positive functions.

The relationship between sound (voice or music) and body has come under close scrutiny by feminist film theorists in the past few years, notably in the work of Silverman, Doane,[40] Carol Flinn, and Claudia Gorbman.[41] According to Silverman's take on the female voice in cinema, as she describes it in *The Acoustic Mirror*, woman is generally not "privileged" by classical cinema, in that she is most often made to inhabit, rather uncomfortably, the body whence sound (prototypically, a scream) is emanating. The "disembodied voice," known by laymen as the "voice of God" in cinema, is most often male. Consequently, Silverman claims, one can observe in classical cinema a tendency to force upon the woman the fact of her embodiment, and the limits that this body brings with it. *Letter from an Unknown Woman* is somewhat unusual in its insistence upon the female voice, a voice that is both trapped in the body of a dying woman and curiously outside of that body.

As Silverman brilliantly argues, much traditional and even feminist criticism emphasizes, seemingly celebrates woman's "enclosure" in the acoustic realm of her own body, within the "enceinte" (a word meaning both "fortress" or walled-in space, and "pregnant") with which she surrounds her unborn child.[42] Woman as "container" becomes the "contained," buried alive in an acoustic realm that may cause her pain or *jouissance*, depending on whom one believes. In a rather polarizing but certainly pertinent move, Flinn also conflates the cinematic "realm of rhythms, music and poetry," with the feminine, and that of "logic, narrative and language" with the masculine, and notes the traditional "supremacy of the film image over the soundtrack."[43] Another essay by Flinn[44] adds the corrective that music does indeed "provide . . . information"—and is therefore also linked with the "masculine," and that the "feminine metaphor used to describe these types of relationships [the listener's "imaginary" fusion with the film score] must be apprehended with extreme care." We will see that *Letter* (as Glynis Kinnan says) can be described as setting up the male-female, image-music, subject-object oppositions that produce both love and violence in the tale, but also as undermining those oppositions even as they are produced—with music perhaps holding the most complex position of all in its identification with femininity, masculinity, heterosexuality, homosexuality, pleasure, and pain.

Both Silverman and Chion describe the maternal voice as the originary "voice-over"; the cinematic teller of tales retains the "symbolic 'trace' of the mother."[45] Ironically, as noted, most of the time that voice is male, and it often comments on the activities of women within the diegesis: "With brand X, Mrs. Jones's clothes are brighter"—or even, "Try brand X for brighter clothes, Mrs. Jones!" Since *Letter* is a fascinating "reversion" to the use of the encompassing woman's voice, Lisa's voice can surround, fascinate, invoke recollection, emotion, pain, and finally death. But within the framed narrative, it is Lisa who is enveloped, seduced, wooed to her death. It is thus doubly interesting that Ophuls uses the seductive powers of voice and music to smooth over conflict in the visual field, to express love and longing otherwise unspoken within the chronological story. What is (as Gorbman observes) "unheard" in most films is—in *Letter*—pointed to before it is internalized, or becomes nondiegetic. Music's offer of *immediacy* is fervently accepted: *these* are the happiest hours of our lives, but, like the letter itself, what these hours hold is recognized only retrospectively, retroaudibly. And music is indeed an ambivalent prize: it is no wonder that Lisa resists being utterly sustained and surrounded by Stefan's music, despite the fact that Ophuls seems to tender it as ointment to the wounds of gender. What Gertrud Koch calls, in her analysis of the film, the "masochistic pleasure of hearing," charms and endangers both man and woman—though its pleasure dwarfs that found for each elsewhere.[46]

A Rug Is Being Beaten

A dissolve from Lisa's ecstatic face as she listens to Stefan through the transom (a scene that, as it is part of the "montage" showing Lisa's preparatory activities, we might suppose to be an example of many such evenings) takes us to another significant event in the etiology of her romance. A particular "rug-beating day"—a regular Thursday occasion in the building, as Lisa tells us in her voice-over account—gives the girl an opportunity to infiltrate Stefan's apartment. The scene opens, as Bacher observes, with Lisa pulling down her rug, "thus opening the curtain on the courtyard 'scene' " (2:430). Because of various changes made during the production process, "Ophuls was able to block the whole action as a continual movement" and achieves impressive fluidity as the camera tracks and pans around the cluttered courtyard (made more expansive, Bacher notes, by the use of a wide-angle lens to shoot it). This fluidity achieved amid chaos bears witness to Lisa's organizational ability, marshaled in the interest of *spying* on Stefan in this scene. By promising to beat *her* rug later (delaying pleasure?), Lisa manages to enlist the lazy Marie to help John carry a large rug upstairs to the Brand lair. When John's back is turned, Lisa looks in the door after him, and, to Marie's amazement, sneaks inside. Lisa's awestruck examination of the "sacred" sheet music (piled beneath a large poster advertising one of Stefan's concerts) ends in the mass of paper falling to the floor, a sound that brings John into the room[47] (he is mute but not deaf, as Lisa has pointed out to her rather smart-alecky girlfriend). Lisa flees, leaving the amused servant smiling behind her.[48]

When she leaves the apartment through the front door leading to the main staircase, the girl confronts a surprising vista. Her mother, standing in front of her own apartment, is being fondled by a corpulent little man. Frau Berndle hastily buttons her shirtwaist and bids her lover good-day, leading the numb Lisa into their apartment while she offers flustered explanations of her behavior. She seats her daughter on the sofa and says, without meeting the girl's eyes, that Lisa must understand that her mother is actually a rather young woman who is quite capable of being in love with a man. Lisa is thus forced to acknowledge that her mother has a sexual life, something she has previously managed to ignore. A reframing of the scene to highlight Lisa's reaction brings to the foreground the smoldering cigar apparently forgotten by Herr Kastner (Howard Freeman), Frau Berndle's fiancé—for, indeed, they are to be married, as the widow now informs her daughter. Horrified at the thought of moving to Linz with her new stepfather (a military tailor) and thus abandoning her love, Lisa runs weeping from the room.[49]

Ostensibly, of course, Lisa's sorrow and wrath are ignited by the possibility that she might be separated from Brand. Her horror might as easily be thought, however, to arise from the grotesque "primal" scene she has just witnessed, whose reminder lies smoldering in the ashtray in the form of the cigar left by her stepfather. If, however, we consider these scenes in their juxtaposition, as they form a belated or *nachträglich* structure,[50] we might observe that they relate to a kind of sexual curiosity, or rather, the first incident in Brand's apartment is a mise-en-scène of Lisa's curiosity, minus the overt sexual component, while the second scene, on the stairway, is a sexual one come upon inadvertently, although Lisa seems to disregard its obvious sexual component. Lisa investigates Brand's apartment as a sacred but also as an erotic place. Her being surprised by John parallels her mother's potential surprise as the daughter spies upon the "parental coitus." Like Lisa, John can hear, even if he does not say anything about it. He is Lisa's rival in listening—and looking, as the mother is the rival for the love of the father (although the stepfather's repulsiveness disguises the latter)—or the father for that of the mother herself.

Family Romances

Returns to the "originary" place of sexual encounter are dwelt upon at length in this film, although the status of these origins is continually questioned, as we can see by "returning" briefly to the very beginning of the film. The film opens on a framing sequence where Stefan Brand light-heartedly discusses his imminent duel in a closed carriage with his seconds, then in his apartment with his valet. His opponent will be Stauffer, although that has little meaning to us as of yet. Brand, knowing that Stauffer is an excellent shot, declares to John that honor is a luxury that "I can ill afford," and orders his bags to be packed within the hour. Before leaving to perform this duty, John presents his employer with a letter that has just arrived. This is, of course, the letter referred to in the film's title, whose reading will delay Brand's departure and reinstate him in the code of honor that demands he both keep his word and fight for the woman who has sacrificed herself for his sake. Modleski makes the

fascinating and surely valid point that if the heart of the film involves Stefan's being "made into a man" by finally accepting "castration" at the
hands of the "father" (words in quotes are my paraphrase), then *Letter,*
thought to be a prototypical "woman's film," is really for and about a
man. If we accept the terms of Stefan's transformation as such, then here
is more evidence that, as some critics hypothesize, "there *is* no such
thing as a woman's film."[51] Modleski salvages the film for women by
locating the feminine voice "elsewhere"—a certain rhythm of time, and
a joy in repetition. Certainly, as we have already seen (and heard), the
woman's voice is located somewhere in this film: this would be evidenced by women's powerful responses to the film, if by nothing else.
But Modleski, Studlar, Silverman, Kinnan, and others amply demonstrate that this woman's voice is nothing short of symphonic—its "presence" is strongly overdetermined in the (perhaps contradictory)
masochistic, paranoid, hysterical, and obsessive structures of the film.

A dissolve brings us from the first words of the letter ("By the time you
read this, I may be dead") to the extended voice-over flashback making
up the body of the film:

> (VOICE-OVER): I think everyone has two birthdays, the day of his physi-
> cal birth and the beginning of his conscious life. The day I came home
> from school and found a moving van in front of our house, I wondered
> about our new neighbor who had such lovely things.

Lisa's first contact with Stefan takes place as she examines these fur-
nishings (the "lovely things" superior to those of her family), about to be
moved into his upstairs apartment. This setting up of the scene of the
couple's *amours* is a specifically theatrical gesture, casting into relief the
staged quality of the original moment of Lisa's fascination. The structure
of sexual latency is repeated in Lisa's "two births," where existence precedes a certain kind of consciousness or where a later moment of awareness acts retrospectively upon the first.[52]

We might assume that Lisa and her mother have lived in this apartment building for years, perhaps since before the death (or departure)
of Lisa's father. Stefan's proximity to the homestead is surely not acci-
dental in the development of Lisa's passion. The fact that Lisa witnesses
her mother's adventure on the *staircase* also has obvious significance in
light of the attention that will be given this staircase with respect to Lisa's
desire for Stefan. This "closeness to home" brings with it the complexi-

ties of social class in the film, where the (petty) bourgeoisie, in this and other films by Ophuls, may represent a repugnant aspect of sexuality—an aspect that will reappear at moments of "disillusionment" throughout the film in relations to cynical servants, in the possibility of marriage to a middle-class man, and so on. Stefan is the man "upstairs," living above Lisa's parents both literally and figuratively, but acting, as well, as their double, as an object that can take up the intensity of feeling Lisa is ashamed to feel for her mother and her father.

After Lisa's mother tells her of her own engagement, with unfortunate results, the film dissolves from her frantic knocking at the girl's door to a scene featuring another melodramatic "return" of the kind mentioned above. At the train station, bound for Linz, the newly formed little family is in a flurry, trying to get the numerous trunks and parcels safely shipped to the Upper Austrian town. The scene opens on Herr Kastner standing at the ticket counter, then crossing and recrossing the large room as the camera tracks and pans, following his movements. He bounces like a rubber ball from counter to anxious wife to luggage, counting and recounting the bags, and checking his watch against the station clock, the parody of the flurried "director-figures" seen in Ophuls' other films. The cigar clutched firmly between his teeth is a rather unpleasant metonymy for the sexual side of this practical little businessman. (As we saw in the previous scene, sometimes a cigar is not just a cigar.) In contrast to Stefan, Herr Kastner is a cheapskate. He asks the porter how long the bags will take to get to Linz "third class," inadvertently revealing his own status in life. The answer, "Two weeks," is satisfactory, although it prefigures ominous losses later in the film (and, indeed, we don't know if these bags ever "arrive," though Lisa, as a piece of the baggage, certainly returns). The parents are both wearing peculiar hats with birds' wings for decoration, and caged birds accompany them on the trip. This odd garb can be related to the hat-gender considerations we will see at work later in the film. Here, the question of "pairing" is linked with the notion of entrapment, as the birds are trapped in their cage. Our sympathies are certainly with Lisa, who is shown in a chiaroscuro medium shot,[53] wearing black clothes and a miserable look on her face. Equipped as it is with such visual metaphors and cruel premonitions, the scene pleases Lisa very little. The camera pans almost 180 degrees, showing Lisa as she slowly moves away from the bustle and, realizing that she "cannot live" without Stefan, flees the station to return to what was once her home. A dissolve picks up the tram as it slows to let Lisa leap down and run toward the apartment building. The camera, which pans to follow her movements, creates the effect of continuous action from the last scene to this, as though Lisa's wish were being fulfilled with dreamlike fluidity. As she explains to the doorman that she (like Stefan) "forgot something," a reverse shot reveals Lisa standing behind the bars of the gate: the visual signs of entrapment have not been left at the train station. She runs up to Stefan's apartment and pounds eagerly on the door—but he is not at home. So Lisa returns to her now-empty apartment, whose rooms, she recalls, were once "filled" with Stefan's music.

> (VOICE-OVER): Would they remain empty? Would [my life]? Only you could say.

The return to the empty home, the wish for the original home to be replenished, made as it was, must remain heartbreakingly unfulfilled. In this scene, which, along with its pendant, has become one of the best-known in the history of American cinema, Lisa waits on the staircase outside Stefan's apartment until, to her anguish, he returns accompanied by a giggling young woman in white. Shot from the top of the staircase, with Lisa in frame (thus "taking her point of view" but also including her as a physical object in the shot), Stefan's arrival with the other woman dashes Lisa's hopes: she leaves for Linz.

Excuse Me, You've Got Linz on Your Uniform

The actual journey to Linz, like Lisa's parents' earlier train trip, is not depicted. The fact that we do not see the journey casts light upon an implicit contrast in the mise-en-scène of Lisa's "authentic" and her "inauthentic" parents. Lisa resembles the child who imagines that she is not really the daughter of these uninspiring people, but who secretly believes that she belongs to a more aristocratic setting. Such, as we observed in the discussion of *Sarajevo*, is the drama of the family romance as Freud describes it:

For a small child his parents are at first the only authority and the source of all belief. The child's most intense and most momentous wish during these early years is to be like his parents (that is, the parent of his own sex) and to be big like his father and mother. But as intellectual growth increases, the child cannot help discovering by degrees the *category* to which his parents belong. He gets to know other parents and compares them with his own, and so acquires the right to doubt the incomparable and unique quality which he had attributed to them.[54]

To the revolting scene inside the train station (where we do not, once more, actually see the train, but only the cumbersome trappings of a voyage) will be juxtaposed scenes of other journeys, real and unreal, which ring truer to the romance Lisa is writing for herself. Lisa's love for Stefan is placed in proximity to visions of grotesque couplings—as in the scene where young Maria brags of her "yellow-haired boy's" roving hands, while Lisa listens, strongly moved, to Stefan's music.[55] Lisa's passion for Stefan is the more intense and the more touching for the tenacity that characterizes her imaginary fixation. This is, in fact, a fixation on the parental figures themselves, though deflected to a more bearable—because more "distant" and more socially prestigious—arena. Thus we are not surprised to learn that Lisa's parental home and Stefan's apartment are actually the same set, slightly altered in shooting the different scenes.[56]

Having joined her parents in Linz, Lisa is thrust into the bumbling niceties of courtship in a "garrison town," as she puts it. Her mother's role as the one who must bend her daughter to normalcy is underlined in the sequence where Lisa is introduced to her young suitor, Lt. Leopold von Kaltnegger (John Good). In another scene changed during the production of the film, the pair is introduced in long shot with a "simple connective flash pan," as Bacher puts it (2:450), during which the lieutenant and his uncle, Colonel Steindorf (C. Ramsey Hill), walk *down* a flight of stairs to join the family placed both literally and figuratively below them. A cart passes by as the young man is about to kiss Lisa's hand, and the two family groups are pressed against the wall behind them. This interruption foreshadows a less-than-fortunate outcome to the events at hand. The scene continues along the trajectory of a "lengthy traveling—perhaps in distance traversed the longest of the American films,"[57] which *very* ironically reiterates the fluid beauty of Fritz's walk with Christine in *Liebelei*, although that sequence was shot with a relatively static camera. *Letter*'s couple's stilted (or, in Lisa's case, evasive) conversation leads to a discussion of the joys of music in Linz, not to be overshadowed, the lieutenant insists, by Vienna's musical scene, to which Lisa is obviously attached. Leopold proudly and, of course, modestly notes that he himself played "second trumpet" as a cadet. Little does he know that he is still doing so.

Not noticing the irony of the mise-en-scène, and upon seeing how meekly Lisa speaks to the young man, the happy mother turns toward the camera, exclaiming to her husband that "there is nothing wrong with the girl if she only meets the right people!" And Lisa does, temporarily, try to placate the mother by taking on the "feminine masquerade" and simulating passivity. Studlar puts it even more strongly: "She self-consciously orchestrates her development into what might appear to be culturally correct, passive femininity—but the film reveals that what she achieves is only a masquerade" (p. 47). Lisa's "choice" of marital partner is overdetermined by the nature of her mother's desire and interdictions. Thus, Leopold is a military man who looks as though he should be a dummy in the sartorial establishment of the military tailor, Lisa's stepfather.

The "engagement" scene that next takes place between them is one of Ophuls' most hilarious comic bits, although Lisa's voice-over studiously avoids acknowledging the irony of her words. A dissolve takes us to the bandleader raising his baton ("Herrup, hup, hup") in the middle of the Corso. A crane shot picks out Lisa and Leopold as they come round the bandstand. Stiffly holding Lisa on his arm, the helmeted and plumed lieutenant (looking very ostrichlike) leads her, in a rhythmic, semicircular traveling shot, past her rejoicing parents to a bench on the Corso. The setting recalls the courtship scene in *Sarajevo*, except that the woman is now seated next to the "statue" rather than below it. The couple's rhythmic movement to the (relatively) melodious waltz hints of a certain ease of motion available to Lisa if she will dance to her parents' conventional music. But as the pair sits on the bench, the static and banal nature of their potential relationship becomes only too obvious, as they are framed frontally and then in an ordinary shot–reverse shot sequence. Lisa interrupts Leopold's embarrassing description of his prospects with an awkward lie that visibly throws the lieutenant for a loop (and, of course, links her to Ophuls' other lying heroines): "You mean you're engaged to be married and your parents don't even know it? Ohhhhhh . . ." Lisa's declaration places her beyond the pale of Leopold's social sensibility. As the music winds down, he again offers Lisa his arm. Applause for the band rains ironically down upon them as they scurry back to the parents' table, walking in time to a march.[58] They indicate, in pantomime, that their break is decisive. The camera tracks in on Lisa as she tells her frantic parents that she had only told "the truth"—that she wasn't "free." Lisa's "poor parents" have lost social status, but Lisa's unfreedom has bought her the larger liberty to return to Vienna. A dissolve once more takes us back to the frame narrative, as Stefan pores over the mesmerizing document.

For Joan Riviere, masquerading in a feminine guise serves to placate the father, showing him the girl's (woman's) "'love' and guiltlessness toward him." The "crimes" the girl has committed are numerous: she wishes to take the place of both the mother and the father and must attempt to disguise this fact.

Both parents are rivals in this [oral-biting sadistic] stage, both possess desired objects; the sadism is directed against both and the revenge of both is feared. But, as always with girls, the mother is the more hated, and consequently the more feared. She will execute the punishment that fits the crime—destroy the girl's body, her beauty, her capacity for having children, mutilate her, devour her, torture her and kill her. In this appalling predicament the girl's only safety lies in placating the mother and atoning for her crime. She must retire from rivalry with the mother, and if she can, endeavor to restore to her what she has stolen. As we know, she identifies herself with the father; and then she uses the masculinity she thus obtains by *putting it at the service of the mother*. She becomes the father, and takes his place; so she can "restore" him to the mother.[59]

One hopes that the fear of the mother reflected in this passage is in part Riviere's denial of the girl's love of and desire for the mother. But, as Lynda Zwinger puts it:

Mother is a problem. She's been figured, refigured, configured, disfigured as (and the following list is partial, incomplete, fragmentary—the usual feminine mess): who we must think back through; who we want to/don't want to/can't/won't be; who is locked up in the attic; who seduces *every*body—really, who is or is not the object, an object, our object; who has or has not, is or is not the Phallus.[60]

In her flight from Linz, Lisa attempts to "abject" the mother in herself, to expel herself from the maternal body—only, of course, to find herself replicating her mother and finding, in Stefan's "unknown goddess," a mother larger and more powerful than any of flesh and blood. "The most properly metonymic feature of this restoration (in Klein's sense of the reconstitution of the good object, the maternal body) manifests itself in the relentless pursuit of perfection . . . to most correctly render the work whose musical quality ends in losing itself to the virtuosity of a transcendent etude."[61] Mother and music are "partial objects" (Lacan's *objet petit a*), representing the "elusive plenitude" of the pre-Oedipal, a site of perfection clearly sought by Lisa. We will see this mother—this maternal body—again. Returning to Riviere's remarks, Lisa's way of "taking the place" of the father is, in any event, peculiar. The initial attempt to placate the parent figures by taking on a suitor is abandoned, as Lisa is tuned to a more primordial (and potentially more rivalrous) desire. Her attempt to restore the father can only take place as a return to the scene of the crime of the originary parental abandonment ("Vienna, about 1900," as the first shot of the film informs us).[62] So, just as the father abandoned his wife (by dying?), Lisa will abandon her mother. She shakes herself free of the familial impediments and goes back to Vienna. Again a dissolve to Stefan shows him absorbing these facts, as the camera tracks in for a closer look at his painful enthrallment.

A joke that I have often made (and which my students have never thought funny) is that if Lisa were really masochistic, she would have stayed with the lieutenant in Linz and listened to the oompah band every Sunday. However, as Studlar (p. 40) has observed, the masochist pays in advance for his or her pleasure through active suffering.[63] By going to Linz, Lisa is certainly paying in advance for the pleasure she intends to take in Stefan's music and presence. In that sense, this sequence constitutes a necessary martyrdom if Lisa is to get what she wants. In "Die masochistische Lust am Verkennen," Gertrud Koch points out that this scene makes a travesty of Lisa's ideal love object by means of its ironic "wedding march," which sets up a systematic contrast between "crude" and "fine" music found in the rest of the film (p. 71). Again, Lisa's "masochism" is characterized by what Studlar calls her "search for submission"—*to the right object* (p. 40). In the scenes involving "bad" music, Lisa's desire is certainly being ironized by the film's process of enunciation, but one senses that Lisa partly *shares* this ironic attitude, characteristic, as we have seen, of the masochist as Deleuze describes "him." The banal music of her parents' milieu is a crucial, if ironic component of Lisa's masochistic project, as well as a chilling reminder of what she would face if she were unable to transcend that milieu. We shall return to the issue of masochism in another context below.

Pursuit and Deflection

A very significant change shortly takes place in Lisa Berndle.

> (VOICE-OVER): Madame Spitzer's is where I found work. It was the kind of establishment where one learns many things.

As she speaks these words, the camera pans from a lovely young woman in a dressing room framed by curtains to Lisa as she stands before a full-length mirror.[64] The shot comes hard on the heels from that of Stefan's face, giving the effect of a point-of-view shot. Lisa is not admiring herself but is preoccupied with struggling into one of the many off-the-shoulder gowns that come to connote her "womanliness" during the rest of the film.[65] She, too, is framed by curtains, which lend a doubly theatrical feeling to the moment. At Madame Spitzer's, Lisa takes on the kind of feminine garb and behavior that will attract the male gaze in no uncertain terms—although several scenes highlight her resistance to this role. She parades, out of necessity, in the furbelows of the female, but she will not succumb to the final meaning of such a display. When, for example, young soldiers peer in admiringly as she (on her hands and knees, in a position of mock submission) arranges a dress in the window, Lisa jerks the curtains shut—a gesture that indicates Lisa's control of male vision through glass and acknowledges the theatrical nature of the modeling job as it closes it off.[66] (She thus stands in contrast to her ancestral Viennese shopgirl, the exhibitionistic Mizzi of *Liebelei*, though the latter also makes use of disguise.) In the next scene, one of a series of "typical" scenes of Lisa's life in Vienna, separated by dissolves, an older soldier crosses the room and speaks to Madame Spitzer, sotto voce, while holding on to the sword that hangs at his side:

> THE OLD OFFICER: Very charming, very charming indeed. Do you think . . . ?
>
> MME SPITZER: [*Smiling wryly*] She's not like that. I don't understand the girl. Every evening as soon as the shutters are closed, off she goes—straight home.
>
> OFFICER: Really?!

Of course, as Lisa now tells us, she does not go home every night—at least, not in the way Madame Spitzer means it:

(VOICE-OVER): I went not home but to the only place that had ever seemed home to me. Night after night I returned to the same spot, but you never noticed me . . . until one evening . . .

On that snowy evening—reminiscent, once more, of *Liebelei*'s courtship scenes—we watch Lisa take her seemingly habitual position on Stefan's street corner. She stands, in long shot, before a niche where the Virgin and Child are enshrined.[67] As she patiently paces back and forth, looking up at his window, Stefan finally does appear at the door of his building. (Lisa "finally awakens Stefan's desire through sheer repetition," notes Studlar, p. 48.) The mobile camera frames his leisurely walk to a waiting carriage. He pauses to pay a group of street singers, then turns toward Lisa, whom we see in a striking long shot established as his point of view.[68] The moment is marked in time, unlike the "typical" scenes depicted just before. He—and we—begin to walk toward Lisa, melodramatic (and bogus) recognition dawning in his eyes and unbelieving rapture in hers. He speaks:

STEFAN: I've seen you here before . . . a few nights ago. Oh, you live near here.

LISA: [*Whispering, in response*] No.

As they walk together, Stefan attempts to introduce himself, but she silences him, saying, "I know who you are." Lisa does not offer to introduce herself. We can see here the peculiar folding of one genre into another operated by Lisa: Although this scene ostensibly takes his point of view, Stefan is also the male object of feminine investigation, according to the conventions of female-oriented Gothic melodrama.[69] And yet, Lisa instates herself as enigma, as in the *film noir* (many of which use this type of flashback structure):

Film noir . . . constitutes itself as a detour, a bending of the hermeneutic code from the questions connected with a crime to the difficulty posed by the woman as enigma (or crime). The fact that the *femme fatale* in *film noir* is characterized as unknowable (and this is the lure of her attraction) has frequently been noted.[70]

According to V. F. Perkins, Lisa actively denies Stefan the opportunity to come to know and love her by avoiding, at significant moments, acknowledgment of their past together.[71] We have, however, already seen that Lisa's actions, her keeping herself at a distance from the object of her affection, may be necessary to the fulfillment of her desire, even, perhaps, to her psychological survival. When Lisa tells Stefan, later in the film (he is bidding her farewell as he leaves for a two-week concert stay in Milan) that he "likes mystery," she is doing more than stating a whimsically arrived-at truth. Stefan's inquiry marks his first and only real attempt to learn more about Lisa, and to break through her silence with regard to the past. He likes mystery, or—to paraphrase Cavell—the pianist is afraid of what he might find out, of what he will claim at the end of the film to have found out about women. Lisa's need for mystery, seemingly designed according to the other's desire, is also a manifestation of the paranoid aggression she knows to be implicit to the attitude that Stefan bears toward her as a woman and an "other," as the reflected image of his own, possibly repressed homosexual desire.[72] And yet she knows that it is only by manipulating that image that she can draw Stefan to her. As a consequence of this play of images, Lisa, quite correctly, fears destruction. This strategic silence is more than a defensive measure: through it she will manage to gain access to the aural pleasure and visual control she craves, and for which she is more than willing to suffer. Indeed, several writers, including Kinnan, Studlar, and Koch, see the suffering itself as crucial to Lisa's happiness.

Although its most poignant moments of desire may be played out on the soundtrack, *Letter*'s "plot" (in the Bordwellian sense) is folded in at least three visual moments. I am thinking of: the initial "look" that shames and excites Lisa—inciting instantaneous love of Stefan; of Lisa's sighting of Stefan during the opera sequence, when the "course of her life" is changed; and of this moment of meeting, when Stefan "sees" the mature Lisa for the first time. Stefan joins his fate with Lisa's in an utterly haphazard fashion. "I almost never get to the place I set out for," is his offhand remark to Lisa as they begin their evening together. In her discussion of the film's "chronotopes" ("spatio-temporal configurations" that Bakhtin calls "the organizing centers for the fundamental narrative events in the novel"), Wexman describes the *street* as Stefan's reigning chronotope. "Stefan exists in an atmosphere of random temporality," she notes, and the street spatializes this temporality. It is "a multidirectional space where time is governed by chance."[73] Perhaps

Lisa realizes subliminally that the street has such meaning for Stefan.

The next scene positions Fritz (the waiter in Brand's local café) as both Brand's social *entremetteur*—keeping his rendezvous with women straight, for a price—and as another locus of observing consciousness in the film. Lisa watches from the doorway while Stefan bargains for Fritz's cooperation, and maneuvers his way around an overly earnest young composer. Fritz (William Trenk) "congratulates" Stefan on his conquest, as Madame Spitzer will later congratulate Lisa on her date with Stefan. Again we can observe a peculiar emphasis on servant-figures in Ophuls' cinema: Fritz echoes John's devotion in a disturbing mirror, in that the waiter accepts gratuities directly from Stefan's hand. Both will, however, be "abandoned" by Stefan. Lisa discovers, in the last scenes of the film, that Stefan is "no longer a customer" of Fritz's café, and John is left standing with bowed head when Stefan goes to fight the duel.

A dissolve takes us to a frontally shot booth in a luxurious, even stuffy restaurant. A cooperative waiter draws the curtains around the pair, emphasizing the stagelike quality of the scene—and anticipating the "private room" where the "girl" loses her (already lost) virtue in *La Ronde* (1950). Stefan places a lobster bib on Lisa, in the first of a number of mutually infantilizing gestures the couple make toward one another. He then questions Lisa about when they can see one another again. His way of phrasing the question repeats the lovers' collapsing of time found explicitly in *Liebelei, Madame de . . .*, and *La Ronde*. Time is presented as cyclical, as the days of the week form a cycle—and thus potentially either comforting or entrapping,[74] responding to Lisa's deepest desires and to her deepest fears. Lobster, it seems, will be served again in a week, but this is too long for Stefan to wait. There is pheasant on Monday, but will she be free? "I have no engagements." "Neither have I . . . so tomorrow it's—Wienerschnitzel!" The aristocratic setting of the scene is deflated by this call to immediate gratification of the desire for love, taken along with a food that, after pheasant and lobster, has a bourgeois—or at least *local*—ring to it. This ironic gesture certainly appears to undermine the glamour that Lisa seems, though ambiguously, to seek. But once again, is it not possible that the relatively humble food figures in this scene as another kind of repetition, a reminder of Lisa's middle-class upbringing? According to the logic of desire set forth in the film, this past must in some sense be what she wishes to repeat, to approximate, peculiar as that may seem in light of her semiaristocratic aspirations. Stefan has become, for a moment, the (pre-Oedipal?) father who promised the exotic (in the "imaginary voyages" they take together, as the film later demonstrates), but who delivered that which was immediately at hand.

If we examine in detail the commonest of these imaginative romances, the replacement of both parents or of the father alone by grander people, we find that these new and aristocratic parents are equipped with attributes that are derived entirely from real recollections of the actual and humble ones; so that in fact the child is not getting rid of his father but exalting him.[75]

The waiter interrupts: would it be possible for Brand to autograph the program from the afternoon's concert for the countess (who has just recognized him)? The program, whose cover is adorned with a large photograph of the pianist, is presented and signed. Brand has gone from being depicted with his instrument, both the symbol of and the "prop" for his authority as a star, to being shown as an idol in his own right, in a close-up framing only his face. His signing of the program, to be echoed in the final scene of the film, is a signature of the contract that delivers his being over to the public, sealing the doom peculiar to such idols in Ophuls' cinema. He is beginning, as Gertrud Koch says, to "abandon the ground of her aural responsiveness" (p. 68)—and to be silenced, himself, while Lisa finds her voice. The signature is, of course, what Lisa will never give.[76] The institution in which she dies, a Catholic convent, will provide her death with a heading (a cross, a note from a nun, that nun's signature), just as Madame de . . . will be provided with, subsumed by a religious monument at the end of that film. Thus, both woman and man are subject to an institutional (military, religious) *fixing* that can function either as phallic immobility or as a site of resistance to the structures of patriarchy.

The dinner scene continues as follows:

> LISA: [*Insistently*] Please talk about yourself. [This line never fails to provoke laughter.]
>
> STEFAN: I believe you really want to hear about me. Why? Oh never mind why. . . . The truth is I've had a rather easy time of it. People accepted my music very quickly. [*Lisa is shown in a full-face medium close-up, listening to Stefan, who continues. She looks up at his hair, an encompassing look that seems to signal real (maternal) love.*] Perhaps *too* quickly. Sometimes it's easier to please others than to please oneself. [*Cut to medium close-up*

of Stefan] You know, you don't talk very much. [*Cut to medium close-up of Lisa, etc. with more frontal views of her face than his*]

LISA: Well, I can't say it very well, but sometimes I felt when you were playing that you haven't quite found what you were looking for.

STEFAN: How long have you been hiding in my piano? Never mind explaining. I'll just assume you're a sorceress and that you can make yourself very tiny. It might be a good thing to have a sorceress for a friend. Who knows? You may be able to help me someday.

This passage is extremely suggestive, in its way of positioning Lisa as the mute spectator of Stefan's "performance," while, visually speaking, the camera privileges her lovely and softly lit face. This is particularly important if the film is encouraging us to see Stefan as the implied spectator of the vision excited by the words of the letter. Lisa's craving to hear about Stefan's life is so violent that the dramatic "realism" of the scene is put into jeopardy: her behavior is odd even by the standards of melodrama. Stefan's search for a reflection of himself has been hollow. He is appalled by comparisons of his talents to those of the young Mozart. These comparisons were made a few years before by a journalist and are, significantly, *quoted* by Lisa from a newspaper article (implicating her in the public response to Stefan's performances). The countess, whose comments are transmitted by the waiter, also draws the parallel between Brand and the eighteenth-century composer. "I *was* very young. There was that much resemblance." Like every lover, or like every artist, Stefan seems to wish to be known for "himself." At another level, he is rejecting the mimetic lure that faces him as performer—the resemblance to another, institutionalized performer.

According to René Girard, the violent potential of mimesis is responsible for the cult of originality conceived with the Romantics and still clinging to our conception of the artistic genius.[77] Lisa seems to want to know the "real" Stefan, and we are given to believe that her observations denote deep insight into his character: she can distinguish the "authentic" from the "artificial" in his character. At least, Stefan seems to credit Lisa with such insight, while to the spectator, these remarks may seem somewhat stereotyped ("You haven't found yourself"). Stereotyped language of this sort deflates the dichotomy between the "real" Stefan and the "false" one, the well-known performer and the private genius. But like the difference between the authentic and the inauthentic parents (or the real and false Charles in *The Exile*), this dichotomy is a superficial one, undermined at various points in the film. Further, the pianist's happiness at Lisa's interest in him disguises the aggressive component implicit to her obsessive watching, her (as Deleuze puts it) "masochistic waiting" for recognition, which paradoxically serves to deflect his grasp on her image-as-woman. Lisa's making herself "very tiny" is, of course, reminiscent of her having listened to the musician as a small girl, but it is also the benign rendition of her fantasy of mastery, whose truth, in the film, comes in the form of the real aggression of Stefan's sneering public, once "too easily" pleased. The tiny, fetal girl, overwhelmed with music, inside the piano-body of her maternal lover, caressed by the strings' vibrations—this, too, is one of the powerful resonances invoked by Stefan's description.

We have observed that Rose characterizes the "paranoiac" film system as setting up certain object relations. According to that view, the cinematic object of vision, being endowed through projection with a kind of pseudosubjectivity (point of view), creates the "imaginary" dyad and the possibility of an aggressive reversal. When Lisa becomes a *conscious* representative of the spectator who takes such proximity to the performer, Stefan is endangered, as she would be endangered by any sign of unified subjectivity on his part (if he were really to recognize her, for example). Stefan is particularly at risk here since, as a woman, Lisa is more "correctly" the object of his vision, a vision made problematic by his never actually recognizing her, leading to her "pent-up" subjectivity raining down upon him with such force at the end of the film. The kind of risk Stefan is running as a public figure is shortly reiterated. but there first occurs another instance of the sexual (gender) confusion that is being brought forth emphatically by the film. Stefan and Lisa ride in an open carriage:

LISA: How *could* I help you?

STEFAN: So that's what you've been thinking about. You're a very strange girl. Don't you have any problems?

LISA: Not important ones.

She leans over to tuck his scarf into his coat. "It's a long time since anyone did that for me," he says tenderly, gazing reflectively before him. Stefan seems to be remembering the ministrations of a maternal figure, a reading of his response reinforced by Lisa's literal mothering of little

Stefan later in the film (nine months later in the diegesis—though the film fudges the gestation period). On Brand's order, the carriage stops at a flower stall, where he buys a white rose from a woman who, oddly, is wearing a broad-brimmed hat exactly like his own, except that hers is tied with a scarf. Lisa says that the white rose will henceforth be "her" flower. When, at the end of the film, she enacts the reverse performance of this scene by turning the tables on Stefan's courtship and bringing him a bouquet of white roses, the man from whom she buys the flowers is wearing a modified top hat of the same kind as her own. This play of hats, a somewhat mundane symbol for the genitals (if I may be allowed a universalizing gesture), does not seem to represent a systematic assigning of Lisa or Stefan to either the active (courting) or the passive (being courted) sexual role, but does seem to suggest that men and women (or men and men, women and women) may take either position, or both of them, at various moments of the narrative. It is also suggestive of the doubling that takes place between men and women in the film, as in both cases it is a man and a woman, similarly dressed, who confront one another.[78]

Another reversal in the complex situating of adulthood and childhood takes place in a scene that occurs shortly thereafter. Standing in front of a candy shop in the Prater (the Viennese fairground where this entire sequence takes place), Lisa takes a candied apple. Stefan contemplates her: "Now I see you as a little girl." She smiles in response, "You do?" The fact that Stefan actually saw Lisa as a girl is something of a red herring in this context, if we are to gather from his comment that it is only Lisa who approaches the situation from the perspective of a child. The emphasis should be placed, rather, upon the continual recurrence of the child-adult pair. Although it is Lisa who positions herself as a child in the scenes at the Prater, it must be remembered that this is actually "Stefan's" place. He has been to the fair in the past, even frequents it. As they approach the park, we hear the sound of a merry-go-round in the distance.

LISA: Do you think it will all be closed?

STEFAN: I never come here in the season. It's more pleasant in the winter. I don't know why.

LISA: It's perhaps because you imagine how it will be in the spring. If it is spring, there's nothing to imagine, nothing to hope for.

STEFAN: Is there anything about me you don't know?

LISA: A few things. For instance [*They pause in front of a plate-glass window where models of a life-sized "Napoleon" figure, the musician Schubert,[79] and a man in a suit of armor are displayed*], I don't know if perhaps one day they'll make a wax figure of you and put you in there because you'll be so famous.

STEFAN: Well, if they do, will you pay your penny to come in and see me?

LISA: If you'll come alive.

This astonishing exchange marks the hypostatization, the creation as a real entity, of Lisa's ardor for Stefan as a public persona. "They" will make a figure of Stefan that Lisa will come to admire. What are we to make of her visit to the wax museum being contingent upon his "coming alive"? Is this an expression of a humanizing urge where, as in the Pygmalion myth, the perverse desire for a literal object of one's own making would be normalized by this object taking on the "otherness" of a living being?[80] Or does it have the resonance of a horror film scenario? Both Lisa and Stefan love "statues," figures displayed for the public—at a price, usually—but which they would like to worship in private. This is the case when Lisa secretly listens to Stefan play only for her, as it is when Stefan gazes at his statue of the "unknown goddess," which he has taken from its public context and adores as a household deity. Lisa perverts the system of desire as defined by the psychic structures of the patriarchal culture in which she exists. In a society in which "man takes his sexual pleasure in woman principally on the Imaginary slope, while she finds hers in him on the Symbolic plane,"[81] Lisa imitates her beloved in that she, too, attempts to take pleasure in him "on the Imaginary slope"—as an image (behind glass) and as a manifestation of her aural drive. In doing so, can she "reverse" the roles of man and woman? Would she even want to? Insofar as the "imaginary" involves the maternal imago, Lisa cannot really "use" the man's image in the same way that he can use hers. And it has been said many times that pure reversal would, in any case, retain the same kind of sexual dichotomy. Lisa seems instead to be trying to play out all sides of the psychic configuration, to act out all roles, to incorporate difference within her own person, to appropriate the image when she can, and to supplement or transcend that image through sound—to have Stefan stand in as her white knight, her warrior, her lullaby-maker, the cardboard sadist to her "performative" masochism (Studlar). Whether or not she is successful, she has managed to displace the terms of the intersubjective relations between the sexes as they are mediated by the image. But in doing so she risks bringing down upon her own head the violence implicit in those relations—just as Valentino, as discussed by Miriam Hansen, produced a kind of generative violence at his death—a violence fed by the complex gender-bending he accomplished in his films.[82]

Public Figures and Private Journeys

In the "woman's film," we often see a coming-to-terms with feminine desire for the masculine public figure—Leonora's (Barbara Bel Geddes) infatuation with Smith Ohlrig (Robert Ryan) in *Caught* (1949) springs to mind as an Ophulsian instance of this phenomenon. However, the female protagonist, who reflects the middle-class ethos of the spectators, is ultimately geared to the private sphere.[83] There is always a tension, in this type of film, between the public and the private. As has been argued above, this tension is expressed in *Letter* in terms of the family romance: a rejection of the middle-class origins as linked to the child's first disappointment in the parent figures. We have seen how, in the earliest months of a child's life, he idealizes the parents, whom he does not see as restricted by class level or financial limitations. In Ophuls' films the exaltation of the love object is invariably mixed with the double-edged attributes of the star, attributes that may destroy the supposedly all-powerful being and that stand in opposition to the "private" virtues of the middle class. Lisa would also have a pecuniary relationship to the statue (paying her penny), just as in *Lola Montès* the men pay a dollar to kiss the dancer's hand. In the Harlequin Romance series, geared primarily to feminine consumption, the female protagonist constantly struggles against the public aspect of the (almost always) powerful and famous man. Of course, the protagonist's desire is incited by these very attributes: thus the "I hate you, I want you" syndrome (first cousin of the "She really wants to be raped" syndrome) is born. This configuration echoes the traditional melodramatic formula in which the lower-class woman falls in love with or is (so to speak) otherwise victimized by an aristocrat. The class conflict reflected in these earlier melodramatic forms, which demanded that the aristocrat be on some level truly an evil character, has shifted, in the later "woman's films," to emphasize the woman's fascination with a man from a more "glamorous" class background than her own, reiterating, in other words, the terms of the family romance as Freud describes it. *Pretty Woman* (1990) meets *Stella Dallas* (1925/1937)/*Stella* (1990) in the boudoir. The denouement of some traditional melodramas and of many later women's films involves the hero's recognition of the superiority of middle-class values, or of his acknowledgment of his own suppressed class background, which may be less exalted than it seems. We know that this humbling of the hero may take a more extreme form than the mere revelation of certain middle-class values he may entertain. The nostalgia for the nonspecular world of the petit-bourgeoisie, so strongly put forth in *Liebelei* and *De Mayerling à Sarajevo*, are of little avail in *Letter*, although it is certainly evident in those moments when Stefan seems to share Lisa's simplicity. Such moments may represent the (ironic) celebration of bourgeois values less than they comprise a transition point for the complete abasement of Lisa's lover.

In women's films, the moment of the hero's acknowledgment of his humbler impulses often takes the form of a rejection of public life. Such a rejection is, however, never completely possible in Ophuls' cinema. Similarly, in von Sternberg's Dietrich films, the public character of the Dietrich persona (who stands in as both hero and heroine of the film) must always subtend her desire for the simple virtues of home. Dietrich, as the phallic/oral woman par excellence, ultimately draws power from her status as a public figure—although, in *Blonde Venus* (1932) and elsewhere, she must suffer to maintain the contradictory poles of her power, the mother and the star, conflating them in the figure of the glittering mother at the end of the film.[84] At the other pole of this dialectic, Stefan the public figure is drained of life until he stands as silently as a wax figure in the window of a museum, while the "private" Stefan is redeemed by his mannequinlike attendance at the duel, or perhaps merely released from his fixation on the "image of woman" and finally able to join the company of men.

Immediately following the scene where Lisa takes candy from the taffy-maker, the film dissolves to a painted backdrop depicting an imaginary view of Venice. The camera pulls back to show Lisa and Stefan in a curtained "railway carriage." It is no wonder that this is the most often-cited Ophulsian commentary on cinematic illusion, for it is very cleverly contrived. Alan Williams writes that the scene is shot exactly as if it were a *real* train sequence in a film, using the same camera angles that are used in filming *Letter*'s diegetically real train journeys.[85] Once again we are struck by the intensity of the desire for myth at work in this film, the very willingness to suspend disbelief, here manifest in this intercalation of codified cinematic "reality" with the obviously illusory.[86] The young man and woman face one another in the car:

LISA: When my father was living we traveled a lot. We went nearly everywhere.

STEFAN: I didn't know you'd traveled so much. Perhaps we've been to some of the same places.

LISA: No, I don't think so.

STEFAN: Where did you go?

LISA: Lots of places. For instance, there was Rio. Beautiful, exotic Rio . . . [*She continues an obviously memorized description of the city*].

As the Venice scroll ends, Stefan goes out to select another country. This is a mom-and-pop operation, with the elderly woman taking the money and her husband providing the power to pedal the images past the booth by means of a modified bicycle.[87] Lisa chooses Switzerland as the next country to "visit," and the couple continues the conversation:

STEFAN: So you were looking down at the flying fish. Then what? Aren't you going to finish the trip?

LISA: Well, there weren't any trips. Do you mind? My father had a friend in a travel bureau. He was an assistant superintendent of the municipal water works. And he used to bring folders home with him. Oh, we had stacks of them. And in the evening he put on his traveling coat. That's what he called it. Of course, I was very young. And he said, where shall we go this evening? And I'd say "Vera Cruz," because it's a beautiful name. And he'd say, "Hmmm, it's summer there. You don't want to roast like a coffee bean, do you?"

STEFAN: So you never did get there.

LISA: No, it was just like our trip to the land of the midnight sun.

STEFAN: What stopped you this time?

LISA: The weather. I thought of India, but then father remembered it was the rainy season.

STEFAN: Your father was an expert on climates.

LISA: My mother used to say that he knew what the weather was everywhere except home. What mountain is that?

STEFAN: That's the Matterhorn.

LISA: Have you climbed it?

STEFAN: Um hum . . .

LISA: Tell me, when you climb up a mountain, what then?

STEFAN: Well, you come down again. [*He moves across to sit beside Lisa*] Tell me more about your father.

LISA: Well, he finally did go away. He had the nicest eyes.

STEFAN: I can see them.

This train sequence has a privileged position in the film. Not only will it later serve as a kind of unconscious primal scene for Stefan Jr.,[88] who will wonder aloud about how "nice" Switzerland must be, but it also sums up the elements of Lisa's wish to *be* her father, to take his place by seeing through his eyes, to *have* him (in the form of her traveling companion, Stefan), and, finally, to *surpass* the father (Stefan really has climbed the Matterhorn). The "stacks" of travel brochures might, by the way, be thought of in relation to the piles of sheet music that Lisa finds and knocks over in Stefan's apartment—an image that brings Stefan into closer connection with Lisa's departed father.

Just as a stagy "reality" (the shooting of the scene according to the standard for railway sequences in films) is contrasted with the fakery of the scenery rolling by, Stefan's "real" relationship with these places is curiously contrasted with his indulgence of the fictional quality of Lisa's traveling fantasy. As he is playing the part of the cultivated gentleman (this is a role, whether he really is one or not), Stefan *must* have performed the requisite gentlemanly mountain climbing. "Aren't you going to finish the trip?" he asks. He does not ask her to finish her *narration* of the trip. This scene is thus a *mise-en-abyme* of the film itself, in which Lisa is telling a more-or-less true story (the letter) to Stefan. In this case, however, they are watching the images unfurl together. It is a moment of parity, then, in visual terms. As in *Madame de . . .*, the screenwriters have taken a nameless character (one who had only an initial, "R.," in the novella) and have this time given *him* the author's first name. Stefan's privileged position as a writer (in the novella) is changed to the more vulnerable, the more exposed one of a concert pianist, who is displayed before us for all to see. And yet, even though this fact seems to make possible the "visual parity" noted between Lisa and Stefan in this scene, he still manages to maintain the upper hand. When Lisa casually remarks that her father's eyes were nice, Stefan will remind her of her status as object of his gaze, subsuming her visual power under the rubric of the to-be-looked-at: "I can see them," he says. As in their first meeting, she drops her eyes modestly.

Mom and Pop and Class Conflict

As noted above, the woman's film of the 1940s tends to shift the focus of what were class conflicts into the arena of the family romance, thus depoliticizing them in a *traditional* economic sense, but bringing in the psychic and political economies of the nuclear family so crucial to middle-class women. Nevertheless, Williams points to a continual intrusion, in this film, of questions of social class. His comments on the *invisibility* of the lower classes to the middle-class Lisa helps us to articulate the terms of the family romance as set forth in the carnival train-ride sequence. As a more or less middle-class woman, Lisa does not rely on the services of domestic help for ironing her clothing and other minor tasks and tends to ignore the presence of servants when they do perform functions for her. Lisa is "more or less" a member of the middle class in that a middle-class woman of her period would probably have at least one servant. (As Williams puts it, she stands *between* Stefan and the servant class.)[89] She is, in this way, more like the middle-class woman of a later period (say, the United States of the 1940s). When she is a model, Lisa approaches working-class status in that she must sell her labor as a shopgirl, albeit a rather special one. Williams connects this ignoring of the serving class to the generally "strong element of self-delusion in Lisa's 'character.'"[90] Although they are invisible to Lisa, the workers in *Letter* are quite visible to the spectator of the film. In this carnival train-ride sequence, the old couple is dealt with only by the more "aristocratic" Stefan, who ostentatiously overtips all the serving people with whom he comes into contact. This contrasts, as noted, with the apparent stinginess of Lisa's stepfather, who is shown to give very small tips to porters at the train station. Williams argues that this foregrounding of the function of servants undermines the conventions of the genre of the woman's film, and analyzes "middle-classness . . . a pervasive and uninterrogated value in all women's pictures."[91] I believe I have amply demonstrated that, on the contrary, "middle-classness" is a value that is *constantly* interrogated in these films (Ophuls' "women's pictures"), although the terms of the debate are often veiled. And certainly Ophuls is not merely an *exception* in this generic self-reflexivity.

Williams has good reason to say that Ophuls ironizes middle-class values, perhaps at Lisa's expense, in this film. But this interrogation is itself being carried out from a bourgeois perspective. It is precisely in the collapsing of class conflicts into the bourgeois family romance that middle-class concerns remain prevalent in the film. Thus, the working-class characters of the film may be more important for the way they reflect the concerns of the bourgeois characters than as a potentially revolutionary group, although it is the fear of that potential that gives the working class its uncanny appeal in films such as this one.

It would be an exaggeration to read the kind of class antagonism into this film that exists in a purer melodrama—for example, one that is set in the same place (the Prater, in Vienna) and time (around 1900–1915): Erich von Stroheim's *Merry-Go-Round* (1923). In that film, an aristocrat falls in love with a young woman whose job it is to turn the handle for the eponymous carousel. Although he is presented with some sympathy in the larger framework of the narrative (in the vein of 1928's *The Wedding March*), the young man is considered a dyed-in-the-wool villain by the girl's family. The hero, a count, pretends to be a mere necktie salesman in order to woo the girl. When the girl's father finds that the count has lied about his origins, he despises the man and never forgives his lie. The fascination with aristocratic life is a force present in the film, but the irreconcilability of the class interests of aristocrat and working class is never compromised. Still, both films represent something of a backlash against pure melodrama, in that they alleviate the working class and petit-bourgeois mistrust of the upper echelons of society, while indulging erotic curiosity and sympathy for the aristocrats (compare John Ford's *The Grapes of Wrath* [1940]). The class lines are slightly blurred in *Letter*, as opposed to those in von Stroheim's film. The old folks in *Letter* are not divorced from the means of production but are, like Lisa, petit-bourgeois who do their own work instead of relying on the services of others. Lisa's stepfather is a shopowner himself, while her father worked as a bureaucrat (for the "municipal water works"). In *Letter* Stefan is linked by his behavior to the aristocracy, but as a performer his position is doubly parasitical—he is supported by a class that is itself often considered parasitical. Interestingly, Stefan seems somewhat more villainous than is von Stroheim's tragic hero, whose tragedy is dictated by the larger-than-life force of class prejudice. Stefan is not "misunderstood" but is understood only too well—and the woman who woos *him* uses her "passivity" as a weapon not so much in the class struggle as in the battle between the sexes. The carousel, like the "imaginary train ride," rhythmically repeats its circuit of pleasurable illusion as long as the money lasts. (Williams has pointed out that the hurdy-gurdy in the background at the Prater is, in fact, playing "Carnival of Venice.")[92] When the old woman at the ticket office tells Stefan, "We have no more countries left," he replies, "Then we'll begin all over again." The fantasy is the product of a group effort in *Letter*—with Lisa ultimately "directing" the action, choosing which country to see. Of course, her control is only partial—the destinations she suggests are unattainable (neither her father nor Stefan can take her where she wants to go). The "Oedipal" male, Lisa's stepfather and her husband, can *really* take her to Linz or home to a fairy-tale existence, but they don't even know about the distant places she desires. As in *La Ronde*, the revolving illusion is obviously engineered, and therefore "ironic." In von Stroheim's *Merry-Go-Round*, the girl, like the old couple in *Letter*, is, in a sense, *creating* the illusion, providing the entertainment. Von Stroheim's heroine is, however, not enlightened by her position as the spinner of her own fantasy, is (along with her parents) a victim of its machinery—whose owner is the real villain of the film.

The old couple in *Letter*, which is certainly not depicted as *abused* (as are the young woman and her parents in von Stroheim's film), might be seen in this context as representatives of the once censuring petit-bourgeois parents, here abased and put to work *for the benefit* of Lisa's desire. To look at the film's "repetitions" from another angle, the old couple can be seen as an ironic, older version of the young people—already relying on images of their past as the source of erotic pleasure. The old man and woman may be carrying the burden of their own past, constructing a cinema of memories that serves to bind them together. Now the possibility of communicating their differences has boiled down to a division of labor that keeps the machinery of their marital union in motion. In Ophuls' films the most sympathetic characters are those who (as we saw in the analysis of *Madame de . . .*) are half aware of their own role in creating the illusions of love, but transcend that knowledge through belief in the spectacle—machinery and all.

Now You See Me . . .

Lisa's softly dropped comment about losing her father is quite ambiguous, and importantly so. "Well, he finally did go away. He had the nicest eyes." Apparently Lisa means to say that he died ("when my father was alive . . ."), but her sentence emphasizes his having . . . disappeared. Appearance and disappearance work actively to develop the notions of loss, memory, and the image in *Letter from an Unknown Woman*. We recall, for example, that Lisa's apartment has literally been emptied of its contents when she revisits it, just as Louise de . . . returns to an empty suite of rooms at the end of *Madame de . . . .* Although it is Lisa who has decided to leave her parents, there is a note of anguish (completely displaced, as before, from the parent figures onto Stefan) in her description of her inner emptiness. Abandonment is a slippery issue in the film: in this case Lisa has arranged to repeat an earlier, perhaps involuntary, abandonment by the father. The film's next scene elaborates upon the theme of appearance and disappearance.

The film dissolves to a group of female musicians in a dance hall that is not particularly elegant, as they play a clunky waltz for Stefan and Lisa, obviously the last clients left. Once again, one can discern a parallel with the ballroom scenes in *Madame de . . .* (where the lovers end up dancing by themselves in a much richer setting), and to *Liebelei*'s oblivious dancing couples, sometimes dancing to music as uninspired as *Letter*'s. (The inadequacy of Fritz's love for the Baroness in *Liebelei* is signaled above all by his inability to be "absorbed" in his waltz with her.) *Letter*'s women musicians are angry:

FIRST MUSICIAN: I'm going home right after this.

SECOND MUSICIAN: I like to play for married people. They've got homes.

One of the women takes a voracious bite of a frankfurter as she glares over her cello at the couple. The musicians then finish the piece and quietly leave, while Stefan and Lisa gaze at one another too intensely to notice the departure.

> STEFAN: Now I know you are a sorceress. Otherwise, how could we dance together in this way? And yet, if we had, I should remember. [Fat chance.] [*He turns toward the musicians, clapping his hands commandingly, but the women are gone. Lisa takes the opportunity to direct Stefan to an out-of-tune piano, where he continues the waltz the small orchestra had been playing. Kneeling by the piano* (in a striking high-angle shot), *she looks at him worshipfully*]
>
> STEFAN: Promise me you won't vanish.
>
> LISA: I won't be the one to vanish.

The musicians wish to play for a married couple because "they've got homes." Lisa certainly does not have one, if we exclude her surrogate home with Stefan. To appear—to vanish: to be the one to vanish is to be the more powerful in the relationship between two individuals. Lisa has learned to play the "fort-da" game, converting her lack of control over Stefan into the imaginary power to make him disappear—and return.[93] It is in this context that any strictly class-oriented reading of the film seems problematic. The musicians are, to be sure, working for Lisa and Stefan, but to say that they belong to a lower class than Lisa is problematical. There is, if anything, an ironic collapsing of difference in this scene: the female musicians, whose castrating powers are emphasized in the voracious munching of the frankfurter, stand as an absurd substitute for the feminized Stefan. (She is also a figure of condensation, like Mizzi in *Liebelei*: a woman in uniform, associated with music, indicating sexual hunger by eating [like Lisa's playmate] etc.) He takes up their music as Lisa watches ecstatically (taking the posture of a small child by the piano). Lisa's union with Stefan is marked by the transvestism of this group, which is the female equivalent of the band that played in Linz during another courtship—that of Lisa and the lieutenant.[94] Lutz Bacher has informed me that Ophuls wanted to place a lesbian couple in the background of Lisa's and Stefan's first romantic encounter on the street. "Local color" for the Vienna of 1905? Perhaps, instead, along with the female musicians, the couple presents another gender sensibility from which to observe Lisa and Stefan.

Lisa "knows" she will not be the one to vanish. Can we find any truth in this statement? After all, soon Lisa more or less runs away from her lover. Perhaps Lisa knows that this evening will hold the only moments when Stefan will come close to knowing her; by her remark she might therefore mean that the Stefan she loves will, for all intents and purposes, be the one to disappear. Lisa indeed repeats her father's vanishing act—but only after she has consummated the relationship with Stefan by means of a homecoming that has many resonances for her.

As the couple enters the door through which Stefan has brought so many young women, the now familiar high-angle shot from the stairway reproduces Lisa's earlier point of view as she watched Stefan on the fateful night when she left, broken-hearted, for Linz. The compulsion to repeat freezes the scene with its colorless irony. But as we know very well, this is not the only scene evoked by a similarity in mise-en-scène. To reiterate: When Brand and his companion (dressed in bridelike white) had entered his apartment earlier in the film, Lisa was given to experience an emotion that we noted to be strangely lacking in or *displaced from* that other scene on the staircase—the one between her mother and Herr Kastner. That scene was explicitly sexual but unremarked-upon in the voice-over narration, as though it were beneath the notice of a Lisa who has just emerged from her idol's inner sanctum. The emotional response to Brand's dalliance fills in the emotional resonance lacking in the earlier scene. Of course, Lisa's reaction to her mother's situation is tinged with implicit contempt. And yet, as noted, Lisa goes to a great deal of trouble to set up a situation similar to her mother's (who was courted on this stairway). She will be a woman alone in Vienna with a child. We feel, accordingly, the echo of Frau Berndle's first nuptials, which may have taken place in this very house and whose product was Lisa. In this way, Stefan is a more literal stand-in for Lisa's own father, who would have taken his bride into the building. He also takes the position of her mother's lover, of whom Lisa, according to the logic of the family romance, is certainly jealous. Thus she becomes the object of her own jealousy, an emotion that feels familiar to women alienated from their bodies and their desires by the culture of the image. Lisa also puts her mother's body into the symbolic fray with her actions:

The child, having learnt about sexual processes, tends to picture to himself erotic situations and relations, the motive force behind this being his desire to bring his mother (who is the subject of the most intense sexual curiosity) into situations of secret infidelity and into secret love-affairs. In this way the child's phantasies, which started by being, as it were, asexual, are brought up to the level of his later knowledge.[95]

Wexman describes the staircase, along with the threshold, as Lisa's "chronotope" in the film. Both the threshold, which represents the "modality of crisis," and the staircase are loci for the "conflicts inherent in Lisa's emerging sexual identity."[96] Climbing the staircase and crossing the threshold of Stefan's apartment, Lisa takes a specific *direction* in her life. For Lisa (though not for Stefan, as Wexman points out), this step takes her into another order of temporality: time takes on what Bakhtin calls a "biographical dimension"—in which birth and death mark definite beginnings and endings. Is this because woman must face biological exigencies to a greater degree than must man? Such "temporal essentialism" seems dangerous. In any event, Lisa—masquerading woman or transvestite man—attains her object in this scene.

The fade into darkness following the couple's passionate kiss is abruptly interrupted by a cut to a pair of curtains immediately thrust apart (creating a vaginal metaphor/metonymy as we retrospectively realize that Lisa has just lost her virginity) by Madame Spitzer, excited by the presence of a new customer who "looks like he'll be a good one." Madame Spitzer's willingness to exploit Lisa's visual potential puts her, to a certain degree, in a "masculine"—or maternal—position. Indeed, Madame Spitzer has some of the qualities of other director-figures in Ophuls' films: it is she who is commanding the performance of the feminine, just as does the madam of the brothel in *Le Plaisir* (1952) and as do the male director-figures in many of Ophuls' other films. John, Stefan's valet, serves, as has been noted, as a kind of director-figure by signing Lisa's letter, and thus signs the narrative, in this way fixing Lisa's image in Stefan's mind. By drawing together all the women of the story—the women (who were all Lisa) Stefan had known under one name—John retroactively makes possible the device of the letter as a subjective vision of his master and of course gives Stefan the motivation to fight the duel. The kind, innocuous John is thus identical to the vicious Montenuovo in his real function in the film.

Lisa puts on the jacket she had earlier been modeling and walks out to the platform where Stefan is seated, playing at being a customer. As she models the dress for her lover, she compliments him on his espionage in finding her. Lisa, of course, seems pleased to see Stefan.

Indeed, her only comment about his planned trip to Milan is to say that it is wonderful. But there are indications that this is not a happy event—at least on the symbolic level of the film. Stefan's observation of Lisa as she displays the gown puts her, in fact, into the kind of danger that she has carefully avoided, that of being bound to herself as an image. While she speaks to Stefan during this scene, pretending to show him the gown she is wearing, we are able see her face for the most part only in a very small mirror placed beside Stefan. This mirroring of Lisa constitutes both a literal and a metaphorical capture, a "very lovely" one. In addition, a new element of this mise-en-scène presents itself for the first time: behind Madame Spitzer stands a wax statue—a mannequin—of a woman modeling a dress. The mannequin, naturally enough, echoes those scenes earlier at the Prater, where Lisa's desire for Stefan is figured in the same way. Just as Stefan could be captured and displayed, immobilized, perhaps by proxy, for public exhibition, so too can Lisa—though here by the mater rather than by the p[r]ater. But the question of *who* is being captured can shift at any moment. When the young woman asks Madame Spitzer if she can leave early (to meet Stefan at the train station for a temporary farewell), the former replies, "Of course, my dear: congratulations!" repeating the comment that Fritz the waiter had made to Stefan on a parallel occasion. Lisa, it seems, has "caught" her man. But another implication, which Lisa will skirt, is also that Lisa has finally become a "normal" girl. Madame Spitzer, an *entremetteuse* not unlike Lisa's mother, must also remain disappointed in her desire to normalize Lisa's sex-life.

Lisa does see Stefan off at the station. As has often been noted, Stefan's promise to return in two weeks anticipates the scene where Lisa sees her son take the train to return to his boarding school (they are similarly shot, certain words—"two weeks"—are repeated, and so on). In one of the more "melodramatic" twists of the film, the conductor "accidentally" seats Stefan Jr. and his mother in a compartment contaminated with typhus, where they converse until Lisa detrains. Lisa's mimetic urge, her imitation of Stefan in flesh and blood, is in this way specifically associated with contamination and is implicated in the destructive mechanisms operating to bring the film to closure. Desire, which came to fruition in the earlier train scenes, finds its logical outcome in the uncontrollable repetition exemplified by the spread of contamination.

However, in the scene following that of her farewell to the "vanishing" Stefan, when Lisa actually does have her baby, the first image we see is a dramatic one: a coiffed nun, lit from below (in the style of Georges de la Tour) by a single candle, walks slowly down a dark corridor toward the camera. (A gothically shadowed nun has been used to similar effect in Hitchcock's 1958 *Vertigo*.) Repeating (ironically but not inappropriately) Madame Spitzer's gesture, she pulls apart the inmates' bed curtains, unveiling and examining a young woman who has just given birth.[97] The camera tracks with her; on the soundtrack women's voices raised in sacred song echo through the convent. The nun rips down a piece of paper over the woman's bed, then moves to another, where she abruptly shuts the bed curtains. There is no troubling male gaze here, as there is in the novella (the student doctors). Women seem, for the moment, to have taken over the function of the inquiring look into Lisa's life. And indeed, Lisa is next. The righteously brutal nun enters the curtained theater of Lisa's martyrdom, where another nun, heard offscreen as the first approaches, asks the new mother about the identity of the baby's father. The camera tracks in to a plaque outside the curtain. The mother, it says, is Lisa Berndle, and the child's name is Stefan—but the father's name remains a blank. Of course, Brand's name *is* on the plaque, in the form of his son's name. The search for identity in this scene anticipates the one at the end of the film. In this case, it is the nun (rather than John) who has signed Lisa's name and has begun to sign that of her lover, but only as a displaced repetition, as the name of the child. In the voice-over narration Lisa says that her silence was motivated by her desire "to be the one woman [Stefan] had known who asked . . . for nothing." In Zweig's novella Lisa's more practical consideration is that the man would probably not believe her if she told him the child was his.

Stefan feels no such hesitation, at least after the fact. He looks eagerly at the photos enclosed in the letter. One is simply a picture of a small child; the third is a picture of the boy a few years later. The second of the three is more interesting. It shows Lisa in a mock-up hot-air balloon basket with her son, still a small boy. The imaginary voyage has continued into the next generation, it seems, and has been captured on film. The complex rapport between mobility and immobility always extant in Ophuls' films is again established, as the motionless voyage crystallizes as the emblem of the drive (*Trieb*).[98]

STEFAN: Say "Stefan" like you did last night.

LISA: Stefan . . .

STEFAN: It's as though you had been saying it all your life.

That moment of departure at the train station, just before Lisa walks off the platform and a fade to black reveals the nun approaching the humble beds of the young mothers, demonstrates the ingenuity of the film in creating a multilayered artificial past, evoked always as already lost to both man and woman, a moment where desires were never satisfied but which still acts inexorably upon the present as the fiction of satisfaction. In breathing Stefan's name to him in this sequence, Lisa echoes the many times in the past she had said it for her own ears, and anticipates that instance when the past and present are about to collapse and she speaks for the last time at the end of the film.

A Birthday That Leads to Death

In the next sequences, Lisa does not dwell upon the difficulties of her early years as an unwed mother but immediately tells of her marriage of convenience to Johann Stauffer.[99] And what convenience: Stauffer is a wealthy, high-ranking officer who wants only the best for Lisa and her child. He knows, Lisa says, the "truth about us [Stefan and herself], and about our child." We see the family on a special night: it is Lisa's birthday, the day of the "second birth" of her passion, as it happens. The scene opens on a shot of Lisa looking at a diamond choker her husband has given her for her birthday. "Oh how lovely," she says with breathless insincerity. (Now she is the judge rather than the possessor of loveliness.) Johann leans over her, placing the necklace around her neck,[100] and stiffly remarks, "Lisa, I am not good at saying such things, but I want you to be as happy as you have made me. . . . You are happy?" Her evasive response: "Why shouldn't I be?" She goes to fetch her white ermine wrap, which he also places around her shoulders. The fur-clad dominatrix last seen in *Venus in Furs* has taken up residence chez Stauffer.

Stefan Jr., we learn, is home from school on holiday. As Lisa prepares for the ball, her son displays his musical talents under the nervous but approving eye of his stepfather. The camera tracks to Stefan's room, following the sound of his harmonica.

STAUFFER: Still another talent? [*He looks at the harmonica*] Made in Switzerland.

We know, of course, that Stefan Jr. was practically made in Switzerland himself. Stefan calls his mother back to ask (in properly Freudian fashion) to be allowed to sleep in his mother's bed. He also asks his mother to bring him an opera program—unlike his mother, he is not reduced to stealing the desired image (though she never does bring it to him). Stauffer awaits his wife downstairs while she has a heart-to-heart talk with her son. She wants the boy to call his stepfather not "sir" but "father": "Supposing you said to me 'goodnight madam'; it would sound pretty silly wouldn't it?" Nevertheless, as she leaves, this humorous exchange ensues:

LISA: Goodnight sir.

STEFAN JR.: Goodnight, madam.

LISA: After all, when a person treats you so much like a son he is, in a sense, your father.

A component of the adult relationship has found its way into the mother-child rapport. Lisa undermines, in this scene, the very notion of genealogy when she describes paternity as role-playing. The scene also reconstructs the virtual image of Stefan Brand's childhood, as elsewhere in the film it is a question of reproducing some version of Lisa's. The stepfather will reluctantly permit his "son" to sleep in the mother's bed, but when it comes to reintroducing the child's father into the picture, then Stauffer must become that instrument of paternal severing described by Modleski in her essay on the film.

We have at last come full circle in this chapter. The next scene is the one where Lisa finally catches sight of Stefan once again. Arriving late, just before the "second act" of *Die Zauberflöte*,[101] Lisa finds her way to the box she and Stauffer share with other wealthy spectators, but she doesn't cease to be tormented by Stefan's presence. All the years that have passed since the first instants of her love "melt away." As Papageno's aria, "Ein Mädchen oder Weibchen" ("maiden or wife") begins to fill the concert hall,[102] Lisa speaks:

(VOICE-OVER): Suddenly, in that one moment, everything was in danger, everything I thought was safe. Somewhere out there were your eyes and I knew I couldn't escape them. It was like the first time I saw you . . .

A tight close-up of Stefan's face brings home to us his permeating presence. The "persecutory gaze," which Lisa has for the most part warded off, now returns to possess her. Modleski, on the contrary, finds additional evidence of the film's "feminization" of its hero in this close-up of Stefan:

> Briefly, we see a close-up of Stefan through a soft focus filter, the device typically used in filming beautiful women. The image appears against a gray background which renders its diegetic status uncertain. The cutting from Lisa to Stefan further enhances this uncertainty, as it is unclear how each is placed in relation to the other and who is looking at whom.[103]

That Stefan is being depicted as an object of desire is irrefutable. The active aspect of his performance has been eliminated; he is now "emasculated," merely an image to be admired.[104] Modleski uses this feminization-effect, which seems to render Stefan passive, as evidence to disregard the voice-over, which places the look on Stefan's side ("Somewhere out there were your eyes . . ."). For Modleski this voice-over indicates a repression of feminine desire manifest on the visual level of the text. Stefan's "searching" look is somewhat vacuous and its penetrating power dubious as he presents his beautiful face for this shot. But there is no need to reduce the meaning of the scene to the material on either sound or image track. Lisa's desire, which does surge up from its source when she sees Stefan, threatens to destabilize the system she has established. She must flee before he *can* reactivate himself and go through the motions of masculine aggression and appropriation of her image. Lisa must and does flee, pleading a headache. But in the foyer, between a statue of a sphinx (sporting a hairstyle identical to Lisa's) and a bust of Beethoven, Stefan awaits her.[105] Low-key lighting dramatizes the scene. He speaks: "Excuse me, you must realize that where there is a pursued there must also be a pursuer." He does not specify who is in which role, and each has, of course, taken each role in turn. Like many of Ophuls' heroines, he has "shuffled faces, like cards, hoping to find the one that lies somewhere, just over the edge of your memory—the one you've been waiting for." Lisa offers him a vision of hope—indeed, he little realizes that she also presents a mortal danger. He tells her that he has stopped giving concerts—his phallic prestige is suffering, though her love for him seems unscathed.

Clément's description of a scene from *Prima della Revoluzione* captures the feeling of this moment, indeed of the entire sequence: "A woman in black, her gaze burning with sadness, watches a newly engaged couple from afar. The man leaves his loge and meets the woman in a long corridor that is white, deserted."[106] Lisa is both the "newly engaged" woman and the one whom Stefan meets in the corridor.

I have mentioned that, in his study of *Letter*, Williams notes that the frame narrative (Stefan's story) and the flashback come to resemble one another more and more in tone and atmosphere as they come closer together in time:

> The letter not only presents information about the "past." It also defines, by opposition, the "present" of the film's "real time"—the time of Stefan's reading. This can be seen in examining the way the "frame" (present) relates to the flashbacks both to establish initial oppositions between them and, later, to annul these oppositions. The lovers' final union, therefore, is not merely thematic. It is a union of their respective domains in the film. It is in this way that Lisa's death may imply—in a sense *contain*—Stefan's.[107]

Thus, Glynis Kinnan's insight into the film's breakdown of oppositions can be substantiated at the most discrete technical level. In particular, the fades and dissolves of the film, which at first distinguish very emphatically between the two levels of the story, are curtailed to the point where Stefan's face (in the frame narrative) is linked to Lisa's new home (after she is married) by a dissolve rather than by fades into white or black after the image is unfocused. At the end of the film both the frame and the narrative itself will be taking place in dark, somber settings until, to reiterate Williams' description, "the final transition from flashback to Stefan's apartment in 'real' time matches two shots which are almost identical, of Lisa writing at a table, Stefan reading at a table, both alone, both about to die. As they will 'meet' in death, so they have already been cinematically joined, 'together at last' within the film's few remaining moments." The "doubling" of Lisa and Stefan is evident in both a thematic and a technical sense at the end of the film. Pursued and pursuer are becoming virtually indistinguishable, despite Lisa's efforts to remain untouched by the mimetic catastrophe she has set off in Stefan's life.

Taking leave of Stefan (who still does not "recognize" her, except as a vaguely familiar image), she gasps to find her husband seated in her waiting carriage.[108] Stauffer attempts to bring his wife to her senses (in a sympathetic and reasonable way, one might add), but she is adamant. When he tries to incite her to use her will to fight her urge to see Stefan, her response is that she has "never had any will but *his* [Stefan's], ever." This remark seems somewhat absurd in light of Lisa's impressive displays of will throughout the film. Her husband clearly finds it hard to swallow, although there are indications that he, too, suffers from Lisa's malady: we have heard him repeat to her the very words she had said to Brand, "I'm not very good at saying these things but . . ." But Lisa's will *is* one with Stefan's at the level of the imaginary dyad, until that moment when the "other" must be recognized as endowed with subjectivity in its own right. The aggression latent in that imaginary relation will be carried out by Stauffer himself, who will (we are led to believe) kill Stefan in the duel. Lisa must now confront Stefan, although her husband—in one of the theatrical moments expressing the overbearing paternal function as a castrating power—stands dramatically in front of his weapons and forbids her to go to him. She bids good-night to her child, who says "Goodnight, father" to his stepfather as he had been instructed by his mother. Lisa is pained by this inadvertent irony. The lie of the family romance is becoming apparent.[109] The next day Lisa takes her son to the train station, to the deadly train compartment, and then goes about her business. Donning a black, man-tailored dress and a top hat, as described above, she makes her way to Stefan's home, stopping "impulsively" on the way to buy flowers.

As the film is returning to its beginning, so must we return to the beginning of this discussion to repeat Rose's description of the functioning of aggression in the film system.

Paranoia is latent to the reversibility of the ego's self-alienation. Furthermore, since the projective alienation of the subject's own image is the precondition for the identification of an object world, all systems of objectification can be related to the structure of paranoia. Aggressivity is latent to the system, but it will also be discharged where the stability of the system is threatened. (p. 88)

The system that seems to stabilize as the woman is paired off in the marital union breaks forth into a series of doublings, culminating in the duel and in the death of all but her husband and the silent John, himself Lisa's double, as has been amply documented. When Lisa goes up the stairs to her old home, Stefan's apartment building, the doorman calls out, "Who is it?" Lisa's response, not to the doorman but to John, who opens the door, is to say her lover's name, "Stefan Brand," exactly as we have heard Brand call out his name to the doorman so many times before. Her husband watches from a closed carriage as she enters the building. Dressed as a duelist (in a dark costume similar to Lisa's), he is both the third term (intruding into Lisa's "dyad" and denying the identity of her will with Stefan's) as well as the agent of her aggression: he will, we assume, shoot Brand.

That her meeting with Brand is disastrous is signaled not only by the fact that he still does not recognize her but, rather, by two other incidents. His sincerity of the night before has once again been displaced by an unctuous seductiveness ("This is just the hour for a little late supper . . . or is it too late? Well, it makes no difference. You're here, and as far as I'm concerned, all the clocks in the world have stopped"). Once again marking time takes on symbolic resonance. To be in control is to be in command of time—something obviously out of Stefan's range of abilities at this point. If only Lisa could believe, however, that "all the clocks in the world have stopped"! Because this would indeed mark Stefan's grasp of her form of temporality. But the circle of time that has captured him is indistinct and undifferentiated, collapsed into meaningless recurrences.[110]

Of course, Lisa is upset when Stefan orders John to bring the "usual" late supper, thus inserting her into an infinite number of repetitions of such intimate little suppers. As Stefan steps out to speak to John, Lisa stands gazing abstractedly toward a clay bust of an idealized woman, which sits upon a low table under a mirror. Stefan returns: "Ah, she fascinates you, too." Lisa smiles as he explains that the Greeks had built a statue to an unknown god that they had always hoped would come to them and that, in imitation, he had acquired this statue of an unknown goddess.

LISA: And you never found her?

STEFAN: For years I never awoke in the morning but what I said to myself, "Perhaps today she will come, and my life will really begin." Sometimes it seemed very near. Well, now I'm older and I know better.

Lisa's face falls as he speaks these last words. And worse: Stefan *compliments her frock* ("You're very lovely; beautiful dress"), devastating her with the permanence of the female masquerade, reading incorrectly both their similarities and their differences, perhaps prophylactically, because of the danger represented by her mimetic appropriation of his identity. (One can see that the man and woman are really at an impasse: both identification and difference lead to violence.) This denial of similarity, however, only comes after an acknowledgment of his failed passion. Stefan's piano is locked; he no longer even plays for himself (as Lisa puts it).

LISA: How could you do that—give it up altogether?

STEFAN: As you're so curious, I'll tell you. One night I came back to this room. I'd given a concert, like all the others. Afterwards they said all the usual things. The things you say when you're not *really* convinced. So I happened to look in the mirror, this one here. The young prodigy was no longer young. He certainly wasn't prodigious. Since then I have found other things to do, more amusing things. [*He lifts her veil; there is a dramatic close-up of Lisa's ecstatic face*] I knew last night. Didn't you?

They kiss. Strains of the air from "The War Between Men and Women," the music of their first night together, can be heard. Just as Lisa seizes the moment to tell Stefan "about us," he reverts to his playboy persona, fetching champagne and chattering to her about his trip to America, where American women had shown him their fondness of Europeans.

LISA: Must have been a wonderful trip.

STEFAN: Do you travel a great deal?

Lisa, listening to Stefan's voice emanating from the other room (his is now the "voice-over") is shown in medium close-up, suffering the torments of the damned as he tramples on their past together. "Are you getting lonely out there?" he asks. "Very lonely," she replies, as she walks out the door. As she goes down the staircase for the last time, she passes John, who gazes back after her (the supper tray in his hands) in mute recognition.

Stefan's discourse to Lisa about himself—his only sincere words to her—sound strangely like a review of his performance with her. Like the critics, he says "all the usual things" to her. After his Dorian Gray-like moment before the mirror, Stefan attempted to step out of the circle of empty performance by giving up his concerts. His expressive power gone, he is left as the hull of a performer, mirroring Lisa's desire for the reification of an image—as she is herself mirrored in the statue and in the looking glass hanging above it. But her victory is obviously a Pyrrhic one. By playing the game of "visual capture," Lisa loses the ideal medium that his music provided—and she cannot be "recognized" if she could never allow herself to be seen. Paradoxically, the "feminized" Stefan can no longer provide the womblike atmosphere she craves (though in addition, as I've implied, the music is not devoid of phallic qualities).

Leaving the building, Lisa meets an old, drunken soldier who offers to "Bring you somewhere, young lady? Anywhere at all? It makes no difference." The "determined" course of her life now takes on a hideous randomness, as the soldier in his most reduced form—without even the stiff masculinity of Stauffer and Lt. von Kaltnegger. Echoing Stefan's callous words, he tells her that her life "makes no difference" in the world she had loved so passionately. No longer is "every step measured," or is time meaningful in itself.

And so once again, and finally, Lisa disappears, walking away in one of the most magnificent shots of the film—a high-angle, static shot, filled with pools of light and shadow cast across a paved square.[111] The voice-over is timed perfectly to match her diagonal walk across the square, through the mist, by the Corso Fountain, from the bottom to the top of the screen:

> (VOICE-OVER): I don't remember where I went. Time passed. Not in days or in hours, but in the distance put between us. When I could think again, I went to my son, but it was too late. He died last night, of typhus, without even knowing I was there. [*The scene dissolves to the room where Stefan Jr. lies dead, and Lisa is writing the letter*] Now I'm alone. My head throbs and my temples are throbbing. Perhaps God has been kind, and I, too, have caught the fever. If this letter reaches you, believe this—that I love you now as I've always loved you. My life can be measured in the moments I've had with you and our child. If only you could have shared those moments. If only you had recognized what was always yours, could have found what was never lost. If only . . . [*Lisa falters and stops writing*]

After reading a note announcing her death from the nun who attended Lisa's deathbed, Stefan drops his head into his hands (to a swell of poignant strings on the soundtrack) and visualizes Lisa in the many settings they had shared (interesting, since he does not yet "know" who she is).[112] John enters. "You remembered her?" Stefan asks. John answers by "signing" the letter: he writes Lisa's name on a slip of paper and gives it to Stefan to read. The clock tolls five times, and the men lift their heads simultaneously. Stefan asks for his things, dresses more or less instantaneously, and silently bids John good-bye. The faithful valet bows his head after his master leaves. Stefan walks out into the dawn, greets his identically dressed seconds, and climbs into the awaiting carriage.

Has Stefan, watching Lisa's girlish image reappear and dissolve before his eyes, "learned" something from her womanly encounter with feeling, from her sacrifice and death? For men and for women in this film, desire is modeled on the process of writing which is that of the letter itself—there is no direct experience, but only the deferred, the distanced, and the interpreted. Stefan can only love *her* as the product of a reading, as the voice of a woman already dead.

Since you come to me from the only place where I don't feel myself loved, I also have the feeling that you are the only one who is able not to love me. And that from that place on the board, you know, the chance of the very first encounter, so improbable and so inevitable: what would have happened if this detail, at such an hour (and it is still a matter of cars and train, and of course, of a letter)[113]

Is this a letter that (as in Lacan's reading of the one in Poe's "The Purloined Letter") "must" return to Stefan, spelling out his obedience to the symbolic order? Or is it one whose meaning disseminates along the way, eroded by the power of Lisa's subversive desire?

From one point of view, we might say that Lisa has moved from masquerade to the more recuperable (male-female, or female-"feminine" transvestism), has been caught in a fatal mimetic snare when engaged in the latter. Stefan represses his recognition of Lisa in transvestite state as "like" him, and persists in seeing only the image of female sexuality, until the last moments of the film when it is perhaps true that he understands better what role the image has played in his life. Transvestism, for the woman, thus leads to a contest of doubles, ending in the duel. For the man, there is a moment when his parade of virility becomes overinvested. He loses the "distance" necessary to performing the phallic function and is feminized. Or, possibly, he is able to put on the masculine uniform and the distance it requires in the service of the feminine. He may then, as Modleski says, use the "feminine" to resist that role, to destroy the "father" within him (as is the case in Deleuzian masochism). This attempt is fraught with danger, however, as he can then become trapped in the fixed, "feminine" image of himself. Lisa, acting the male part, comes to Stefan's apartment seeking both the phallus and a woman's voice—piano and music—but she finds instead the "frozen" head of a woman. She makes her obeisance and departs. The "alternative" scenario in which same-sex desire finds expression lies buried in the film's heterosexual masquerade.

Flashback to the Opera: A Political Note

Virginia Wright Wexman and others have observed that *The Magic Flute*, usually performed in German, is sung in Italian in *Letter from an Unknown Woman*. She sees this and the fact that a Frenchman (Jourdan) was sought for the role of the Viennese musician (although that was, in fact, not Ophuls' decision), as well as other elements in the film, as evidence of Ophuls' avoidance of a certain history—that of the Vienna in which "the first public programs for the elimination of Jews from the life of Europe were devised and proclaimed."[114] Ophuls' many artistic returns to a city where, as we know, anti-Semitism was part of his personal experience, certainly implies, as Wexman suggests, his attempt to work out a "historical contradiction," partly figured as a conflict between nationalism and internationalism—a conflict displaced onto the female body and into the private realm. Indeed, in *Der Kampf* (interesting title, actually), Ophuls describes how "the international producer anxiously avoids any political avowals."[115] We know that these avowals are made nonetheless in Ophuls' work—and like Wexman wonder whether Marcel Ophuls' "stylistically unadorned documentaries probe the processes of history" partly in reaction to his father's seeming ahistoricism.

I will at this point risk making certain connections, in concluding this chapter, between Ophuls' peculiar ahistoricism and the issue of masochism, as articulated by Studlar. My risk is double, first in that Studlar's essay on Deleuzian masochism challenges the roots of my argument derived from the work of Freud, Rose, Modleski, et al., and second in that I see the relation between Ophuls' films and masochism in the context of these films' references to the psychological injuries of the Jewish subject who survived the Holocaust. (Again, I don't claim that Ophuls' subjectivity is directly operative in his films, but that it is part of their overdetermination as texts.)

In "Masochistic Performance and Female Subjectivity," Gaylyn Studlar argues that masochism has been defined too narrowly in discussions of the woman's film. These discussions (Doane's *Desire to Desire* is cited as exemplary of the view that female masochism in fact de-eroticizes or denies pleasure) have, according to Studlar, described masochism almost exclusively in terms of the pain and restriction of women's lives wrought by female masochism (we are speaking here in the context of the cinema). Studlar answers feminist criticisms of her use of the "male-centered" Deleuzian model of masochism, and places a special emphasis on the possibility of discussing female subjectivity in light of Deleuze's formal system. Studlar thus addresses the highly politicized issue of the value of masochistic pleasure in the woman's film. In doing so, she gives the female masochistic scenario its due in a way that, for example, Tania Modleski and Kaja Silverman have not, the former tending to "translate" masochism into anger or other more obvious forms of resistance to patriarchy, the latter having followed Reik in presenting male masochism as by definition more "subversive" of patriarchal values than female masochism.[116] When I say that Studlar gives the female masochistic scenario its "due," I mean to say that she acknowledges its *force*, its all-consuming quality—elements that Reik saw ("that blind unrestricted rush of self-destruction") as missing from female masochism, but which, like Studlar, I believe are crucial to any understanding of what films like *Letter from an Unknown Woman* offered and continue to offer to women.

According to Studlar, Stefan is not the blind hysteric described by Modleski (in a gesture that strangely undoes earlier feminists' efforts to show that hysteria could be a passionate means of expression for women in the nineteenth century). Rather, he "better represents the typical pattern of pathological narcissism in which the individual channels infantile fantasies of grandiosity into professionally and socially acceptable pursuits: here, a career (music) and a pastime (women)" (pp. 45–46). Because of his narcissism, Stefan fits more easily into Lisa's masochistic project, which, as I have mentioned, though using a more Freudian mode of analysis, must operate at a distance. In this version of Lisa's story, she is much more in control of the fantasy than I have given her credit as being, certainly the "director" of her own story. The "dangers" involved in the return of the gaze, in the capturing of the woman as image, and so on, which I have outlined above, would according to Studlar be rather beside the point. Perhaps the crucial difference between what I have to say (and this serves as well in the context of *Madame de . . .*) and what Studlar claims for Deleuzian masochism involves the intactness of the woman's (or man's) fantasy. I continue to see a potential for violence, directed mostly toward the woman, despite the existence of the duels in the films, in the collapse of the masochistic fantasy. Studlar notes, in fact, that the feminization of Brand that many have noted in the film makes it possible for him to "embody the necessary sadistic (bad object) element in the masochistic fictionality that must construct him carefully to prevent him from emerging as a potential other subject who might wrest control of the scenario away from (and disfantasize) the masochistic subject" (p. 44). It is this emergence and wresting for control that seem to me redolent of the potential for violence toward that mother figure (in this case, the unknown goddess) idolized by the masochist but also feared and even hated by the Oedipalized male. The question may ultimately be to what extent, as Studlar puts it, "this kind of pre-Oedipal conflict has defensively organized all later relations," so that the masochist's disavowal of the sadistic father can ultimately work to restructure the political unconscious. One's reading of the ending of the film—as the triumph of Lisa' masochistic project which denies the persecuting father his place, or as the return of the father in the form of the duel—depends upon how strongly one believes that the masochistic heterocosm can hold up in the face of the cultural devaluation of women. Of course, Lisa's final devotion to a female figure—a feminized Stefan or the goddess herself, may also indicate an even more radical exclusion of patriarchy via lesbianism. In a male homosexual economy, Stefan's turn from Lisa's "boyish" adoration to the sword of the father may indicate that the punishing father still acts as an important fantasy object. Perhaps my tendency to emphasize the "sadistic" potential of the films also echoes my involvement in them as part of an "auteurist" project—in which I am made continually aware of Ophuls' deep ambivalence toward the potential for directorial abuse in the audio/visual realm. The divergences between the "implied director's" and Lisa's points of view in the film in this way reinforce the sense that a consciousness other than Lisa's may be in control—measuring every moment, counting every step, as she says. The "truth" probably lies somewhere among the models and systems we are invoking, and certainly changes over time, even as we look (repeatedly) at the "same" film.

Recent feminist criticism of *Letter* has a way of both invoking and avoiding the question of the author, no doubt for the same reasons that incite my discomfort in making claims about textual continuities, much less about what the films may or may not reflect about Ophuls' psychic state at the time of their making. At the very least, no critic has over-looked the way this film seems to play into Ophuls' predilection for turn-of-the-century Vienna. Wexman points to the strange process of political avowal and disavowal that goes on in *Letter*,[117] noting that the film may rework the trauma Ophuls experienced in his "German fatherland" (and Vienna itself, I'll add, when he was dismissed from the Burgtheater because he was a Jew), but that it also contains not one word of Ger-man (even translating Mozart into Italian), thus, I assume, repressing Ophuls' contact with the mother tongue.[118] "Thus," Wexman continues, "an impulse originating in history is transformed into one anchored in sexuality, and politics is transformed into style." I would take Wexman's statement one step farther and say that style and sexuality are themselves the fabric of history. Just as medieval illuminators drew lines that creat-ed a religious era, *Letter* redefines the history of cinema in its distillation of the Hollywood vision of female suffering and pleasure, of Ophuls' hopes that this film in particular would open Hollywood's doors; in its condensation of Lisa's fate with the meaning of exile and suffering in Ophuls' identity as a Jewish filmmaker. I will cite once again Wexman's statement that "the career of the director's son Marcel, whose stylistical-ly unadorned documentaries probe the processes of history, completes the Oedipal trajectory" (p. 12). But Marcel Ophuls' films respond not only to what is "lacking" in his father's work but also to what they pro-duce as historical documents that express as well as repress, place as well as displace, the problems of nationalism, sexual and religious identity, historical change, and artistic desire.

$\mathscr{F}\!ive$

✦

To Hear Is to Obey: The Acoustical Imperative
in *La Signora di Tutti, Werther, Lachende Erben*

All of us directors should never cease to fight against the velvety clarity of Hollywood sound conception. We should be courageous and rather accept a non too perfect dialogue with real atmospheric sound than looping and wild lines, etc. You know that.
—Max Opuls, Inter-office Communication to Walter Wanger[1]

And now I've just cut myself shaving. Perhaps because I got carried away by my insistence on the priority of the image.
—Max Ophuls, "The Pleasure of Seeing"[2]

In the modern careers in spectacle, publicity [advertising] plays a large role: this publicity that I so despise, I had decided to give it a place in my film. The questions that the circus audience asks Lola were inspired by the wildly immodest radio game shows aimed at advertisement. I find frightening this vice of wanting to know everything, this lack of respect for mystery. Lola's circus could exist on Broadway, whose motto seems to be: sell man before man.
—Max Ophuls, "Publicity Must Be Killed"[3]

Pierre Lazareff: A small, gnome-like man talking much too fast, too eager—the "what makes Sammy Run" type. Nobody should ever overlook him. He once ran the Paris-Soir and L'Intransigeant and had his hands in many creative pies; bankers and brokers, lawyers and Moroccan princes, their mistresses and museum directors asked him before doing anything themselves. Then Hitler came and destroyed all that beauty, and Lazareff had to leave. Then started the resistance and the Invasion and the Liberation to bring back Pierre. To the same spot where he had been before. He is wonderful.
Rizzoli. Italian Hearst, specializing in magazines. Lives in Milan. Backed my Italian picture LA SIGNORA DI TUTTI. Is, like all good faschists [sic], back in power.
—Max Opuls, Inter-office Communication to Walter Wanger, 1949

◆

At the Juncture of Sound and Image

In an interesting article, Martina Müller has traced the history of
Ophuls' fascination with the sound medium.[4] Müller postulates that
Ophuls' considerable experience in both theater and radio profoundly
affected his "acoustical mise-en-scène" from the earliest film works.[5]
Ophuls' work in sound is far more subtle than I have perhaps indicated
in the preceding chapters: Müller points to, for example, the complex
mood created in *Liebelei* by the *lack* of Viennese accents. Wolfgang
Liebeneiner speaks Prussian "Hochdeutsch"; Magda Schneider's accent
is Bavarian; upper-class Viennese society is represented by a Rhinelander
(Gustof Gründgens) and a Russian (Olga Tschechowa) (p. 68). As in
Letter from an Unknown Woman (1948), the "local" quality of the Viennese
sets is undermined by the film's complex linguistic realm. (I have always
had a peculiar fixation on Louis Jourdan's carefully coached English: "I
haven't given any concerts in Vienna latelehhh . . ." A French accent with
slightly clipped British edges produces a very "Viennese" effect, indeed.)
Along with its "cosmopolitanism" (noted by Virginia Wright Wexman),
and the privileging of music in one way or another, Ophuls' soundtrack
often presents a kind of "acoustical panorama" (p. 67) that puts the spoken word in the background. Although Ophuls' dialogue is not as
blurred as Robert Altman's or as intricately overlapped as Orson
Welles's, it does present a sort of acoustical paradox, as "one voice" (the
meneur de jeu's, the music's, the heroine's) tries to break through the
"polylogue" of the films' soundtracks. Spoken words *by themselves*, Müller
notes, give no "assurance" in Ophuls' films (p. 71). Thus such assurance
is sought in juxtaposing words with image and music. However, as Glynis
Kinnan observes in a commentary on the divergence between Lisa Berndle's words and the image track of the film, "This deliberate separating
of the visual and the auditory discourages the latter's subsumption by
the former."[6]

It is precisely at the juncture of image, music, and word that the
archaeology of woman's relation to sound in Ophuls' films can be carried out. This chapter focuses primarily upon the woman's vexed relationship to sound in *La Signora di Tutti* (Italy, 1934), in which the prob-

lem of "subject formation" seems to hinge on the woman's relation to the sound-image. I find supporting evidence for this reading of sound in *Signora* in films from *Lachende Erben* (1932) to *Werther* (1938)—and, of course, in *Letter from an Unknown Woman* (1948).

Ophuls' experimentation with sound and image brings to the surface anxieties about the role of sound also observable in the "classical Hollywood cinema." Carol Flinn has pointed to the curious troping of the film soundtrack in terms of deficiency and lack. First, according to Flinn, film music in the average Hollywood movie is not considered autonomous: musical scores cannot stand on their own as can, say, a symphony. Second, paradoxically, film music is thought to be able to compensate for the deficiencies of other aspects of the film, or deficiencies of language itself.[7] As both Mary Ann Doane and Flinn emphasize, music's power to "fill in"—to give the apparatus "a sense of plenitude and unity"—also causes it (as the preceding chapter makes clear) to carry (per Flinn) "the threat of denying that completeness and of exposing the material disunity of the apparatus, the separateness, for example, of the sound track and image track" (p. 44).

Perhaps even more than music, words that are torn from their synchronicity or displaced within the film's diegesis can represent a powerful threat to the "subject" postulated by the film (characters, spectators). In *La Signora di Tutti* both music and words are most pain-inducing, and most constitutive of female subjectivity, when they are displaced from their diegetic function. Synchronous sound wards off spectator awareness of the separation of the sound and visual tracks, the fissure in the reconstituted 'reality' of narrative cinema. Thus, when synchronicity is disrupted, the film is literally "haunted . . . by the specter of a loss or absence."[8]

Music serves as a point of stress in Ophuls' films, a place where the possibility of fragmentation and disaster is in conflict with a vision of idealized love and subjective homogeneity that is also part of the romantic notion of music's potential. The stress point that music exacerbates thus often focuses on the emergence or formation of subjectivity, particularly female subjectivity. The project of unifying subjectivity seems most often to involve integrating past states into the present, perceived as the locus of possible but never achieved plenitude. Flinn comments:

Repeatedly cast into scenarios of loss and restoration, the score is treated as if it were able to restore an original quality currently found wanting, operating as a souvenir or trace of lost, idealized moments. Scores are constantly associated with anterior states . . . or with other kinds of lost objects. . . . [Her examples are Max Steiner's score for *Gone With the Wind* (1939) and David Raskin's score for *Laura* (1944).] In theoretical accounts this sense of nostalgia is frequently linked to the idea of a lost humanity. (p. 37)

Flinn makes this last remark with regard to critics who believe(d) that music restores a human dimension to the heavily technological apparatus of film. *La Signora di Tutti* won the prize for technique at the Venice Film Festival when it appeared and is, from any perspective, a technically complex film, using ingenious tracking shots, a great many "impressionistic" dissolves, montage sequences, and numerous voice-overs.[9] This praise for the film's technical aspect is highly ironic in that the subject of the film is the alienation of woman through technology—including the camera, the printing press, and the auditory devices of telephone, phonograph, and radio. Like the soundtrack that Flinn describes, *Signora*'s protagonist is fragmented, frighteningly disunified.

The plot of the film is as follows: Gabriella Murge (Isa Miranda) is a young woman who has no mother and lives with her strict father (a retired colonel), her aunt, and her sister Anna (Nelly Corradi). Gaby causes a scandal in her school when the music master falls in love with her and flees abroad. Forcibly sequestered at home, she is finally invited to a ball by Roberto (Federico Benfer), the son of a rich family, and is befriended by his lame mother Alma (Tatiana Pavlowa). Gaby becomes her close companion. The father of the house, Leonardo Nanni (Memo Benassi), falls in love with the young woman during a performance at La Scala. Alma dies ambiguously soon thereafter when, during a desperate search for Gabriella (who is at that moment amorously engaged with Leonardo in the garden), she and her wheelchair go hurtling down the staircase. Roberto wants to marry Gabriella, but Leonardo will not permit this and marries her himself. After a wedding trip tortured by guilt, the couple returns to the villa, from which they are soon driven by Gaby's aural hallucinations of the opera music heard on the radio the night of Alma's death. Roberto renounces Leonardo, who is led by his passion to financial ruin and prison. Gaby goes off to Paris to become Gaby Doriot, a film star, and Leonardo is finally run over by a car just outside the theater where the premiere of Gaby's new movie is being held. At the request of the French film producers, Roberto comes to France as a character witness to defend Gaby's reputation. Their love seems to be renewed, but he confesses that he is married to Gaby's sister Anna and has children with her. Distraught, Gaby attempts suicide but is found by her agent. The film ends with Gabriella's death on the operating table, which provides the frame for the film narrative.[10]

The Audio/Visual "Nature" of Female Subjectivity

Although the representation of the woman in La Signora di Tutti may seem less worked out, less radical than is the case in Letter from an Unknown Woman, the former film is by no means merely a rudimentary version of Ophuls' later works. It has an intricate structure and takes up the problem of feminine subjectivity in a detailed and probing fashion.

The film opens, with a circular wipe, on the image of a spinning gramophone record, and ends on a "frozen" image of the star, a publicity photo produced on a printing press at the moment of her death. In the first scene, Gaby's recorded voice wails plaintively that although she is "everyone's lady" there is no one man for her. The producer and agent who listen to her record argue about what Gaby is worth. She is trapped in what Andrew Sarris calls the "banal dialectic of stardom and heartbreak."[11] If one taps into the film, however, one begins to see that this dialectic of the star's position is anything but banal. As in Letter from an Unknown Woman, the last scenes in the film function to "reëstablish visual dominance" over the star,[12] who, like Lisa Berndle, attempts but fails to elude final "capture" as a cinematic image through her painful relationship to music. In both films the intense form of feminine pleasure represented by music is thwarted as the auditory world is shown to be hopelessly intertwined with the visual, making it impossible for the auditory world to live up to its promise of being an ideal medium for the expression of love, imagined (erroneously, of course) as an immediacy without danger. Just as the masochistic tenor of Lisa's relationship to Stefan's music conceals her iron will to pleasure, Gaby Doriot's far more stricken aurality holds the only possibility for expression of her sexual being. The disingenuousness of the young girl's voice, its vulnerability to commodification can be observed in a number of Ophuls' early films (notably, Liebelei and La Signora di Tutti). In Letter the woman seems to be passive with respect to music but is actually, paradoxically, able to desire most actively in response to music. Under the surface of that effort there lies, however, a troubled history in which the rhythmic circularity of the waltzes scattered throughout the films seems to represent a moment of "equality" between the partners, while a more or less violent libidinal discharge, leading toward death, is taking place. In *La Signora di Tutti* the premise and danger of music are reiterated in the young girl's voice, the opera, the radio, and most disturbingly, in auditory hallucinations.

In her reading of *Letter* Gertrud Koch appropriately places considerable emphasis on the scene of Lisa's disillusionment with Stefan.[13] What she characterizes as Lisa's willingness to maintain a masochistic relation to Stefan ends abruptly when Lisa discovers that he is no longer interested in playing the piano. The violent termination of the relationship comes about through a combination of the cessation of the woman's pleasurable relationship to music and of the mesmerizing and violent effects of the *visual* elements of this and other scenes. In both *Letter from an Unknown Woman* and *La Signora di Tutti*, paranoia, especially female paranoia (the fear of the destructive return of what was formerly pleasurable), is produced at the *juncture* of aural and visual motifs. In *Letter* this "juncture" occurs when Stefan's piano-playing is superseded by his image. In *Signora* paranoia is unleashed by the juxtaposition of a woman's painting and her disembodied "voice," which takes the form of music. Lisa is far more able than is Gaby to take control of her own visibility, to play the man's game of possessing the other's image on his own terrain. Gaby's only refuge from male possession of every commodifiable aspect of her being will be in a return to the guilt-inducing realm of the mother.

Lost Immediacy and the Maternal Image

Like *Liebelei* (1932) and *Divine* (1935), *La Signora di Tutti* is a tale of innocence, the story of a fundamentally nontheatrical (that is, unselfconscious) woman endangered by (and dangerous *in*) her role as performer. The motif involving performance is understated in *Liebelei*, sustained in that film, as we have observed, only by Christine's brief appearance as a charming songstress and by her father's profession as musician. Gaby Doriot is both a singer and a film star. Though Lisa Berndle is not as emphatically "innocent" as Christine and Gaby, her passion is, like theirs, inflamed (though in her case not begun) at an opera performance. Oddly enough, it is the less innocent Lisa (less innocent because she *acts* as an agent of her own desire, although her "suffering" is meant, to some extent, to disguise this fact) who is not herself a musical performance artist. This is peculiar because performance is generally associated with an arch self-display. But Lisa recognizes both that only music displaced from direct bodily presence can evoke her desire, and that any kind of performance is potentially dangerous for the performer. (By the time she "performs" her letter, she is already—dead.) In *Signora*, on the other hand, Gaby represents the paradoxically guileless woman who, through her self-display, endangers others despite her own artless wish for love.[14](Doane comments, aptly, that "the woodenness of Isa Miranda's acting, the clumsiness or awkwardness of her gestures, underscore her lack of deliberation in relation to emotionality or intentionality," p. 125.)

In these early films Ophuls seeks an oxymoronic coupling: the nontheatrical performance. Music should be not self-display but the guileless outpouring of a being absorbed in sound. The woman's voice and physical presence seem at first to hold, *for the man*, a promise of such a precommodified "authenticity." But this authentic purity is always already accessible only when transformed into the plaintive siren's song that opens the film and into the mesmerizing and entrapping image. Woman suffers the slings and arrows both of the "embodiment" that Silverman describes as the female's relation to sound in cinema and the "abstraction," or dismembering, that Doane observes in *Signora*. Gaby's quavering, childish voice inevitably turns into the mechanized and commodified version we hear at the beginning of the film, cruelly divorced from the "body" of a woman who is elsewhere, attempting suicide.[15]

In *La Signora di Tutti* Leonardo is shown to seek a form of immediacy with respect to the woman: he desires her bodily *presence*. He will, in fact, be driven to suicide because of his melancholia over the loss of an imagined immediate access to the woman.[16] The woman's relationship to voice and image is more complex than the man's because she is both object and spectator/auditor: in this film it is never a question of the *man* occupying the role of the commodified audio/visual object. In addition, the woman, too, suffers from the melancholy of lost immediacy: she cannot reach out with her "authentic" self to the ones she seeks to love (in particular, to the mother figures of the film). When the motherless Gaby is about to succumb to the effects of the anesthetic gas, she murmurs a single word—"mama." It is this loss of closeness to the mother, who is the primary libidinal object for both male and female, that is the most damaging trauma for the young woman. And yet, at the same time, because she physically resembles the mother whose love she wants (in that as a female her body is "like" the mother's), Gaby is also in danger of being too closely identified with and finally absorbed by the woman-as-image. In this film the problem of the woman's dangerous *closeness* to the image is repeatedly conflated with issues of maternity, while the mother represents, with respect to the *sound track*, the distant judge of the daughter's behavior (although the lure of the maternal "sonorous envelope" still beckons). As Doane comments, speaking of American films of the 1930s and 1940s, "motherhood is conceived as the always uneasy conjunction of an absolute closeness and a forced distance."[17] The woman cannot strike a middle distance with respect to the maternal/female imago. Instead, she can only pay homage to that "mother" by reproducing her fragmentation and death. Or as Doane notes in "The Abstraction of a Lady": "Above and beyond the Oedipal rivalry between father and son, the text invests much of its energy in delineating the place (or perhaps non-place) or the difficulty of the maternal" (p. 128).

In this analysis of *La Signora di Tutti*, I examine how repeated sounds—embodied and disembodied, diegetic and nondiegetic—work in conjunction with still and moving images in the film as it progresses, within the framed narrative, from musically induced *jouissance* to suicidal despair. I also discuss the "family romance" as it figures in the film and delineate the importance of the mother fixation underlying Gaby's obsessive or masochistic love and her suicidal guilt. This guilt will be shown to have a close relationship to the debt incurred by Leonardo, as interior and exterior polarities of similar situations. An analysis of Ophuls' use of "adjacent spaces" in *Signora* and of the intricate deployment of communications devices draws together several of these thorny issues.

A Hot Little Number

Both *Letter from an Unknown Woman* and *La Signora di Tutti* are framed by stories telling the "last hours of a life."[18] As the reader may have gathered, the narrative framing *Signora* is one of the strangest on record.[19] Having attempted suicide, Gaby Doriot, Italian queen of the French screen, lies only half-conscious on the operating table. From her point of view we observe a large gas mask descending from the ceiling to cover her face.[20] "Narcotically induced dreams" of her past life (we are informed by a lengthy intertitle) constitute the main body of the narrative. Emphasis is placed on the woman's *immobility* in the frame narrative, as in *Lola Montès* (1955) and in *Letter*—underscoring the woman's double role as actor and spectator of her own life. Ironically, the search for Gaby in the first scenes of the film (she is late on the film set) is characterized by a highly mobile camera—a mobile camera that is often linked to Gaby's desire during the course of the film. The film tracks along in two parallel sequences, in which the assistant director searches among the props and people of the film studio, calling Gaby's name, and her agent seeks her at home—only to find her immobilized behind the door of the bathroom where she has cut her wrists.

As in *Letter*, the narrative of *Signora* is by and large only loosely connected to Gaby's "consciousness" (or lack thereof, in this case). But unlike Lisa's, Gaby's voice emerges only twice as a voice-over narrating agent. This disembodied voice is immediately recuperated by the diegesis (the "world" implied by the images we see on the screen), first as a conversation with Roberto's mother about the events of the previous night (when Gaby's tryst with Roberto has been interrupted by his father driving by), then as a discussion with her agent/manager about her autobiographical radio broadcast.[21] In the middle of the midnight tryst, a voice begins narrating the events—establishing the scene retrospectively as a flashback. In the latter case we are also utterly unaware that we are watching a flashback within a flashback: Gaby's narrative control comes as a shock. By contrast, although her agent and the diegetic film producers do not in fact have control of the sound or image track, several scenes emphasize their access to an infinite number of "communications devices," including intercoms, telephones, radio, and other systems for projecting the voice, as well as to the printing presses and cameras used to reproduce the image.

Although Gaby is almost never empowered to control its visual elements, the film is nevertheless at pains to establish itself at least partially as her final deadly vision, become that of the audience. We have the impression, as is also the case in *Letter*, that certain flashbacks are more "directly" authorized by Gaby than are others. Sometimes this "authorization" is subliminal, as when the credit sequence unfolds against a gaseous background like the one Gaby sees as she begins to breathe the anesthetic gas. There are other moments when the camera seems to identify with Gaby's predicament, even when it does not adopt her point of view. But despite these efforts to place the woman as an authorizing consciousness with respect to the image track, it is as listener that Gaby is most decidedly constituted as subject. In her discussion of *Sorry, Wrong Number* (1948), Amy Laurence terms this interpellation of the subject-auditor the constitution of the female subject as the "One Who Hears" (p. 22).

With respect to the image track, Gaby is far more likely to be the suffering object rather than the subject of vision (though she is occasionally both). But there *is* a profound tension in this film between the woman's passivity and the ambiguous effort made by the frame narrative to endow Gaby with subjectivity, by lending her explicit narrative authority from time to time. We will see that this tension stems from the film's strategy, an ambiguously feminist one, which makes Gabriella the *ground* of any possible subjectivity, although she herself cannot really occupy the subject-position. Indeed, Gaby finds virtually no relief from the tyranny of the image in this film. She is more radically and immediately punished for the use of her image to her own narcissistic ends (if we can even say that this ever really occurs) than are the women in Ophuls' later films—who have devised strategies, however imperfect, to circumvent co-optation and to obtain what they desire. Gaby's moments of pleasure in vision occur when she is preparing herself first for the ball, then for the opera, and gazes at length at her own image in mirrors. In both cases these flirtations with narcissism precede the beginning of destructive love affairs and signify the mysterious power of Gaby's poisonous beauty as well as her dangerous absorption in her own image.[22] Gaby's pleasure in music is similarly brief, whether she produces or only listens to it.

La Signora di Tutti's narrative hinges on the strategic placement of telephone calls. This is also true of *De Mayerling à Sarajevo* (1940) and *The Reckless Moment* (1949), among other films by Ophuls. As has been noted, the final phone call of *The Reckless Moment*, for example, serves to reestablish the patriarchal order absent during most of the film, as Lucia Harper receives a phone call from her husband while she is still wracked with grief over her "lover's" death. And Montenuovo's call at the end of *Sarajevo* is the call of fatality, of historical destiny. In *Signora* Gabriella's call to her husband Leonardo and Roberto's call to Gabriella both function with many of the other disembodied sounds in the film as calls of *conscience* (as I will show later in this chapter). Both *Letter* and *Signora* are structured on the abrupt interventions of *communications from a distance.* In the former film it is of course the letter that arrives at the beginning and that finally (literally) awakens Stefan to the moral world. In the latter film two phone calls intrude upon the narrative (as do two telegrams and a written invitation), acting as the "calls to conscience" that will determine the destinies of the protagonists. In contradistinction to Laurence's claim that aurality as it is exemplified by the telephone represents a feminine challenge to dominant (masculine) visuality,[23] in both *La Signora di Tutti* and *Sorry, Wrong Number* the "call" that interpolates differentially the man and the woman does not operate to the woman's final advantage. (Of course, Laurence's view of the telephone as a challenge to male dominance is supported by many other cultural cues—including the frequent eruption of men's anger at women talking "endlessly" with their women friends on the phone.) The woman's "difference" from the man—a difference whose psychological roots are shown to lie in her relationship of desire, identity, and rivalry with the mother, and which is nurtured by discriminatory treatment toward girls as they are growing up—does establish her in a separate sphere with its own distinct powers, but those powers are most often finally held in horror or subsumed to the production of the dominant masculine subject. Laurence notes, in fact, that in *Sorry, Wrong Number* the woman is, ultimately, only listening in on a phone call that spells her doom. In *Signora* it is Gaby herself who is called, but she too is called only to the inevitability of her demise. Both films arrive at the impasse of feminine subjectivity, but from different angles.

From Shame to Guilt in Waltz Time

The framed narrative of *La Signora di Tutti* opens with a fade to a "narcotically" clouded image of the young Gaby singing with a group of uniformed (or plainly dressed) girls. This is a school singing class being carried out under the direction of a bespectacled young woman. Our delving into Gaby's past thus begins with the offscreen sound of young voices raised in song: we are lured into the past via the sound track. Gaby stands out in this crowd of young girls—she is centrally placed and is wearing a gown with a bold plaid print. The depiction of a girl growing into womanhood, using the same actress to play both girl and woman, is familiar to viewers of Ophuls' films, since both *Letter from an Unknown Woman* and

Lola Montès use the same device. Among the three films, only Joan Fontaine's portrayal of a child in *Letter* could be termed "successful," according to conventional standards of realism. The others retain an awkwardness that is perhaps of interest for what it reveals of the sexual precocity and sexual latency that provide an important tension in the films.

We soon discover, in this scene of *Signora*, that the schoolmistress is only standing in for the usual choirmaster, who is mysteriously absent. When the female teacher leaves the room to see what has happened to the choirmaster, the other girls mill around Gaby and tease her about her apparent infatuation or flirtation with him. One girl holds a pencil under her nose in imitation of a mustache and pretends to direct the singers, thus placing emphasis on the question of sexual role-playing in conjunction with the performance of music in the film. The school principal soon arrives to announce that "an accident has happened" involving their singing teacher. On hearing this, Gaby faints (in another of her recurring moments of unconsciousness in the film), murmuring, "What fault is it of mine?" Blended together in this scene are the elements that will come to punctuate all critical moments later in the film: the abrupt arrival of a message that prompts one of the protagonists to constitute him or herself as potentially guilty (a coming to consciousness in guilt), intercalated with the story of a love that takes root through a musical relationship.

A dissolve to a close-up of the principal's face takes us to his office, where Gaby has been transported for interrogation. She describes her motherlessness, speaks of her teacher's declaration that he could no longer live without her (which will be echoed), and wishes aloud that she had married him before this terrible event (the teacher's departure, or possible suicide) had occurred. "A man with a wife and children!" is the principal's horrified retort. Her wish is not only impossible but deeply shameful. He bitterly repeats one of the phrases that will later constitute Gaby's paranoid aural hallucinations: "Vergogna, vergogna, vergogna!"—"Shame!" The rudimentary form of feminism guiding the surface of this film is evident in this pointed injustice shown to Gaby, who cannot "rationally" be held responsible for her own fatal attractiveness. (One assumes that her voice as well as her face is alluring, since her music teacher is enamored with her.) On a more fundamental basis, the woman is held by the film to be necessarily responsible for the damage done by her compelling presence. Or perhaps, the film shows us that contemporary society holds her thus responsible.

The principal's hissed word, "vergogna!" overlaps into the dissolve that takes us to the next scene (a family dinner at Gaby's house), and recurs later while Gaby watches the clock during the ball at Roberto's house.[24] A similar pattern of obvious injustice meted out by patriarchal authority can be observed in the dinner scene, which opens with a medium shot of the family gathered around the table, quickly followed by a dissolve onto an extreme close-up of the father's censuring face as he angrily stares Gaby down. The Colonel calls his other daughter, Anna, into an adjacent room and begins to shout about Gabriella (she is to be taken out of school, to work at home, to be punctual at table, and so on, in order of decreasing severity). Gaby miserably walks down a hallway to the rear plane of the image, shot in deep focus, as the tunnel-like walls seem to close around her. She can hear her father's shouts, and her sister's cry when he slaps her and bids her to be silent. Once again, a fissure opens up between soundtrack and image, although this remains within the diegetic space.[25]

I have noted in my previous readings of Ophuls' films that the military man takes the role of blustering interdictor. Even in this early film, however, the father's function is as much *pointed to* (ironized) as it is used in any straightforward way. Gaby can live under the "military discipline" of her father, whose anger is not treated with absolute seriousness by the film. (I might also point out that the father is shown, at one point, waxing sentimental over a picture—subject matter unknown—he has just found in the attic: controller of images? mesmerized, in his turn, by them?) Gaby can, in other words, bear to be *shamed*. Only her guilt toward the all-powerful, crippled, and destructive mother (a guilt experienced as the return of a sonorous ghost) incapacitates Gaby.

The Family Romance: The Case for Space

The dining room scene, which begins with the echo of the principal's voice and ends with the equally "disembodied" shouts of the father heard from the next room, is not the first in the film to linger in one space while in an adjacent offscreen space violent, often sexual, activities provide the real focus of attention—nor will it be the last scene of this kind. A dissolve from the Murge family dining room to a shot of the house's garden gate is followed by a pan to Gaby tending the plants, not unhappily, under her father's direction. The "inside-outside" dichotomy signaled by the gate is underscored when the Colonel immediately reproaches his daughter for looking outside through its bars. Very soon afterwards, a fight takes place outside the iron bars of the garden fence. The still unknown Roberto Nanni is battling his comrades, who insult Gabriella because Roberto wants to invite the scandalous girl to a ball at his home. During the squabble, a ruler is broken over Roberto's face, scarring him for life.[26] A piece of wood flies to Gaby, who picks it up and reads (in close-up) the initials "R.N."—the Italian letters roll sensuously off her tongue. This momentary violence, this bridging of two spaces by the "broken rule(r)" will join Gaby's fate to Roberto's. The wooden emissary from Roberto also serves to open up the series of written communications from him: first the invitation signed with his whole name in the next sequence, and finally the telegram to his father asking him never to write him again. As is many times the case in *Letter from an Unknown Woman*, this scene contains elements that can best be understood in *juxtaposition* with subsequent scenes in the film. The father's presence in the garden with his daughter in this scene might, for example, pass unremarked-upon were there not another such pairing later in the film, involving Gaby and Leonardo in a garden, with drastic consequences (see below).

The scene of the ball is notable for many reasons, not least of which is the 360-degree swish pan signaling the camera's "identification" with Gabriella, made happily dizzy by her waltz with Roberto. (Roberto, be it noted, sees Gaby from the landing of a staircase as she sits below, waiting to be asked to dance.) Then, while the couple wanders in the garden, Alma sends for her son. As Gaby sits in the anteroom to Alma's chambers, watching the clock, she anticipates a similar scene of a later Ophulsian heroine—Sophie Chotek in *Sarajevo*. Gaby's wait for Roberto is shot with low-key lighting; the camera tracks in first on Gaby, and then on the clock. As its ticking grows louder, Gaby's school principal's voice can be heard repeating "shame, shame," as the image dissolves to show the passage of time. (Dissolves are also used in a "nonclassical" manner, as punctuation of a shot–reverse shot series in the next, intimate scene between Alma Nanni and Gabriella.) As the image blurs, becoming spatially and temporally disjunctive, the disembodied voice strikes dread in the young woman.

After Gaby has been introduced into the wealthy Nanni family by means of the ball, she is invited by the doting Alma to make use of their box at La Scala for an evening of (solitary) pleasure. As Gaby dresses for the occasion (gazing at herself in the mirror as she had before the ball), a car arrives outside, making a noise that the women can hear in Alma's bedroom. (Cars are strongly associated with Leonardo in both the novel and the film.) Since the servants are busy elsewhere, Gaby offers to run down to open the door. The "visitor" in question is Leonardo Nanni, an elegant businessman, the master of the villa. Gaby's first meeting with Leonardo takes place on the staircase—a moment whose resonance with respect to the Ophuls film corpus can hardly be overestimated. Attired in a borrowed black evening gown, Gaby presents a striking picture as she pauses shyly on the bottom steps. The *visual* impact of this moment, as much as the *aural* dimension of their quickly blooming passion, produces repercussions throughout the rest of the film. As Gaby holds out her hand to Leonardo for the first time (on the stairway), Alma's voice floats down, startling both her husband and the girl. Only a moment later will the handshake be accomplished, in hasty embarrassment. (One is reminded of Lisa's interrupted introduction to Lt. von Kaltnegger in *Letter*—an interruption that also signaled a hitch in the smooth Oedipalization of the female protagonist.)

As has been mentioned, the love or passion between Leonardo and Gaby is ignited at (by) an opera performance, or, more specifically, during the *retelling* of this opera's plot at the bedside of the lame mother (Alma) later that evening. For the moment, music and the telling of a story kindle the romance *in the absence of the image* (we never do see the opera stage, even when Gaby and Leonardo are looking at it). Or rather, it is Gaby herself who is still the primary object of vision even when she is looking at the stage. Not only do we watch Gaby and Leo instead of the opera, but Leo himself is shown looking only at Gaby during this scene. As is the case in several other films by Ophuls, the plot of the opera within the film has a strong thematic tie with the events of the film itself, though Leo recounts only a short segment of the opera at Alma's bedside.[27] The story (set in the nineteenth century) goes as follows: A young officer is shot while a crowd gathers triumphantly beneath balconies laden with flowers and spectators. During the ensuing silence, a young woman steps forward and goes to the officer, who is "healed by her presence." (While he tells this part of the opera, Leonardo fixes his eyes on Gaby, who stares at him, enchanted by her recollection of the opera, but as yet ignorant of Leonardo's growing passion.)[28] In the next act (the second), the woman rides away on a military campaign with the officer, now her lover. When they finally have a chance to be alone together, the

emperor himself intervenes—carrying the woman away to a series of foreign cities, to which the young man follows them, searching every night
for his lover and calling her name in the streets. The young man finally
goes mad in prison, for love of the young woman.

In the midst of recounting, in tandem, this part of the opera, the couple has moved into Gaby's room, adjacent to Alma's, to find a cigarette
for Gaby. As Gaby describes the young man's plight, she says his love is
"magnificent," that his imprisonment and death for the woman are also
"magnificent." The couple is already framed in a tight close-up as she
whispers these words. Leonardo tries to kiss her, but confusion or her
awareness of Alma's nearby presence makes her raise her hand to his
mouth to prevent it.[29] Clearly, Leonardo sees himself in the role of the
emperor who abducts the young woman from the arms of her more suitable lover. The intervention of the paternal figure is not precisely the
appearance of the placeholder of the Law: indeed, as in *Lola Montès*, it is
the emperor/father who willingly commits the incestuous transgression
with the symbolic daughter. This "father" may be "healed" by the
embodied woman, by her presence—which is also always mediated by
her potential as captivating image. Moreover, it is Leonardo, rather than
Roberto, who "goes mad" in prison.. Leonardo wishes to play *all* the
roles in the film's version of the opera. This pattern involving the desire
of the father for a surrogate daughter is less common in Ophuls' films
than is a more typically Oedipal schema (an emphasis on the "daughter's" desire for the father, the misbegotten "Electra complex"). Even
more obscure in most of the films is that structure whose outline we
could barely trace in *Letter*, but is the overriding emotion of this film
(although it is absent from the operatic passion-tale as recounted by
Leonardo): the daughter's hallucinatory sense of guilt toward the mother she wishes to or indeed has replaced.

Alma's death scene, the culminating point of a number of the film's
motifs, ought to be one of the best-known in the European cinema of the
thirties, for its sheer bravado as well as for its visual dynamism. One night
(to be the last of Gaby's protracted visit), Alma lies in bed, confiding to
the solicitous Gaby her old fears concerning Gaby's character, the scandal over the choirmaster, and so on. Now all her anxieties are calmed,
and she extends an emotion-laden thanks to Gaby for the difference the
latter has made in her life. Alma turns on the radio as Gaby retires to her
(adjacent) chamber, where Leonardo awaits her, hoping to lure her to
a tryst in the garden. When the music on the radio turns out to be the

music from the opera, Alma calls out to Gaby, who does not answer since she has been obliged to silence Leonardo by creeping outside to meet him. As crosscutting between the two scenes indicates, Alma becomes more and more upset, finally struggling to her wheelchair as she screams for Gaby. Whether or not she realizes that her husband is making love to Gabriella in the garden is, as Andrew Sarris puts it, "tantalizingly ambiguous."[30] Alma wheels faster and faster, as shots of the hallway are crosscut with shots of Gaby and Leonardo about to kiss (she only half willingly, especially after he repeats the choirmaster's prophetic words, "I can no longer live without you"). As Alma nears the staircase, we only see the shadow of her wheelchair. When she gets to the staircase, she first tries to walk down assisted by her cane. But her urge to find out what is happening "offscreen" overwhelms her: getting back into her chair, she appears to fling herself downwards, in what seems to be a suicide, as the wheelchair crashes to the floor.

With this final gesture, Alma once again manages to interrupt her husband's physical contact with Gaby as they stand in the adjacent space of the garden, alerted that something is amiss by Alma's "disembodied" scream and the crashing sound of the falling wheelchair. As I implied above, this scene casts a different light on the earlier one where Gaby is "in the garden with (her real) father," as well as on the outdoor walk with Roberto during the ball scene (only incestuous when read in retrospect—after Gaby becomes his stepmother), where they were "spied" upon by his mother and then interrupted through the intermediary of a servant. At a number of other moments during the film, a seemingly "incestuous" pair lingers in a space barely separated from a jealous or interdicting party. This is already the case even in the scene where Gaby describes to her principal how she and the choirmaster had walked together in the schoolyard. What was apparently an uninflected relationship—that between the stiff and unprepossessing Colonel and his daughter—now reappears in the trappings of the girl's "romantic" vision of a paternal figure who is wealthier and more powerful than her own. The father's importance as a love-object is shown to be far greater than is his potential as law-giver. Roberto, the "realistic" love, is also blocked by maternal interdiction (as he later puts it, "If only I had kissed you then, perhaps none of this would have happened"). This aspect of the maternal function is taken over by Gaby's sister Anna, when she marries Roberto and has children with him, effectively insuring that Gaby will never possess him.[31]

Honey, I'm Home

When Gaby and Leonardo rush in from the garden to see what has happened to Alma, Gaby trails behind her lover, half-smiling in her shock. Running past the ruined wheelchair and up the steps where Leonardo first saw her, she pounces on the still-blaring radio and smashes it to bits. A fade to Alma's portrait above the mantelpiece brings us to a conversation, not many days later, between Roberto and his father. Reproaching his father's profound grief as contrary to what Alma would have wanted, Roberto declares his intention to marry Gaby. Leonardo walks across the room, contemplating his son's words, finally barking out a brief but definitive "No!" An extremely rapid cut takes us to the exterior of a train, where the tormented Gaby and her husband Leonardo are on an extended wedding trip. This complex montage sequence includes images of the train compartment, its wheels, the couple's baggage receiving stickers from many ports, a ship, and the scarcely audible murmurs of the couple attempting to soothe one another's anguish at being together in culpability.

Leonardo and Gaby are called back to the villa by an urgent telegram (most likely related to Leonardo's business), but they find the mansion too haunted by Alma's presence for Gaby to remain in it. After they are welcomed home by the servants, Gaby moves to the fireplace where Alma's full-length portrait is enshrined. As light streams in from the windows, a shadow in the form of a cross falls across the painting. With a gesture reminiscent of Madame de . . .'s final dedication of the earrings, Gaby places flowers on the mantel shelf, in homage to the woman she has replaced—as she had, earlier in her life, "replaced" her own mother. (Again, this shot–reverse shot sequence is connected by dissolves rather than the more conventional cuts.) The castrated (lame), now dead mother returns as the sound of a music only Gaby hears—the strains of the opera's symphonic overture coming up from the fireplace.[32] The "perverted hearing" described by Koch has moved from the realm of sexual obsession to the related one of ineradicable guilt. Gaby moves to the stairway only to have a nervous fit (asking wildly that the no-longer-existing radio be turned off), thus going back to the scene of her original self-display to the erring father (Leonardo)—the "chronotope" of the staircase, which in this case (as in *Letter*) resurrects a painful past. The role of the visual in the etiology and the horrifying collapse of love is inextricably mixed with the seductive effects of the sonorous. The mother's call from beyond the grave immediately shakes Gaby to the depths of her being.

P. S., I. O. U.

At that moment in the film when Gaby and Leonardo arrive home from their sad honeymoon, Leonardo returns immediately to his office, mostly to get hold of some money so that he can buy another house for his bride. Since he has already borrowed huge sums from the firm, he is met at his office with accusations of embezzlement. With an image that repeats in a displaced manner a configuration that opens and closes the film, Leonardo finds himself surrounded by a group of businessmen— just as Gaby's turning record is surrounded by her debating film agent and producer, and as her inert body is surrounded by the team of surgeons. Like the other men "masochistically" connected to women in Ophuls' films, Leo is feminized by his association with the woman, as is evident in his adoption of this archetypically feminine position. His indebtedness has led him to a criminal act for which he is now about to be imprisoned. Although Gaby's predicament is the film's focus, *La Signora di Tutti*, even more than *Letter from an Unknown Woman*, also depicts with great detail the man's masochistic agony. Like Louise in *Madame de . . .*, Leonardo will be stripped of all his possessions because of his love and will finally die (without Louise's compensation) because of his fascination with this woman's "dangerous" image.

One similarity between *Letter* and *Signora* lies in the man's ambiguous enslavement to the woman's image, ambiguous because it also entails her capture and death. The woman's image (the "maternal" superego or, perhaps, Deleuze's "oral mother") functions to render vestigial the paternally based superego. When, in the scene at his office, Leonardo attempts to talk his way out of his partners' accusations, they rise up against him one by one, shouting "No!" as he had shouted to his son earlier in the film. The paternal interdiction is turned back onto Leonardo, but its effect is only felt when indirectly relayed by the dead mother: the phone rings—it is given to Leonardo. From the other end of the wire, Gaby tells him in a trancelike voice that he must be true to Alma, to "stay" with her even if she is dead. Her train is waiting; Gaby leaves the phone's receiver hanging from its cord—an umbilicus that is never cut—and goes to begin her journey to France. Leonardo's only response is to weep. In this scene,

Leonardo is clearly *humiliating the paternal function as it exists in himself,* putting himself in the position of the one to whom "no" is said. Deleuze describes this humiliation of the father-in-himself as a primary goal of the male masochist. Nevertheless, the emphasis in this film may fall on the poisonous effects of the female image, rather than on the man's culpability for desiring or for commodifying and controlling the woman.

Leonardo encounters death when, freshly out of the debtor's prison where his love for Gaby had sent him, he allows a car to mow him down. This ambiguously voluntary death occurs after Leo gazes tearfully at hundreds of photos of Gaby displayed at the premiere of her film. These images, which serve to dominate the man, are reified as the emblem of exploitation itself and, of course, repeat Gaby's mother's and Alma's reduction to an "image." Gaby's life also reaches its painful climax as a result of her husband's encounter with her photographs when, to defuse the scandal brought on by Leonardo's death, the French production company convinces Roberto to come to France to defend Gaby's good name. Only after their reunion and nostalgic walk together does Roberto later confess over the telephone that he is married to Anna and has children with her. "I'll see you in your films" is his final promise to Gabriella. As much as anything else, these words serve to precipitate her suicide. Roberto's "call from afar" spells out for Gabriella that she is ineluctably commodified as *la signora di tutti.* The "realistic" love she had known has now been absorbed into the prostitution of her stardom. Roberto is one of the multitude fascinated by her screen-image.

In this discussion of Leonardo's *debt* and Gaby's *guilt,* we are on familiar territory, insofar as Ophuls' films are concerned. As we saw in great detail, it was a sense of *irredeemable* debt that drove Louise to protest her situation in *Madame de. . . .* There is no question, for Louise (nor for Lisa or Lola Montès) of internalizing guilt. Although Gabriella's subjecthood is otherwise in doubt in this film, she is the one who takes on the burden of *internalization,* "the development of a soul"—whose name in this case happens to be "Alma." Samuel Weber comments upon a well-known passage from Nietzsche's *On the Genealogy of Morals* concerning the "material" origin of *Schuld* as *debt* (though the word means both guilt *and* debt): "The opposition consists in the nature of the obligation thereby designated: whereas *guilt* is construed as a debt that is essentially unredeemable (by the debtor, at least), the earlier, more original, more tangible notion of *Schuld* was predicated precisely upon the essential quality of its being *repayable.*"[33] That Gaby's irredeemable debt is a debt to a parent, in this case the "mother," is a situation also illuminated by Nietzsche's remarks: "The civil-law relationship between the debtor and his creditor . . . has been interpreted in an, historically speaking, exceedingly remarkable and dubious manner into a relationship in which, to us modern men, it is perhaps least intelligible: namely into the relation of the present generation to its ancestors."[34] What Freud sees as *fundamental* (in *Totem and Taboo* and elsewhere)—the sense of guilt toward the ancestors—is described (sarcastically) by Nietzsche as almost unintelligible to moderns. Indeed, it is Freud who *made* this notion intelligible to nineteenth- and twentieth-century Westerners by giving it precisely the kind of context to be found in *La Signora di Tutti,* that is, a *familial* one.

Although Leonardo is able, in prison, to redeem debt brought upon him by his desiring relation to the young woman, he cannot withstand the power of her image, and like Gaby in front of Alma's portrait, Leonardo buckles when he is confronted with Gaby's multiplied image hanging in the theater's antechamber. Through her *irredeemable* guilt Gaby grounds any possible subjectivity in this film. It is the man's reaction to the woman's image, to something *external,* that drives him to despair, while Gaby dies as a result of the inmost truth of her being, from a sense of guilt, caused by the double bind of obligatory identification and rivalry with the mother, that leads to suicide. If Gaby experiences her painful relationship with the mother as masochistically pleasurable, it does not seem to be because this pain will purchase a later, guiltless pleasure. Instead, the death drive seems to be invoked as a fundamental aspect of subjectivity.

In a gesture that may help us to open up the role of debt and guilt in this film, Jacques Derrida and Samuel Weber have described the effects of the Heideggerian call to conscience by means of the figure of the *telephone call.* In *La Carte Postale* Derrida tells of receiving a collect call from the United States from a certain "Martini Heidegger"—a call that he very quickly refuses ("It's a joke, I do not accept").[35] Weber juxtaposes Derrida's quick refusal of a "debt" (the "collect call" from Heidegger) and Derrida's obsessive concern, in *La Carte Postale,* with Freud's rapid dismissal of his intellectual debt to Nietzsche and to philosophy. Concerning the phone call, Weber comments:

The discussion of *Schuld* in *Being and Time* is also the analysis of a "call" (*Ruf*), or rather, of an "appeal" (*Anruf*). Or perhaps of a telephone call. Indeed, coming to section 58 with that other [Derrida's] call in mind, it becomes impossible *not* to read the *Anruf* of conscience (*Gewissen*) as just such a telephone call. In the first place, the call is very definitely long distance: "The call is from afar to afar" (*Gerufen wird aus der Ferne in die Ferne*) (p. 316). Secondly, the call is in a certain sense uncalled for, it comes as a surprise, interrupting and deranging. Thirdly, if the call deranges, it is because, ultimately, nothing is said: "The call asserts nothing, gives no information about world events, has nothing to tell" (p. 318). It announces nothing, except perhaps the nothingness of the called, of the addressee."[36]

Earlier in this chapter I describe the man's need to find a certain "authenticity," also defined as "immediacy," in or with respect to the woman. The call to conscience involves precisely such an appeal to the authentic self: the woman, far more than the man, is shown to be capable of responding to the call to authenticity. The woman, however, cannot be authentic *for herself*: she is "everyone's"—even her relation to herself is owned by someone else. As the recipient of the mother's "call," the musical reminder of her fundamental guilt, Gaby Doriot is confirmed in the nothingness already shown to be her lot in terms of the image track—in that the film within the film, the one about Everybody's Lady, is caught up, as Doane has indicated, in a *mise-en-abyme* structure centered on the woman as absence: that film within the film (also entitled *La Signora di Tutti*) is never seen. In her role as the receiver of musical terror, Gaby is reenacting the mother's position as *auditor* "and [is] hence the recipient of the text's greatest degree of violence" (p. 134). Only insofar as she is linked to the mother through the medium of sound will Gaby also be able to enact the role of the caller: she calls Leonardo not to provide him with information but to remind him of his essential duty. But even though Leonardo seems to share the "same" fate as Gaby (in that he, too, kills himself), everything having to do with the debt that Leonardo assumes is less profound than Gaby's guilt. When Gaby begins to forget her irredeemable debt to the mother, by thinking that she might be able to resume her relationship with Roberto, her own sister Anna intervenes indirectly (her sister, now a mother), via Roberto's phone call, to remind Gaby of what has gone before. In this demonstration of the woman's positioning vis-à-vis the structure of guilt and debt, as well as in his comparison of "woman" to the cinematic machine, Ophuls deconstructs the woman's otherwise (in this film) "naturalized" role as fatal cinematic object.

In my discussion of *Madame de . . .*, I commented upon the situation of the protagonist of Dickens's *Little Dorrit*, who occupied the debtors' prison with her father. Although, like Gabriella, Dorrit is "innocent," the novel is structured on her primordial participation in the debt of her husband/father, not that she must *repay* it, but she must share in the guilt brought about by the situation. The reader may recall that for a moment, and for that moment only, Dorrit rages at her friend Clennam, saying that her father should not be made to repay the debt in years and now in money, too! Later, Dorrit recognizes her own guilt in retrospect as precisely that momentary inability to distinguish moral truth, to recognize the real nature of the debt. So, too, we have seen, did Gaby momentarily dismiss her own debt to the "ancestor," to the mother who bore her and who returned in surrogate form in the person of Alma. In *Signora* Gaby's relationship to the film's "hearing world" has been described as privileged because, although Leonardo is also affected by the music of the opera and is, in the eyes of the law, a man *in debt*, he does not share Gaby's profound guilt, depending upon her, rather, to constitute the possibility of morality itself, even if she cannot herself *be* moral. (Woman is not the "custodian" of truth but, as Gayatri Spivak has commented, its "mysterious figure.")[37] Gaby is the addressee of conscience's call: she is, finally, a "nothingness."

The demises of Leonardo Nanni and William Dorrit are not dissimilar. In both cases, *after the debt is canceled*, the man returns, in fantasy, to the scene of primordial loss (Dorrit hallucinates his prison life; Nanni is confronted with the hallucinatory multiplication of Gaby's picture). This hallucinated return to the past announces Dorrit's sickness and impending death. Leonardo turns away from Gaby's image, still mesmerized by it, and permits himself to be killed. Leonardo's debt is not to the woman or women he loved but to the society that bankrolled his involuntary fascination with Gaby. That this social debt is absolved is indicated in his son's ability not to carry on the paternal tare. Instead, he leads a "normal" life, only moderately allured by Gaby's cinematic image. Although Gabriella attempts finally to absolve guilt by facing a voluntary death, inflicting it upon herself, she dies without issue, still culpable with respect to the maternal essence now embodied in her sister. She must die because it is possible that she will sin again. In her dying Gaby also hallucinates—she sees and "projects" the film that we are watching. In her final moment of consciousness, Gaby turns not away from but toward the maternal image that haunts her, the "mama" whose name she calls out at the last.

Your Seams Are Showing

We have seen that it is at the confluence of the aural and the visual—portrait and music—that the "repressed" opera returns. The nostalgia for the past, Gaby's past, asserts itself as horror: the seams of the unified sound-image are showing. In Ophuls' 1938 French film, *Werther*, adapted from Goethe's *The Sorrows of Young Werther*, the female protagonist's (Charlotte/Annie Vernay) response to music is emphasized at the expense of the narrative of male heartbreak and suicide that Goethe's text comprises. Again, guilt and regret are figured as a menacing eruption of sound, and a disturbance in the synchronicity of sound and image. Werther (Pierre-Richard Willm), a music and poetry lover, comes to a new town where he is employed as chief clerk by Albert, Charlotte's fiancé, a judge (technically, an "assessor," or assistant to the magistrate). (Werther's arrival by carriage recalls the opening scenes of *The Bartered Bride.*) Although he is thus the official "upholder of the law," Albert actually presents himself initially as, like Werther, a lover of Rousseau (some intense male bonding takes place when they discover they have both underlined the same passage in their "forbidden" copies of the *Social Contract*). But Albert becomes more and more the oppressive husband, the hanging judge, during the course of the film.[38] Like Charlotte's father, and the elderly presiding magistrate, Albert is concerned with punctuality—while Werther is habitually late, indeed something of a bon vivant. The motherless Charlotte cares for her many younger brothers and sisters. (One of her brothers meets Werther in the carriage and swaps hats with him, in a familiar Ophulsian play with headgear. This makes the boy late for dinner, for which he is heavily reproached.) Music is both symbolic of pleasure and liberty and part of the slowly tightening paternalistic society. Werther's love for music is clearly meant to make him a desirable, "sensitive" man; but the obligatory chamber music recitals set up by the magistrate are more and more oppressive. Werther attempts to reform the musical predilections of the town by convincing the mayor to change the song played by the carillon in the tower of the "palais de justice," where Albert and Werther are employed. Like the typical Romantic, Werther insists that a local poet's words, put to music, should take the place of the current selection. Interestingly, a scene with the mayor (featuring displays of numerous suits of armor) indicates that he does not really care what music the bells play, as long as he doesn't have to pay to reconstruct the "mechanism." So despite the song's "melancholy" words (which, his assistant points out, no one will hear or remember), the mayor signs the proclamation.

When Albert leaves town on business, Werther, unaware that Charlotte is "taken," even less so that she is Albert's fiancée, courts her assiduously despite the shrill objections of Charlotte's aunt. (Her raucous shrieks at Charlotte's improprieties are not taken as effective interdiction, despite their ridiculous stridency, and Charlotte continues to dance and make merry with Werther.) But Charlotte is a "nice girl," and their courtship is cut short when, during an outdoor scene unusual in the Ophuls corpus,[39] she finally tells Werther of her secret engagement to Albert, which she feels duty-bound to honor. As she runs away from the devastated young man, who has been cruelly interrupted in the midst of his marriage proposal, Charlotte hears the town's bells playing the simple song Werther had championed (and offered as an engagement gift to her). As she runs screaming through the streets, shots of the ringing bells are superimposed over her face and body. Her pain is clearly agonizing; she finally collapses.

Charlotte marries Albert. (The occasion is depicted in a series of scenes very much anticipating the marriage of the Archduke Franz Ferdinand and Sophie Chotek.) Werther's behavior deteriorates more and more—he begins to frequent taverns and prostitutes, and in one scene tries to slash his wrist with a wine glass! This peculiar moment is interrupted by the innkeeper. But Werther manages to appear at one last weekly musical soirée, organized by Albert. Charlotte weeps at her piano, and returns a poem of Werther's to him. They bid each other adieu.

In one of the last scenes of the film, a sinuous tracking shot reveals the trollops in the bawdy house, who steal a poem from Werther's pocket and read it aloud. His pain on hearing his words mocked links him to Charlotte's painful relationship to the "hearing world." Charlotte receives a letter from Werther recounting this scene, and she realizes he is doomed. Like the Baron in *Liebelei*, Albert searches for his wife, who has gone out not to rescue her lover but to confess: "I must love my husband, and I always think I feel the other's look upon me. I only want to love my husband, and always I hear the voice of the other who speaks to me. . . . I didn't lie, and I didn't tell the truth. Is there a lie in me?" The priest sends her back to her husband. Werther is called to the courthouse, where he interviews a man who killed a faithless woman. He has the man's chains removed, but Albert arrives and immediately reverses the order. They argue about the case before them, with Albert insisting that "there are limits to passion" set by moral tradition. Werther finds extenuating circumstances in the "bitterness of solitude" and derides the law.

As Werther prepares to leave town, he gazes out of the rain-streaked window, listening to the carillon. The camera tracks toward him; his image is connected by dissolves first to the bell tower, where "his" song is playing, then to Charlotte, who also gazes out her window toward the "palais de justice." She screams horrendously, as the camera cuts to the servants and tracks and pans with them as they run to her aid. Once again, the film's visuals seem to insist on matching the intensity of its soundtrack: Charlotte is framed through yet another window, as one servant watches the other minister to her. (All of this is completely absent from the novel, as are Werther's democratic notions, the deadpan treatment of his passion, and Charlotte's "true love" for him.) Werther sends for the pistols that he had loaned Albert, which the latter gladly returns. (The suicide thus has overtones of the familiar Ophulsian duel, just as the love triangle, which completely betrays the Goethe text, is reminiscent of those in *Liebelei, Letter from an Unknown Woman, Madame de. . . .*, and elsewhere.) As Charlotte prays for him, Werther shoots himself, offscreen. We only hear the sound of the shot.

The woman's relation to the sound track is in this film overtly a tortured one. Like Gaby, Werther dies by his own hand, and is tormented by what he hears, but his plight is given less cinematic sound and fury than is Charlotte's auditory response to his song, and his death. And when the woman's painful response to the "sound world" is most emphasized, the film's visuals are always in disarray; dissolves and superimpositions emphasize the fragile juncture between image and sound, image and image. Charlotte's "guilt," her sense of loss, does not seem to be immediately connected with a maternal entity. Nevertheless, Werther is certainly a "feminized" man, in his relation to music (more ardent than the other male characters'), his protests against the law, his (Willm's) Ashley Wilkes looks. And Charlotte's mother, like Gaby's, has died and left her daughter with a stern, restrictive father.

Interestingly, this series of "feminized" sound-images has its "origin" in what might be termed a paternalistic film—the 1932 *Lachende Erben* (discussed in chapter 1).[40] The reader will recall that that film is a lighthearted and rather trivial comedy about the trials and tribulations of the nephew of a deceased wine industrialist. The old man, Herr Bockelmann, has left his fortune to his nephew, Peter Frank, on the condition that the latter abstain from alcoholic beverages for a month. It is the "format" of Herr Bockelmann's will that makes the document relevant to our discussion of *La Signora di Tutti* and *Werther*. In an early scene in the film, the Bockelmanns' extended family gathers in the parlor of the dead man's mansion, where the will is to be read. Over the mantelpiece, a large portrait of a substantial man looks down upon the "mourners" (most of whom are only interested in his money). As Bockelmann's voice (seemingly) booms forth from the portrait, the camera tracks back from its low-angle medium-long shot to reveal a phonograph on the mantel. Bockelmann's will—his last wishes—are recorded for posterity. First, he sends all his annoying relatives out of the room—everyone except Peter, who will be the sole heir if he can carry out the will's dictate. Like Franz Josef's statue in *Sarajevo*, the portrait is given point-of-view shots in a shot–reverse shot sequence between the nephew and "his uncle." Peter listens, obedient and chastened (an impression increased by the high-angle shots from the portrait's point of view). The uncle's position as law-giver turns out to be nothing more than a parody of the "virile display." The will, it seems, has a codicil that insures Peter will inherit only *if* he disobeys his uncle and shows his love of wine—by drinking it even at the risk of losing his fortune. Peter does so, wins his bride, keeps the fortune, and lives happily ever after.

In the "gap" the film opens between the visual (the immobile painting) and the aural (the "living" voice on the record player), and in its baring of the *device* producing the auditory element of the film, *Lachende Erben* provides a matrix for Ophuls' later experimentation with sound and image where erotic derangement is brought on by the possibilities inherent in the cinema's mechanisms. The "call to conscience" experienced in *Signora* and *Werther* as grounded in the feminine (pre-Oedipal), though taken up by the male characters, is given a more traditionally masculine (Oedipal) origin in *Lachende Erben*. But as we've seen, guilt (and the related masochistic response to guilt) and its relation to subjectivity is much more a feminine than a masculine concern in Ophuls' films.

Ophuls' last films seek quite emphatically to dissociate the "dangers" of image and sound from any implied *essential* relationship to femininity. Woman, nonetheless, continues in *particular* to act as the lightning rod for disturbances in the visual field. The next chapter treats the three sketches from *Le Plaisir* (1952) and certain aspects of *Caught* (1949). *Le*

Plaisir's last female protagonist is shown to conflate the behavior of Gaby and Alma to arrive at a more stubborn, if not more positive, approach to the treatment she receives as a potentially destructive image, and as an "irritating" source of sound. *Caught*'s Leonora Ames (Barbara Bel Geddes) must also learn the hard way how to deflect the trouble her image has attracted. And in both of these films, as in *La Ronde* (1950), which is also discussed, theatricality and masquerade provide a possible response to the oppressiveness of the directorial imperative.

Six

✦

Spectacle, Economics, and the Perils of Directorship in *Le Plaisir, La Ronde,* and *Caught*

Ein paar Hauptthemen ziehen durch Maupassants Leben und seine Arbeit: Geld—Krieg—Bauren (aus seinem Heimatland, der Normandie)—Wasser (Flüsse, das Meer)—Spuk—Aberglaube—wir wählten: "Pläsier."

—MAX OPHULS,
"MAUPASSANT WÄRE HEUTE FILMAUTOR,"
KASSELER POST (JANUARY 24, 1953)

Contagion is a phenomenon of which it is easy to establish the presence but which is not easy to explain. It must be classified among those phenomena of a hypnotic order. . . . In a group every sentiment and act is contagious, and contagious to such a degree that an individual readily sacrifices his personal interest to the collective interest.

—SIGMUND FREUD,
GROUP PSYCHOLOGY AND THE ANALYSIS OF THE EGO

[Caught was made in] the Orson Welles idiom—overlapping conversation, dramatic lighting, a sultry sense of claustrophobia; but it is an idiom on which the director, Max Ophuls, has magnificently improved.

—PAUL DEHN, SUNDAY CHRONICLE [1]

✦

Authorial Relays and Ghostly Voices

We have seen that Ophuls' films, by foregrounding the contradictions that fuel the representation of women in mainstream Western films, give us occasion to reflect on what it means to idealize, to scapegoat, to torment, to dote on the beauty or recoil at the horror of woman. The films examined in this chapter present further permutations of these issues. First is a brief analysis of Ophuls' *Le Plaisir* (1952), an adaptation of three sketches by Guy de Maupassant ("Le Masque," "La Maison Tellier," and "Le Modèle"). Next we take a look at several related scenes from *La Ronde* (1950), and from *Caught* (1949), Ophuls' superb penultimate American film, whose protagonist suffers a fate not unlike that of *Le Plaisir*'s Josephine.

In *Le Plaisir* issues of directorship, theatricality, circulation, and feminine self-expression take particularly complex, though aesthetically economical forms. To some extent, Ophuls can be thought of as posing his most *probing* questions about sexual difference in *Letter from an Unknown Woman* (1948). And clearly, *Lola Montès* (1955) must be regarded as the most extreme representation of feminine sexual aggression. Of course, no single Ophuls film, even any of those from his last two periods (1946–1949, 1950–1955), forms an adequate basis for summarizing the representation of sexual difference in his films. Still, I am tempted to say that *Le Plaisir* brings together the filmmaker's most "typical" concerns.

"Le Modèle" is the second of three sketches in the English version of *Le Plaisir* distributed in the United States. It was originally presented as the last segment of the film—and does provide a more satisfactory if less optimistic ending than the "Maison Tellier" piece that replaced it.[2] Georges Annenkov, who designed the costumes in all of Ophuls' late French films, documents the numerous production difficulties suffered by Ophuls and his crew during the early phases of making *Le Plaisir*. Halfway into the process of setting up the film, the original producer dropped out and was replaced, after some anxious moments, by François Harispuru.[3] The changeover had at least one important effect on the material dealt with in this chapter. Ophuls and his collaborators had originally intended to adapt the story "La Femme de Paul" as the film's third and final sketch. However, the new producer thought that the tale of a man brought to suicide by his mistress's lesbian affair might be too much for the cinema-going public to accept.[4] According to Annenkov, Ophuls was attracted to the plastic possibilities of "La Femme de Paul" as much as he was to its subject matter. The aquatic setting of the story (which takes place around a river in Normandy) offered the opportunity to practice cinematic pointillism. Some traces of these plans exist in the river scene from "Le Modèle."[5] Although this forced alteration of his film disappointed Ophuls, I tend to agree with Alan Williams's assessment that "Le Modèle" "works as well or better than 'Paul's Woman' might have."[6] With the excellent technical crew—including Ophuls veterans Christian Matras as cinematographer, Jacques Natanson as dialogue writer, and Jean d'Eaubonne as set designer—already in place, Ophuls' rapid adaptation of "Le Modèle" has the force of a quick sketch drawn by skillful hands.

Ophuls' major thematic concerns are reiterated in the piece with assurance and with a tender irony. Despite the "success" of the substituted story, "La Femme de Paul"'s subtle pattern of authorial intervention seems to have appealed to Ophuls at the time. There is evidence that Ophuls would have preferred to retain the voice of "Maupassant" as an entirely disembodied phenomenon, as a ghostly presence rather than as an on-screen narrator. From Kaja Silverman's point of view this "ghostly" presence would be a more powerful force than the embodied narrative voice. But unlike "La Femme de Paul," "Le Modèle" requires a visible narrator since it is recounted in flashback from the perspective of a "friend" of the male protagonist. The on-screen presence is not necessarily that of Maupassant, but the link is strong, especially in Ophuls' interpretation. Although the voice-over narrator of the film (Jean Servais) states that he is giving his voice to "another," this "other" is played by—Jean Servais. Williams observes that the appearance of the on-screen narrator in this sketch contradicts the initial voice-over in the film, when the narrator declares: "They wanted to photograph me, but an author's pleasure is to be heard, not seen."[7] Indeed, this narrator loves the anonymity of "the darkness." He continues, "I thought that the best thing would be if I just told you these stories myself as if I were sitting beside you and, well, who knows? Maybe I am."[8]

"Maupassant's" statement recalls the opening of La Ronde, which like Le Plaisir begins with an overt declaration by an authorial or directorial agent. In La Ronde this "agent" is Anton Walbrook, whose role as meneur *de jeu* is ambiguously that of playwright, master of ceremonies, or film-maker. Dressed in formal evening wear and walking about on a misty theatrical or cinematic soundstage, he speaks his monologue: "And what am I in this story? The Author . . . ? A Passerby? I am, well I could be anyone among you. . . . But where are we? In a Theatre? In a studio?"[9] In both films the narrator insists upon a certain unlocatability of the space he inhabits. This "unlocatability" is particularly emphasized at the beginning of *Le Plaisir*, in which the author addresses us while there is nothing but blackness on the screen. Not surprisingly, he prefers *disembodiment*, which is tantamount, as has been noted, to mastery of the offscreen space.[10] And, as usual, it is the woman's body that is decidedly visible.

"Le Modèle" is an intriguing story for Ophuls to have adapted because it is within the world of images that this author-figure, a word-smith and a musician, is defeated by a woman whose manipulation of her own image is deft, if self-destructive. Ophuls, as image-maker and as enunciating agency, holds an ambiguous place in these proceedings.

Masked Men and Filles publiques: Pleasure and Contagion

Before moving to the final sketch of the film, we will look at the "directorial relays" and related themes in the first two sketches.[11] The initial "pleasure" in the film is that of the author ("to be heard, not seen"), the first of many kinds of pleasure, and one that will be shown to have a sadistic element as well as a necessary social function. (Of course, such figures often *suffer* along with the actors' mise-en-scènes.) Such is the case in "Le Masque," which, amazingly enough, is a tale of *masculine* embodiment and its effect on women. The story is a simple one: a strangely rigid man (Jean Galland) dances in the chorus line at a public ball in Paris so frantically that he collapses. He is revived by a doctor (Claude Dauphin) called to the scene. The doctor discovers that the man is masked, and asks for scissors to release him. The man turns out to be old and withered beneath the youthful mask. The doctor accompanies his patient home to a seedy apartment on the top floor of an old building. Denise Ambroise (Gaby Morlay), the old man's wife, puts her husband to bed while she relates the old man's exploits in the ballrooms and bedrooms of Paris to the doctor. M. Ambroise wants to relive the days of his youth, when he was a popular hairdresser to actresses and a master seducer of women. Each night in those days he would return home and brag to his wife, "Yet another one, Denise, another one." Even as she explains her voluntary servitude to his youthful beauty, the wife hastens to answer the infantile demands of her husband, who calls her name out petulantly. Thus, the woman suffers through both the youth and the old age of the "embodied" man.

The doctor is visibly appalled by the story and vows to take a lesson from it, but his response to the old man's depravity is, in fact, to follow suit: he calls for a carriage to take him back to the public ballroom so that he may continue his night of debauchery.

The mise-en-scène of this sketch makes it one of the finest instances of "French" cinematic skill in existence. The opening voice-over, the neon letters of the sign for the BAL, from which the camera pans down into the crowd, following first one couple, then another, tilting, canting, and cutting among the various "types" that populate a nineteenth-century Paris ballroom—all contribute to a sense of movement, grace, and irony scarcely to be found again in the French cinema. Ophuls would most assuredly have become a force to be reckoned with in the French *Nouvelle Vague* ("New Wave") if he had lived into the late 1950s.

The ugly little masked man, M. Ambroise, seeks pleasure in creating the illusion of youth. But he is unmasked, and the truth of his situation is revealed: all in all, an edifying moral tale. This "moral" is spoiled, however, by the doctor's final plunge into the same behavior that was "condemned" in the old man. Like Lola Montès in her circus act, the old man is caught in the perpetual performance of what he once was. The narrator's voice describes M. Ambroise as a "figure in a wax museum": he is, therefore, also what Stefan Brand might have become if he had not gone to the duel. Like Stefan at certain phases of his career, M. Ambroise is trapped in a masquerade of his virility, one that collapses when the shocking visage is revealed beneath the mask. The doctor, as witness to that mimesis and as demystifier of the spectacle, is *infected* by the old man's behavior, implicated in the very "distanced" participation that was his in the event. Demystification does not render innocuous the mesmeric power of the spectacle—and M. Ambroise is doubly playing a part, in that he wears a mask and is invited to replace an absent performer in the choreographed bacchanalia of the dance. The old woman, his wife, is still under the spell of her husband's imagined attractiveness. Despite years of "demystification" in the form of her husband's repellent behavior and accumulating wrinkles, she still loves and reveres the image of the youth he once was. She even helps him to reconstruct the "fetish" of that former self, willing to be seduced despite her knowledge of his loss of virility. Is this "true love"? Quite possibly it is.

After the old man and the doctor have left the ballroom, a short exchange takes place between the director of the *palais de la danse* and one of the female professional dancers employed there. This man had been seen at the beginning of the sketch, drawing people into the ballroom and handling the matter of the collapsed dancer. Here, as they watch the odd pair drive away in a carriage, the entrepreneur turns and rudely commands the woman, in long shot on the steps of the ballroom, to go inside and continue her work. This ruthless director of pleasure is clearly another relay for the initial offscreen voice: Ophuls' mania is always to "suture" the role of enunciator. "Le Masque" presents the vacillation between identification with the image and distance from that image in the figure of the doctor. The doctor, as a scientist, a man of medicine, rips off the mask in a ritual purgation and reveals the hideous reality of "embodiment" underneath. But the man of medicine is also a "medicine man": he effects the cure only by identifying with the evil, by imitating it and channeling it through his own person.

In the "Maison Tellier" segment of *Le Plaisir*, Ophuls lays emphasis upon prostitution-as-performance in order to reveal its role in catalyzing and maintaining social order. One might regard this part of the film as a humorous reversal of those films where, as in John Ford's *Stagecoach* (1939), the expulsion of the prostitute from the community is carried out in an effort to resolve conflicts within that community. I have already observed that the prostitutes in this film are (with a couple of exceptions) linked with the middle class. Madame Tellier (Madeleine Renaud) is described as a respectable woman, who has inherited the family business from her uncle. Her husband, a former merchant, dies from overindulging in the pleasures of the table soon after they inherit the bordello.[12] The first part of the segment implies that prostitution has the power to prevent violence. That is, the *absence* of the prostitutes (who have gone away to attend a first communion) provokes rivalrous conflicts between the French and English sailors who gather outside the locked doors, and then between the more elite citizens of the town. In their disappointment at finding their favorite haunt closed, these gentlemen almost come to blows when one of the men makes salacious remarks about the daughter of another. The group of prostitutes (each one with her particularized role as "the beautiful Jewess"[so-named in Maupassant's tale] or the "good-natured country girl") acts as a sexualized family—it is a family business, run as a matriarchy—which functions to expel excessive sexuality from the community's family structures.

Only insofar as the women produce a spectacle in which others participate can they carry out their function of maintaining social order. In the train ride on the way to the first communion of Madame Tellier's niece, Rosa (Danielle Darrieux, the "star" of the sketch) launches into a formidable recital of the attentions of her husband, a dashing viscount. Her story is told under the bulging-eyed gaze of a pair of peasants. Rosa's own eyes widen as she describes the imaginary gifts he brings her. "He says such wonderful things to me," she sighs ecstatically, and everyone strains forward to hear what the viscount could have said that had so thrilled his wife. "Unfortunately, I've forgotten them," she continues, looking ruefully at her disappointed audience.

Rosa continues to act as the lightning rod for group responses later in the sketch when, during the communion ceremony, she begins crying. The scene is sumptuously decorated and shot, and uses music and voice poignantly. As the children troop in and begin to sing, Rosa is so moved that she must weep. Her tears are infectious: soon the entire congregation is sobbing. The priest, who has been watching the scene, comes forward to "direct" the worship of the assembly, with the tears streaming down his own cheeks. Once again a "director-figure" or stand-in for the author is caught up in the contagion of the emotion aroused by the performance of the very ritual that he is celebrating. This will also be the case for Madame Tellier herself. She discourages her brother's "advances" to Rosa (in Maupassant's story it is an attempted rape). (The brother is played by Jean Gabin, which considerably glamorizes the dull farmer in the story!) At the end of the sketch the ladies return home to the bordello. Breaking the house rules, Madame Tellier for the first time grants her sexual favors to one of the "regulars." Although she had previously resisted becoming personally involved in prostitution, she finally does succumb (for a price) to the contagion of "pleasure."

Much has been said about Ophuls' "toning down" of both Maupassant's and Schnitzler's mordant social commentary. Ophuls was, however, surely attracted to these authors' common view that what seems to be excluded from a society can in fact form the basis for its functioning. We have seen that this is a typically Ophulsian concern. But what of the claim that Ophuls has hopelessly glamorized these often bleak works? Certainly the prostitutes of the "Maison Tellier" segment of *Le Plaisir* are more attractive than are Maupassant's deformed caricatures of women in his short story. (Among other things, Ophuls changed Rosa from a character who *eats* to a character who *drinks*—we have seen the connotations of eating in earlier films!) Williams defends Ophuls against accusations of betraying his source material by showing how Ophuls' irony is "of a different sort" than that of these two authors.[13] While I concur with the spirit of that assessment, I disagree with the particular view of Ophulsian irony exemplified, for Williams, by such scenes as the one where Rosa weeps in church. While Ophuls visibly relishes some elements of Maupassant's irony and, indeed, introduces some ironic touches of his own ("overloading," as Williams puts it, "image and soundtrack with more symbols of religiosity than the event can bear"), the scene must also be read in perfect seriousness. Ophuls never entirely abandons his sense that participation in the ritual of spectacle offers a transcendental experience, though that experience need not be qualified as a religious one. While Maupassant finally connects the transcendent to the bestial itself in his descriptions of the irresistible brutality and beauty of nature,[14] Ophuls returns to the experience of the spectacle. In his adaptations of both Maupassant and Schnitzler, Ophuls always shifts the focus of the literary or theatrical work toward the paradoxes situated around the spectacle—artifice, community ritual, the scapegoating process, pleasure, self-realization, and death.

The Woman Out of the Window

The final part of *Le Plaisir*, "Le Modèle," is one of the most elegant expressions of Ophuls' cinematic concerns. In the frame narrative of this sketch, the Maupassant figure (or his incarnation) also appears as a character who narrates the extended flashback that forms the body of the segment. According to this same narrator, the episode of "Le Masque" was a story of "pleasure and love," "La Maison Tellier" was one of "pleasure and purity," while this last episode tells a story of "pleasure and death." However, this last description is not precisely correct.

The story opens on two men (in medium shot), circa 1890, who are contemplating an elderly married couple (in long shot), as the husband pushes his wife (Alma's reincarnation?) in an invalid's chair along a seaside boardwalk. For the distance between them, the two onlookers might as well be in another world from the elderly couple—as indeed, we discover, they are. One of the two men asks the other how it is that the elderly fellow married a crippled woman. The Maupassant figure replies that, in this case, "the accident came about in a special way." The narrator continues: "He married her as one marries anyone . . . by foolishness. The little one risked all for all. . . . How can one be sure of women? They lie without knowing it, and yet they have a frankness, sudden reactions which rout our reason and completely upset our plans. . . . I was present at their first meeting."

The scene shifts to the foot of a large double staircase in an art school or museum. A young artist, Jean Summer (Daniel Gélin), and his friend, the narrator (Jean Servais), are standing at the foot of the immense staircase engaged in aesthetic activities that soon deteriorate into girl-watching. Summer is painting the figure of a woman from a nude and headless marble statue, certainly the least troublesome kind of model. At this time, according to the narrator, Jean dislikes both still lifes and landscapes and only paints nudes. A lovely young woman, Josephine (Simone Simon), passes by to climb the stairs. Intrigued by her beauty, Jean follows her up the stairs. "He did not know that she was a painter's model, but was overwhelmed by her childish face and her wasp waist," intones the narrator. The pair returns down the other side of the staircase, walking hand in hand. Jean gaily waves his hat to his friend as he trips out the door with his newfound love. Although (or because) she is a model ("like any other model," as the narrator later insists), Jean has fallen instantly in love with her. Desire has a mechanical quality that, in this case, can be ascribed to the woman's possession of the characteristics of a "model," that is, of a creature who by definition imitates an ideal and is imitated, reproduced by the artist.

Indeed, this is the outcome of their meeting. The infatuated Jean paints an endless series of portraits of his young mistress. With his first success they decide (in a scene absent from Maupassant's story) to buy an old house with such romantic touches as a lightning-struck tree. This emphatic "typicality" of their aspiration is not simply a device for ironic deflation but underscores the imitated or derived nature of their desires. They set up housekeeping together. In one scene in this house, Josephine—wearing a short "Greek" dress and seated on a carousel horse of the type found in *La Ronde* (perhaps an oblique reference to that film's carousel of love)—poses in a mirrored studio. The next scene includes a prettily wrought and rapid montage of Jean's perceptions of his sweetheart's adorable gestures—getting into a carriage, raising her arm, eating a sardine, and so on (a sequence much admired by Godard). Jean's visual fascination is complete.

The scene of the couple's first quarrel is one that repeats almost exactly a scene that occurs in "La Femme de Paul." In that story the protagonist is walking with his beloved by a river and comes to realize, as her silly song shatters the harmony of the evening, that her head is "empty, empty!" So, too, in "Le Modèle" does the first disillusionment take place beside a river, as the three friends take an evening stroll. The narrator, the third person who is both witness and catalyst in this scene, pompously intones in the voice-over about the need for real suitability of character and taste in love relationships. It is clear that the two men would have preferred to walk alone in the evening air, without Josephine's noisy, babbling song "spoiling the landscape," as Jean puts it. Interestingly, the *embodied* female voice grates on the masculine ear. The silence of the portrait is ultimately preferred—although the men finally do what they can to evoke the woman's scream, which Silverman describes as the sound the Hollywood cinema soundtrack is most eager to extract. It is not only in Hollywood that we find "the identification of the female voice with spectacle and the body, and a certain aspiration of the male voice to invisibility and anonymity."[15]

Matters now go from bad to worse for our protagonists. Three months later, the couple is seen in the throes of another violent argument. As in the "Tellier" sequence, this scene is shot through the windows of the house as the couple runs from room to room—Jean closing the shades furiously all the while (as André had closed them gently in *Madame de . . .*). The chase continues (Jean wants the key Josephine is holding) until they begin to smash paintings and other objects, finishing by smashing their reflections in the large mirror in the studio. The carousel horse, on which Josephine had posed for Jean when their love was young, is visible at the edge of the frame, linking this with the earlier scene (and with *La Ronde*): modeling, painting, the growing fascination with the feminine image, these ultimately lead to mutual or self-destruction. But as in "Le Masque," the disenchantment does not lessen the contagious power of the image. Even (especially) during the violent eruptions of hatred, Jean continues to paint, and to paint only Josephine. There is an immediate dissolve onto a large portrait of

Josephine, as the owner of the art gallery examines Jean's endless portraits of the young woman.

GALLERY DIRECTOR: At least you work.

JEAN: I love only work. [*The artist takes his money and leaves*]

GALLERY DIRECTOR: He needs more and more money.

COLLEAGUE: Perhaps a separation gift.

GALLERY DIRECTOR: Painters don't know how to break off.

If Jean does not know how to break off his affair, he will certainly try, with the narrator's help, to do so. One night Josephine returns home to find a note bidding her adieu. The envelope also contains money meant to buy her absence from the painter's life. Scenes of Josephine going through the motions of life without Jean are crosscut with shots of Jean and the narrator as they climb the stairway to their new abode, a two-story garret. They discuss the perfect harmony brought about by their both having "quiet occupations." Meanwhile, "out of love or vanity," as the narrator puts it, Josephine searches everywhere for her lover. After going from the art gallery to the museum stairs, and so on ("revisiting the scenes of their youth," so to speak), "one evening about nine," she finally rings their doorbell. Jean's "quiet" occupation has become a noisy one: he is making a linoleum or woodcut and hammers loudly with a wooden mallet throughout the scene, as he tries to block out Josephine's words. (Maupassant's story does not mention what Jean is doing during this scene.) Evidently, Jean and Josephine are equally capable of creating a disturbing fracas, despite the narrator's claims.

Before Jean answers the door, the narrator remarks with uncanny foresight, "It is she, you know." Jean nods and his companion opens the door to the furious Josephine: "I should have known that you [the narrator] would be here. You have always detested me." She turns to Jean, who merely stares at her as he hammers.

JOSEPHINE: I don't want your money and I don't want your dismissal. I don't want to be treated like a trollop [*une fille*]. I didn't seek you out. You took me, now keep me.

JEAN: You're not going to impose yourself on me until death!

Seeing that things are getting out of hand, the narrator takes Josephine aside. He sits down at a small piano: "Let me explain. Above all, no dramas, no dramas! Don't take life tragically; it does no good. He still loves you . . . only he . . ." The narrator/friend begins to play and chants with the music: "It's the classic story. His family wants him to marry. He must obey. Do you understand now?" Josephine nods, "Yes." "Then no dramas." He plays a quick dance piece (the theme music of the film) as she goes to bid farewell to Jean.

JOSEPHINE: If you marry, I'll kill myself.

JEAN: Then kill yourself. The window is up there. [*He points with his mallet*]

Josephine accepts the dare, "risks everything," and begins to climb the staircase, as she has climbed so many already in her love affair with Jean. During Josephine's climb, a lengthy displaced point-of-view shot shows the stairs, her legs, and her shadow (as in the staircase suicide scene in *La Signora di Tutti*). She rounds the curves of the spiral staircase, opens the window—and jumps from it, crashing (with the camera) through the skylight below. The woman is later brought up, the narrator informs us, with both legs broken, never to walk again. Remorse leads Jean to marry her at last, breaking, as well, the homosocial union that sought to exclude the model.

The little model, another Ophulsian gambler, "risks all" in following to the letter the directions of her lover, accompanied by the narrator's piano music and by his contradictory invocation: "No dramas, above all no dramas." (Although Jean's friend does take Josephine aside for this discussion in Maupassant's story, there is no piano and no discussion of "drama.") Her "directors" order the model-actress to kill herself, and in a jump repeating Christine's in *Liebelei* (1932) and anticipating Lola's final leap in *Lola Montès* (1955), and reversing the movement of ascension Josephine had accomplished in her passionate climbing of the stairs, we share her vision. It is the vision of a headstrong woman who follows her cues too exactly, who subverts the masculine scenario by carrying it out to the letter. While the homosocial contract offers in this sketch (as in "La Femme de Paul") a less violence alliance than does the heterosexual one, both are based on exclusion, expulsion, even death. Their treatment is in this way, at least, even handed.

Throughout the sketch (and film), the economic issues at work in Ophuls' other films continue to regulate the interchanges between the characters. Of course, Jean has appropriated and sold Josephine's image, and now he uses the same money to try to buy her honor. This she refuses, as she has refused to be silenced. The narrator holds a more complex position regarding the economics of the situation. Like Ketzal in *Die verkaufte Braut* (*The Bartered Bride*, 1832), he is trying to bring the young man back into the fold, to help him accomplish the socially correct marriage desired by his family. Ophuls' sympathy seems to belong to the woman who has risked everything, trying to buy happiness by putting her image, and finally her body, up for sale.

At the end of *Le Plaisir*, the narrator finishes his story while he watches the couple on the beach. Hilary Radner sums up the action of the sketch:

When, to the painter's chagrin the young woman cannot remain mute like her image, [she] inscribes her rage at her lover's betrayal upon her own body by throwing herself from the window. . . . The only way, then, that she could keep her lover was to render herself completely powerless. But with her loss of mobility, she also loses her capacity to represent his desire: subsequently the artist will paint only landscapes. Immobilized, the woman can no longer reflect back herself as the object of his desire; her body becomes the emblem of the fixity of death, of the terror of castration. (The woman, here, is doubly castrated; not only is she a woman, but she has broken both legs.)[16]

Muteness and mobility, fixity and the intrusion of sound, exchange and expenditure. We have seen that none of these terms can be absolutely valorized in favor of the woman nor can it be said that any of them always works against her. The woman who was accused of breaking the silence comes to the men's apartment to be greeted with a rash of aggressive noises (hammering, piano music, words). Continually immobilized as an image that is then used to torment her, she "ironically" obeys her direction to the letter and succeeds not only in immobilizing herself as a cripple but, at the same time, in taking her place in the loveless world of middle-class marriage. The horror is, of course, that the woman "inscribes her rage" on her own body. And in the decades of cinematic production since the film was made, such mutilations continue to be perpetrated, while simultaneously women struggle to externalize the inscription, to carve their stories into celluloid.

The Theater of Desire in La Ronde

Ophuls' fourth "Viennese" film, *La Ronde*, is the first film he directed after returning to France in 1949–50. Initially, Ophuls had gone there under the auspices of Walter Wanger, with whom he was to have worked on several film projects. These were to include not only *La Duchesse de Langeais* (retitled *Lover and Friend*), starring Garbo and James Mason, but an adaptation of *The Ballad and the Source*, already in script form when Ophuls returned to France. But these plans came to naught, and Ophuls was approached by Sacha Gordine Productions to direct another film based on a Schnitzler work (his play *Reigen*)—*La Ronde*. This film accomplishes perfectly the vision of circularity that had haunted Ophuls from his earliest days as a filmmaker, and no doubt as a theatrical director. It is also Ophuls' most successful comic film, the only one that seems to capture the dry wit evident in Ophuls' biography and other writings. But, of course, this comedy is a dark one.

Unlike the narrator in *Le Plaisir*, *La Ronde*'s *meneur de jeu* (Anton Walbrook) manages to stay out of the "contagion" of love, pleasure, lust— and, perhaps, disease. He does, however, have his own problems! And his relationship to the female characters, if less noxious, is equally problematic. Both play and film consist of ten "dialogues" between men and women, each of which ends in a sexual act. One of the partners then moves along to a new partner, then one of those two moves along to another, and so on. The social status of the characters goes from very low to very high, and back to very low, with representatives from almost all social milieus in between. The film begins with a common prostitute (Simone Signoret) and an ordinary soldier (Serge Reggiani), then links the soldier to a maid (Simone Simon), the maid to a bourgeois young man (Daniel Gélin), the young man to a married woman (Danielle Darrieux), the married woman to her husband (Fernand Gravey), the husband to a "*grisette*" (a very fast young woman, Odette Joyeux), the fast young woman to a poet (Jean-Louis Barrault), the poet to the actress (Isa Miranda, from *La Signora di Tutti*), the actress to the hilarious Count Bobby (Gérard Philipe), ending with the count and the prostitute (Simone Signoret, once again). Anyone familiar with French cinema immediately recognizes that this cast represents some of the best French actors of the era. The production itself is equally lavish, featuring the talents of Ophuls' French "team"—Matras, d'Eaubonne, Annenkov, Natanson, and Oscar Straus, who also composed the music for *De May-*

erling à Sarajevo (1940), just as d'Eaubonne had decorated its sets.

Ophuls' main addition to Schnitzler's piece is, not surprisingly, the *meneur de jeu*, who questions his own role in the film, as well as his "location," as mentioned above. He is "the author," "a passer-by," finally, "anyone among" the audience. And we are certainly not surprised that Ophuls also emphasizes the passage of time in the film and adds the "chronotope" of the carousel, which acts as Walbrook's stage and symbolizes the turning of the circle of desire. (During the sketch with the young man and the married woman, the carousel's breakdown indicates discreetly that the young man can't maintain an erection!) This celebrant of the carnival, the *meneur de jeu* is "the incarnation of your desire, your desire to know everything": "Men never know but one part of reality. And why? . . . Because they only see one aspect of things. Me, I see everything, because I see all around [*en rond*], and that allows me to be everywhere at once" (p. 7).[17] And, indeed, this overworked and omniscient "author" acts as the intermediary between each couple. He also repairs the carousel when it breaks down, and is seen editing the film itself when things get too steamy—a humorous commentary on Ophuls' problems in the United States with the Production Code. The *meneur de jeu* is also a "performer"—like the ringmaster in *Lola Montès*, he occasionally bursts into song: "Turn, turn, my characters. . . . this is the circle of love."

As Williams observes in his remarks on the film, in "Keeping the Circle Turning":

It is the male characters who in each case are common to the paired sketches, and it is the women who change at each boundary. This occurs in the play, of course, as a result of its structure, but Ophuls emphasizes the pairings by having the women who "bridge" the pairs of episodes speak directly to Walbrook in his role as Leader (as noted, the men only see him disguised as minor characters). (p. 45)

The female characters' greater access to the *meneur de jeu* reflects, as Williams puts it, "their relatively greater self-awareness and reflexiveness in the film." The familiar dialectic between woman and director, freedom and destiny, directorial control and actor's will, are reincarnated in the fatalistic turning of the carousel of desire, and in the actions of the *meneur de jeu* as controlling force—and as a guy who is just doing his job. The *meneur de jeu* does not present the women of the story as the unilateral "victims" of the men. Both men and women are ground under the wheels of sexuality, gender roles, and social status. However, *La Ronde*'s men do seem to fit, almost without exception, Robert Chamblee's description of them as "cads."[18] The sexual equality implied by the women's "freedom" to move from partner to partner in the film is belied by details of each encounter. The prostitute is mocked for giving her services away instead of exchanging them for money (what she wants in trade is respect and love); the maid is seduced and abandoned by the soldier; the married man, though later deceived by the *grisette*, nonetheless holds the purse strings—and will feed her only if she succumbs to his caresses; and so on. Walbrook's innocuous air stands in contrast with the "author" in the later *Le Plaisir* but, as Williams notes, there is a "demoralizing" effect in the *meneur de jeu*'s refusal to judge.[19] This extraordinarily conscious, everyday work of leading women to the various humiliations and small triumphs of love has the painful clarity and inexorable quality of daylight.

Mimesis and Exchange: A Carhop's View

Like Lisa Berndle before her, and Josephine a few years later, *Caught*'s Leonora (Maude) Ames (also spelled "Eames"), played by Barbara Bel Geddes, trades on her work as a model. And like them she makes a deal that will destroy her health and her capacity to desire. We will see that aspects of Leonora's fate coincide with the underlying logic of Josephine's, as with that of the ambitious women of *La Ronde*.

Beautifully photographed by Lee Garmes in chiaroscuro and deep focus, in both subject matter and technique *Caught* is Ophuls' *Citizen Kane*.[20] Classified variously as a "woman's film," and as film noir, it is the story of naive and lovely Maude Ames (or Eames), who comes to Hollywood from her hometown of Denver to make it big however she can. But Barbara Bel Geddes does not make a convincing golddigger or aspiring starlet. This casting seems to have been a deliberate choice by Ophuls and his producers. Unlike *Signora*'s Gaby, Leonora is no femme fatale: she is a "nice girl" whose fantasies about beautiful clothes and jewels come true when a Prince Charming comes to her rescue. Saving her pennies to go to Dorothy Dale's School of Charm, Maude changes her name to Leonora as part of her attempt to root out her bourgeois instincts, substituting for them awkwardly mimed upper-class manners. At her first modeling job, Leonora is spotted by a rich man's *entremetteur,* Franzi Kartos (Curt Bois), a glorified pimp of uncertain nationality and sexual preference. Franzi drafts the pretty girl to come to a party on his employer's yacht. But Leonora is left waiting on the dock until a mysterious man in black appears in a small craft and says he will take her to the yacht—later. A brief conversation reveals that he is Smith Ohlrig (Robert Ryan), the rich man himself, a moody, somewhat deranged individual, who intends to use Leonora as such women are usually used by rich men. Leonora resists, which increases her value in Ohlrig's exchange-oriented mind. When his psychoanalyst (played by Art Smith, Stefan's valet in *Letter*) quietly observes that his patient probably wouldn't get married, Ohlrig "makes arrangements" to prove he's wrong—despite his conviction that Leonora, like everyone else, only sees dollar signs when she looks at him. Ohlrig calls Franzi to set up wedding plans with Leonora. The empty marriage deteriorates as Ohlrig absents himself, and Leonora is left in enforced isolation in the "Xanadu" her husband owns on Long Island. A particularly abusive episode sends her back to her middle-class milieu, and she again becomes a working girl, this time a doctor's receptionist. One of her bosses, dedicated pediatrician Larry Quinada (James Mason), finds her society-lady act annoying and scolds her into adopting the good old American work ethic. A brief reconciliation with Ohlrig leaves Leonora pregnant, just as she is falling in love with Quinada. She again returns to her husband, for the baby's "security," but sequesters herself in her room away from his abuse and demands. A confrontation with Quinada, who wants Leonora to come away with him, and then Franzi's betrayal cause Ohlrig to have one of his "heart attacks," which in turn triggers a miscarriage for Leonora, who chooses not to help her stricken husband. Quinada comes to the rescue, and both are taken to the hospital, where the baby (and possibly Smith Ohlrig) dies, leaving Leonora "free" of Smith Ohlrig and free to marry her average Joe (who also happens to be James Mason).

Mary Ann Doane's brilliant reading of the film focuses on the problems of female desire and "the woman's relation to processes of imaging" within the woman's film.[21] Doane considers both *Caught* and Hitchcock's *Rebecca* (1940), also analyzed in her essay, "limit texts," in that they "expos[e] the contradictions which inhabit the logic of their own terms of address as women's films" (p. 169). In the most familiar of these "contradictions," there is an "inexorable" pull between woman's desire, the "female Oedipus," and "the force of the tendency to reduce the woman to an image" (p. 156). Even as this binary opposition between the apparatus and female desire falls apart, it is crucial to consider this "woman's dilemma" in examining Ophuls' films. The women considered to be of sexual interest in the films are "caught" between possessing the desiring look or sound and becoming an object of spectacle/audition.[22] This is true to some extent even with women whose roles are primarily "maternal" or "domestic."

Doane spells out the many double binds of femininity in her reading of *Caught.* High on the list is the woman's relationship to her own image—as it is projected outward to mime that of the glamorous models in fashion magazines and elsewhere. Doane's argument is one that I have discussed earlier in these pages. Woman's relationship to "her" body, to the female body in the world of representation, is often one of desire: it is a desire to imitate and to appropriate but, for Doane, can only present itself as a form of transvestism. The woman takes on the "look" of a man in order to see how to see this body. But to reiterate, because woman is "so close" to her own body, Doane claims, she has difficulty with such projection: the distance between the desiring woman and the image she wishes to become collapses, leaving her stranded in two dimensions. She no longer is able to *desire* this image, because desire requires distance. Although I believe that women may indeed look with desire at other women—with a gaze that does not only imitate the "male" gaze or reduce itself to lack and negation—Doane's points remain relevant in discussing certain aspects of classical and current cinema. Doane is right to emphasize the disappearance of female desire in this film; the desire that is destroyed is the woman's for the still image of the commodified female body, and for its associated "signifiers." (Doane also discusses the *moving image,* as we will see below.) Does female-female desire persist nonetheless in *Caught?*

The film opens with a bombardment of economic metaphors as they pertain to the American woman. Maude (Leonora) and her roommate Maxine (Ruth Brady) are looking at fashion photos in a glossy magazine (the photos also make up the title sequence of the film, drawing "us" into the spectatorial position occupied by the two young women). We hear their conversation in voice-over. This lends an abstract quality to their covetousness. As Doane notes, the roommates are reveling in fantasies of appropriation: "I'll take this one." "This one's for me." They are actually pointing to drawings and photos of jewelry (bracelets and necklaces) rather than other women as they say this, but Doane's point is essentially correct: the comments on the photos are "the indexical actualizations of the female appetite for the image" (p. 156). Their fantasies are indeed "complicit with the fashion industry" and with the "commodity fetishism which supports capitalism" (pp. 156–57). Fixating on one particular object as the primo "signifier of economic wealth," the mink coat, Maude and her Maxine pragmatically assess their situation in the world of exchange. As she is, Maude has only her manual labor (she is a carhop with aching feet) and her sexuality to trade, something neither finds acceptable: both options are dead ends. The camera pulls back to reveal their room, and much of the conversation is carried out with one woman in the extreme foreground, the other in the rear field, *Citizen Kane*–style. "You're never going to meet a real man," her roomie laments. Maxine is in the slightly better position of trading off her looks by working as a model in a department store, a trade both deem more acceptable than carhopping. Adopting a 1950s coed's pose, with her feet up on her bed, Maude spins a Rosa-like tale about what a real man would be: a millionaire who can buy both Maude *and* her mother a mink coat. (The mother-as-appendage is thrown in in true woman's film style.) So Maude counts up her expenses and finds that if she spends just twenty-five cents a day on lunch, and doesn't wear stockings, she can afford charm school.

Although the charm school is presented ironically, as a pathetic means of income for otherwise socially useless women, Maude very earnestly believes in its transformative power. In the first scene she reads aloud its claim to fame (as advertised in its brochure), which I take as a barely veiled obscenity: "Dorothy Dale places all her graduates in the finest positions." Maude thinks Dorothy Dale is a "nifty number," but both "girls" agree that the photo is probably retouched. Well, that's the beauty of images, isn't it?

When Maude slips into the school one day, the receptionist (played by Sonia Darrin, the evil Agnes in *The Big Sleep*) calls out, reminding her that she must pay her tuition "in advance." Chastened, Maude makes a down payment, has her pronunciation corrected, and then trades in her name, announcing that she's changed it to the more socially correct "Leonora" (which the receptionist approves). The assumption, as we know, is that woman is mutable—in name, economic status, and social class. Despite the paucity of its props, the charm school manages as another locus of fantasy: women act out tea parties and other hoity-toity social occasions, as Dorothy Dale (Natalie Shaefer) looks on. She takes out a cloth coat: "Believe it or not, this is a beautiful mink coat," she declares, as she drapes it on Leonora's shoulders. And, indeed, a dissolve takes us to a low-level shot of a mink coat over a woman's legs. The camera tilts up to show us that this is Leonora in an elevator, looking very chic. Has her dream come true? No, this is a department store, and Leonora is modeling the coat for men and women. (Two women are especially attracted to it. One, played by Barbara Billingsly, asks the other if "Wally [has signed] his contract with Metro yet." Since the answer is no, she'll have to have the old one glazed, although $5,000 is "not too bad" for a mink. "I'd rather make him buy me a new bracelet anyway"—a *Madame de . . .* in the making. Her desire of course reiterates that of the young women in the opening scene.) Leonora is well aware of the double meaning of her words ("Forty-nine ninety-five"—i.e., $4,995) as she offers the coat to a small man with a hard-to-place foreign accent. He asks to see "the lining," forcing Leonora to display her body to him. It seems to pass inspection since he offers her an invitation to a party on a "business associate's" yacht. He gives her his card: "Franzi Kartos, Personal Representative for Smith Ohlrig." And, indeed, Franzi "represents" Ohlrig: he comes close to doing what her fantasy millionaire was supposed to do (walk up to her at the perfume counter of a department store). At first she refuses to take the invitation Franzi tenders, but relents when he suggests she not "be a silly bourgeois, dahling" and points out that they both "have work to do": his, to "represent" a rich man's desires; hers, to represent their fulfillment. Like the *meneur de jeu* in *La Ronde*, Franzi is just doing his job.

Another dizzying array of economic issues for women begins to unfold. The next scene shows Leonora unhappy with her image in the mirror ("I look terrible") and getting cold feet again. She "resents the whole setup" because it makes her feel "cheap." Maxine, vicariously excited, convinces her that it is a "good investment." Leonora replies, dutifully, "I know I should think of security."

MAXINE: And what is security? Money.

LEONORA: Period.

MAXINE: Exclamation point!

Reinforcing the fairy-tale motif, Leonora's roommate insists that she would "be glad to be in [L.'s] shoes," even as she chides her roommate for wanting Prince Charming to appear on a golden horse.

But Leonora's shoes can't walk on water. A dissolve from her confused expression in her room takes us to her forlorn figure sitting near the bay. Franzi has forgotten to send anyone to pick her up, so she lingers on the dock. Out of the dark, however, a boat finally arrives. A man in black, whose white face is picked up by a key light, comes up the steps. Leonora is disappointed when she finds out he's not her ride. However, his take-command attitude ("Don't say yacht, say boat") turns out to be more than simple rudeness. He is, in fact, the Prince himself: her bored host, Smith Ohlrig, the object of her ambitions. (Leonora's object of *desire* is still her own image in a mink coat, covered with jewels.) She gives up her initial destination to go with him. As they drive toward the city, Ohlrig rudely interrogates her about her background: "Family poor? Who paid for your charm school? How many weekend yachting trips have you been on?" The answers are "Yes," "Me," and "None." But Ohlrig (Oil Rig?) is even more interested in what *his* image is—what she knows of him. He orders her to light a cigarette, then proceeds to question her:

OHLRIG: What do you know about me?

LEONORA: I know you're from the East.

OHLRIG: New York. What else?

LEONORA: I know that you're sort of an international something.

OHLRIG: Well, that just about describes it.

LEONORA: I know you've never been married before.

OHLRIG: [*Abruptly*] And I'm not going to be either.

Ohlrig keeps his "date" waiting in the car as he discusses business deals around town (we hear him ordering his associates around offscreen). And thus begins, in true masochistic form, Leonora's life of waiting. A voice-over by Ohlrig makes a sound bridge to the next scene, a brilliant shorthand sketch of Ohlrig's character, which takes place in his psychiatrist's (or analyst's) office. At the beginning of the scene, both men are lying down, one in a chair, the other on the couch: bodies take similar forms in the front and rear planes of the image. As the scene progresses, and Ohlrig becomes irate, he moves around the room. The doctor (Art Smith) remains static, and yet, through his calm, manages to convey analytic "control" of the situation. Ohlrig's psychiatrist seems to be the only person who is willing to tell him the truth about himself — at least at this point. As the millionaire rants and raves about everyone (including Leonora) wanting only his money, the analyst quietly reminds him, "I thought you said she was sweeter than the other girls." He goes on to tell Ohlrig that he believes his "heart attacks" are only "nervous reactions," simply Ohlrig's way of saying that he's "not all-powerful." They are, in short, a plea for help. Ohlrig refutes this furiously, claiming (in an unconscious play on words) that he has a "bad heart." In defiance of the doctor's opinion, he declares that he *will* marry—and he will marry Leonora (whose last name he doesn't recall), adding, "Sorry to cut off a major portion of your income, doctor, but you won't see me again." The analyst seems unmoved (and, indeed, doesn't budge): "You've only done this because you're angry with me, and to prove no one has authority over you." Ohlrig leaves and, as far as we know, never returns.

It is not only the economical and highly expressive acting that makes this scene so effective. I believe that Ophuls is, oddly enough, handing the film over to Smith Ohlrig—to the lean, taut Robert Ryan with his dark, impenetrable eyes. I must echo Tania Modleski's assessment of Stefan in *Letter from an Unknown Woman*: Ohlrig is hysterical (and narcissistic, of course). His "conversion hysteria" is acted out in his illness (again, the same illness that plagues Louise de . . . and Ophuls himself). Perhaps because of his highly problematic relationship to the "father," and to figures of authority, Ohlrig also experiences the disintegrating effects of paranoia. Locked in a universe in which he and his money are the specular center, in which everything is, by definition, an extension of his own narcissistic sense of self, Ohlrig continually fires the actors who "represent" him. As one by one the people in his life begin to assert themselves as "others," Ohlrig begins to collapse. But the poor little rich boy, whose diagnosis is laid out on a platter for us, is the film's most complex, most compelling character. Having inherited four million dollars from his father (which he has increased twenty-two and a half times), Smith Ohlrig is the ultimate economic victim. He has the power to trade in people and objects, but his money is a cancerous invasion. (Such a sympathetic view of Ohlrig may recall to mind Gayatri Spivak's warning that "psychoanalysis and counterpsychoanalysis can easily become the gift of capitalist imperialism to the cause of feminism.") The possibility of infinite exchange, infinite mobility, sits poorly with a man whose paternal inheritance holds sway in his psyche. Often dressed in black against black backgrounds (rather like Lisa Berndle), continually away from home, Ohlrig is a blank space whose absented "presence" casts a pall of dread and menace throughout the entire film. No wonder Leonora scurries back to her own social class!

The marriage accomplished, Leonora's "transformation into the image" has been "completed by the newspaper montage sequence announcing the wedding, framing and immobilizing her in the photograph" (Doane, p. 159). And still Leonora is not having fun yet. She is spending yet another (we are told) endless night in Ohlrig's mansion on Long Island, with only Franzi for company. This "dazzling set piece,"[23] bears a strong resemblance to the scene between Josephine and the narrator in "Le Modèle" and leads to a confrontation that is pivotal in Doane's analysis of the film.

It is three o'clock in the morning and snowing outside—as the first image shows us. A slow panning and tracking shot takes us to Franzi as he sits at the piano playing "Tales from the Vienna Woods" while Leonora, in an evening gown, lies on the couch, "Susan Alexander"–style, awaiting the master's return. (This visually striking scene opens with Franzi in the foreground and Leonora in the rear field, shot in deep focus. Soon the positions are reversed, with Franzi at the piano in long shot, and Leonora close to the camera. A shot–reverse shot sequence traces their conversation.) Because it brings up a number of relevant issues, I quote the dialogue of this brief scene in its entirety:

LEONORA: Franzi, will you stop playing?

FRANZI: Just this one, dahling, it's so lovely.

LEONORA: I wish I could go to bed.

FRANZI: So do I.

LEONORA: It's almost three o'clock, Franzi. [*She lies down*]

FRANZI: Take a pill.

LEONORA: I've lived on pills ever since I came East. That's ten months. I won't any more.

FRANZI: [*Hums and sings*] Go play with the necklace he gave to you for your anniversary.

LEONORA: Instead of that honeymoon trip we'll never take. Instead of going to Denver to see my family. Instead of having dinner together, spending time together, being together like other married people.

FRANZI: [*Hums*]

LEONORA: No, all he wants me to do is sit here and wait until he phones or comes home. Then I see him for exactly one hour. Two if I'm lucky.

FRANZI: [*Cutting in*] Tough. You got what you wanted, dahling. You're wearing it. You mustn't expect him to pick up your handkerchief, too.

LEONORA: Maybe money's enough for you.

FRANZI: [*Breaking in*] Of course, isn't it enough for you?

LEONORA: No.

FRANZI: Why else marry a madman like that?

LEONORA: But he wasn't like this before we got married.

FRANZI: He was a bachelor.

LEONORA: He was a human being.

FRANZI: Tough. Buy yourself a new hat. Tough, darling, tough.

LEONORA: [*Screams*] Will you stop saying that? Will you stop playing that piano? Will you stop? Will you stop??

FRANZI: You know, you're a greedy little girl. And you're getting greedier every day. This part is divine . . .

LEONORA: Greedy—how dare you! Greedy . . . ! [*She crosses the room, the camera panning and tracking after her*]

FRANZI: I remember hearing it in a Viennese café—

LEONORA: [*Interrupting him in mid-sentence, she slaps both his cheeks and the cigarette falls from his lips*] I'm sorry!

FRANZI: It's all right. Saves him from getting hit. That's what I get paid for. [*There is an approximately 150-degree cut to a low-angle tilt as Franzi keeps playing*]

LEONORA: [*Shouting*] Stop playing! Will you stop playing? [*As she slams the piano lid down, a car horn honks outside and they both start. Camera pulls to level angle as she moves to the back of the room and gets her purse*]

FRANZI: Here he is. Get ready. Report for duty.

LEONORA: My comb?

FRANZI: Yes, here it is.

LEONORA: I'm sorry.

FRANZI: That's all right.

[*Leonora combs her hair next to the piano and then runs to the door in the rear field. Cut to foyer where Smith Ohlrig is arriving with numerous business guests to show them a film of his own activities*]

Leonora, we know, has demonstrated that her only interest in the image is in the appropriation of a particular kind of woman's "look," as exemplified by the fashion photograph she imitates and finally becomes. And it is Franzi who responded to her successful approximation of the fashion image and recruited her for one of Ohlrig's parties. Now, having put her image into the cycle of exchange by marrying Ohlrig, Leonora is obliged to remain fixed (evening gowned and combed) in that image, not for her own pleasure but for the tenuous pleasure of an absent husband. Franzi dramatizes the theater of Leonora's despair, even as he offers his body as a substitute for Ohlrig's. His cynical claim is that she has chosen, *as a free subject*, to exchange herself for the objects she is wearing. According to Franzi, Leonora is now able to command commodities as well as being one herself. But she is a "subject" only insofar as she consumes. And Leonora's status as object is caught up in her role as consumer and as spectator of her own image: when, at the end of the film, she has ceased to be a rich man's ornamental wife, the doctor at the hospital discards her mink coat—she doesn't need it any more. At the same time, any "subjectivity" achieved, any "authentic" expression of her own desire dissipates. Although the social circumstances of the two films' settings and release circumstances are to some degree not comparable (nineteenth-century French artist's model versus twentieth-century American carhop-model; Parisian filmgoing public versus the more easily "shocked" American spectators), both *Le Plaisir* and *Caught* depict women who trade upon, then fight to leave behind their status as a commodity-image. Both are mocked by impresario and/or director-figures who attempt, in one way or another, to intervene in the circulation of women, acting as middlemen who dramatize sexual exchanges. These men are ambiguous characters: Franzi, an "international something" himself, seems almost a parody of the "Viennese" Ophuls and is both "slimy" and sympathetic. (Ophuls was certainly good-natured to allow aspects of his own personality to appear in Franzi.) He is her makeup man, her agent, the assistant director under Ohlrig. But he is loyal to the woman, finally leaving Smith Ohlrig (who terms him a "parasite") when she does. (His parting words are, "I think I'd prefer to be a headwaiter again, Mr. Ohlrig." Is this the sordid American career of *Letter*'s Fritz?) "Maupassant" stands in opposition to the woman, seemingly a representative of the patriarchal double standard. Neither male character here can be said to be the more typical stand-in for the process of image-making although Smith Ohlrig can and does. But Franzi's close identification with the woman—they are ultimately *both* actors for a higher directorial power—represents another dimension of the "directorial" position.[24]

A confrontation between Leonora and Ohlrig, who has brought home what she (an unwilling "signora di tutti") calls "so many men," takes place as Leonora tries to go to bed. She is partway up the enormous, curved staircase (where, naturally, several confrontations of this kind take place), when Ohlrig orders her back to play hostess. The scene immediately following this one (they actually form one long sequence) is analyzed by Doane for its use of the *moving picture* by Leonora's husband to humiliate and to subjugate her. Like Hitchcock's *Rebecca*, Doane observes, *Caught* incorporates the cinematic apparatus into the diegesis as *props*: "Camera, projector, and screen are explicitly activated as agents of narrativity, as operators of the image" (p. 156). The "projection" that is so difficult for the woman seems to come easier to the man. Ohlrig has a private theater, into which he now invites his entirely male audience—and Leonora. The film he shows is one featuring his own business exploits. He is thus, as Doane puts it, "the most prominent spectator" as well as the image on the screen (p. 159).

But as in "Le Modèle," the woman's voice spoils the narcissistic male moment (bonding with nature, with one's friend, with oneself). Just as Ohlrig is admiring his own directorial prowess, Leonora laughs aloud at something one of the men says to her. A shot–reverse shot sequence follows (described in detail and illustrated by Doane), which also exploits the deep focus, slightly wide-angle effect seen in much of the film. This sequence places Ohlrig and Leonora either in medium close-up, or in extreme long shot. As Doane notes, there is a false eye-line match effect—the characters face the directions they would be facing if they were looking at each other, but the planes of the image that they occupy are so divergent that this is impossible (p. 162). Ohlrig dismisses his wife's partner in crime and proceeds to take her apart cell by cell. Since Leonora refuses to participate in the moving spectacle of his narcissism, Ohlrig humiliates her in front of the group of men. She leaves the room, and soon leaves Ohlrig, but she "takes a piece of the image with her—the mink coat." Ohlrig tacitly admits that her "silent complicity" was necessary to his cinema: he stops the projector when she leaves (pp. 162–63).

While the stakes of identifying with the projected image are different for men and women, I believe it is worth noting that Smith Ohlrig is as caught in his own image as Leonora is in her own virtual one. The "subject-object opposition," which Doane describes as so difficult for women (and it is), has certainly broken down for Ohlrig. His solipsism makes it almost impossible for him to perceive anyone as an "other" except in the moments of the aggressive return of the "partial objects" of the look and the voice.[25]

I have mentioned that Leonora's class and economic position are normalized through her work and love for Larry Quinada. The dream, once again, is for equivalent exchange, for the purchase of "real value" for one's money or labor. But even as the film advertises these values, *Caught* undermines any sense that it is really possible to achieve such a healthy sociosexual economy. As Doane points out, the mise-en-scène indicates in more than one way that Leonora is just as "caught" and just as diminished in her relationship with Dr. Quinada as she is in the one with Ohlrig. For example, as Quinada discusses his dawning feelings for his receptionist to his wise partner, obstetrician Dr. Hoffman (Frank Ferguson), the camera tracks back and forth between them, emphasizing Leonora's absence from her desk (p. 169). The camera, the only piece of the apparatus missing from Ohlrig's projection room, and whose appearance in the diegesis would be the most *disruptive* to classical cinema, "demonstrates its potency" through the woman's absence. At the end of the film, Quinada declares her "free" only after she has miscarried and is flat on her back in an ambulance, visually crushed (from a high-angle shot) into a hospital bed. Once again Leonora is caught "between" the two men who are deciding her fate (p. 172).[26] Thus woman herself, as well as her desire, are obliterated, leaving Leonora as the object of the "medical gaze" Doane describes so well.

Interestingly, Leonora presents her love of wealth as a kind of addiction from which she is having trouble weaning herself. Her rationale for her return to Ohlrig for the "security" (or name) of her child is not convincing. (Nor is her love of wealth, actually. Leonora's incoherent motivations may be a result of the Breen office having instigated policies assuring that Leonora could only *react* rather than *act*.)[27] A scene late in the film, after Leonora has left her husband for the second time but knows she is pregnant with his baby, contains interesting background on Quinada's—and Leonora's—relationship to money. The night after Quinada makes Leonora a present of a cloth coat, they go to a dance hall together. The following conversation takes place while they are seated at the bar:

QUINADA: I was mad at you that day . . .

LEONORA: Was that because I talked about marrying rich?

QUINADA: It always makes me see red when people talk that way. My parents made themselves absolutely miserable by having an exaggerated sense of the importance of money. [*An attractive woman interrupts him for a light and says, "Muchas gracias"*]

QUINADA: Your hair looks good that way.

LEONORA: Thank you.

QUINADA: You look very lovely. Is there something worrying you?

LEONORA: No, I'm very happy. Go on about your parents.

QUINADA: Oh, they just wasted their lives pretending to be rich, conniving and finagling. Never working, of course.

The same woman cuts between them again, this time giving something to Quinada, which he says isn't his: "This isn't mine." "Don't you want it?" "No." "Muchas gracias!"

LEONORA: I can't imagine you pretending to be rich—or pretending anything.

QUINADA: Oh, I did for a while, until I pulled out of it . . .

LEONORA: Larry, was it difficult?

QUINADA: No.

LEONORA: That's because you don't care about money.

QUINADA: You've got to care about money to a certain extent. How else could I take you out to dinner when I want to? But I care more about other things, like doing the kind of work that interests me . . . [*Their conversation is soon interrupted once again by the adventurous flirt, who grabs a drink from the bar. Both Quinada and Leonora laugh at her*]

QUINADA: That's a wonderful smile you've got . . .

Unaware of her marital status or her pregnancy, and still wondering where he has seen her before (he doesn't quite remember the publicity her marriage got in the papers), Quinada tries to make an honest woman out of Leonora. He instructs her in living authentically, in using her smile (described by Dorothy Dale as a woman's "greatest asset") not as legal tender but to ensure one man's happiness. As an added attraction, he also deflects the flirtatious young stranger's extremely blunt advances. In this way he places the besmirched Leonora firmly in protected "good girl" territory, at the expense of the naughty woman in black. He also refuses the mysterious "exchange" the woman wants to make—and tells her to keep the lighter (or whatever it is). Although she thanks him, she is obviously disappointed. Quinada urges Leonora to focus on money's *use value* (really its exchange value)—but that use is, in his case, as with the dark lady's, not just food (or drink, or a light), but seduction. Quinada's "inheritance" stands in contrast to Ohlrig's: the former was born into pretense, poverty, and, no doubt, debt. But he was able to learn more manly, as well as more "American" values.

Leonora's plea of addiction to money—which makes her the object of a "hygienic" if not medical gaze—seems to be contradicted elsewhere, particularly in the scene where Ohlrig comes to visit her in her shabby apartment. Although he succeeds in wooing her back home, it is with promises not of wealth but of togetherness. She opines that it is "not such a bad room." Leonora now seems to be neither a nice girl with properly directed desire nor a narcissistic golddigger. The camera, that, with its framing of Leonora's empty chair, as Doane puts it, writes her "absence," writes the truth. Without convincing character motivation, it is doubly important that Leonora (like Louise de . . .) remain attached to the signifier of her wealth. But Louise, more knowledgeable about her own desire than is Leonora, refuses to part with that signifier. And the sincere Quinada, who has spent so much time complaining about

Leonora's "fanciness," himself has a fastidiousness of manner and enunciation (after all, it *is* Mason's dulcet voice), which we now learn is the
product of the "wasteful" family pretense to be what they are not. Are
Leonora and Quinada, like Stefan and Lisa, much more alike than they
had thought?[28] Or is Ohlrig's tortured relation to money and to his own
image really closer to Leonora's?

An abrupt marriage proposal follows this conversation and takes a
familiar Ophulsian form. The couple is dancing and enjoying being jos-
tled by the crowd. The camera, of course, tracks with them:

> QUINADA: Why don't we go out again on Saturday and then spend Sun-
> day together.

> LEONORA: And Monday, too.

> QUINADA: Sure. Tuesday? [*They move across the dance floor*] Then we can go
> dancing again on Saturday night, and then spend Sunday again. You
> know, it would be simpler if we were married. Then we wouldn't have
> to make dates.

Preoccupied by her pregnancy, Leonora puts off responding to his proposal except in a vaguely encouraging way. Despite Quinada's lecture on
money, and the proposal marked by the Ophulsian signifier of true love
("Monday, . . . Tuesday . . ."), which stands in contrast to Ohlrig's indirect telephone proposal using Franzi as an intermediary, there are interesting parallels in the two men's attitudes toward Leonora. In particular,
both men see her as an "employee." (During the men's confrontation
chez Ohlrig, the latter comments that he's "just interested in employer-
employee relationships" such as that between Quinada and Leonora.
"After all," he adds, "she was an employee of mine. In a way, she still is."
Quinada: "What do you mean?" *Ohlrig:* "She's still my wife.") Both men
have played Pygmalion with Leonora, Ohlrig scraping off the charm
school veneer (the product of Leonora's problematic self-molding), and
Quinada inspiring her to undertake a complete "professionalization"
and to purify herself of the love of money. And despite Quinada's well-
advertised love of children, neither he nor Ohlrig seems particularly
interested in Leonora's baby except for Ohlrig's suspicion that it's
Quinada's, and Quinada's lukewarm expression of regret at its death.

Indeed, the sleepless night Leonora and Quinada spend together taking care of a sick child is, in my opinion, a displaced admission that this

blithe sacrifice of Leonora's baby is troubling. Returning to the office after a busy day, Quinada greets with exasperation Leonora's news that little Lorraine Rudecki's mother has called *again.* Apparently Mrs. Rudecki habitually harasses Quinada with Lorraine's imaginary stomach ailments. But once he hears that the child is "seeing double," he sends the faithful Leonora to fill a prescription while he rushes to the humble Rudecki flat. The girl, it turns out, has botulism, contracted by eating unrefrigerated potted meat. Quinada leans over her wrought-iron crib, worriedly. He can't guarantee the child's survival and blames himself aloud to Lorraine for ignoring Mrs. Rudecki's calls. Little Lorraine's vision problem acts as a trope for Quinada's ability to see through apparent hypochondria to real sickness. (It is a "double vision" problem, too, in that Quinada also had to see through the hypochondria to the wellness underneath!) Thus, Quinada reproaches himself for his insensitivity to a child—and, indeed, as with Leonora's child, he is partially responsible for her calamity. Interestingly, Mr. Rudecki sees this as the appropriate time to pay Dr. Quinada for the past two months. When, later that morning, Quinada offers Leonora a cloth coat (unconsciously trading it for her mink), it is with Rudecki's money that he purchases it. The bartering of human life thus seems to occur in Quinada's profession, as in Ohlrig's. The film's radical gesture of sacrificing Leonora's baby—exchanging it—for a "happy ending" is reflected and cauterized in Quinada's close call with the Rudecki girl.

In Conclusion

As Williams observes, and as we have seen, in *Caught* "the evident and repeatedly emphasized differences between the two men [Ohlrig and Quinada, the nice "middle-class" doctor Leonora probably marries], so necessary to Leonora's 'choice,' is subtly undermined by a series of visual, gestural, and verbal equivalences."[29] When Ohlrig dies (or lets go of her, depending on which version you follow), leaving Leonora free to marry Quinada, she enters into a new life as alienated as was her old one. This is made amply clear, despite the humanizing touches given to the selfless Quinada character. Perhaps Leonora will be able to return to her fold of female friends—to mutual admiration in cloth coats rather than the worship of the distant woman in mink.

To summarize the women's relations to themselves as commodities and as images in the films examined above: Leonora wishes to maintain an erotic relationship with her own image (she wishes to enjoy the way she and other women look but finds that she cannot when she is Smith Ohlrig's possession). Josephine's only relationship to her image is to sell it for what she thought was marriage, but was merely a pittance. She finally smashes the mirrors and destroys the paintings that have brought her only unhappiness. *La Ronde*'s heroines roll with the punches, less plagued by the image itself than by the social mechanisms that also crush Leonora and Josephine. Both Leonora and Josephine realize that to possess money (which they can use only to buy themselves more ornaments) is not fundamentally to alter their own commodity status. Although Leonora is married, it is not, according to her definition, the "real" marriage that would confer subjecthood upon her—only a return to her own class can even pretend to do this, although the pretense is hollow. For Josephine, too, the impossible dream of moving up the social ladder (in her case, to the bourgeoisie) is accomplished only through a thorough destruction of any possibility of pleasure. The "bourgeois solution" advanced in some of Ophuls' early works seems to be completely gutted, despite *Caught*'s surface "moral of the story." Only the community of women in "La Maison Tellier" continues to find pleasure in their middle-class home—where men are only visitors. Ambitions of social mobility on the part of the women in the rigid world of *La Ronde* seem even less feasible, and perhaps less desirable, than in *Le Plaisir* or *Caught*. In all three cases, it is clear that this solution is no real solution at all. Thus movement through society, like the moving image, may seem actually to restrict even as it seeks to liberate women. In *Lola Montès*, the subject of the next and last chapter, mobility of all sorts is deconstructed, and the paradoxes it presents for female desire and for filmmaking "rout our reason, and completely upset our plans," as "Maupassant" says in *Le Plaisir*.

$\mathcal{S}e\,v\,e\,n$

✦

Closing the Circle: *Lola Montès, Divine,* and *La Tendre Ennemie*

Look. In the middle of the ring, a luminous circle lit by white spotlights and a trainer wearing a ringmaster's uniform magnificently decorated, officer-style. He holds a long whip in his hand as if to tame a wild cat. In fact he has a wild animal act. Here comes the wildest of all, the animal that spelled man's ruin: the snake. Enter the marionette woman: this is the prima donna. . . . When the jump is over . . . Lola in a flannel bathrobe, stripped of her tutus and the fragile, black swan's crown, is exhibited in a cage. Where wild animals are kept. Men can pay a dollar to touch one of the two hands dangling through the bars. And two endless lines wait to kiss this woman's hands, to kiss a bit of a serpent. Here ends the story of a woman who, to make her living, acts out her life in performance.

—CATHERINE CLÉMENT[1]

One day during the coldest week in February, I was at the Billancourt studios, where fifty young women, half-naked, were filming music-hall scenes. For seven consecutive hours, sheltered under the heavy special makeup, they underwent the temperature extremes of a cloth-covered courtyard, iced by the east wind and then briefly overheated by a catastrophe of Klieg lights. Following Max Ophuls' quick commands, they climbed up and down the raw wood steps unprotected by guard rails, running and turning with inexhaustible grace. . . . At a cry from Ophuls—"We can hear the feet on the stairs! Take off your shoes!"—fifty young women, Simone Berriau among them, took off their shoes without a word and ran barefoot over the unfinished wood, among serpentining cables, metal shavings, rubble, and nails. . . . This was the same day on which the hands of an animal trainer were to drape over Simone Berriau's shoulders a live python, almost as heavy as a man. . . . [A]t the top of her gilded headdress, the python's head reappeared, raised itself like a rattler. . . . Simone Berriau's large eyelids fluttered downward, hid her eyes, and Ophuls allowed her to be rescued. . . . But I think he was more moved than she.

—COLETTE, ON THE FILMING OF *DIVINE*[2]

Queer Beasties

By the mid-1930s, Max Ophuls had already found his sea legs in the French film industry, which was not yet in the state of disarray discernible in *De Mayerling à Sarajevo*, although the major works of French Poetic Realism were also yet to be made.[3] After completing the French version of *Liebelei* and the lost film *On a Volé un Homme*, Ophuls made two films which, like his last film *Lola Montès* (1955), depict woman as a beast in need of training, or as the victim of the beasts who feed on spectacle. These films are *Divine* (1935) and *La Tendre Ennemie* (1936). Both films star Simone Berriau (who also produced *Divine* through her Eden production company), a talented actress but not a particularly powerful screen presence—rather, an ingenue type. Both were adapted from works by well-established authors: Colette's novel *L'Envers du music-hall* (*Backstage at the Music Hall*) became *Divine*; André-Paul Antoine's misogynist *L'Ennemie* became the more indulgent *La Tendre Ennemie* (*The Tender Enemy*).[4] (Colette and Antoine collaborated on the adaptation and/or dialogue for their respective films as well.) Both films were produced by Paul Bentata, and while *Divine* was a commercial and critical washout, *Ennemie* won the Prix Lumière and represented France at the Venice Biennale.[5] The latter film was made at the same time that Ophuls was working on his two musical shorts as well as on *Komedie om Geld*.[6] *Ennemie* is piquant and rather polished, visually speaking (not surprising, since Eugen Schüfftan directed the photography).[7] It is not an especially distinguished film: light-hearted but tritely moralistic ("tragi-comic," in Ophuls' words)—close, in short, to French boulevard theater, as well it might be since that is its origins. Ophuls, in fact, had directed the Antoine play in Breslau. It must have been a pleasant experience: when, despite the failure of the previous year's *Divine*, Bentata allowed him free choice of subjects, Ophuls choose *L'Ennemie*. The script is, indeed, very much to Ophuls' taste, as he himself comments in his autobiography. It was not, however, pleasing to Ophuls' wife. As Ophuls puts it: "Curious fact: a lot of women didn't like this film. My wife still detests it today."[8] Thus, it may not be surprising that a female critic (me) should, in solidarity, find *Ennemie* less interesting than either *Divine* or *Komedie om Geld*.

Even so, the plot structure, several sequences, and a number of technical devices from the film repeat or anticipate important moments in
Ophuls' other works, and it is, on the whole, a well-made and clever film.
Just what it is that the female spectator (of which Ophuls' wife is a special case) finds difficult about the film may have to do, precisely, with
how female spectatorship is structured into the film.

The frame narrative of *Ennemie* involves three ghosts ("ectoplasms," as
Ophuls terms them), who meet on a park bench and discover that they
have something in common: each was married to or in love with Annette
Dupont (Berriau); each died as a consequence of her behavior. (The
third ghost actually does not appear until the end of the film—he turns
out to be the lover Annette left behind when she married. He committed suicide.) As in *Letter from an Unknown Woman* (1948) and *Lola Montès*, this is a story told mostly in flashback, though the flashbacks are not
(for the most part) "authorized" by the female protagonist but by the
men who "loved" her. The occasion of their reunion is the posh engagement party of Annette's daughter. The impending marriage threatens to
be unhappy, one arranged, like Lisa Berndle's first engagement, by the
girl's mother, though her daughter is actually in love with a young pilot.
(The latter makes an appearance with his airplane several times in the
film, anticipating the function of the airplane in Jean Renoir's *La Règle
du jeu* [*The Rules of the Game*, 1939]). Like Lisa's lieutenant, the fiancé is
appallingly respectable and deadly dull (we see him slurping soup and
overhear him discussing his business prospects). The ghosts (like *Letter*'s
implied narrator) are eager to stop the marriage because they believe
that an arranged marriage is what turned Annette into such a monster.
Each tells the story of his experiences with her. The other ghosts listen
raptly. They then proceed to play ghostly pranks (with the help of the
terrified servants usually found in humorous ghost stories) that enable
the daughter to elope with her lover. The ghosts' moans and groans and
complaints ("It tickles when humans walk through me") are comple-
mented by droll gestures (lifting their hands in the air and waving their
wrists limply when they want to change locations) which produce a
strong comic undercurrent in this not-always-humorous film. A delight-
ful device is used to indicate their "ghostliness": not only are they always
shown in filmy superimposition, the two (then three) men are also
wrapped in a cellophanelike substance that gives them an amusingly
dime-store quality otherworldliness. Barry Salt points to another of the
very interesting aspects of the film's mise-en-scène:

The scenes set in the past are distinguished by having very stylized sets, consisting of not much more than furniture and props in front of a blank background onto which is projected a dappled pattern of abstract light and shade continuously streaming from one side to another. These flashbacks were also marked off from the rest of the film by being tinted pink and lavender.[9]

This pattern represents a "reversal" of the premise in *Lola Montès*, in that the "present" is stylized, while the "past" is treated more realistically. Although both films make use of a male "narrator," *Lola Montès* enters (partially) into the subjectivity of its heroine—its narrator (the ringmaster) is not privy to the flashbacks—while *Ennemie* "abstracts" its heroine's past, the male narrators being supernaturally omniscient. Of all Ophuls' female protagonists whose pasts are revealed in flashbacks, only Lisa Berndle unites voice-over narration with seeming (though problematic) "control" of the image track, and uses these devices to present her story to a particular interlocutor. In *Ennemie* Annette's point of view seems particularly blocked—not one but *three* male narrators are needed to bring her life story under control: it is a story exchanged *between men*. Even her own momentary access to the flashback narrative is thoroughly mediated by the male narrators, who use it as a device of persuasion.

Salt shows little charity toward the female pro- or antagonist of *Ennemie*:

La Tendre Ennemie introduced the Ophuls woman in the extreme form: vain, spoilt, selfish, and directly responsible for the death of one lover and another admirer also. She is the enemy of the film's title, and it seems likely to me that Ophuls regarded her tenderly, though the author of the original play did not, just because she is pretty and charming. We shall meet her again, particularly in *Madame de . . .*, but also elsewhere.[10]

Sometimes I resent Ophuls' penchant for beautiful women, too. And it's true that Ophuls, characteristically, took the bitter edge off Antoine's play by having the film give mitigating circumstances for the woman's behavior that were absent from the play (the abortive elopement). Contrasting film to play, Richard Roud observes that "In Antoine's play, Annette ruins the lives of her fiancé, her husband and her lover, because woman is the natural and hereditary enemy of man,"[11] while her destructive penchant is rationalized by the film. Still, although Ophuls does add mitigating circumstances, this is a less sympathetic portrait of woman-as-dangerous-force-of-nature than is the case in either *Madame de . . .* (1953) or *La Signora di Tutti* (1934). It is in the mise-en-scène of the woman's desiring look that *La Tendre Ennemie* stands apart. Thus, as mentioned above, this is a film that excludes—or punishes—by proxy its female spectator.

If Marie of *The Bartered Bride* had married the bourgeois simpleton, then run away with the circus later on, the film would be close in content to certain aspects of *Ennemie*. The ghosts describe how Annette, unhappy in her marriage, takes up with the exciting, though rather oily circus star, who had not intended that the liaison should become more than an affair. The scene where she first sights her lion tamer is reminiscent of the one in *Blood and Sand* (1922) in which Doña Sol gazes upon the matador played by Valentino. Miriam Hansen's brilliant analysis of the dynamics of erotic contemplation in Valentino's films is helpful in this context:

The notion of ambivalence is crucial to a theory of female spectatorship, precisely because the cinema, while enforcing patriarchal hierarchies in its organization of the look, also offers women an institutional opportunity to violate the taboo on female scopophilia. The success of a figure like Valentino, himself overdetermined as both object and subject of the look, urges us to insist upon the ambivalent constitution of scopic pleasure, the potential reversibility and reciprocity of roles.[12]

As is the case with Valentino (and, to some extent, with Stefan in *Letter*), the "to-be-looked-at-ness" of the circus performer in *Ennemie* "destabilizes his own glance in its very origin" (p. 279). Like the sexually vampiric Doña Sol, Annette sits with another man and looks down at the performer in the ring, admiring his domination of and vulnerability to the beasts he attempts to master—and humiliating her escort. (Thus, if she is identified with the wild animals, her attraction to their trainer/tamer is both sadistic and masochistic.) Annette's husband Georges is the one who sits next to her at the circus as her devouring gaze takes in the baroque spectacle of Rodrigo, the stereotypically slick, monocled, and tailored performer, surrounded by tigers (Rodrigo's image is continually echoed by his posters in this part of the film—indeed he looks a bit like Valentino). Like Doña Sol, Annette looks *first*, marking the man as her prey. Unlike Mizzi and Christine in *Liebelei*, Annette has no binoculars to drop, no embarrassment about her own desire that urges her to its symbolic negation. Instead, as her husband pursues her in a carriage (anticipating Monsieur de . . . and General Stauffer), and the unfocused background whirls like a carousel, Annette makes a beeline for Rodrigo. Although he is amenable to her advances, the lion tamer is perturbed when she moves in and begins ordering him around. His ghost confesses (in the frame narrative) to that of Georges that he was eager to give her back to her husband, but the latter had disappeared. The two ectoplasms chuckle together over this reluctant exchange of the woman.

Returning to the flashback, Rodrigo describes how Annette drove him to his death. Worn out from weeks or months of lovemaking, he decides, on the advice of his doctor, to take a vacation before his next big show, which would be too dangerous in his depleted condition. (His headaches and vapors are curiously hysterical; meanwhile Annette sings lustily at the piano.) Annette follows him to the train station and tearfully persuades him to let her come along. She refuses, in other words, the kind of parting that Ophuls traditionally places in railway stations. Of course, Rodrigo gets little rest on his trip and is later torn apart in the ring under the horrified (and eroticized) gaze of his mistress. The scene of his death is stylistically atypical of Ophuls, as well: it features a montage of Annette in medium shot and close-up, tigers in fragmented close-ups, brief glimpses of the wounded man. The power of the woman's gaze seems to splinter the screen as the camera virtually "zooms" (through fast tracking) to the face of a roaring tiger, then cuts to the pained and enthralled woman. In the meantime, Annette's husband has also expired, in the arms of a wryly businesslike strumpet, while they dance to a peculiarly mechanical piano performance in a cabaret—perhaps a send-up of a similar scene in *Liebelei*. As he falls, the scenery whirls 360 degrees (a common transition device in the film but here specifically attached to Georges' condition): as for Gaby in *Signora*, the camera identifies with the (in this case male) protagonist's emotion, and in the process the man is emasculated and dies. Thus, Annette is also shown to be capable of killing at a distance—not through her image, as did Gaby, but through her look. The scene fades back to the older Annette at her daughter's engagement party, seeming to imply that to some extent the flashback *does* comprise her consciousness as well, and that the recital of Rodrigo's and her husband's deaths comprise the beginning of her remorse and ultimate reform later in the film. In this way the ghostly narrative acts upon its object, apparently influencing her in her decision to allow her daughter to escape the dreaded marriage.

Annette's behavior in these and other scenes is unpleasant and casually abusive in a manner uncharacteristic of Ophuls' other heroines, however "cruel." The film's depiction of female sexual aggression, seen as clinging, frightening, obsessive, is rather conventional. In *Ennemie* woman is a beast who must be tamed: it is the trainer who, disturbed by her presence, ends up being devoured. The only antidote to such an obnoxious form of femininity, we are left to conclude, is itself a dubious salute to female self-determination. One must make sure that young girls marry men who satisfy them sexually—or else the kind of devouring need experienced by their "mothers" will find additional prey. If it were adequately stretched, this could be a description of most of Ophuls' films. But in *Ennemie* the ambivalence toward female sexual power is tilted toward the pole of blame—amusingly, even "tenderly" cast blame, but blame nonetheless. The woman in this film is culpable in "pursuit," or merely as a seductive, "drawing" image. However, the power of spectacle is not *itself* thoroughly questioned, as in *Lola Montès* and elsewhere. *Ennemie*'s men are victims, dead through her devices, and yet they are quite safe, (literally) wrapped in cellophane, as they narrate the events of the woman's life without recognizing that it is the machinery of desire, rather than one of its cogs, which is responsible for the destruction left in its wake.

And yet . . . the film takes on the poetry of *Liebelei* in its penultimate sequence, during which the mysterious sailor presents himself to explain Annette's unhappiness and consequent cruelty to his fellow ghosts. The young woman's attempt to elope is cut short by an interdictive mother, who screams at her daughter about marrying a man who will bring her debts and starvation (by contrast, the respectable fiancé claims not to have any "gambling debts"). The sailor lingers on the beautifully lit docks (one sees Schüfftan's hand here) and gazes into the distance, waiting for his beloved to appear. Instead, his look is deceived (one of Annette's crimes, perhaps—the deception of the male look), as the approaching figure proves to be Annette's maid, with a letter of farewell. As he walks away, a shot rings out, and he falls victim to suicide. After hearing this sad story, the ghosts—using a spyglass to ascertain the daughter's movements—go to work to assist her departure. (The permissive father in *Liebelei* has been multiplied and his vision enhanced.) They (and the filmmakers) amuse themselves with creating various "ghostly" effects to distract the servants as the girl slips out the door to meet her pilot. The obligatory Ophulsian communications devices, including a telegraph ticker tape announcing the daughter's departure, now take over the narrative: Uncle Emile panics and calls the police. Annette is, oddly, inspired to take this opportunity to look through a box of mementos. A series of flashbacks unfolds as she looks through the box—all of them images drawn from film, thus from the ghostly narrative and not from her own visual memory; then the three ghosts begin to speak to her, urging her to "think of her youth"—using "her" vision and *hearing* to persuade her to let her daughter go. Tears on her cheeks, she runs to the phone as the camera tracks nimbly with her, and her shadow is etched in slow motion on the wall in a fashion reminiscent not only of Schüfftan's later work in poetic realism, but, tellingly, of the mother's suicide scene in *La Signora di Tutti*. But this is a benign mother, who picks up the phone to convey not guilt but release. Annette's face is crosscut with shots of her daughter running toward her lover's plane. A clock (always a device of external control in Ophuls' films) falls on the "patriarch," Uncle Emile. The job well done, the ghosts bid each other adieu and close the doors behind them.

The contradictions of the female address are located in the very space where the registers of the look and those of narrative and mise-en-scène intersect. In offering the woman spectator a position structurally analogous to that of the vamp within the diegesis (looking at Valentino independent of his scopic initiative) identification with the desiring gaze is both granted and incriminated, or, one might say, granted on condition of its illegitimacy.[13]

The illicit look at Rodrigo early in *Ennemie* is not *legitimated* but, perhaps, retroactively "tamed" by the appropriation of the woman's flashback at the end of the film.

The Milk of Human Kindness: Divine

Divine, made in 1935, one year before *Ennemie*, is a film in the tradition of the American backstage musical of the early 1930s, but with a perverse twist. Adapted from Colette's script with her input, the film presents some of the anxieties about single women's economic survival also to be found in American films of 1930–35. *Divine* did not catch fire at the box office, and on the whole has been, I think, sadly underrated.[14] The film features some of the most extreme interrogations of the process and results of spectacle in Ophuls' work. The spectacle depicted within the

1935 film, though quite impressive, is not nearly as flamboyant as that of *Lola Montès* —what could be?—but the dangers and allure of spectacle are presented with style and depth and certainly anticipate the later film. Ophuls himself was confounded by the film's lack of success (it barely made up its production costs). It was, he said, written by a "great author," produced by a "solid studio."[15] In his autobiography Ophuls wistfully remarks that he thought the film was good, even though it was the "biggest failure" of his career to that point. Alain and Odette Virmaux regard the film's failure as a result of its inability to maintain the "schematic opposition between an unhealthy environment (the music hall, debauchery, artifice, drugs) and a healthy one (the country, the outdoors, animals, simplicity)." Ophuls ended up privileging the "artificial and baroque" qualities of the music hall, which prefigures the milieu of *Lola Montès*'s frame narrative.[16]

Ophuls' films do demonstrate a discomfort with dichotomies (as we have seen many times in earlier chapters), and urban-country, spectacle-purity are among the most mutually contaminated dichotomies in the film(s). Thus, if he felt himself obligated to follow Colette and the producers in creating a simple moral tale, with the urban as "bad" and the rural as "good," it is no wonder that the film did not do well. Ophuls does seem more "comfortable" directing the music hall scenes, and this is certainly at odds with the "condemnation" of the music hall Colette has written into the script. But Ophuls' films are anything but a simple celebration of the "unhealthy" theatrical world. It is very true that the loss of the music-hall atmosphere is also the loss of desire. The return to mother Ghea required of Colette's heroines is only convincing in Ophuls' films when it is presented as already, utterly doomed. And, indeed, the publicity packet's "Promotion Advice and Ideas" suggested that theater owners "emphasize the morbid side of DIVINE, developed in a gripping fashion, at the same time playing up its very moral conclusion." This contradictory injunction points to the only-partly resolvable double bind in which the film's protagonist finds herself, and no doubt indirectly represents perceived contradictions in French women's relationships to the working world during a period of intense urbanization in France.[17] As we have seen, the "bourgeois" (or, in this case, kulak) solution to the problems of the displaced young woman (who could be French, Italian, Austrian, German, American, depending on the specific Ophuls film)— with the statistical two children, a middle-class husband with steady work, and some of the modest luxuries of life—is panned even in Ophuls' "conservative" films. However, a rise, or at least a *change*, in social class is almost always a major issue for the women in this body of works.[18]

Divine (Simone Berriau) is the stage name of Ludivine Jarisse, "the very pretty daughter of a small farmer" who has died and left his daughter the farm as her only financial resource.[19] A childhood friend, Roberte Meunier (Yvette Lebon, who was to have starred in the film but became ill), who has become a Paris showgirl, returns and shows the naive farm girl her beautiful car and clothes, which she owes to a male benefactor as well as to her job. Roberte has a fractured ankle; it occurs to her that Divine might make a good replacement (ironic in the context of Berriau's replacement of Lebon). Looking over Divine's lovely body, as they get ready for bed, Roberte insists that Divine could make better money and have a glamorous life if she were to go back to Paris with her. (As in *Caught*, the "modeling" industry acts as a relay for female-female desire.) Divine hesitates: who would take care of the pigs and chickens, till the garden, keep her ailing mother company? But farming is hard work, marriage seems out of the question, and she only makes eighteen francs a day at the candy factory (her "country" life being thus already *industrialized*). The forty francs per day promised by Roberte excites Divine's innocent fantasies of wealth, luxury, and fame. She leaves for the city.

Divine's disillusionment begins quickly in Paris. Roberte's apartment is in the wild disarray of the typical showgirl and filled with things the young woman could not have bought for herself. Divine, playing Ruby Keeler to Roberte's Ginger Rogers (à la 1933's *Forty-Second Street*), good-naturedly picks up the soap and gives the place the order of a snug country kitchen. But her job at the little neighborhood music hall, the Empyrée, is less easy to "clean up." Soon after Divine's arrival, the police come to speak with the harried director (Marcel Vallée) about the drug-smuggling that is going on at the theater. The director himself has called them in. Colette's pithy dialogue paints the director's character vividly:

DIRECTOR: If I've decided to tell the police commissioner, it's because I couldn't figure it out by myself, right? After fourteen years of running this show, you can imagine what I've seen. Thefts, babies, sudden death! . . . And now I learn that my theater's a drop for snow. Personally, I don't give a shit! The private life of my artists isn't my business.

POLICEMAN: Couldn't a packet of drugs have got in here accidentally?

DIRECTOR: [*Sarcastically*] Oh, accidentally! Do you know people who sniff coke accidentally? Not me. And I'm the boss! [*Another knock; another intruder; the director blows up*] Come in! Get out! I've had enough! [*He throws files at the intruder's head, who retreats. Another knock*] Come in! [*It's Victor, who gestures to stop the director, who is ready to throw anything, it doesn't matter what, at his head*][20]

Victor (the assistant director, played by Paul Azaïs) is there to complain that the star of one number is afraid of the live snake used in the act. The director cries out for "one woman who's healthy and sane!" who might not be afraid of a snake (an interesting definition of sanity!). Divine, of course, has arrived ex machina. In a scene reminiscent of the Dietrich character's debut in *Blonde Venus* (1932), Roberte shows off her modest friend's charms to Victor, who grudgingly admits that Divine "will be good fresh meat for the slave market." She is only one of many chorus girls, not a star, and she gets along well with the other girls. Soon after the drug scare, several of the girls bamboozle the doorman, who's supposed to search their bags, into letting one large bag slip through. Opened in the dressing room, the bag contains a baby, which (in a gorgeously lit shot composed by cinematographer Roger Hubert)[21] its mother begins to nurse. To follow the milk's metonymic pathway, Back at the apartment, Divine has attracted the attentions of the handsome milkman (Georges Rigaud), who brings her "farm fresh" milk and eggs and flirts with her when she uses her good country sense to doubt their freshness (though not his). An accident had occurred with milk on the stairs a day or two before (a kid knocked the bottle over in front of Divine's door, spilling the milk all over the landing and the stairs), so the concierge orders the milkman to ring Divine's doorbell when he drops it off. In a description anticipating Madame Spitzer's of Lisa Berndle, the concierge remarks that Divine "never goes out, and she never has callers, not so much as a cat." This chastity clearly makes the girl even more attractive to the milkman, since he no longer sends his assistant but always delivers the milk himself (and refrains from boyish "spilling" on her doorstep).

At the music hall, Divine's beauty and "sanity" attract directorial attention, and soon she is taking part in the risqué snake number, which requires her to remove her clothes and allow the python to slither over her seminude body. Despite the sinister quality of the act, the technicians' and other actors' pretensions and bouts of hysteria lighten the atmosphere as they prepare for the performance:

SET DESIGNER: [*Following his idée fixe*] The serpent will be striped black and white, with a cross on the stomach and a cross on the back. If the serpent doesn't have a cross on his back, it will ruin my whole decor!

The sleazy animal tamer, an obese man whose stage name is Nero (Coirol) and who sports a toga, continually accosts Divine, under the guise of offering her "advice." It is opening night, and Divine is getting a bit frantic about having to work with the snake:

DIVINE: Can't you tell me anything [about the snake]?

NERO: Tell you anything? But I can tell you everything and even do everything with you, my Andalusian! [*He tries to press her up against him; she escapes*] (p. 185)

But the chubby Nero is really the least of her worries. The "fakir," Lutuf-Allah (Philippe Hériat), appears and gives her instructions.

DIVINE: [*By the fakir*] Monsieur, I came for the serpent . . .

FAKIR: [*Superior*] What's the matter? Look me in the eyes. . . . You aren't afraid, are you?

The mysterious Lutuf-Allah is the owner of the python, and the male star of the sketch where Divine must strip. His body is painted in gold lamé, and he has a mesmerist's power to make others do what he wishes, to project a powerful gaze *from* the stage: cinema looking back at its spectators. Divine goes through the number in a hypnotic state, obeying the fakir's penetrating voice and eyes ("Are you my faithful slave? Then take this serpent!). It comes off without a hitch—though Divine's clothes stay on.

But such modesty is made more difficult with Divine's next number, this one with Nero. The "Slave Market Number" requires the girls to stand on a pyramidlike structure and, as Nero cracks his whip, to undress one by one. Divine freezes, refusing to comply. Before the director has time to become furious, the audience begins to applaud—they love her resistance to the whip! Thus, she is able to resist displaying her own body, but remains locked in the gaze of the powerful man. A success in spite of herself, Divine eats out with the other impecunious showgirls, then returns home where the milkman is waiting with flowers to congratulate her on her opening night. He leaves, and Divine writes a letter to accompany a check to her mother, a good country woman now profiting from her daughter's nefarious career. Even mom's purity is being sullied, via the economic realm from which Ophuls so frequently draws his metaphors.

The fakir's "mistress," Dora (Gina Manès), who is obviously meant to be a lesbian, continually eyes Divine, offering her strange-tasting candy and other weird goodies. Here is a gaze even more perverse than Annette's in *Ennemie,* and Dora seems to be working as the fakir's *entremetteuse* as well as for her own pleasures. Before long the young girl has been invited "for tea" to Lutuf-Allah's plush apartment with a heteroclite "Oriental" decor. The couple's attempts to get Divine to smoke opium are interrupted by the police, who know that Lutuf-Allah is dealing drugs. The fakir slips a packet to Divine and sends her out the back way. Of course, the packet contains drugs of some sort. Soon poor Divine has been coerced into delivering Lutuf-Allah's packets all over town.

Meanwhile, however, the romance with the milkman (whose name we now discover is Antonin) is also heating up. He persuades Divine to let him take her to his farm. Despite her apprehensions about missing work, she agrees and falls in love with the baby chickens and other farm animals she had missed so much. The lovers begin the typical Ophulsian chorus (even though it is Colette's script), listing together the various chores that must be done every day around the farm. Back at the Empyrée, things are literally heating up. The search for drugs has narrowed down to the fakir, Dora, and Divine. (The latter falls under suspicion mainly because of a postcard from Roberte in Cairo, who asks Divine if she's gotten her car yet.) The police begin to search for Divine, as Lutuf-Allah sets fire to his dressing room to destroy incriminating evidence. By the next morning the dance hall is seriously burned. Divine—just setting out for her trip with Antonin—wonders if she should do something, but he persuades her to go with him anyway. When they return that evening, Antonin leaves Divine in his milk truck as he goes to make inquiries at the theater. The police won't let him in, but he notices that one of them is looking at a newspaper photo of Divine and is moving toward the truck to arrest her. Antonin rushes back to the truck and engages the quick-witted Divine in a "mom and pop" conversation, confusing the cop and enabling them to get away. They go immediately to the city hall to get married. However, the clerk, an old friend of Antonin's, also recognizes Divine and goes into the back room to recheck her photo in the paper. He's thrilled to be catching a drug smuggler. But when he calls the police he is told that the case has been cleared up. Divine is free. He returns to the couple, who are picking the petals off a flower, and offers his congratulations on their marriage. The End.

From the virtually Eisensteinian fragmentation of the early "auto arrival" scene in *Divine* to the last shot of the clerk's family looking out the window to see the newly married couple kiss, the film is a complex and beautifully filmed commentary on the nature of theater, the theater of nature, and a woman's role in both. Roberte brings with her into Divine's chaste room aspects both of the public's eyes and the director's, and of the "model" to be imitated, if Divine's desires are to be fulfilled. She orders Divine to walk back and forth across the room, then she saunters across the floor doing her "Queen of the fountain" walk, to Divine's amusement. Roberte wants to be taken seriously, but the two young women end up making a game of it. So the theater is a game to Divine, but more importantly it is a "real job," a way to make honestly needed money. So despite the close resemblance between this scene and the opening one in *Caught* (1949), the nature of Divine's desire is much less clear than is Leonora's in the later film. The woman's desire seems divided between mother, farm, factory job, baby, glamour, admiration, husband, and so on, without a clear focus on any—except perhaps the baby chicks. *Because* women's desires (time, socioeconomic possibilities) are impossibly divided, the premise of the film is excellent. But the attractions of farm life seem too rosy, and the corruption of the music hall too absolute, presenting, according to Alain and Odette Virmaux, a narrative that is (though only *on the surface*) too easy to resolve—by contrast, even if Leonora's "addiction" to money is not completely convincing in *Caught*, her desire to incarnate a certain image *is*. If Divine had smoked a bit of the opium, found herself oddly attracted to Dora, had an argument with her saintly mother, or generally bitten a little more deeply into the apple, the corruption of the country girl by the spectacle would have been more evident than it finally is. In comparison to Ophuls' other heroines, Divine's fate in the theatrical world is not very harsh: Gaby, for example, is destroyed by the workaday star business and by her own "fatal" beauty. Salt complains of the relative arbitrariness of Divine's theatrical career, seeing it as a caprice on her part:

The eponymous heroine of *Divine* (1935) also chooses to become an actress without the slightest necessity to do so, though she is unusual amongst Ophuls' heroines in rejecting the profession after having tried it. The story of this film is an unskillful cobbling together of bits and pieces of Colette's music hall anecdotes, and in general the way it is shot presents the beginning of Ophuls' retreat to conventional film-making in the later part of the nineteen-thirties. (p. 363)

Although Salt's research on Ophuls' technical style is far more extensive than mine, I can't follow his lead and agree that this film is "conventional," or close to it. Its unusual use of dissolves and close-ups in the first sequence; its panning and tracking shots "caressing" the girls' apartment; the amazing 360-degree shot marking Divine's first entrance into the backstage area; the neat dissolve (anticipating *Caught*) from a drawing of her costume to the costumed girl; the superb crane and tracking shots on the stairway as a female assistant directs the showgirls' choreography for the male director (described by Colette above); the jarring 180-degree cut in the director's office; the montage of spectators' eyes coming toward Divine, superimposed upon Nero's face as she takes the whip and strikes him; the Sternbergian treatment of the fakir's apartment with its many rugs, veils, screens, and Asian doors, all shown in tracking shots; and many more scenes—all make the film's visuals extraordinarily compelling.

Regarding the issue of Divine's character, Salt expresses a general impatience with Ophuls' female characters because they seem to choose their misery—the profession of acting, of putting themselves on display is, he says "not forced on them" (p. 378). Salt overlooks the fact that there are many kinds of force, among them the economic, and even the force of ambition. It is, moreover, important not to succumb to the simplistic notion that spectacle is simply "bad": certainly Ophuls did not. Regarding Divine, however, because her capacity for desire and pleasure does not seem to hinge upon playing out the destiny that Lisa, Gaby, Lola, and so on seem more profoundly *driven* to contend with, her choice of the theater may seem a bit random. Her role as an empty vessel is exaggerated and approaches the passivity of *La Signora di Tutti*'s protagonist. Perhaps the very point is that Divine has no desire at the beginning of the film—only duties. She must feed the chickens, care for her mother, and so forth. Marriage seems to be a boring or difficult prospect, and she has tried a factory job. The pure and beautiful girl seems to have few avenues, and because of her concern about money (eighteen versus forty francs a day), she becomes caught up in the force of Roberte's desires and ambitions. When Divine sees what it is like to live the life of the spectacle, she does reject it—and she is, unlike Lola and her sisters, able to do so (though not without having been dragged deeply into it). But Divine's "rejection" is not a simple one. Indeed, because of the complexity of her response to her newfound life in the country, the film does not fall into simple dichotomies. She does not return to an unaltered world or, rather, that world is now filtered through another model for desiring—Antonin.

Milk runs through *Divine* and takes on several roles. It functions as metonym for the country; it is the excess of male arousal pooled at her door (much to her concierge's disapproval); it is the milk of a young mother nursing her child backstage. But even this last scene does not constitute simple praise for the simplicity of mother-love. The group of young women gazing "tenderly" on gives the act of nursing a theatrical air and makes childbirth an exciting secret (smuggled in like drugs in big valises) among women. When the milkman knocks "three times" at Divine's door, he is giving the traditional signal for the opening of a play in the French theater: *les trois coups.* And when he begs her to open the door to the apartment a little more, so that he can see in, is he not repeating Nero's demand that Divine reveal all? What Antonin does is bring the love of the countryside to Divine's door in a *theatrical* form: of course, the location for this courtship is on a staircase, a fundamentally *theatrical* space for Ophuls.

The "directorial" functions in the film are divided among several characters—the vaporous director himself, who works only with the girls paid two hundred francs or more; the crudely pragmatic but amiable Victor, who deals with the "cheaper stuff"; and the "oriental" Lutuf-Allah, who combines every form of hypnotism, Svengali-ism, mes-merism, drug use, and blackmail that a negative "director-figure" could have in an Ophuls (or even a Fritz Lang) film. Even the basically harm-less Nero, who stands "theatrically" under a prop trellis to proposition Divine, cracks the "ringmaster's" whip, demanding that Divine display herself to the public. Only insofar as Antonin fills in the directorial role—announcing the opening of the "play" with his three knocks, throwing Divine her lines as they make their getaway, and so on—can he incite her desire and her loyalty. (Incidentally, the farm that he is sup-posed to "own" actually belonged to Simone Berriau herself.) Divine does turn the whip back on her "tamer," and does break away from the Svengali ruining her life. But her future happiness, almost ruined by a newspaper photo identifying her as a criminal suspect, seems as dependent on the newfound theatricality of the farm as it does on any escape from the evils of theater life. Of theater life itself, we retain the vision of the beleaguered, put-upon director, and his hapless assistant, sitting in the ruins of their theater and wondering just whether it is possible to "purge" it of its most dangerous and exploitative components—without spoiling the show.

As the above section-title for the discussion of *La Tendre Ennemie* indicates, the world of women in spectacle is full of "queer beasties." Most often, the beasts seem to be the women themselves—the serpents men flock to kiss (as Clément puts it) in *Lola Montès*, the lions who tear up their master out of sympathy for their fellow "cat," the "tender enemy" herself. Divine is, on the other hand, oppressed by the snake that kisses *her* on the lips, the snake that seems to be a phallic extension of Lutuf-Allah's ability to hypnotize her into doing his will. But the real danger is that the woman might *become* snake, the snake that revealed itself exclusively to her at the beginning of time. That she was, according to myth, *approached* by a snake, oddly, makes her one in the eyes of men. In Ophuls' film we have seen the director who uses beasts to force his will upon the woman—it is not clear whether he or the woman is most beast-like. We have seen the director who is convinced that woman herself is the only dangerous beast. And, more rarely, we have seen the man who himself is placed in danger of being torn apart by beasts *alongside* the woman he directs, knowing that he, too, has a beast-nature. These dialectics between man and woman, beast and beast, director and star are never resolved. They can only be traced in their endlessly spiraling patterns, through the films of Max Ophuls.

Lola Lola Squared[22]

Although it is neither his most aesthetically pleasing nor his best-structured film, *Lola Montès* is an immensely rich culmination of Ophuls' career as a director. Ophuls' only film in either color or CinemaScope, it takes a boldly experimental approach to both, with the help of many of the technicians who had worked on the earlier French films: Matras (cinematographer), Annenkov (costumes), d'Eaubonne (set design), Natanson (script and adaptation), and many more. Despite its sometimes bleak subject matter—the life and times of a failed dancer—the film is often quite comical. The quiet tone that Ophuls wanted to impart to this story of a king and his mistress was blasted to bits by demands on the part of the producers that *LM* be a superproduction. Ophuls did his best, but the film was marketed as a vehicle for sex symbol Martine Carol—contrary to his wish to make it a complex and demanding, only marginally salacious film. As is documented in the introduction to this book, *Lola Montès* was both a terrific flop and a critical bone of contention when it came out in 1955. A major Franco-German international effort, shot simultaneously in French, German, and English, the film did not come anywhere close to covering its enormous production cost of 648 million old francs. Although it was hooted at the box office, the film gained the inalienable admiration of serious filmmakers and critics, including Jean Cocteau, Roberto Rossellini, Jacques Becker, Jacques Tati, as well as Rivette, Truffaut, and the rest of the *Cahiers du Cinéma* crowd. Ads defending the film were run in the daily newspaper *Le Figaro* by its adherents, while more casual support was expressed by fisticuffs in the aisles. The producers reedited the film in an effort to make its structure more conventional (and distributed it in the United States in this form, as *The Sins of Lola Montez*), but to no avail. It was still a flop. Ophuls died of heart failure less than a year later, deeply disappointed in the film's reception but also aware of staunch critical support for the film and, as always, completely involved in many other projects.

Lola Montès picks up the major concerns of almost all of Ophuls' previous films. Like *The Bartered Bride* and *La Tendre Ennemie*, it features a circus, though it goes much farther than the earlier films in depicting what we have called the "carnivalesque," after Bakhtin.[23] The carnival is a place where hierarchies are overturned, and in all these films this "revolution" results from unbridled female desire. That the carnivalesque does not necessarily represent woman's access to freedom (Mary Russo's point, which I raised in chapter 2) is written in flames in *Lola Montès*. Like *Komedie om Geld* and *La Ronde, Lola Montès* features an overt director-figure, although this one directs within rather than outside of the diegesis. As in *The Exile* and *Sarajevo*, a king's frustrated love for a commoner plays an important role. Stardom, the sale of women within marriage and without, the woman who belongs to "everyman," the "back side" of the music hall—all are met with in this film as they are in *The Bartered Bride, La Signora di Tutti, Divine, Sans Lendemain, Caught . . .* During the course of this discussion, spectacle, the role of sound and image, the exchange of women, the ever-more-difficult director-star relationship, and the question of Ophuls' return to his Weimar days (and even to "primitive" cinema) are traced through several scenes from the film. *Lola Montès* opens on the circus act in which Lola (Martine Carol) earns a living by acting out scenes from her scandalous past as the mistress of many famous European artists, politicians, and noblemen. The "Mammoth Circus," which thus employs her, is an American one. A cynical, cigar-smoking clown, looking rather like a sinister version of the Karl Valentin character in *Die verkaufte Braut*, doubles as the manager of the circus. He makes a number of appearances in the film, mostly in consultation with Lola's concerned doctor (Willy Eichberger), whose warnings of imminent disaster are (literally) muffled by the sound of the manager counting money. Lola is indeed ill. The ringmaster (who also seems to be her lover, played by Peter Ustinov) frets over her weak heart—asking her about the results of her recent medical examination. Yet he encourages her to continue the strenuous performance. Like Leonora Ames, Lola only keeps going by means of pills and potions— and both women have to shell out cash for them. The former courtesan's weakened state causes her to lapse into recollections of her past, presented as a series of flashbacks triggered by the names and dates cited during the performance of her life story.

The film's flashbacks, which comprise its main action, take place in Italy, France, Scotland, and Bavaria, depending on which epoch of Lola's life is under review. Thus, the narrative crosscuts (or cross-dissolves) between heavily stylized circus representations of Lola's parents, of herself as a child, as a young adult, and so forth, and Lola's own audio/visual recall of particular events from the past. All this takes place as she climbs, during her act, to the "top" of her career as courtesan and, simultaneously, to the top of the circus tent via a series of trapezes. *Lola Montès*'s moment of greatest tension occurs when its heroine is to leap from her platform, without the benefit of a net, to a trampoline below. Her physician threatens to call the police if Lola makes the netless leap. Refusing the intervention of the law on her behalf, and gathering her courage, she jumps anyway. To her ringmaster's relief, and the delight of the crowd, whose male members subsequently line up and pay a dollar to kiss her hand,[24] Lola has survived another fall.

Ophuls must be credited, in *Lola Montès*, with yet another of the most offbeat premises for a flashback on record.[25] Surprisingly, the events of Lola's life, other than the circus act itself, are mostly factual,[26] as reported by the film, although their treatment is almost antirealistic, and certain events are exaggerated or glossed over. Lola's experiences at the

American circus are fictional, although it is true that Lola spent time living and performing in San Francisco during the gold rush. Even when
the historical Lola was alive, it was hard to tell what was truth and what
fiction in her creative autobiography. Lola Montès (or Montez) was born
Eliza Gilbert in Limerick, Ireland, in 1818. She claimed, however, to
have been born in Seville in 1823, and that her real name was Maria
Dolores Porres y Montez. Her father was (in fact) an ensign in the British
army. He married Lola's mother when he was eighteen and she only thirteen or fourteen years old (sources vary) and already pregnant with
Lola. Ensign Gilbert was soon sent, along with his family, to Calcutta,
where he died of cholera not long afterwards. Mrs. Gilbert remarried
quickly, and Lola's stepfather, Captain Patrick Craigie, sent her back to
Scotland to be brought up by relatives. When her daughter was eighteen,
Lola's mother attempted to marry her off to a sixty-year-old man, Judge
Abraham Lumley, but Lola refused and (as is shown in the film) eloped
instead with her mother's traveling companion, Lt. Thomas James. They
were married in Dublin in 1837, went to live with the young man's family in rural Ireland, and were then dispatched to the Punjab in India.
Apparently, Lieutenant James abandoned his wife—although the film
depicts the contrary—and ran off with the wife of another officer. On
her voyage back to England, Lola became involved with a Captain
Lennox: this liaison resulted in a court case being brought by her
(apparently hypocritical) husband. At this point Lola began her "career"
as a dancer, although she was generally regarded as more of a curiosity—
a *personality*—than an artist. Often she would manage to get booked at
important European theaters, only to be jeered off the stage. In 1844
Lola became the friend or mistress of Franz Liszt, and in 1846 she
became King Ludwig I's companion, with many musicians and writers
(Chopin, Dumas père, Mérimée, and others) in between. Lola was a
powerful orator and a brilliant strategist. Well before she met King Ludwig of Bavaria and became his "uncrowned queen," Lola had been active
in politics, riding on the coattails of various members of the English par-
liament, German princes, and others. She often showed up in political
hot spots, and was more than once suspected of spying (for the Russian
czar in revolutionary Warsaw, for example). These qualities and experiences, as well as her beauty, obviously impressed the king. But her often
successful attempts to dismiss ministers and run the government of
Bavaria alienated her from both the Church and the nobility of the
country. Eventually she was ejected from Bavaria, during the putsch of

1848. Like Liszt, Lola Montès went through a religious, or mystical, phase toward the end of her life. She ended her years as a "penitent," under the influence of a powerful spiritual mentor.

Lola's dancing was apparently always dreadful, or at least controversial. Ophuls' film certainly reflects the artistic ambiguities of her career: was Lola Montès an accomplished performer or simply a buxom and scandalous beauty, whose large blue eyes had a peculiarly penetrating quality? Perhaps not coincidentally, similar questions were being posed about Martine Carol, the star of the film, whom the producers imposed on Ophuls over his strenuous objections. The film is not a defense of Lola's (or Martine's) merit as an artist. One senses, rather, that the lack of clarity in Lola's—and Martine Carol's—status as an artist gives Ophuls free rein to concentrate on the issue of representation, the meaning of performance, and the question of mediation (by painting, film, and so on)—as well as on the meaning of female "exhibition."

If Louise de . . . is a liar, Lola is false through and through, but hers is an earnest falsity, one that Ophuls permits us to admire without reserve. Nothing indicates to us, for example, that we should doubt the veracity of her flashback recollections—although their status as representations is constantly asserted. The film's complexity is created by this doubled narration: circus act and flashbacks. The circus act is an amazingly dense set of metaphors for the production of woman as a commodity and as spectacle, as marginal and as central to the production of machines of desire, picking up on images found throughout the Ophuls opus. The "severed head" floating in the psychological background of *The Exile* reappears here as a multitude of baskets shaped like Lola's head on a stick, in which red-garbed valets gather coins for the benefit of "fallen women" (*filles perdues*). The circus "spectators" are mostly black-and-white cardboard figures behind black netting, as befits the hollowness of this repetitive and concentrically encircled narrative. The flashbacks themselves are famous for, among other things, the color schemes that lend a surreal touch to the "realistic" sequences telling the tale of Lola's life. As Alan Williams notes, the color systems of the film are "far from capricious" and are "related to the division between performance and flashbacks."[27]

In the circus, action inside the ring takes place in all possible colors, distinct and of great intensity. One dwarf is a brilliant red, another bright orange, another white. Lola's face is seen at various times illuminated by lights of bright orange, green and blue. Outside the ring all is black and white. . . . The flashback episodes, on the other hand, each have a dominant color scheme which is maintained in all details. The scheme of the Liszt episode . . . is red and gold. Ophuls went so far as to paint several kilometers of roadway red and spray neighboring trees with gold paint for the outside shooting. For Bavaria, the colors are white, dark blue, and grey.[28]

The tension produced by the distinct division between the various registers of narration (and subconsciously promoted by the color schemata) is comparable to that produced in *Letter from an Unknown Woman* by the separation between the sound and image tracks. That "separation" is not a clean one, but during most of *Letter* there is a temporal gap between Lisa's voice-over letter (accompanied by the frame narrative of Stefan reading) and the flashbacks of her life inspired by it. In both films the "gap" closes as the flashbacks get closer in time to the frame narrative. In both films, as well, the flashbacks seem to be, for the most part, inspired by the mental processes of the female protagonist. This is much more clearly the case in *Lola Montès*, which does not get interference from the narrative's "addressee" (Stefan, in *Letter*). The ringmaster stands in as narrator in that he introduces the chapters of her life—often in voice-over—which seems to give him some access to the "scene of production" of the image track. An "enunciative agency" is at work in the sound and visuals of both films, providing a larger range of knowledge than the heroine can possibly have and introducing what Judith Mayne has called an intersection of narrative authorities.[29] Ophuls uses CinemaScope partly to reveal Lola's isolation in the heart of the vast mechanisms that have sprung up around the telling of her life story. And yet, through masking, shooting in restricted spaces, intimate dialogue, and other devices in the flashbacks, Ophuls also manages to retain some of the quiet intensity of his original project—which would have been, one assumes, closer to the tone of *Letter*.[30] Obviously, the similarities with *Letter* do not end here, as a look at a sequence early in the film will confirm.

The first flashback in *Lola Montès* occurs after the extraordinary and disturbing opening circus scene, one of Western cinema's great feats of choreography. The circus prologue features chandeliers descending from the ceiling as a low-angle camera tilts to follow their descent, platoons of uniformed giants and dwarfs, a "parade of wildly leaping, top-hatted lovers," the collection of funds for fallen women, juggling Lola lookalikes, foregrounded paste crowns pulled up and down on strings to emphasize vertical space, canted camera angles producing bizarre Cine-maScope effects, complex tracking shots, various kinds of music (some of which comes from an African-American orchestra led by an Uncle Sam figure—the first people seen in the film, interestingly), and, not least,the booming voice and masterful presence of the ringmaster, Peter Ustinov, who emerges cracking his whip from between curtains depicting scenes of Lola's life. Lola, wearing sparkling white garments and a crown with veil, but whom the ringmaster describes as a "bloodthirsty monster with the eyes of an angel," is brought in on a litter.[31] Close-ups reveal Lola's deep distress, her faintness, and her determination that "it will be fine" ("*ça va aller*"). During the "wildly immodest" question-and-answer period about Lola's life,[32] the ringmaster answers almost all the questions. As he does, he speaks Lola's motto: "*Femmes fatales* do not stay . . . do not stay anywhere." The voices of the questioners about the size of her bust, the location of her children, and so forth, begin to echo in Lola's ears (and we experience this along with her): "Does she remember. . . . Does she remember?" The flashbacks thus triggered are "hallucinations" of Lola's past, which both disturb and fascinate her—in any case, they are very painful.

An extraordinarily complex superimposition/dissolve takes us from Lola's face in close-up to a carriage traveling a country road, headed toward Rome in the company of Franz Liszt (Will Quadflieg). The carriage, more elegant than Lola's (which accompanies them), is equipped with bed, piano, samovar, and other accoutrements of the itinerant late-Romantic musician's life. *Letter*'s Stefan Brand again takes his show on the road—though not by train this time. The camera cranes to look through the windows into the interior, where Lola is lounging barefoot on the bed. Liszt moves to the window and, like many of his Ophulsian brethren who wish to "protect" their women from any gaze but their own, closes the curtain. A cut, however, foils this attempt to frustrate our vision. Dialogue between the couple immediately reveals that their love affair has grown stale: "Things are going very badly with us, you know," comments Lola, not unkindly—or with much regret. (Indeed, her own carriage has been following the couple in anticipation of her voluntary split with Liszt.) Lola is prepared but not certain to take off on her own at the next stop, an inn where she, her servants, and Liszt will stay the night. The scenes in the carriage and the inn are brilliantly executed, showing at its most pronounced Ophuls' tendency to layer the objects in the field of vision. Inside the carriage, a restricted space which must have been a challenge to film, Ophuls (as was his habit even in his American films) violates the 180-degree rule, creating a sense of spatial disorientation not dissimilar to that practiced by Yasujiro Ozu during the same period. Both technically and thematically speaking, this scene is a curious permutation of the givens of *Letter* since Franz Liszt is, of course, the composer of the piano piece "Un Sospiro," which Stefan Brand plays while Lisa Berndle listens yearningly to him from the courtyard. As the magnetic and hyperbolically spec(ta)cular virtuoso of late Romanticism, Liszt personifies the kind of emotional epiphany sought by Lisa in Stefan.

A shared vision of the virtuoso is only one of the elements common to the two scenes. Some of the most interesting "similarities" reveal the more radical nature of *LM*'s approach to female sexuality, desire, and will, as compared to Ophuls' earlier films. Although Liszt is a musician, and thus readily comparable to Stefan Brand, it is Lola whose many sexual partners and whose tendency to move from man to man, from place to place, are emphasized, thus identifying her—as well as Liszt—with Stefan. Ophuls finally directs the film about Don Juan he said he had always wanted to make (a desire no doubt influenced by his love of Mozart). During this first scene with Liszt, Lola states her philosophy: "Life, for me, is movement," a statement that, of course, stands in opposition not only to the traditional passivity of women but to Mary Ann Doane's observation that the moving image in cinema is more oppressive to women than the still image. (This does not mean that Doane's analysis of *Caught*, where she advances this argument, is faulty, merely that in the larger context of Ophuls' films still and moving images have many meanings.) *Lola Montès* is Ophuls' vision of what happens when the woman is permitted—or determines upon—the same sexual rootlessness usually acted out by men like Liszt—or Stefan. Lola "suffers from reminiscences" even more acutely than do the characters in *Letter*. Perhaps Lola feels the pain Stefan began to experience when his blindness to his past was cured. Both Don Juan and Doña Juanita finally meet their "man" of stone: Stefan's is Johann Stauffer, or Lisa herself—or even his unknown goddess. Lola's is King Ludwig (Anton Walbrook), the ringmaster (Ustinov)—perhaps even herself as immobilized image. Is Lola a "transvestite" (as was the historical Lola), taking on the trappings of male sexuality? To a certain extent this is the case, since men have for centuries been the most obvious models for active sexuality in most cultures. But according to the scenario written over the course of the past centuries, even when woman actively pursues man there is still the moment when she stops, allowing him to take in her mesmeric charm, drawing *him* to *her*, as Gaby does inadvertently—and Lola deliberately. Just who is in control? "Fate"? The problems of activity versus passivity become very complex when we delve beneath the roles generally assigned the sexes and see how variegated they really are. Lola's extravagant desire for men and her extravagant desirability certainly open the film to "queer readings" of many kinds: indeed, a "straight" reading of the film is a stretch of the imagination. Lola is the queerest of all Ophuls' characters—a veritable cipher of possible gendered and sexual identifications.

As though in imitation of Lisa's and Stefan's night at the opera, Lola's and Franz Liszt's farewell scene at the inn involves a (spoken) fantasy in which the two meet on equal ground—at a performance—each abandoning a lover to go to the other. The inn scene is magnificently shot. We see the sleeping Lola through iron grillwork while Liszt is on the other side of the room, under a stone arch used to create a frame within the CinemaScope image (as do the many maskings and curtains used throughout the film). Liszt is writing his "Farewell Waltz," dedicated to Lola, and tries to give it to her as a parting gift. When she feigns sleep, he tears it up in frustration (though she later gathers up the pieces). "Do you hear me?" he asks, "Do you want to hear me?" Significant words, coming from a musician. However, as he begins to leave the room, Lola, eyes still closed, complains that it would be nicer to say good-bye, and asks for a farewell kiss: she did indeed hear him, though she was at first mute. The kiss leads to the fantasy of reunion, arranged through the offices of "coincidence" (which arranged things so well for Donati and Louise in *Madame de . . .*). Fantasy and kisses lead to a lingering foretaste of what that reunion would be like. Lola's life of movement apparently does not brook closure, only the circles of eternal return, marking her as a powerfully Nietzschean character. She transforms the woman's nightmare of a man sneaking out of her room after a night of love into something actively wanted, and by gathering up the pieces of the waltz, she remains "faithful" to the man's music—and to her own free will, (in direct contrast to Lisa Berndle). Free will, individual self-determination, ultimately reveals itself to be at least in part illusory. Political circumstances enforce Lola's abrupt departure from the kingdom of her beloved Ludwig. But not chance, nor fate, nor Ophuls' beloved "coincidence," nor even politics is the only force determining Lola's fate. The laws guiding Lola's movements are written into the Western codes surrounding representation and, as we have so often seen, the "circulation" of images, money, and women. The upheavals of Ophuls' peripatetic life, the advent of "international" filmmaking in the form of superproductions, even the history of political "conquests" in European history are all written into this costume drama.

The most lyrical scene in *Lola Montès* may be the one when the teenaged Lola and her mother take a ship across the Channel to sell the girl to an English lord. Although (the ringmaster informs the spectators) we are not to ask questions about Lola's mother, this sequence tells us much about the pain that drives Lola's extraordinary desires. Lola and her mother, Mrs. Craigie (Lise Delamare) are met as they board the ship by Lieutenant James (Ivan Desny), once Lola's father's aide-de-camp. As Lola and her mother wend their way into the bowels of the ship, toward the cabins, Mrs. Craigie awkwardly explains that Lola must sleep in the dormitory since the lieutenant has reserved only a single cabin for the mother. Lola is dejected and complains that she'll be lonely without her mother, who makes fluttering excuses and then leaves to meet her lover. The forlorn girl asks the cabin boy who helps her with her luggage if there are very many singles. His reply is that there are almost none, inadvertently revealing the mother's ruse. She settles into the dormitory under the inquisitive eye of a shrewish governess, who asks her how old she is. Lola cries on her bunk. (This is not one of the finer moments in the acting career of Martine Carol, who makes a very unconvincing "child." One savors Joan Fontaine's Lisa all the more.) The "maternal" gaze is ever an appraising one in this film, sometimes negligent, sometimes sharp and penetrating.

At dinner, just when the musicians are warming up, Lola's mother reminds her, emphatically, that "it is *time*" to go to bed—an echo of the familiar Ophulsian concern for time and its relation to performance. Again, Lola is polite but wistful. As she leaves the dining room, her mother and Lieutenant James are framed by a window. They are brightly lit and seem to be floating in a fishbowl or, at least, in a realm completely removed from the dark, windy deck where Lola has been exiled. Once again, her mother is behind glass, seeable but utterly removed. She moves toward the prow of the ship, the camera tracking with her, and gazes at the sea, listening to the music. The camera tilts up to show the stars, drawing us into the child's melancholy state and her aesthetic nature. A dissolve takes us immediately to another starry field, but this

one is a curtain, a theatrical curtain which has just been dropped at the
end of the first act of a play. (Lola, as "trickster" figure,[33] is at the pivot
of the shift between nature and theater.) Lola, her mother, and Lieutenant James are in the audience. The girl stares raptly toward the curtain, unwilling to let go of the magic of the moment—still stargazing—
but she follows her mother obediently when called. They leave the theater itself and head toward a towering staircase, which they climb. At
each landing we see them walk by, and the camera slowly cranes up the
several stories. Ironically, Lola's first "rise" is into maternally sponsored
prostitution, which she rejects. Mother and daughter argue while the
lieutenant remains discreetly silent. It seems that Mrs. Craigie is low on
funds and wants to trade in her daughter and her debts to an old
baron—a banker—who was once Lola's father's friend. Lola suggests
(with Oedipal sarcasm) that her mother marry the man herself. The
baron himself, it turns out, is not there, his gout having sent him to
Baden-Baden. But the assistant (Franzi's ancestor) is overwhelmed by
Lola and bubbles over with compliments. He had seen her portrait but
was not prepared for the real thing—"My compliments, Madame" (to
the mother). One of the many paintings and portraits acting as important props in the film, this depiction of Lola has been used as a catalog
of her charms, one that disarms men but is profferred by Mrs. Craigie
rather than Lola herself, who remains out of the circuit of control. We
overhear Mrs. Craigie admit that "there is no fortune at all" in her family—"actually, it's the contrary"—confirming the fact of female endebt-
edness as the motivating force behind the sale (as though Lucia Harper
had handed her daughter over to the blackmailers in lieu of payment).
As her mother and the banker's assistant quietly decide her fate, Lola
and the lieutenant sit in the foreground, facing one another and providing a striking frame for the conferees in rear field.

A few moments later, when the lieutenant's back is turned, Lola disappears; the mother sends her lover in hot pursuit. We follow the pair as
they descend the stairway, watching Mrs. Craigie's staircase plot unravel
on the way down. By the time they reach the bottom, Lola has learned
that Lieutenant James "loves her a lot." Turning this over in her mind,
she heads for the door, obliging him to chase her once more (a pattern
that is reversed later in the film as Lola's desires become more active).
"Well, then, do something. Marry me! Are you coming?" As the young
man rushes to join her, the screen is masked on both sides, framing their
exit. An usher in powdered wig stands up and walks slowly around the

foyer with a bell: "Second Act, Second Act." And, indeed, this wonderfully self-reflexive moment signals that the second act of Lola's life has begun with her elopement. Even in the *framed* narrative, thus, "reality" is marked by theatricality: this is a story that was drawn from the histories purveyed by novel and play, from the Bildungsroman and Gothic tales of the eighteenth century to the melodramatic plots of the nineteenth century. Lola's marriage quickly falls apart, and the young woman begins her notorious travels. But one wonders if her disgust with her drunken and abusive husband is not overshadowed by her recollection of her mother's betrayal. Having been on the auction block once, Lola later insists that she is not for sale and resists reliving the circumstances of maternal treachery. It is, however, very interesting that in Bavaria she falls in love with an older man—certainly as old as her father (or the banker) would have been. He is also quite rich. However, it is not he but his wife who goes away for cures at public baths, a twist on the compulsion to repeat that also acts as a determining "force" in Lola's life.

Lola takes her mother's lover, drawing the Oedipal noose around her neck. But her strongest desire, her truest love, strangely coincides with the scenario her mother had planned for her. Was her mother like her?—the question is posed by a spectator of Lola's circus act. Certainly she was, if only because, like Lisa Berndle, Lola acts out an exaggerated version of her mother's story, using parody and masquerade in her complex weaving of submission to and defiance of the maternal will. In her promiscuity she achieves perfect fidelity. Her frustrated desire for her mother becomes identification—in the proper female Oedipal pattern. But desire for mother is never gone, and identification is never complete.

During the flashback narrative, we see many instances of Lola's tendency to move forward—not in circles, but in a straight line—straight to what she desires.[34] Leaving the theater to elope with Lieutenant James is the first of her beelines toward freedom, the first of many. Lola's flashback journey through the various capitals of southern Europe (closely followed, mimed, broken down into code in the circus act) culminates in her scandalous success on the Côte d'Azur. Despite the "cheerful" subject matter of this part of the performance, the circus's Lola falters and must be prompted by the ringmaster to begin telling the story of her affair with the conductor Claudio Pirotto. By contrast with this passivity, in the flashback (whose importance is underscored by the double wipe that introduces it), when she learns from another dancer both that the conductor is married *and* that his wife is present, Lola acts without hesitation. She leaps down from the stage where she is performing her "Spanish" dance to the rhythm of Pirotto's music, past Pirotto, whose baton she breaks, straight up to his wife's box, to the scene of a more important performance: the seat of the female spectator. As a mark of her integrity, Lola presents a bracelet to Mme Pirotto which is, she claims, that woman's rightful property as it was a gift to Lola from M. Pirotto. Her gesture is curiously "masculine," repeating mockingly Pirotto's courtship of Lola or his wife, as she stands below the box, tendering the bracelet, daring (like Lola Lola in *The Blue Angel*) to cross the line between audience and performer, mistress and wife. One might compare this *deliberate* behavior to that of the Lola in *Madame de . . .*, who gambles away the jewelry given her by Louise's husband, losing control of it through bad luck rather than defiant honor. If only Louise could have thrown the earrings in the faces of her husband and lover—LM would not have put up with them for five minutes! Or if Donati, like Liszt, had *thanked* her for her lies, the lies that Lola, like Louise, uses to balm her lover's ego, allowing him to think it was he who was leaving. Instead Donati petulantly refuses the balm and insists on his privilege as the abandoning male. If only Gaby had shoved Leonardo's cigarette into his face, with Lola's comment: "I don't have much respect for married women, but I detest cowardly men!" If only Gaby had told the music teacher (like Pirotto, a married man), what to do with his stick! If only Lisa Berndle had gotten tired of Stefan, (as Lola tires of Liszt), slammed his piano shut, and called for her own carriage instead of being ambushed by her husband's. "If only . . . If only. . ." These are Lisa's last words. But we, and "Ophuls," know that these women, our mothers and grandmothers, could not always walk away. Somehow we must stop blaming them and instead take note of where they found their pleasures.

The Pygmalion Industry

Our Lola valiantly attempts to control the circuit of exchange by running away from her arranged marriage. But the frame narrative belies this possibility even as we applaud (along with the other spectators at the dance) her defiant gesture. The flashback's Lola attempts to avoid the implications of being "caught" in the image she creates onstage. Thus she avoids classical dance, with its fixed formulas and tight control, performing instead (rather badly, to be sure) iconoclastic, "Spanish" dances to the rhythm of Pirotto's music. But the caged Lola is gently forced by her ringmaster to tell the story. Her words now mean big bucks at the box office. A woman both demanding and beautiful, defiant of the laws of men but enjoying men without shame—such a "beast," with the frisson of danger its presence evokes—can be transformed into a cash cow.

Having made a sensation on the Riviera, Lola is visited by the local aristocracy. And the ringmaster himself "did not miss the rendezvous." It is an appointment of his own making. As Lola, dressed in pure white, paces her brightly lit room, her maid Josephine (Paulette Dubost, one of the prostitutes from *Le Plaisir*) announces a man: "He's bizarre. He scares me." "Nobody scares me." is Lola's jaded reply. She looks out a window down the steps to watch the man ascend. As he enters the room, the camera cants sharply to the right, framing Ustinov and the cane that he extends stiffly toward Lola:

> RINGMASTER: I am a circus man. I'm the one who found Barnum's three-headed woman and the only elephant who can play "On the Bridge of Avignon" on the piano.

A curious shot–reverse shot sequence ensues, marked by a severely canted camera, which keeps Lola leaning to the left (although there are also level shots of her—making the ringmaster more "off balance") and the ringmaster to the right. He compliments her performance of the night before.

> LOLA: So you liked my dance?

> RINGMASTER: You don't know how to dance. But you know how to produce scandal. [*Lola closes the physical distance between them as he continues*] In the whole world scandal is gold. In America there are no limits. . . . I'll sell you very high . . . "the most scandalous woman in the world." . . . We'll show everything the woman in the street wants to do, but never has the courage to do.

Lola as *skandalon*, a screen for fantasy, ultimate scapegoat. Strangely, Lola allows the ringmaster to put her through her paces. "Stop walking. Be still." She freezes. But as she does so, as though enacting Mulvey's description of the power of the female image in cinema, he begins to fall under her spell:

RINGMASTER: [*Seated behind a barred window, as if caged*] You are beautiful, terribly beautiful.

LOLA: [*Standing before a full-length mirror*] Despite what you think, I'm not a scandal machine. I do only what pleases me.

RINGMASTER: The elephant thought so, too. But he finally learned to play the piano. Now he likes it.

Who is in control here? Both the ringmaster and Lola have a mesmeric power, though hers is clearly stronger. She needs no whips or contracts, refusing the latter as Sophie Chotek had refused Montenuovo's. The ringmaster points out that the elephant didn't want to play the piano either, but he ended up liking it. The maker of music has been reduced to its most mechanical, most pathetic incarnation in Ophuls' works. "If you see me again," she tells the ringmaster, "it will be for the worst. Don't wish it." The ringmaster's economic advantages, his ability to market her, may outweigh the power of Lola's image, of her dynamic motion. But as he leaves, he pauses to kiss her. "Don't be stupid, like all the others," she sighs. Too late.

The last part of the circus act is beginning: "Lola accedes to power," the ringmaster announces, as Lola climbs up trapezes and ropes, up to the top of the platform high above the circus floor. With her is the trapeze artist playing Ludwig of Bavaria. A close-up under blue lights shows that Lola is gasping and perspiring with the effort of her climb. Her "ascent" in the world of the past is equally fraught with danger. Crossing over the border into Bavaria, Lola has lost her way and commandeers a young student (Oskar Werner) to show her the way to Munich. Drawn by her beauty and beckoning gaze, the student gets into her carriage and goes back the way he came, accompanying Lola along her "straight line." Lola and her entourage reach an inn and are led from the first floor, where the most expensive apartments are located, to the second, then the third, as the innkeeper finally realizes that the impecunious Lola really does want something "simpler." As in the theater, where the student later watches Lola dance, the "top" of the summit in the European dwelling coincides with the bottom of the social ladder. This ambiguous coding of the meaning of height makes the overturning of hierarchies even more difficult to trace. As they reach the top floor of the inn, however, a letter arrives from the Ballet Royal, granting Lola an audition. They take the bottom floor.

Unfortunately, the ballet officials "don't appreciate Spanish dance," and Lola leaves the theater disconsolate. The chronotope of the street reappears, as the dancer sends her carriage away and begins to walk at random away from the theater. A soldier accosts her, but this is not an old drunk, as in *Letter from an Unknown Woman*, but a handsome young officer, with a tall, plumed helmet, like Count Bobby in *La Ronde*. The depressed woman ("No one can help me") grows more alert when she hears that the officer is one of the Royal Guards. However, the next scene reveals the officer to be as uninteresting as *Letter*'s Lieutenant von Kaltnegger. Lola is forced to blaze another "straight line" for a more direct achievement of her aims. Seated on horseback, the pair gazes across the parading troops up to a gazebo atop a hill. Lola wants to be introduced to the king—after all, her new lover has bragged about knowing the king. His insulting response is that "You don't introduce a dancer to the king in six weeks." He hazards that in another month . . . "Too late," Lola replies abruptly. Spurring her horse, she gallops through the parade, up the hill to the king.

Seconds later (after a shift of scenes), the king himself remarks on the irony of the situation: "You attacked a lieutenant of the gendarmes. This is serious. I should have demoted him and expelled you. Instead, I gave you an audience and named him captain." By giving Lola an audience, he gives her a voice, precisely, it would seem, because she *has* transgressed the law. (In fact, things are not that simple. Lola is only accorded a voice to the extent that she agrees not to use it except to speak the king's desire.) In his interview with the dancer, King Ludwig reads the charges, as well as the results of her audition with the Ballet Royal. She was found, he informs her, to be without classical training (a more serious offense than her assault of the king). Lola responds with fiery words, decrying the "laws and ordinances" of classicism, as well as kingdoms.

KING: You can't give up all laws and ordinances.

LOLA: Too bad.

She continues her inflammatory rhetoric, declares the audition invalid ("What is an audition? You weren't auditioned to be king!"), and proclaims the death of the stiff figures of classical dance. Stamping her feet, she insists that only the bolero, the fandango, the seguedilla are "alive!" Lola demonstrates the dances spontaneously, catches herself, and apologizes, dropping to a curtsy. But the king is intrigued and encourages her to continue. Lola comments bitterly that the committee only made these charges because "they couldn't say that she was badly shaped." The king replies that it is precisely on that score that doubts were raised! Infuriated anew, Lola grabs a letter-opener and rips open her bodice. A ("censoring") cut takes us instantaneously to the footmen in the hall, in response to the king's urgent ringing. He demands a needle and thread, and a remarkable sequence of events ensues as the order is passed from footman to soldier to chambermaid, until dozens of men and women are running down the most immense staircase in all of Ophuls' films in search of the items the king desires. Moments later, the ladies in waiting withdraw silently, backing toward the door away from the king and Lola, whose bodice is now mended. She assumes the posture characteristic of her appearance in the circus, stiffly upright, with her wide skirts drawn around her.

The "chain of command" demonstrated in the needle-and-thread search is familiar from many scenes in Ophuls' films. I have discussed such scenes in *Sarajevo, The Exile, Madame de* . . . , and elsewhere. But the social structure that can unleash such displays of hierarchy and group actions is very fragile. Later in the film, on another staircase in another palace, the king will realize he has lost control of his country because of Lola. Just as important is the king's "gallant gesture" toward Lola. Gallant it is, but it also signals that Lola may not expose her body, master the field of vision, show the naked "truth" about herself without the king's permission. His obvious fascination with Lola, a fascination that remains almost entirely in the visual realm, is held in abeyance by his ability to command her actions.

Lola is allowed her night on stage, and she is a smashing success. The scene opens on a close-up of the king's fingers, dancing on the edge of the Royal Opera Box. Very rarely does one come to the front of the Royal Box in Ophuls' films! The privilege of the king as ultimate spectacle and as most masterful spectator is examined in close-up, as he mimes the woman's onstage movements. As usual, we do not see the stage itself— only the reflection in the king's eyes and motions. The masking of the screen that created "curtains" for the fingers' dance dissipates, and we see that the queen is watching her husband's excitement with maternal indulgence. She does not understand his complicated explanations of the figures of the Spanish dances, but she *does* understand, as she puts it, that she "must go take the cure at Wiesbaden." "When?" her husband curtly demands, cupping his ear while his eyes are on the stage. The power relations involved in looking and being looked at are dizzyingly complex here: transfixed by Lola, the king is "caught" more surely than Lola is caught as object of his gaze (at this point, in any event). But the look he levels upon the dancer, his invocation of a superior (though feminine?) knowledge of the intricacies of Spanish dances, work to put his wife in her place as betrayed spouse. She doesn't understand—but she can *see* what larger pattern is being revealed.

And so she goes to Wiesbaden, and the king takes time in his hands, in an attempt to keep Lola with him as long as possible. He decides to have her portrait painted. A group interview with the best painters in the land is arranged. The king glances at each painting, but more important is *how long* each painter took to paint it (just as Lola was anxious about how long it would take her officer to introduce her to the king). The artists, misunderstanding his motive (to keep Lola there as long as possible), competitively cite ever-shorter times to complete a painting. Finally, however, a wry little white-haired man announces that it took him three months to paint his unprepossessing canvas. "Three weeks?" asks the deaf king. "Three *months*." "It's you," the king proclaims. So Lola begins a long series of sessions with the artist, who paints her riding in a sleigh, with her fur hood, gloves, and a lap robe. The king inspects it and, with the sly cooperation of the artist, agrees that many changes must be made. Lola smiles cooperatively. The irony of her stillness is enhanced by the fact that she's being painted in a sleigh—one reminiscent of *Liebelei*'s, of *Sans Lendemain*'s—a means for lovers to take a straight line out of town, away from interfering eyes. But Lola is alone. With her fur hood, against a snowy background, she is the very picture of Deleuze's "cold oral mother," the Venus in Furs. The "masochist," the king who worships her to the point of losing his kingdom, is mesmerized by her image. And yet the balance of visual power is still uncertain: Lola has been fixed as an image, one that does not represent her desiring fantasy, although the king is also caught like a fly in oil. If, as Williams says, one source of Lola's attractiveness *is* her movement, does Lola lose this quality when she is at rest? I'm not sure this is the case. Perhaps it is only that her movement draws men, who then feel compelled to still her. In any event, as Williams also observes, desire for Lola does seem to follow Girard's delineation of *mediated* desire: one desires her because everyone else does.[35] Again, such desire trips on its own contradictions because "possession" (a traditional, though not universal, male aim with regard to the woman he loves) means withdrawal from others. Here we discover yet another of the roles played by representation in the trajectory of desire.

Unlike the couple in *Le Plaisir* who destroys the image that holds them, the king and Lola try to hang the painting of Lola in a public building. The portrait has metamorphosed into what appears to be a fake Ingres, the "Odalisque," with Lola's head attached—mimesis, begun with the king's imitation of Lola, seems to have gotten out of control. The couple is continually rebuffed in their efforts to place the painting by ministers who believe that it is indecent. But Lola can't keep it in her palace: "It would seem like I'm advertising!" (Advertising is one of the institutions Ophuls specifically sets out to critique in this film.) And Lola has no need to advertise. She has refused again and again to sell herself as pure commodity, and she is not about to start—not yet. This refusal is illustrated in one of the circus sketches when Lola stands amidst a group of men with coins for heads, who are throwing dollars around freely, while the ringmaster intones that she rejects the idea of living off men. Like Leonora Ames, she wants honest work. And like Leonora, she moves from performance (modeling, dancing) to the role of nurse—taking care of her king. Although Lola has, in effect, been bought by the highest bidder, the king, it is a "love-match," which serves to disguise, if not alter, the nature of the exchange. Despite the inevitable intervention of the dangerous world of representation, she is the one who makes her choice. But why, then, must the painting be hung in a public space? Is the king's desire propped upon Lola's continued role as "la signora di tutti"?

One of the last scenes between Lola and her king reveals another way in which *Lola Montès* and *Letter from an Unknown Woman* are tantalizingly alike, and subtly different—that being in their use of sound. The stakes of man's and woman's relationships to sound are familiar to us from *La Signora di Tutti*, *Werther*, and *Madame de . . .* , not to mention *Letter*. Each of these films performs a profound exploration of female subjectivity via the sound track. We have seen that because Lola is a dancer rather than a singer or musician, she seems more caught up in the visual rather than the auditory realm. In addition, she does not *narrate* the events of the flashbacks but *sees* them. But the importance of hearing, not just as a medium of female pleasure and pain but as another potential gap in masculine perception, comes back to haunt Lola at a pivotal moment, near the film's dénouement. This scene seems to be connected only tangentially to the unfolding of the plot of the film although it can easily be linked to the earlier scene with Liszt, through various subtexts.

Lola's relationship with the King of Bavaria has proceeded apace, and Lola is now more wife than mistress. Ludwig is extremely hard of hearing, which frustrates Lola, so she takes him to see an eminent ear doctor, also a very old man (Gustav Waldau). The king is examined and receives a prescription for "eleven pills a day" and a change of attitude—morale being the most important influence on hearing, according to the doctor. As the doctor extols the virtues of being able to hear Mozart (not Wagner) and "Madame's pretty voice," the camera wanders to an enormous model of an ear. The outsized quality of the ear is more or less justified by its placement in a doctor's office. Still, it is a strange object —one that would seem more appropriate in the fantastical world of the circus than in the "realistic" flashback. In a film in which visibility—Lola's dancing, her figure, her *look*—is of paramount importance, Ophuls seems to be signaling, with his usual strong comic sense, that the king's blocked hearing is also symbolically laden. Among other things, the spirals of the inner ear resemble those of the staircases Lola must climb to reach the king. (Indeed, it is by virtue of an "audition"—which has the same double meaning in French as it does in English —that Lola comes to the attention of the king in the first place.) The ear doctor and his wife suggest to the king that, for example, he is "deaf" to the protests of his people against the presence of Lola Montès. (Her image is burned in effigy in a subsequent series of dissolves.) Perhaps we are also to compare him to the General in *Madame de . . .*, literally only a little hard of hearing but tragically deaf to Louise's plea for mercy.

Just as Lola is "faithful" to Liszt's music when she gathers from the floor at the inn the discarded shreds of the "Farewell Waltz," she remains faithful to the deaf king, wishing to open his ears to the lover's music he does not know, as well as opening his eyes to the figures of the dance. We might recall that *Letter*'s mute valet, John, does not share the moral shortcomings of the "deaf" men in other films. He *does* have some control over narrative events by giving Lisa's letter a voice and then a name—but his relationship with the woman seems to be almost entirely sympathetic. Although he is in love with Lola, Ludwig—with Lola's support—nevertheless upholds the law that Lola finds so restrictive. When riots break out around the palace, he places himself in the hands of his ministers and bids his mistress adieu. Monarch-scapegoat, placeholder for a tradition that kills his own desire, Ludwig is perhaps the saddest of all Ophuls' male "trophies." Lola leaves the kingdom under the protection of the revolutionary student who had showed her the way to Munich. (Thus her Bavarian experience is circular.) Not surprisingly, she expresses indifference about revolutions, which are by definition circular, "whether they be from the right or the left." Her demand for greater freedom is not guaranteed by either political wing. Assured by the earnest young man that their putsch is from the left, she does seem relieved. But his vision of "woman's place" is no less limited than the king's was: as the young man rides with her in the carriage leaving Bavaria, he proposes marriage, a home, children. Lola listens sympathetically, and refuses. Despite what the boy thinks (for he is still a boy), she did love the king. And now, she says, something in her is broken.

Max Ophuls' *Lola Montès* (1955), most "writerly" of woman's films, and more a film about classic cinema than a participant in it, subdivides its diegesis in similar ways [to *Singin' in the Rain*] by confining its female protagonist . . . to a circus ring, and obliging her to offer prewritten answers to the questions posed to her by the ringmaster. . . . The ringmaster is represented as being outside the spectacle, in a position of discursive control. Because he remains to one side of the drama, and because his voice at times speaks "over" the image of Lola, he seems less diegetically anchored, and hence closer to the point of textual origin. Indeed, during Lola's pantomime repetition of her earlier rise to fame and fortune, he maintains a running off-screen commentary, much like a disembodied voiceover.[36]

The ringmaster, who has in fact thoroughly linked his fate to Lola's, may be more involved in the diegesis—more "embodied" than Silverman takes him to be. Although he is certainly in a position of "discursive control" throughout the film, his role also exacts a price. At the end of the film, the ringmaster asks for a glass of whiskey from one of the many valets (this one distinguished by his raucous voice). As soon as he hands the ringmaster the glass, the valet demands payment for the whiskey—fifty cents. Even the master of the ring has no line of credit. But the ringmaster takes his pleasure in directing Lola, despite his knowledge of the mechanisms of the circus, despite the fact that he must pay for his involvement in the performance. Money and images circulate through him, and he does not always emerge unscathed. Indeed, the ringmaster is the masochistic spectator of the woman he loves, who—like von Sternberg's Lola-Lola—exposes herself to the masses. He holds a contract for Lola's services, but it is a double-edged one: he holds his "monster," his showpiece, in awe: "the more she ill-treats him, the more wantonly she toys with him and the harsher she is, the more readily she quickens his desire and secures his love and admiration. It has always been so, from the time of Helen and Delilah all the way to Catherine the Great and Lola Montez."[37] True enough. But despite the ringmaster's "masochistic" enslavement, male domination, as usual, ultimately triumphs. When, near the end of the film, Lola is about to jump from a platform high above a pitifully inadequate trampoline, her doctor arrives to protest, to call in the *police* (his emphasis), if Lola does not use a net. Knowing that, like "Le Modèle"'s inveterate gambler Josephine, she must "risk it all" in her leap, Lola silently refuses the net—although, as a matter of fact, her ringmaster never really poses the question to her. He "knows" what her response will be. "Are you ready Lola?" "Ready." A point-of-view shot (again, like the one depicting Josephine's fall) takes us down, down, down to the net below, inscribing the woman's "vision" unforgettably into the eye of the camera. A cut reveals Lola in her cage, with the men from the audience lined up to kiss her hand. The camera tracks back, getting lost in the converging lines of men moving "straight" toward her. Acrobats confuse the frame with their leaps, and we back through the curtain, which is drawn closed—on Lola, on all of Ophuls heroines, on Ophuls' career as a filmmaker. The ringmaster stands beside Lola, whispering endearments, as she accepts the kisses and the dollars. Ringmaster and performer are partners in exploiting her woman's body, both part of the machinery of the spectacle, both outlaws, marginal, yet within the circle. When, someday, Lola finally does fall to her death, the ringmaster will probably smoke a cigar, and weep. Then he will go find the next three-headed woman for the Mammoth Circus.

Echoes of Weimar, and the Origins of Cinema

When we last see Lola, double lines of men swarm toward her, all in hope of kissing her hand for the low price of one dollar. The "two endless lines . . . wait . . . to kiss a bit of serpent," writes Clément in her lyrical passage on the film.[38] But Lola, too, is caught in the coils of the lines of men, a caged lioness re-creating the Laocoön.

In adapting the story of Lola Montès to the screen, Ophuls went back to his Weimar roots. The flashback structure of *Lola Montès* seems to be partially derivative of Berg's opera *Lulu*, adapted, like Pabst's 1928 film *Pandora's Box*, from Wedekind's dramas. Like *Lola Montès*, *Lulu* opens with a circus prologue, and the female protagonist is referred to as a "wild and beautiful beast," just as Lola is "un fauve."[39] Like Wedekind's, Berg's, and Pabst's Lulu, Lola is perceived as possessing a "malignant" femininity. Like Lulu, too, she is perceived "largely in economic terms" but remains "outside" the class system.[40] Doane traces the significance of the metaphors that arise around Lulu and her lover Alwa:

In Kracauer's analysis, subordination to or dependency upon a woman is collapsed onto social disintegration. From this point of view, Alwa would exemplify the conflict-ridden male psyche of Weimar Germany. Alwa's two addictions in the film are Lulu and gambling, linking a peculiarly modern conceptualization of free sexuality with the idea of unrestrained speculation at the economic level; in both cases the returns can be either extremely pleasurable or unpleasurable. But both addictions also manifest a desire to escape history, to move into the realm of the infinitely repeatable idea or gesture. [41]

Lola's seemingly endless desire, her ability to generate large sums of money, her childlessness, her "specularity" all tie her firmly into the systems of exchange, speculation, and inflation that have been among the governing terms of my discussion of Ophuls' films. In 1955 Ophuls described the "social disintegration" of Ludwig's mid-nineteenth-century kingdom by way of Weimar Germany, World War II, and the relocation to the United States suffered by both himself and Lola. (Thus, the mob scenes in the film take on a different flavor, as Lola's image is burned in effigy: she is purged like the scapegoat-Jew in Hitler's Germany.) Ophuls is not attempting, however, to "escape history" through his fascination with the femme fatale. As one of the first major international coproductions in the 1950s, *Lola Montès* (filmed in several languages) represents Ophuls' return to Germany as an "international" filmmaker, one whose name, like Lola's, has changed in every country. A metaphorical relationship to the history of the twentieth century is established, ironically, by means of a woman who has stepped out of time into the eternal recurrence of the same: her circus act. Doane points out that the "modernity" of *Pandora's Box* is "in a somewhat paradoxical manner . . , constituted by its ahistoricity" (p. 156). The kind of ahistoricity she describes is that of the factory, exemplary tool of capital, where work on the assembly line consists of "constantly repeated gestures" that "bear no necessary connection with each other, insure no continuity through time" (p. 157). And, indeed, Lola's repeated words and gestures constitute a factory for spectacle, linked, in Benjamin's words, to the repeated motions of gambling, separate throws of the dice or drawings of cards in which no act is related to the other. "With its valorization of chance, gambling disallows the cause-effect determinations which support historical understanding." But the use of the metaphor of gambling, and the invocation of ahistoricity in the factory, are themselves historically placed. Like the workers Doane describes, Lola is deprived of her history and must set about to reconstruct it on a daily basis. Interestingly, card games and roulette wheels are associated with the determinations of *fate* in Ophuls' films (*Sarajevo, Madame de . . .*), as though to reinject the cause-effect absent from gambling itself. The circle upon which Lola is turning may be regarded as no more than a gigantic roulette wheel, like the wheel of fortune in *The Bartered Bride*, a wheel whose next turn may bring her death, and whose movements she cannot "crook."[42] So, too, did the film *Lola Montès* prove to be more of a speculation, more inflationary, more of a gamble than its financial backers could bear.

Although Alwa is identified as the authorial relay in Wedekind's play, Doane points out that Pabst's "filmic discourse promotes a broader view of sexuality, seduction, speculation, and spectacle" (p. 158). *Lola Montès* also takes a "broader" view on these issues than is available from the perspective of any of the characters. However, the presence of the mediating figure of the ringmaster in the latter film points to the way in which Ophuls remains closer to the "Brechtian" aspects of Weimar than did Pabst, whose films notoriously lack the self-reflexivity of Wedekind's play (or Brecht's *Threepenny Opera*).

The "director-figure," whom we have traced throughout Ophuls' cinema, brings to light another aspect of Ophuls' relation to specular praxis of the past: a return to the "exhibitionist" structure of early cinema. As Yamaguchi observes, Ophuls' Brechtianism was learned, in part, from Karl Valentin, the well-known and immensely talented comedian who plays the circus owner in *The Bartered Bride* and who was Brecht's close associate. "He was," notes Yamaguchi, "Brecht's teacher of the streets" (p. 62). In his most "modernist," if not "postmodernist" work, Ophuls returns emphatically to the itinerant origins of theater and of cinema, the fantasy of the ultimate circus spectacle.[43] As Mayne notes, the director-figure has a special role in the early cinema, in which the grammar of "classical" film narrative has not yet been established. Mayne discusses what she terms "primitive" narration in light of the use of the "primitive" in avant-garde women's films later in the century. Rather than speaking of "early cinema," Mayne retains the often reviled term "primitive" in quotation marks in order to "foreground its problematic implications" in women's films.[44] Mayne traces the evolution of the "classical" narrative's system of enunciation. In early cinema

the narrating function fulfilled by the lecturer, by intertitles, and by the "invisible hand" of Griffith's films is primarily one of linear continuity and referential information. Other, more limited kinds of narrating functions are fulfilled by those figures who appear to direct, mediate, or otherwise act out the visual pleasures of the cinematic scene. I will refer to these characters as "primitive" narrators or the absolute agents of "primitive" narration—i.e., they are objects of the camera's view at the same time that they act out the emerging visual and narrative capacities of the film medium. (p. 168)

The "primitive" narrator, exemplified by the part Méliès plays in films including *The Living Playing Cards* (1905), is *present on-screen*, like the object—or woman—he is showing to the spectator. Like Ophuls' "director-figures," this personage (in Silverman's terms) makes himself vulnerable even as he asserts narrative, or *exhibitionist* mastery.

In discussing early cinema, Mayne refers to Tom Gunning's valuable work on what he calls the "cinema of attraction." Gunning contrasts the ostensive or exhibitionistic quality of early films, which emphasized the cinema's penchant for a visible display *not* mediated by the fetishizing, anthropomorphisized gaze of classical Hollywood's camera, with the "storytelling" film, which took off in 1906–1907, and utilized the "diegetic absorption" familiar to modern audiences, thus prefiguring classical narrative film. The "primitive" narrator was, Mayne notes, absorbed into the movement of the camera in the storytelling film. But the cinema of attractions, Gunning notes, "does not disappear with the dominance of narrative, but rather goes underground, both into certain avant-garde practices and as a component of narrative films."[45] The narrative style of *Lola Montès* certainly sustains Gunning's point. One can feel "Ophuls" being torn between the laying bare of cinema's ability to *show*, to exhibit, and the more occulted, fetishizing powers of the camera unmediated by a "director-figure." As Mayne observes, in moving from the exhibition context for early motion pictures, "where fairgrounds and sideshows would appear to have created a quite literal exhibitionist frame . . . motion pictures marked the *erasure* of popular entertainment as performance" (p. 166, emphasis added). Thus Mayne discerns a more active repression of the exhibitionist's frame than does Gunning. And we can certainly see in Ophuls' work a broad exploration of the historical "displacement of exhibitionism by fetishism, by the separation of subject and object, and by the distance between performer and onlooker" that Mayne describes.

What are the implications of this exploration for the representation of women? Mayne has a course corrective for Gunning's read of the role of women in the cinema of attractions: contrary to Gunning's claims for the *alterity* of these films, early cinema's exhibitionism, says Mayne, *evokes the register* of fetishism, of the classic representation of the female body, which existed in painting and theater—and the circus—long before cinema was born. In his postmodern reworking of the modernist concern for the stakes of representation; in his attempt to move back to the origins of cinema, perhaps to "free" cinema from its fetishistic qualities, to celebrate the woman's ability to *exhibit,* Ophuls reveals a process of breakthrough and recuperation that is never resolved but continues to circle through "revolution" upon revolution.

Postmodernism or "a case of culture falling into the world"[45]

In the ongoing debate about the relationship between modernism and postmodernism,[46] and about the political stakes of postmodernism itself, *Lola Montès* occupies a pivotal site. Through its "complexity and ambiguity of language," its irony and "construction of [an] elaborate symbolic system"—seeking a kind of interpretive, philosophical, and historical depth—*LM* incarnates many of the (elitist) modernist traits that Fredric Jameson describes as having been "repudiated" by postmodernism (p. 4). And so I have traced a modernist, auteurist trajectory in my obsessive linking of moments from the various films, in my pairing of these moments with historical events, and in my writing of a "master narrative" of Ophuls' films, of which *LM* is another kind of master narrative—as George Eliot might have put it, "the key to all mythologies."[47] In turning to the postmodernist aspects of the "Ophuls" text, I am no doubt looking to rescue myself from the charge of naïveté such a project attracts. But the political naïveté of an auteurist/modernist study is not only theoretical but also, appropriately, *economic*. One-author (or director) books don't sell, I have been told. In order to maximize the marketability of my work, Ophuls must be hooked up to the totalizing machinery that will make him "useful" to current criticism. And, of course, my project has also been to enact just such a totalizing event, which is also traceable to my relationship to the "father": a filmmaker my graduate adviser liked; a director born in 1902, along with two of my grandparents; a man whose last film was made the year I was born.

The emergence of postmodernism is, for Jameson, "materially tied . . . to the rise of American capital on a global scale, dated to the late fifties and early sixties" (Stephanson, p. 8). Postmodernism coincided with the "collapse of modernism and mass culture" into one, a "falling" into the world of consumerism that appropriates history without depth, without coherency. It is a spatialization of time (Jameson, p. 6), just as Lola's circus act is the simultaneous display of her past, present, and future, arranged in concentric circles; just as the final sale of her body is a "fall" into a world of consumerism that Ophuls obviously finds reprehensible ("Il faut tuer la publicité"). And Lola's past is not only her own but, analogically, that of all of Ophuls' heroines "spatialized" within the context of many strips of celluloid—modernistically totalized, postmodernistically bringing the masses (the circus) to the trough of bourgeois culture (all can take a piece of "her" body): the cinema. *Lola Montès* is also a history of modern colonialism: Lola moves from Ireland to India, is returned to the Empire, adopts the identity of a Spaniard—the European and Asian "third worlds" invade the bastions of European imperialism.

Are these factors evidence of "neoconservative" postmodernism, which "appropriates" and depoliticizes history, or what Hal Foster and others have called "post-structuralist" postmodernism—an artistic and political movement that calls into question the categories of historicism, abstraction, the "artist," and so on?[48] Is this film to fall under the heading of the "nostalgia film," as Jameson describes it (p. 18), which cannibalizes images of the past and offers them up as truth? It seems easy to say that Ophuls' work is too "complex" (modernistic?) and self-reflexive (ditto) to fall into such an easy retailing of images. But is there not a sense in which Lola's past is brought forth in the framed narrative as truth? In any case, Lola's postmodern "autobiography" acknowledges the multiplicity of subjectivity. "Lola" exists as "Ophuls" does—through a layered, historically dense subject-effect.

However we respond to these questions, it remains crucial to recognize the role that gender continues to play even (especially?) in the postmodern text. Jacqueline Rose comments on the "postmodern" aspects of neurological disorders as discussed by theorists of postmodernity: "The joke is clearly at the expense of the woman who finds herself caught in a perceptual crisis that flouts the limits of anything recognizable or knowable as a world. . . . Recent writings on postmodernism . . . bypass . . . this question of the woman on which they could equally be said to rely."[49] Postmodernism brings with it a "loss of spatial coordinates," an inability (as Jameson describes it) for the postmodern body to locate itself in space, "cognitively to map its position in a mappable external world."[50] Woman/women remain(s) the *site* at which such unmappability is deployed, the emblem of man's/men's epistemic difficulties—celebrated or deplored. Lola's space is "knowable" to the ringmaster who leads her through her act; Lola as "individual" has been peeled away in a series of images that can't be reedited and made right. She is knowable; she is not knowable ("Where are your children, Lola?"); mappable (Irish, Spanish), unmappable. But even if as a commodity she continues to sell, as a participant in the market she remains marginal. Even if Lola takes the profits from her circus act and buys, say, a jewelry store, or stock in AT&T, woman as commodity, as "brand name," prevails. From another political perspective, it doesn't much matter to exploited Third-World labor if First World women have stock in AT&T or Dow Chemical.

Rose reminds, or informs, the reader that there are feminist artists who "have set themselves up systematically to interrogate the operations of that fantasy at the very point at which it turns the woman into its stake" (p. 246). Feminism may be, Rose believes, "one way of rethinking the temporal narrative (nostalgia, breakthrough) on which so much writing on postmodernism seems to be based" (248). Interestingly, it is in the discourse of *aging*—a discourse of particular interest to the women's movement and to the woman "taking stock" of herself" in midlife—"the narrative of the woman who ages"—that Rose finds the hint of such a rethinking. "For the woman, nostalgia is always an addiction to the image and fantasy of a flawless self" (p. 248). Lola Montès literally "takes stock" of herself in the final scenes of the film—as both commodity and individual. Is it, we might ask once more, strategically "essential" to grant individuality, the power of "self-mapping," to the woman trying to break free of or at least interrogate the commodity system that holds her? Do we want for her economic power in the safe environment of the shopping mall, where women can exercise the right of the *flâneuse*—mistress of its glass-lined space—until she is kidnapped from the parking lot, a body "exchanged" for the fantasy some man is carrying around in his head? The aging woman of color, the aging white woman (First or Third World-er), all are devalued, shopworn, in the culture of late capitalism, though their power as "consumers" may differ. But women of different ethnic groups, educational levels, class levels, nationalities are not *equivalent* either in their devaluation or in what de Beauvoir has called the *force* of age. Can Rose really speak of the stakes of nostalgia (a painful look at her mystified youth) for women in general? Women of European extraction, occasionally relieved by their "exotic" Third World sisters, have had the dubious and mostly fictitious "privilege" of being at the center of the ring of Western representation. Looking back at the "flawless," fictional women who take this privileged place in the center of the (artistic) history that men have made need not be only nostalgic— although our look(s) at history cannot be "purified" of nostalgia. Longing itself arises contextually and disseminates its meanings. Nor must recollection be only painful for the women who are engaged in appropriating, in the best sense of that word, the narratives and images of "women" past. Even our past selves are not ourselves: let us be attentive to the deflected dreams of the others both within and outside, to the words we do not always, at first, understand.

The first image of *Lola Montès* is that of an Uncle Sam figure leading a band made up of African Americans, providing the "sonorous envelope" for the film and, symbolically, for America—an America made up of cardboard spectators of a circus that is both "revolutionary" and fascist, a place where "the other" is playing the music all along. The ambivalence toward the masses to be found in *Lola Montès*, as in Ophuls' other films, comes forth as the figuration of mass culture in politically ambiguous terms: bloodsport and carnival of gaiety, scapegoating and "entertainment," terror and transcendence. In the midst of this oscillation, the woman, both marginal and central, remains a site of interrogation, the place where Ophuls poses questions concerning the birth of the individual in violence, and the roles of spectator, actor, and director. It is my hope that Ophuls' films can help us in the interrogation of our histories, in our construction of possibilities for the future. *Ça va aller.*

$\mathcal{N}$otes

✦

$\mathcal{I}$ntroduction

1. Gayatri Chakravorty Spivak, "Displacement and the Discourse of Woman," in Mark Krupnik, ed., *Displacement: Derrida and After* (Bloomington: Indiana University Press, 1983), 186.

2. Spivak, "The Problem of Cultural Self-Representation," in Sarah Harasym, ed., *The Post-Colonial Critic: Interviews, Strategies, Dialogues* (New York: Routledge, 1990), 57–58.

3. Claude Beylie, *Max Ophuls* (Paris: Editions Pierre Lherminier, 1963; rpt. 1984), 5. All translations from this work are my own. Further page references appear in the text.

4. For contemporaneous discussions of the *Lola Montès* scandal, see François Truffaut, "Lola au bûcher," and Claude Beylie, "Le Dossier de presse de *Lola Montès*," *Cahiers du Cinéma* 55 (January 1956): 28–31, 55–57; Jacques Rivette and François Truffaut, "*Entretien avec Max Ophuls,*" and Charles Bitsche and Jacques Rivette, "Biofilmographie de Max Ophuls," *Cahiers du Cinéma* 72 (June 1957): 7–25, 52–54; and also the numerous commentaries on and by Ophuls in the posthumous issue, *Cahiers du Cinéma* 81 (March 1958), dedicated to Ophuls' career. For additional critical commentary dating from this period see also Richard Roud, *Max Ophuls: An Index* (London: British Film Institute [BFI], 1958).

5. Roud, *Max Ophuls: An Index*, 3. Roud also comments that Ophuls' "stock" went up during the 1950s with the release of such films as *The Earrings of Madame de . . .* (1953). This economic metaphor is of interest when read in light of Ophuls' complex relationship to economic tropes of all kinds (to be examined in upcoming chapters).

6. For a discussion of this term, used throughout Freud's works, see Sigmund Freud, "The Neuro-Psychoses of Defense," in *The Standard Edition of the Complete Psychological Works*, 3d ed., trans. and ed. James Strachey, 23 vols. (London: Hogarth Press, 1953–66): 3:43 (hereafter cited as *SE*).

7. For the crucial distinction between *woman* as theoretical construct, and *women* as historical beings, see Teresa de Lauretis, *Alice Doesn't: Feminism, Semiotics, Cinema* (Bloomington: Indiana University Press, 1984), 5; and Judith Mayne, *The Woman at the Keyhole: Feminism and Women's Cinema* (Bloomington: Indiana University Press, 1990), 6. See also Gayatri Spivak's subtle explication of the problems involved in defining or speaking for "woman" in "French Feminism in an International Frame," in *In Other Worlds: Essays in Cultural Politics* (New York: Routledge, 1988), 134–53.

8. Some recent critical studies not *primarily* motivated by issues directly related to women's studies include Paul Willeman, ed., *Ophuls* (London: BFI, 1978), an anthology of articles spanning several decades; Alan Williams, *Max Ophuls and the Cinema of Desire: Style and Spectacle in Four Films* (New York: Arno Press, 1976); Mary Ann Doane, "*Madame de . . .* and the Desire for Narrative," in "The Dialogical Text: Filmic Irony and the Spectator" (Ph.D. diss., University of Iowa, 1979), 223–58; Robert Chamblee, "Max Ophuls' Viennese Triology" (Ph.D. diss., New York University, 1981); Barry Salt, "Stylistic Analysis of the Films of Max Ophuls," in *Film Style and Technology: History and Analysis* (London: Starword Press, 1983), 351–79; Lutz Bacher, *Travails/Travelings: The American Career of Max Ophuls* (New Brunswick, N.J.: Rutgers University Press, 1995), a revised version of his "Max Ophuls's Universal-International Films: The Impact of Production Circumstances on a Visual Style," 2 vols. (Ph.D. diss., Wayne State University, 1984); and William Karl Guérin, *Max Ophuls* (Paris: Cahiers du Cinéma, 1988). Works that consider Ophuls' films from a feminist perspective or simply as they depict women are cited below.

9. It is insofar as Ophuls' films have been particularly defined as (female-oriented) *melodramas* that they have received critical contempt. Thus some authors have attempted to rescue Ophuls from the "accusation" of melodrama by emphasizing the irony of even his most sentimental sequences. A contrary movement, which finds value in melodrama itself as a genre potentially subversive of "dominant ideology," has gained strength in film studies. See especially Robert Lang, *American Film Melodrama: Griffith, Vidor, Minnelli* (Princeton: Princeton University Press, 1989); Christine Gledhill, ed., *Home Is Where the Heart Is: Studies in Melodrama and the Woman's Film* (London: BFI, 1987); Patrice Petro, *Joyless Streets: Women and Melodramatic Representation in Weimar Germany* (Princeton: Princeton University Press, 1989); and Mary Ann Doane, *The Desire to Desire: The Woman's Film of the 1940s* (Bloomington: Indiana University Press, 1987).

10. Robin Wood, "Ewig hin der Liebe Glück," in *Personal Views: Explorations in Film* (London: Gordon Fraser Gallery, 1976), 122; reprinted in Virginia Wright Wexman, *Letter from an Unknown Woman: Max Ophuls, Director* (New Brunswick, N.J.: Rutgers University Press, 1986), 226. Page numbers will refer to latter edition.

11. Roud, *Max Ophuls: An Index*, 6. Alan Williams aptly points out (in a passage devoted to the dangers of trying to construct, as Roud does here, a filmmaker's "ideal film") that the "love" felt by Lisa in *Letter from an Unknown Woman* (1948) is not iden-

tical to that of Lola Montès, and that there are, in fact, some Ophuls films that do not take "women in love" as their subject at all. See Williams, *Max Ophuls and the Cinema of Desire*, 10–12.

12. I translate (loosely): "What [other] filmmaker will ever touch upon the so quivering, the so wounded [flayed], the so bleeding [qualities] of femininity?" (Beylie, *Max Ophuls*, 98).

13. Ophuls, who was very much interested in nineteenth-century literature and theater, draws, in his films, on a concrete tradition of fallen and unhappy women. Ophuls speaks, for example, of his interest in Balzac in Rivette and Truffaut, "Interview with Max Ophuls" ("Entretien avec Max Ophuls"), in Willeman, ed., *Ophuls*, 15–30. See also Beylie, *Max Ophuls*, 23–27, for a discussion of Ophuls' literary influences (including his fascination with Stendhal); and Masao Yamaguchi, "For an Archaeology of *Lola Montès*," in Willeman, ed., *Ophuls*, 61–69, for the sources of the femme fatale in Ophuls' last film.

14. Nina Auerbach, *Woman and the Demon: The Life of a Victorian Myth* (Cambridge: Harvard University Press, 1982), 157–58. Further page references are cited in the text.

15. Auerbach (*Woman and the Demon*, 159) is referring to the view of prostitution put forth in, e.g., William Acton, *Prostitution* (1857), available in an abridged edition edited by Peter Fryer (New York: Praeger, 1968), and more recently in Judith Walkowitz, "The Making of an Outcast Group: Prostitutes and Working Women in Nineteenth-Century Plymouth and Southampton," in Martha Vicinus, ed., *A Widening Sphere: Changing Roles of Victorian Women* (Bloomington: Indiana University Press, 1977).

16. For a discussion of one of Ophuls' middle-class heroines in the context of film noir see Robert Lang, "Lucia Harper's Crime: Family Melodrama and *Film Noir* in *The Reckless Moment*," *Literature/Film Quarterly* 17, no. 4 (1989): 261–67.

17. Stephen Heath, "The Question Oshima," in Willeman, ed., *Ophuls*, 87. See also Jacques Lacan, "The Meaning of the Phallus," in Juliet Mitchell and Jacqueline Rose, eds., *Feminine Sexuality: Jacques Lacan and the Ecole Freudienne*, trans. Rose (New York: W. W. Norton/Pantheon Books, 1982), 84, for a discussion of the feminine masquerade in relation to the phallus as signifier. In her introduction to this collection of essays, Rose notes that "sexuality belongs for Lacan in the realm of masquerade. The term comes from Joan Rivière for whom it indicates a failed femininity." For Lacan, "masquerade is the very definition of 'femininity' precisely because it is constructed with reference to a male sign" (*Feminine Sexuality*, 43).

18. For a definition of this phrase see David Bordwell, Janet Staiger, and Kristin Thompson, *The Classical Hollywood Film: Film Style and Mode of Production to the 1960s* (New York: Columbia University Press, 1986). Like the auteur, the classical Hollywood cinema is a fiction that is sometimes useful, sometimes perniciously totalizing.

19. It is Laura Mulvey's germinal but pessimistic description of Hollywood cinema as necessarily excluding feminine subjectivity that opened this debate. See "Visual Pleasure and Narrative Cinema," *Screen* 16, no. 3 (Autumn 1975): 6–18, reprinted in Constance Penley, ed., *Feminism and Film Theory* (New York: Routledge, Chapman and Hall, 1988), 57–68; and Mulvey, "Afterthoughts on 'Visual Pleasure and Narrative Cinema' Inspired by *Duel in the Sun* (King Vidor, 1946)," *Framework* 15–17 (1981):

12–15, reprinted in Penley, ed., *Feminism and Film Theory*, 69–79. (Citations of these texts will be taken from Penley.)

The best responses to Mulvey open up the possibility of tracing or shifting the terms of feminine subjectivity in Hollywood cinema. See, for example, the texts on melodrama (cited above) as well as Miriam Hansen, "Pleasure, Ambivalence, Identification: Valentino and Female Spectatorship," *Cinema Journal* 25, no. 4 (Summer 1986): 6–32, a more complete version of which appears in Hansen, *Babel and Babylon: Spectatorship in American Silent Film* (Cambridge: Harvard University Press, 1991); de Lauretis, *Alice Doesn't*; Tania Modleski, *The Women Who Knew Too Much: Hitchcock and Feminist Theory* (New York: Methuen, 1988); Kaja Silverman, *The Acoustic Mirror: The Female Voice in Psychoanalysis and Cinema* (Bloomington: Indiana University Press, 1988); and especially Mayne, *The Woman at the Keyhole*.

In *Femmes Fatales* (New York: Routledge, 1991) and *The Desire to Desire*, Mary Ann Doane is more cautious than are some of the above critics in assessing the possibility of women's self-expression in mainstream cinema. Her work on Ophuls is examined in some detail in my discussion of *La Signora di Tutti* (Italy, 1934) and elsewhere. Silverman is discussed in next section, "Ophuls as Auteur."

20. For a discussion of the status of authorship in the European art film of the 1950s and 1960s see David Bordwell, "Art-Cinema Narration," in *Narration in the Fiction Film* (Madison: University of Wisconsin Press, 1985), 205–33.

21. Per Guérin, *Max Ophuls*, 71: "the consenting victim of the pleasure of man" (all translations from this work are my own).

22. For a complete listing of and credits for Ophuls' films, see the filmography in this book.

23. *Spiel im Dasein: Eine Rückblende* (Stuttgart: Henry Goverts, 1946) was translated into French by Max Roth (*Max Ophüls par Max Ophüls* (Paris: Robert Laffont, 1963) but is as yet unavailable in English. It was, according to Lutz Bacher, dictated to Ophuls' secretary, Renata Lenart, and covers the early years of Ophuls' life (through 1946). I do not agree with Karen Hollinger's translation of the title of the book as *A Play About Survival*, in her "Biographical Sketch" of Ophuls in Wexman, ed., *Letter from an Unknown Woman*, 19. The volume also contains the shooting script and a number of essays about the film, including a useful one by Wexman. The title of Ophuls' autobiography might better be translated as *Play in Existence: A Flashback*, or even *Existing in Play*. In any case, either of the latter titles is more reflective of Ophuls' light touch than is the former. (Thanks to Susan Z. Bernstein for her consultation on this translation.)

24. Helmut G. Asper, who is currently completing a biography of Ophuls, has uncovered documentation concerning the unfortunate circumstances of Ophuls' departure from the Burgtheater in 1926. Ophuls was forced to leave his position as director there because of the profound anti-Semitism of the high officials of the theater. The details of his departure are presented in Helmut G. Asper, "Die Affäre Ophüls: Antisemitismus am Wiener Burgtheater 1926," *Theaterzeitschrift* 22 (1987): 135–42. For more on Ophuls' theatrical career, see Helmut G. Asper, "Das andere Ufer—Max Ophüls und das Theater," in Asper, ed., *Max Ophüls: Theater, Hörspiele, Filme*, Vorträge des internationalen Max Ophüls Symposiums im Filmhaus Saarbrück-

en vom 6 bis 10 mai 1992 anlässich des 90.Geburtstages (St. Ingbert: Röhrig, 1993), 101–24. Thanks to William Paul for his help in translating essays from this volume.

25. Marcel Ophuls, director of *The Sorrow and the Pity* (*Le Chagrin et la Pitié*, 1970) and *Hôtel Terminus: The Life and Times of Klaus Barbie* (1988), documentaries treating issues related to the Holocaust, and other films, wrote an amusing piece on "what it's like to be Max Ophuls' son," modeled on one of Cyrano de Bergerac's defiant speeches. See "Confessions d'un fils à papa," *Positif* 232–33 (July–August 1980): 4–7. The highly politicized work of the younger Ophuls seems to me to be in part a response to the (not apolitical but *otherwise* political) films of the father, as is discussed in chapter 4 of the present volume.

26. See Beylie's comments on *Yoshiwara* (*Max Ophuls*, 60). For Ophuls' own remarks on the film, see Rivette and Truffaut, "Interview with Max Ophuls," 18. Guérin, *Max Ophuls*, 22, discusses the negative effects of the war on Ophuls' films. And in his "Stylistic Analysis," Salt describes the films of the early French period as stylistically conventional. A part of my project is to bring a new theoretical perspective to some of Ophuls' less admired films, perhaps echoing what David Bordwell has described in *Making Meaning: Inference and Rhetoric in the Interpretation of Cinema* (Cambridge: Harvard University Press, 1989), 49, as the "explicatory project" of early auteurism which also sought to salvage the minor films of admired directors. My interest does not lie only in showing that there is "thematic continuity" in Ophuls' films, or in enhancing his reputation, but rather in tracing a certain logic concerning the representation of women through the intermediary of Ophuls' works.

27. During this broadcast Ophuls recommended that Hitler could get to sleep by counting not sheep but the countries that had fallen victim to his war machine. A filmscript ("The Man Who Killed Hitler," 1943), adapted from this radio play and from an unpublished novel by Ophuls, is housed in the USC film archives. See also Helmut G. Asper, "Max Ophüls gegen Hitler," in *Gedanken an Deutschland im Exil* (Munich, 1985), 173–82, and "The Man Who Killed Hitler: Die Darstellung des widerstands in Roman und Filmdrehbuch," in *Der Zweite Weltkrieg und die Exilanten: Eine literarische Antwort*, ed. Helmut F. Pfanner (Bonn/Berlin, 1991), 107–14.

28. Ophuls could have left for the United States directly from Switzerland if he had let himself be declared a deserter from the French army. Instead, he made the dangerous voyage back to France before embarking for America. For details of his departure from Europe see Ophuls, *Spiel im Dasein*, as well as the exhibit catalog *Von Babelsberg nach Hollywood: Filmemigranten aus Nazideutschland* (Frankfurt am Main: Deutsches Filmmuseum, 1987), 36–39, which documents the flight of German Jews to Hollywood during the 1930s and 1940s. The exhibit and catalog were organized by Ronny Loewy. See also Lutz Bacher, "To 'The Highlands' with Ophuls: Paul Kohner's Management of Max Ophuls' American Career," *Film Exil: Stiftung Deutsche Kinematek* 2 (May 1993): 4–20, and Bacher, "The Max Ophuls File: A Guide to the Paul Kohner Sammlung," ibid., 21–23.

29. Screen tests of Garbo made in anticipation of this film were actually shot, with James Wong Howe and William Daniels acting as cameramen for producer Walter Wanger. The tests were aired on *Entertainment Tonight* on April 25, 1990, soon after Garbo's death.

30. There are other collaborators on Ophuls' films who worked with him (often intermittently, and in more than one country) over the course of many years. Franz ("Frank") Planer, for example, photographed both *Liebelei* and *Letter from an Unknown Woman* (and *Vendetta*, in a very brief collaboration); Ralph Baum was assistant director on films from *Liebelei* to *Lola Montès*; Isa Miranda acted in *La Signora di Tutti* and *La Ronde*; the great cinematographer Eugen Schüfftan photographed *Dann schon lieber Lebertran* (1930) and several of Ophuls' French films in the thirties. Although the last four French films have the greatest continuity of personnel, Ophuls tended to work with actors and technicians on more than one film—a superficial count enumerates thirty-five people who worked on at least two of Ophuls' films.

31. Incidentally, Ophuls had the umlaut removed from his name in the credit sequence of *Le Plaisir* (Beylie, *Max Ophuls*, 16).

32. Sources for this biographical information include Ophuls, *Spiel im Dasein*; Beylie, *Max Ophuls*; Karen Hollinger, "Biographical Sketch," in Wexman, ed., *Letter from an Unknown Woman*; and Paul Willeman, "Familmographic Romance," in Willeman, ed., *Ophuls*, as well as various other materials as noted. Thanks to Lutz Bacher for factual corrections and additions.

33. This last is Beylie's claim (*Max Ophuls*, 16–17).

34. It is apparently Douglas Fairbanks, Jr. who worked with Ophuls on *The Exile* (as star and producer), and who had Ophuls change the spelling of his name: "I am to blame for having Max respell his name for English-speaking audiences. My reason was that people began jokingly to call him 'Awfuls,'which I thought was unkind and unfair. I had him change it to 'Opuls.' He didn't like this idea at all and when he returned to Europe reverted to the correct original spelling" (letter dated October 27, 1975). Thanks to Lutz Bacher for providing me with this citation from his correspondence with Fairbanks.

35. See Willeman, ed., *Ophuls*, 1, for a cautious approach to the "set of discourses in which 'Ophuls' was/is embedded," and Williams, *Max Ophuls and the Cinema of Desire*, 1–15, for a discussion of auteurism and Ophuls.

36. For the definition of this term and some debates about its advantages and disadvantages, see the special issue of *Communications: Enonciation et Cinéma* 38 (1983). All these terms—"enunciation," "voice," "commentary by an author"—should be used with caution since they imply the unified presence of a single consciousness in the creation of a film and in the guiding of our perceptions. Clearly this is not the case. For further discussions of these issues see Edward Branigan, *Point of View in Cinema* (Berlin: Mouton, 1984), as well as "Objectivity and Uncertainty," in *Narrative Comprehension and Film* (London and New York: Routledge, 1992), 177–91; and Christine Saxon, "The Cultural Voice as Collective Voice," in *Cinema Journal* 26, no. 1 (Fall 1986): 19–30. On the issue of authorship after 1990, see Dudley Andrew, "The Unauthorized Auteur Today," in Jim Collins, Hilary Radner, and Ava Preacher Collins, eds., *Film Theory Goes to the Movies* (New York: Routledge, 1993), 77–85. See also Sandy Flitterman-Lewis, *To Desire Differently: Feminism and the French Cinema* (Urbana: University of Illinois Press, 1990), and Mayne, *The Woman at the Keyhole*, for their insights about women's authorship in cinema. Flitterman-Lewis's discussion of Marie Epstein

in the context of French cinema of the 1930s is helpful in placing (ideologically and otherwise) Ophuls' French films of the period.

37. Raymond Bellour's psychoanalytically-based "auteurism" is articulated in "Hitchcock the Enunciator," *Camera Obscura* 2 (Fall 1977): 69–94.

38. Bordwell, "Art-Cinema Narration," 211.

39. See George Wilson, *Narration in Light* (Baltimore: Johns Hopkins University Press, 1986), 135. Extrapolating from Wayne Booth's terminology, Wilson uses the phrase "implied film maker" to describe the personage to whom we attribute "the peculiar sensibility and intelligence that we find manifested in the way the narration has been crafted" (134). Rather than directly attributing that sensibility to the "flesh and blood author or film maker," though we may suspect that he or she "had, in reality, the personal qualities that we find thus manifested," Wilson suggests that we posit the implied film maker—which "permits us to articulate the character of the relevant impressions and experience without incurring any direct commitment about the artist's psychic biography" (134–35).

40. Wilson, *Narration in Light*, 135.

41. Bordwell, "Art-Cinema Narration," 211.

42. For the distinction between story and discourse see Emile Benveniste, *Problems in General Linguistics*, trans. Mary Meek (Coral Gables, Fla.: University of Miami Press, 1971). Roughly speaking, "story" does not show marks of a speaking subject's enunciation (first and second person pronouns, certain temporal markers, etc.), while "discourse" does show such marks.

43. See Sandy Flitterman, "Woman, Desire and the Look," in John Caughie, ed., *Theories of Authorship* (London: Routledge and Kegan Paul, 1981), 242–50, in which she claims that Hitchcock's presence as "enunciator" in his films subverts the dominant Hollywood practice of maintaining authorial invisibility.

44. Linda Williams, "*Mildred Pierce* and the Second World War," in *Female Spectators: Looking at Film and Television* (London: Verso, 1988), 28.

45. In "Vom Souffleurkasten über das Mikro auf die Leinwand: Max Ophüls," *Frauen und Film* 42 (August 1987): 60–71, Martina Müller documents the frequency with which Ophuls made use, in his theatrical productions, of a "Spielleiter-Figur" who was not in the original material being adapted. The *meneurs de jeu* and other surrogate directors inserted into the films are sometimes minor, sometimes major, characters and most often do not exist in the source material.

46. Fredric Jameson, "Imaginary and Symbolic in Lacan: Marxism, Psychoanalytic Criticism, and the Problem of the Subject," *Yale French Studies* 55–56 (1977–78): 340n.

47. Silverman, *The Acoustic Mirror*. Page references will be cited in the text.

48. See also Silverman's work on Fassbinder in *Male Subjectivity at the Margins* (New York: Routledge, 1992).

49. See Modleski, "Woman and the Labyrinth: *Rebecca*," in *The Women Who Knew Too Much*, 43–55.

50. Modleski, "Woman and the Labyrinth: *Rebecca*," 55, cited by Silverman, *The Acoustic Mirror*, 210.

51. Gertrud Koch, "Positivierung der Gefühle: Zu den Schnitzler-Verfilmungen von Max Ophüls," in Harmut Scheible, ed., *Arthur Schnitzler in neuer Sicht* (Munich:

Wilhelm Fink, 1981), 314. (Thanks to Susan Z. Bernstein for her careful translation of and commentary on this text.) There seems to be some argument as to whether Ophuls actually takes the point of view of the heroines whose lives he describes so intimately. See, for example, Jean-Loup Bourget, "Le Tombeau de Max Ophuls," *Positif* 232–33 (July 1980): 25–29, who claims that there is always "a subtle game between the sentimentality of the heroine . . . and the gaze that Ophuls directs towards the adventure" (28, my translation).

52. For an introduction to the issues involved in the conjunction between Freudian and Lacanian psychoanalysis and feminist theory, see Juliet Mitchell, *Psychoanalysis and Feminism: Freud, Reich, Laing, and Women* (New York: Pantheon, 1974; rpt., New York: Vintage, 1975); the introductions to Mitchell and Rose, eds., *Feminine Sexuality*; and to Penley, ed., *Feminism and Film Theory*.

53. Angela McRobbie, "Strategies of Vigilance: An Interview with Gayatri Chakravorty Spivak," *Block* 10 (1985): 7.

54. Gaylyn Studlar, *In the Realm of Pleasure: Von Sternberg, Dietrich, and the Masochistic Aesthetic* (Urbana: University of Illinois Press, 1988), 3.

One. Circulation and Scapegoating

1. The coins to which I refer are in *The Exile* (1947). They are stamped with the head of the (recently decapitated) King Charles I and are sent into circulation—spent—by his son at the beginning of the film. Nietzsche associates the invention of money and the inscription of coins with the establishment of guilt and punishment as systems of exchange in *On the Genealogy of Morals*, trans. Walter Kaufmann and R. J. Hollingdale (New York: Vintage, 1967). See Gayatri Chakravorty Spivak, "Scattered Speculations on the Question of Value," *In Other Worlds: Essays in Cultural Politics*, 154–75, for a discussion of Marx and Nietzsche on the relation between value, morality, and the "subject." See also Marc Shell, *Money, Language, and Thought* (Berkeley: University of California Press, 1982), 185, for a brief consideration of Nietzsche's numismatics. See chapter 2 of the present volume for a continuation of this discussion.

2. For suggestions about "some of the ways in which such accounts of action and intention, and such instances of *agency-talk*, lend themselves to an idealization of the market criteria of self-possession and self-identity," see parts 2 and 3 of Mark Seltzer, *Bodies and Machines* (New York: Routledge, 1992).

3. Ophuls' version of the opera combines some unusually static episodes with the camera movement typical of his later style (such as the circular motion showing Kezal as he runs singing around the bargaining table, or the tracking shots following bustling people in the frenetic pig-chase). The songs in the film combine spoken dialogue with bits from the most famous pieces, something that shocked music critics at the time, although, as Barry Salt points out ("Stylistic Analysis of the Films of Max Ophuls," 351), it was a typical tactic in German musicals during this period. A detail I hesitate to interpret is the fact that Jarmila Novotna, a well-known star from the Berlin Opera who plays the female protagonist, was visibly pregnant during the shooting of the film. See Ophuls, *Spiel im Dasein*, 151–52 (Roth, *Max Ophüls par Max Ophüls*, 141–42).

4. The "musicality" of Ophuls' *The Bartered Bride* resembles that of René Clair's

Le Million (1931), which, interestingly, concerns a lost Dutch lottery ticket and in which the characters sing their dialogue. Salt also sees Ophuls' early film style as derivative of Clair's *A Nous la Liberté* (1931) and of von Sternberg's films ("Stylistic Analysis," 353).

5. Thanks to Michael Koch and Anette Schwarz for translating this and Ophuls' other German-language films. Ophuls' *On a Volé un Homme* (1934), which is about financial speculation, has unfortunately been lost.

6. In *The Bartered Bride*'s credits, Kezal (Otto Wernicke) is called simply the "marriage broker." Willeman calls him the "impresario."

7. Alan Williams discusses the relationship between René Girard's theory of mimetic desire and the configurations of desire in Ophuls' cinema in *Max Ophuls and the Cinema of Desire*, 155–58. For an account of the relationship between mimesis and literary history see René Girard, *Deceit, Desire and the Novel: Self and Other in Literary Structure*, trans. Yvonne Freccero (Baltimore: Johns Hopkins University Press, 1965). Girard rejects historical readings of his own work in *Violence and the Sacred* and in *Des choses cachées depuis la fondation du monde: Recherches avec Jean-Michel Oughourlian et Guy Lefort* (Paris: Grasset, 1978). Girard's work has often been critiqued for its privileging of male heterosexual desire. Toril Moi analyzes Girard's biologistic tendencies in " The Missing Mother: The Oedipal Rivalries of René Girard," *Diacritics* 12, no. 2 (Summer 1982): 21–31. See also Sarah Kofman, "The Narcissistic Woman: Freud and Girard," *Diacritics* 10, no. 3 (Summer 1980): 36–45, for a discussion of Girard's "fear of feminine self-sufficiency." One feminist writer who has successfully integrated Girard's work into her own is Eve Kosofsky Sedgwick in *Between Men: English Literature and Male Homosocial Desire* (New York: Columbia University Press, 1985).

8. As noted in the introduction, Gertrud Koch makes the strongest case for Ophuls' "femininity neurosis" in "Positivierung der Gefühle: Zu den Schnitzler-Verfilmungen von Max Ophüls."

9. Actually, Ophuls claims to have been (happily) amazed at the enthusiasm with which his Italian cameraman filmed this 360-degree shot (see Ophuls, *Spiel im Dasein*, 187; Roth, *Max Ophüls par Max Ophüls*, 179–80: further citations are from Roth's translation, but some readers may wish to check the German text for variants, which are often significant). It is certainly not the only 360-degree shot in Ophuls' films, however. In *The Bartered Bride*, Kezal runs around a table while a series of pans is made to approximate a 360-degree movement. And 360-degree shots occur in *Divine* (1935), *Komedie om Geld* (1936), *Le Plaisir* (1952), and *Lola Montès* (1955), among others.

10. Frieda Grafe, "T*he Bartered Bride*: Smetana as well as Ophuls," in Willeman, ed., *Ophuls*, 58. Further page numbers appear in the text.

11. Ophuls cowrote the script with Jaroskav Kvapil and Curt Alexander. The latter cowrote four of Ophuls' films from the 1930s.

12. Ophuls' version of *The Bartered Bride*'s narrative begins when the wheels of Hans's coach stop spinning—one of them breaks as the coach passes by the town where Marie lives, just as the circus is arriving. The halting of the motion-cycle brings Hans into town (to fix the wheel), where he finds Marie spinning a wheel of fortune. She wins a pig, which runs out into the town square and is caught by Hans. (This

entire sequence is not to be found in Smetana's opera, which opens with the young couple, Hans and Marie, already in love, meeting in the marketplace during festival time in Bohemia.)

13. See especially Mikhail Bakhtin, *Rabelais and His World*, trans. Helene Iswolsky (Bloomington: Indiana University Press, 1984), and Bakhtin, *The Dialogic Imagination: Four Essays*, ed. Michael Holquist (Austin: University of Texas Press, 1981).

14. Mary Russo, "Female Grotesques: Carnival and Theory," in Teresa de Lauretis, ed., *Feminist Studies, Critical Studies* (Bloomington: Indiana University Press, 1986), 218.

15. Georg Simmel, *The Philosophy of Money*, trans. Tom Bottomore and David Frisby (London, Henley, 1978; Boston: Routledge and Kegan Paul, 1978). Simmel's original German text was published in 1900.

16. The character (played by Max Schreck, the original Nosferatu!) is Native American in the film. In the opera he is a Fiji Islander.

17. As Salt has commented ("Stylistic Analysis," 357), "The stuttering brother-in-law who was the hero's rival was handled more sympathetically in the film, which is not surprising, since his infatuation with a show and its performers against the wishes of his parents almost exactly matched Ophuls' involvement with the theatre."

18. "Other social historians have documented the insight of the anthropologist Victor Turner that the marginal position of women and others in the 'indicative' world makes their presence in the 'subjunctive' or possible world of the topsy-turvy carnival 'quintessentially' dangerous; in fact, as Emmanuel Le Roy Ladurie shows in *Carnival at Romans*, Jews were stoned, and there is evidence that women were raped, during carnival festivals" (Russo, "Female Grotesques," 217).

19. Roth, *Max Ophüls par Max Ophüls*, 143. Valentin also participated in "surreal" Wilhelmine film comedies. See Thomas Elsaesser, "Early German Cinema: Audiences, Style, and Paradigms," *Screen* 33, no. 2 (Summer 1992): 208.

20. Of course, the circular structure traceable in many of Ophuls' films is repeated here in the shape of the circus ring. In *La Ronde*, Ophuls' 1950 film that thematizes circularity, the *meneur de jeu* plays "The Bartered Bride" on a pianola—the name of the tune is, ironically, placed right beside the coin slot.

21. Reported in Claude Beylie, *Max Ophuls*, 30.

22. Paisley Livingston, *Ingmar Bergman and the Rituals of Art*, 44. Livingston also notes (66) that in many countries (specifically, Sweden) the cinema has itinerant origins, often making its first appearance with the traveling circus as a sideshow attraction. Further page citations appear in the text.

The best-known work on carnival folk culture is that of Bakhtin, who writes approvingly of the heterogeneity and social upheaval made possible by ritual spectacle and festivals. As "outcasts" on the edge of society and the outskirts of town, the circus folk may be considered "liminal," as defined by Victor Turner in "Betwixt and Between: The Liminal Period," in *The Forest of Symbols: Aspects of Ndemba Ritual* (Ithaca, N.Y.: Cornell University Press, 1967), 93–111. *Sawdust and Tinsel*'s series of humiliations culminates in a scene of bear-baiting in which the circus director (Albert) himself ends up taking the role of the taunted bear.

23. The existence of such "founding moments" is, of course, highly problematic. Girard's claims for the historical facticity of the primordial acts of violence are cri-

tiqued in Cynthia Chase, "Oedipal Textuality: Reading Freud's Reading of Oedipus," in *Decomposing Figures: Rhetorical Readings in the Romantic Tradition* (Baltimore: Johns Hopkins University Press, 1986), 182–83, 192–93.

24. See Moi, "The Missing Mother," 29 (further page references appear in the text). Because, according to Moi, Girard's version of the Oedipal triangle (and all "triangular desire") ultimately excludes the mother (and all "'objects' of desire"), his theory of mimetic desire "cannot account for feminine desire" (ibid., 23).

25. Philippe Lacoue-Labarthe, "Typographie," in *Mimésis des articulations*, ed. Sylviane Agacinski (Paris: Aubier-Flammarion, 1975).

26. Giles Deleuze and Félix Guattari, *Anti-Oedipus: Capitalism and Schizophrenia*, trans. Robert Hurley, Mark Seem, and Helen R. Lane (Minneapolis: University of Minnesota Press, 1983), 7.

27. As Salt notes in "Stylistic Analysis," Marie and Hans's visit to the exhibits at the fair anticipates the several scenes of "imaginary travel" taken by lovers in Ophuls' later films, including *Yoshiwara* and *Letter from an Unknown Woman*. The constellation of the Napoleonic battle scene and a pair of lovers recurs in *Madame de* . . . .

28. The problem of memory, a pervasive concern in Ophuls' cinema, is thus made explicit as early as this film.

29. Catherine Clément, *Opera, or the Undoing of Women*, trans. Betsy Wing (Minneapolis: University of Minnesota Press, 1988), 6–7.

30. Seltzer, *Bodies and Machines*, 212.

31. Mulvey, "Visual Pleasure and Narrative Cinema," 11.

32. Presumably, the narrative "movement" is threatening to the woman because it leads either to the sadistic (Mulvey's term) unmasking or punishment of the woman, or else to her recuperation into the patriarchal family structure.

33. Basically, the fetish, as defined by psychoanalysis, is an object (or group of objects) that acts as a substitute for the woman's (the mother's) penis. See Sigmund Freud, "Fetishism" (1927), *SE* 21:152–57. Also of interest in the context of the "frozen" image used apotropaically (as a warding-off device) is Freud's "Medusa's Head" (1922), *SE* 18:273–74. See Neil Hertz, "Medusa's Head: Male Hysteria Under Political Pressure," in *The End of the Line* (New York: Columbia University Press, 1985), 161–93, for a discussion of the political implications of castration anxiety. For various studies of the economic, philosophical, and psychoanalytic significance of the fetish, see Emily Apter and William Pietz, eds., *Fetishism as Cultural Discourse* (Ithaca: Cornell University Press, 1993).

34. Gaylyn Studlar's important work on von Sternberg is discussed in chapter 2.

35. Guérin, *Max Ophuls*, 102. In "Female Spectatorship and Machines of Projection: *Caught* and *Rebecca*," in *The Desire to Desire*, Mary Ann Doane supports the notion that the moving camera acts to prop up masculine structures of desire.

36. Guérin, *Max Ophuls*, 26–28, 64, 76, 86, 103–104, 112, 114.

37. Like Stephen Heath ("The Question Oshima"), both Paul Willeman ("The Ophuls Text: A Thesis," in Willeman, ed., *Ophuls*, 70–74) and Stephen Jenkins ("Lang: Fear and Desire," in Jenkins, ed., *Fritz Lang: The Image and the Look* [London: BFI, 1981], 38–124) regard Ophuls' camera movements as permitting a "breakthrough of excess" related to the psychoanalytic notion of the return of the

repressed—the repressed itself being, finally, the feminine. "To freeze Ophuls' flow of flowing images . . . would clearly be working against the grain of the text, where movement is all," Jenkins concludes. Jenkins and Willeman ignore the paradoxical element in Ophuls' films whereby the desired freezing or halting on the beloved image is also shown to be productive of horror and death (notably, at the end of *La Signora di Tutti* and *Le Plaisir*).

38. They are present as disembodied voices saying the word, "eternity." For a discussion of the implications of disembodied sounds in Ophuls' films see the section on *La Signora di Tutti* ("Lost Immediacy and the Maternal Image") in chapter 5.

39. For a discussion of the theatrical space in the skiing sequence of *Die verliebte Firma*, and for several well-documented discussions of the problem of vertical movement in Ophuls' films, see Robert Chamblee's chapter "*Liebelei*" in "Max Ophuls' Viennese Trilogy," 10–11, 64–66, and passim.

40. Catherine Gallagher, "George Eliot and *Daniel Deronda*: The Prostitute and the Jewish Question," in Ruth Bernard Yeazell, ed., *Sex, Politics and Science in the Nineteenth-Century Novel: Selected Papers from the English Institute: 1983–1984* (Baltimore: Johns Hopkins University Press, 1986).

41. One of Hans's passengers (identified as the rather absurd "financial consultant" by Grafe) almost forces him to leave the scene of the action prematurely because of an urgent need to transact some business with the Rothschild bank in Vienna.

42. For a glimpse of the logic that, during the early twentieth century among the German Freikorps, linked together women, Jews, and communists as an inchoate mass in need of destruction, see Klaus Theweleit, *Male Fantasies*, vol. 1, *Women, Floods, Bodies, History*, trans. Stephen Conway, Erica Carter, and Chris Turner (Minneapolis: University of Minnesota Press, 1987). A "Bavarian drawing of Lola Montez, beloved of Ludwig I," in which Lola displays her genitals to a group of men passing by in a boat, can be found in Theweleit's text (1:178).

A supposedly intimate connection between Jews and the origins of capitalism was traced by the influential economist, Sombart, at the beginning of the twentieth century. Not meant specifically to be an anti-Semitic text, Sombart's treatise nonetheless seemed to provide academic legitimation for the worst kind of anti-Semitic theories. George L. Mosse describes how Sombart's text was taken up by the ideologues of the German fascists: "Economic prejudices were always prevalent in anti-Semitism and they attained academic respectability with Werner Sombart's treatise *Die Juden und das Wirtschaftsleben* [*Jews and Capitalism*] (1910). This eminent economic historian linked the growth of capitalism to the role played by the Jews. As usurers in the Middle Ages and entrepreneurs in modern times, the Jews had been a vital force in building the capitalist system. He asserted that their restless character had made them the motive force of capitalism, a role which Max Weber more astutely ascribed to the ethos of Protestantism. . . . [Sombart's treatise] agreed broadly with Völkish thought, which described the Jews as 'the shiftless, rootless, conniving middleman and stockjobber, hoarding the gold coin and bleeding Germany dry.'" Mosse, *The Crisis of German Ideology: Intellectual Origins of the Third Reich* (New York: Grosset and Dunlap, 1964), 141–42.

The figure of the Jew is thus associated with both a harmful stillness (hoarding) and a suspicious kind of movement that has its roots in the restlessness of the "race" (entrepreneurialism). Shell has astutely observed (*Money, Language, and Thought*, 55) that the exchangeability between money and human life (*Wergeld*) seen in, for example, *The Merchant of Venice* is a Christian rather than a Jewish concept. And in Bottomore and Frisby's introduction to their translation of Simmel's *The Philosophy of Money*, it is noted that "'Weber had never forgiven Dilthey, Rickert and Windelband for concertedly blocking the call to a full professorship for Georg Simmel—who in his eyes was the most significant of contemporary German philosophers—because he was a Jew'" (3; quote taken from E. Baumgarten, *Max Weber, Werk und Person* [Tübingen, 1964], 611).

43. As Alan Williams states in a discussion of *La Ronde*, "Ophuls does not see desire and the social system as representing two warring levels [as Schnitzler does], but as necessarily implying one another." Sexuality is not *repressed* but circulates just as money does, though sometimes this circulation creates countercurrents. See Alan Williams, "Reading Ophüls Reading Schnitzler: *Liebelei* (1933) [*sic*]," in Eric Rentschler, ed., *German Film and Literature: Adaptations and Transformations* (New York: Methuen, 1986), 75.

44. I have mentioned, for example, that in *Le Plaisir*, the prostitutes are humorously portrayed as, precisely, *bourgeoises*, unashamed either of their merchandise or their status as tradeswomen. (There are also working-class prostitutes downstairs in the Maison Tellier.) According to the system of signification which regards both Jews and performers as inherently destabilizing, the Jewish actor must be a very special case indeed. Significantly, almost every reference Ophuls makes to the fact of his Jewishness in his autobiography is humorous, though indignation at the anti-Semitism of the other parties involved may be read in Ophuls' conspicuous silence on the topic. One of the most striking—and hilarious—instances of Ophuls' wry indirectness concerning his encounters with anti-Semitism involves his first role as a "leading man," for the Austrian troupe, "Theophile Brandt and His Actors." After his audition, Brandt offered Ophuls a role as a salesman whose name is "Rabbi"—so that the audience will understand that he is Jewish. (Ophuls took the part, by the way. See Roth, *Max Ophüls par Max Ophüls*, 60.)

45. Grafe, "*The Bartered Bride*," 58. Alan Williams has also pointed out that Ophuls emphasizes not a "focused dramatic space" but *transitional* space, spaces *between* things ("Reading Ophüls Reading Schnitzler," 78). Doane connects this emphasis on the transitional spaces with narrative postponement, digression, and delay in *Madame de . . .* ("*Madame de . . .* and the Desire for Narrative," in "The Dialogical Text," 235).

46. Koch, "Positivierung der Gefühle."

47. *The Bartered Bride* can also be associated with what Russo terms the "grotesque body," which seeks to connect with "the rest of the world," while *Liebelei* is linked to the "classical body, which is monumental, static, closed, and sleek, corresponding to the aspirations of bourgeois individualism" ("Female Grotesques," 219).

48. The order of Ophuls' early films is disputed. See Beylie, *Max Ophuls*, 157, where he refutes the claim made by other film historians that *Lachende Erben* was filmed in 1931, right after *Dann schon lieber Lebertran*, a children's film made in asso-

ciation with Emmeric Pressburger. Salt opts for the 1931 production date of *Lachende Erben* ("Stylistic Analysis," 356), but claims that the film profited from a more modern soundtrack than *The Bartered Bride* since it was released only in 1933. Helmut G. Asper and Ophuls himself place *Lachende Erben* after *The Bartered Bride*, thus in 1932 (Ophuls, *Spiel im Dasein*, 157; Roth, *Max Ophüls par Max Ophüls*, 149), with a March 1933 release date. I assume that Ophuls' date is correct, although it is easy to see why Salt maintains that *Lachende Erben* is an earlier film: in both subject matter and technique, *Die verkaufte Braut* is closer to Ophuls' later films. Ophuls did not think highly of *Lachende Erben*, despite its commercial success. He called the scenario "inept, insipid, full of platitudes"—although he was pleased to work with Heinz Rühmann (Roth, *Max Ophüls par Max Ophüls*, 149).

49. See chapter 5 for a discussion of *La Signora di Tutti* and Herr Bockelmann's will as "audio/visual" device.

50. Patrice Petro comments that both the female spectator and women's stories have been largely ignored by critics of Weimar cinema, whose "analyses of crisis. . . almost always return to questions about male subjectivity: unresolved Oedipal conflicts serve to symbolize the political and economic situation of Germany in the 1920s, and narrative is said to enact the drama of male passivity and symbolic defeat which supposedly organizes both the history of Weimar and its cinema" (*Joyless Streets*, xviii). The theory of a crumbling Oedipal facade as a causal agent in the rise of fascism figures in many of the psychological studies of the rise of Nazism. This view is promulgated, of course, by Siegfried Kracauer, but more subtly and less narrowly by Klaus Theweleit in his history of the proto-Nazi army officers who fought Rosa Luxembourg and the "Reds" in the late 'teens and twenties. (Although it is set at the turn of the century, *Liebelei* is clearly questioning the attitudes of the military regarding not only dueling but the role of women as "purifying" and "contaminating" entities, issues dealt with at length by Theweleit.) Petro points to the way that mass culture was (at that time and is even now) conflated with threatening (contagious) femininity, while women themselves as historical agents have been pushed aside. One can see in *Happy Heirs* as in *Liebelei* the dialectic of female and male spectator/"Oedipal" subject. These films were made, interestingly, during a period (1931–32) in which Petro observes a "return to femininity" from the fashionable androgyny of the 1920s in German popular culture, part of the attempt to "stabilize" female identity (*Joyless Streets*, 105–32). Ophuls' films always deconstruct both the need for and the possibility of any such "stabilization" of female identity. The Oedipal scenario invoked in discussing *Happy Heirs* is not meant to extract the "unconscious" of the film, but to point to the flow of production and consumption (of wine) in the context of social legitimation.

51. As Simmel notes in discussing marriage for money as a variation on prostitution, "This view holds that it is polyandric just as much as it is polygamic but because of the social superiority of the male only the consequences of the polygamous element, the degradation of the female, takes effect in marriage for money" (*The Philosophy of Money*, 381).

52. Spivak, "Scattered Speculations on the Question of Value," 156.

53. Ibid.

54. For a radical critique of "semiological," "postmodernist," and "Derridean post-

Marxist" collapsing of sign systems and Marxist economics, see William Pietz, "Fetishism and Materialism: The Limits of Theory in Marx," in Apter and Pietz, eds., *Fetishism as Cultural Discourse*, 119–51.

55. Chamblee, "Max Ophuls' Viennese Trilogy," 64. Further page references appear in the text.

56. Kaja Silverman, *The Acoustic Mirror*, 217–18.

57. Koch, "Positivierung der Gefühle," 311. Further page references appear in the text.

58. Chamblee ("Max Ophuls' Viennese Trilogy," 51) cites Martin Swales, *Arthur Schnitzler: A Critical Study* (London: Oxford University Press, 1971), 182, on the figure of the *süsses Mädel*, the lower-class girl of "easy virtue," in Schnitzler's work. As a shopgirl Mizzi seems to belong to a lower class than Christine, who is rendered "classless" by her affiliation with the art world.

59. In "Max Ophuls' Viennese Trilogy," Chamblee states that these two sequences are connected by a dissolve (115). My print, which appears to be in excellent condition (taken off German television during an Ophuls festival) definitely shows a fade to black at this point in the film.

60. Before making *The Bartered Bride*, Ophuls was offered the direction of a military subject ("une farce militaire") starring Heinz Rühmann, who plays the lead in *Lachende Erben*, and whom Ophuls "adored." After two months, finding the script too clichéd, Ophuls threw in the towel (Roth, *Max Ophüls par Max Ophüls*, 137). Perhaps he found it frustrating to treat the military one-dimensionally—as farcical.

61. The military and social hierarchies are, of course, not unrelated. Fritz and Theo are upper-class men; Christine and Mizzi are, at best, petty bourgeois (Mizzi might be called working class, of course). Chamblee observes that even Christine and Mizzi are dominated by the military hierarchy: Mizzi explains military rank to Christine, observing that the latter need not concern herself with the meaning of gold braid since it is "not for us" ("Ophuls' Viennese Trilogy," 88). Captain is the highest rank such women can hope to be associated with. Chamblee sees the resistance to the military way of life shown by Theo in *Liebelei* as the film's major political statement. Attributing Ophuls with more foresight than he may have had, Chamblee conjectures that the filmmaker "saw the collapse of the Austrian monarchy [depicted as imminent in *Liebelei*] as prefiguring a catastrophe in his own country. Even before *Liebelei* opened he felt compelled to take his family out of Germany. In light of Ophuls' own need to leave Germany, it is interesting to consider to what degree he chose Schnitzler's fin-de-siècle play to adapt into a film so that through it he might alert German citizens of the holocaust to come" (41).

62. As Chamblee points out, this pneumatic tube is certainly evidence of Ophuls' "fascination with communication devices" ("Ophuls' Viennese Trilogy," 73).

63.For a more philosophical discussion of vision in this scene, see Lars Henrik Gass, "Ironie der Schaulust: Ophüls' kinematographische Maschine der Sichtbarkeit am Beispiel *Liebelei*," in Helmut G. Asper, ed., *Max Ophüls*, 50–67.

64. Chamblee (ibid., 71) notes that *Liebelei*'s structure is circular in that it involves returns to the theater on the part of almost all the central characters (Fritz is the exception).

65. Chamblee, "Max Ophuls' Viennese Trilogy," 85.

66. Mizzi's profession is ironically linked to her role in "selling a bill of goods" to Christine. A brief but effective scene (anticipating the scene in *Letter from an Unknown Woman* when Stefan visits Lisa at the dress shop) has Christine visiting Mizzi in the glove shop where the latter works. When their whispered conversation about their plans to meet the men attracts the attention of the shopowner, Mizzi concocts the story that Christine wanted "baby gloves." The image is interesting in itself—with its tender evocation of the baby who never was—and it also serves to link the women *between themselves* to the motif of exchange, "alienated" even in their friendship.

67. Robin Wood comments that the army is "an extension of the 'theater'" in Ophuls. See "Ewig hin der Liebe Glück," in Wexman, ed., Letter from an Unknown Woman, 224.

68. In her book on female spectatorship in Weimar Germany, Petro (*Joyless Streets*, 66–68) describes Kracauer's ambivalence toward the "little shopgirls" as "distracted" cinema spectators—exemplary of the fragmented subject of modern life, yet curiously concentrated on the cinematic image. See Siegfried Kracauer, "Die kleinen Ladenmädchen gehen ins Kino," in *Das Ornament der Masse* (Frankfurt am Main: Suhrkamp, 1977), 279–94.

69. Petro, *Joyless Streets*, 8.

70. As Lacan has so aptly put it, "In the human being, virile display itself appears as feminine" ("The Meaning of the Phallus," in Mitchell and Rose, eds., *Feminine Sexuality*, 84).

71. Leslie Fiedler, *Love and Death in the American Novel* (New York: Criterion Books, 1960), 266.

72. Helmut G. Asper describes this situation in "Die Affäre Ophüls: Antisemitismus am Wiener Burgtheater 1926."

73. Jane Feuer, *The Hollywood Musical* (Bloomington: Indiana University Press, 1982), 42.

Two. The Economy of the Feminine in Madame de . . .

1. Catherine Clément, *Opera, or the Undoing of Women*, 5.

2. Quoted in E. P. Thompson, "The Grid of Inheritance: A Comment," in *Family and Inheritance: Rural Society in Western Europe, 1200–1800* (Cambridge: Cambridge University Press, 1976), 348–49.

3. Charles Dickens, *Little Dorrit* (1857), ed. John Holloway (Harmondsworth: Penguin, 1967), 472.

4. On this point see Nancy Chodorow, *The Reproduction of Mothering* (Berkeley: University of California Press, 1978).

5. See Sigmund Freud, "Female Sexuality" (1931), in *Collected Papers* (hereafter, *CP*), 5 vols., ed. James Strachey, trans. Joan Riviere (New York: Basic Books, 1959): 5:252–72, or Freud, *SE* 21; and Freud, "Femininity" (1933), *SE* 22:112–35.

6. "Ophuls did not like realism in the cinema, but he enjoyed the realist novelists of the nineteenth century—Stendhal, Maupassant, Balzac. . . . For Ophuls realism is a literary process, not a recipe for depicting reality" (Frieda Grafe, "T*he Bartered*

Bride," 55). *Madame de . . .*'s exposé of the situation of the woman who is tragically revealed to be an object of exchange places Ophuls' film and Vilmorin's novella in the tradition of works such as Dumas fils's *La Dame aux Camélias* (1852).

7. Translations from the film are my own. The original reads: "Madame de . . . était une femme très élégante, très brillante, très fêtée. Elle semblait promise à une jolie vie sans histoire. Rien ne serait probablement arrivé sans ce bijou."

8. Ophuls acknowledges not a *debt* but a resemblance between his work and that of Clair. See Chapter 7, note 5, for more on Clair and Ophuls.

9. Mary Ann Doane is an exception to this trend. See *"Madame de . . .* and the Desire for Narrative," in "The Dialogical Text," 231. Further page citations appear in the text.

10. Chamblee, "Max Ophuls' Viennese Trilogy," 22. Roy Armes is usually cited as the major proponent of the notion that Ophuls' characters lack "depth." See Armes, *French Cinema Since 1946* (New Jersey: A. S. Barnes, 1970), 63.

11. A detailed discussion of the notion of the "character" as it relates to the cinema and as an historical problem is to be found in Richard Dyer's *Stars* (London: BFI, 1979), 99–149.

12. The remark was originally cited by Georges Annenkov in *Max Ophüls* (Paris: Le Terrain Vague, 1962), 67.

13. In discussing the meaning of spectacle for women, Mary Russo asks if "women are . . . so identified with style itself that they are estranged from its liberatory and transgressive effects as they are from their own bodies as signs in culture generally. In what sense can women really produce or make spectacles out of themselves?" ("Female Grotesques," 217). These questions are addressed further in chapter 4 of the present volume.

14. See Thomas Keenan, "The Point Is to (Ex)Change It: Reading *Capital*, Rhetorically," in Apter and Pietz, eds., *Fetishism as Cultural Discourse*, 161. Naomi Schor's remarks on the aesthetic history of the "detail" may be of significance in discussing the earring as (commodity) fetish: "[An] imaginary femininity weighs heavily on the fate of the detail as well as of the ornament in aesthetics, burdening them with the negative connotations of the feminine: the decorative, the natural, the impure, and the monstrous" Naomi Schor, *Reading in Detail: Aesthetics and the Feminine* (N.Y.: Routledge, 1987), p. 43. The decadence associated with the detail in art also informed the aesthetics of the German National Socialist Party. Ophuls' "baroque" style, which glorifies the arabesque and the detail, undermines the "classical" severity of the Nazi monument.

15. The names of the film's characters were altered with respect to those in the novella by Louise de Vilmorin. This issue is discussed below.

16. Louise de Vilmorin, *Madame de* (Paris: Editions Gallimard, 1951). A number of differences between the novella and the film can be discerned, even in this very general outline, which omits some exchanges of the earrings that take place in the film. Major alterations made by Ophuls include the addition of the entire Constantinople gambling sequence as well as the duel scene and the ultimate fate of the earrings. The role of Louise's Nanny (especially her predilection for fortune-telling by using playing cards) is expanded in the film.

17. Alan Williams, *Max Ophuls and the Cinema of Desire*, 106–107. It is in the unusual frequency of exchanges that a certain "frenetic" movement may be found in the film, as well as in rapid pans following "intermediary" and principal characters. Chamblee claims (and I agree) that Ophuls' cinema is wrongfully stereotyped as exhibiting frenetic motion: see, for example, Noel Burch, *Theory of Film Practice* (New York: Praeger, 1973), 77, where Burch writes of the "arbitrary and frenetic arabesques around the actors' movements characteristic of the films of Max Ophuls."

18. According to Doane's reading of the film (in "The Dialogical Text," 223–58), *Madame de . . .* is the site of a "dialogue" (in the Bakhtinian sense) between conventional narrative structures and their ironization through excessive repetition. Doane's interesting argument shares some theoretical commonalities with the work of Alan Williams, who writes about the "two films" at work in *Letter from an Unknown Woman* (1948) (*Max Ophuls and the Cinema of Desire*, 17–41).

19. This textual echo is noted by Molly Haskell in "*Madame de:* A Musical Passage" in Philip Nobile, ed., *Favorite Movies* (New York: Macmillan, 1973), 143–44, and by Williams (*Max Ophuls and the Cinema of Desire*, 119). Haskell's essay also appears in Patricia Erens, ed., *Sexual Stratagems: The World of Women in Film* (New York: Horizon, 1979), 65 (for this passage).

20. On the question of coincidence, chance, and the barter of woman, see Mary Ann Doane, "The Erotic Barter: *Pandora's Box*," in *Femmes Fatales*, 157–58.

21. For a discussion of the necessary mystification of the ideas of "chance" and "coincidence" in bourgeois capitalist life, see Georg Lukács, "Reification and the Consciousness of the Proletariat" in *History and Class Consciousness*, trans. Rodney Livingstone (Cambridge, Mass.: MIT Press, 1971), 102. In brief, the laws of the market cannot be completely "rationalized" or even fully "knowable," for if they were, then one individual or entity could come to monopolize the economic realm.

22. Doane, in "The Dialogical Text," 254.

23. As the editors (among them, Doane herself) of an excellent collection of feminist writings on cinema have remarked, "Symptomatic of the limitation and exclusions involved in the woman's relation to language is the image of the 'old wives' tale.' A discourse which is marked as the possession of the woman is simultaneously marked as seriously deficient in its relation to knowledge and truth." See Mary Ann Doane, Patricia Mellencamp, and Linda Williams, eds., *Re-Vision: Essays in Feminist Film Criticism* (Frederick, Md.: University Publications of America and the American Film Institute, 1984), 12–13.

24. As we shall see, Louise's "lies" (her manipulations) do, in fact, turn out to be the truth. This becomes clear when she dies at the end of the film from a condition thought to be either a social fiction (the faint) or hypochondriacal.

25. André's deafness is reminiscent of that of another tolerant patriarch, King Ludwig in *Lola Montès*. Perhaps it is to be read as an instance of the "rigidity" of the patriarchal figures who are deaf to the needs of others. In *Lola Montès* this rigidity, in combination with Lola's presence, will lead to a revolution. The king's deafness is given elaborate treatment, both cinematic and medical, in that film.

26. The earrings are heart-shaped diamonds, iconically echoing the suits of Nanny's cards. Thanks to John Jones for this insight.

27. As Alan Williams observes, the distinctions between the costumes of Louise and Nanny and between those of André and Fabrizio become less and less marked as the film progresses (*Max Ophuls and the Cinema of Desire*, 123).

28. It is difficult to assign any special significance to the name "André." It does, however, happen to be the name of Louise de Vilmorin's brother, who also edited her works and wrote a preface to the edition of the book cited above. Perhaps this is a joke on the part of the authors of the scenario, or it might be yet another coincidence.

29. Catherine Gallagher, "George Eliot and *Daniel Deronda*," 55 (further page numbers appear in the text). See chapter 1 (at note 38) for earlier remarks about this article. In *Daniel Deronda* Gallagher also discerns a "close connection between selling oneself as a sexual commodity and selling oneself as an artist" (53)—not only for writers but for performing artists as well. The performer, who offers him/herself (more likely, *her*self) as a commodity often commands an "inflated market value," which Gallagher sees as a link to the stereotypical usurious Jew: "It is thus little wonder that Jews have only two professions in [*Daniel Deronda*]"—that of money changer and that of singer or theatrical performer (55).

30. Mary Ann Doane, *The Desire to Desire: The Woman's Film of the 1940s*, 25.

31. For an excellent analysis of consumer tie-ins as they relate to female spectators of the 1940s, see Maria Laplace, "Producing and Consuming the Woman's Film: Discursive Struggle in *Now, Voyager*," in Christine Gledhill, ed., *Home Is Where the Heart Is: Studies in Melodrama and the Woman's Film*, 138–66.

32. The contract is referred to indirectly when Louise mentions her "wedding day" at the beginning of the film. Compare this scene's use of the "patriarchal portrait" to that in *Lachende Erben*.

33. I am grateful to Richard Macksey, who pointed out to me that an inscription in the alcove where Louise goes to pray identifies the "sainte" who is Louise's patron as Ste. Geneviève, and added that in her role as patroness of Paris and as King Clovis's initial adversary, Geneviève is a figure with particularly strong local resonances for a Parisian woman. Further, the notorious *chastity* of both the Parisian Geneviève and the Geneviève de Brabant who figures in Proust's *Du Côté de chez Swann* (*Swann's Way*) has a nicely Ophulsian irony.

34. This "old woman" serves to remind us that there is a strong maternal association with religion in this film, starting with the plaint at the beginning of the film when Louise wishes her mother were there to advise her, as she simultaneously knocks her missal (it is , I believe, not a bible) from the shelf. Louise's belief in the power of her mother is emphasized by her remark. She also mentions that her cross is a gift from her mother. Later in the film the earrings will be (falsely) marked by the maternal inscription when, in order to deceive Donati, Louise claims that her mother had given them to her. (This issue is taken up in some detail below.) Superstition, as a variant of the religious impulse, is associated with Louise's old nanny. Alan Williams also mentions the maternal aspect of Louise's possessions and of her patron saint (*Max Ophuls and the Cinema of Desire*, 131–32).

35. A propos of Louise's behavior in the church scene at the end of the film, her words to the saint indicate—although Williams (ibid., 134) thinks otherwise—that

the union between Louise and Fabrizio was never sexually consummated. Addressing
her patron saint, she states: "Save him, my saint. You know that we are guilty only in
thought." A similar line of dialogue occurs in *Divine* (1935).

36. For an interesting description of the language games in this scene, see Doane,
"The Dialogical Text," 240–43.

37. On the ambivalent status of the female desiring look in *Blood and Sand* (1922),
see Miriam Hansen, *Babel and Babylon*, 269–77. Further discussion of Hansen's work
is found in chapter 7.

38. This sequence repeats a courtship ritual that takes place in *Liebelei* to the tune
of a turn-of-the-century jukebox (time stretching forward as a kind of infinite repetition of days and hours), as well as in the restaurant scene in *Letter*.

39. An intriguing detail near the end of *Madame de . . .* seems to make light of the
tendency to read causality into the destructive "look." When Louise is forced to give
her earrings to her husband at the final ball scene, she begins to feel faint, perhaps
"really" so for the first time in the film. In one of Ophuls' typically ironic asides, a man
who had seen her faint at the hunt (where Donati fell from his horse) remarks: "Every
time I see her, she collapses [*s'écroule*]." Is the man merely remarking on the coincidence of constantly seeing Louise faint, or does he believe (absurdly) that his looking may have some causal connection to these fainting fits?

40. The opera being performed on this evening is Gluck's *Orpheus and Eurydice*,
which tells the story of another kind of loss, the irrevocable departure of Orpheus'
beloved wife, caused by his inability not to *look* at her. Alan Williams remarks on the
irony of the use of the aria ("Che far òsenza Euridice?" sung in Italian) announcing
the loss of a wife. Louise has not, at this point, truly lost her earrings, but her greater
loss is anticipated by the opera: "The use of the Italian score, though it is never performed at the Paris Opera, heightens the narrative parallel, since in that version
Orpheus is played by a woman—whereas in the French version the role was rewritten
for a tenor" (*Max Ophuls and the Cinema of Desire*, 132).

41. The director of the opera house reassures M. and Mme de . . . that the earrings
will be recovered. In doing so he states, with curious emphasis, that if they are not
found the *police* will be called in (a threat echoed in the doctor's words at the end of
Lola Montès). The woman being suspected of a theft is a topos that can be linked to
Freud's theory about woman's desire to castrate man after he has taken her virginity.
For a discussion of the woman's hostility toward the man who initiates her into sexual intercourse, see Sigmund Freud, "The Taboo of Virginity" (1918), *SE* 11:191–208;
and Jean Laplanche, *Castration Symbolisations* (Paris: Presses Universitaires de France,
1980), 101–107.

Freud states that the woman's initial sexual experience wounds the woman's narcissism and revives penis envy, throwing her back into her earlier "immature sexuality," when she still felt competitive with the male. "Behind this envy for the penis,"
Freud writes, "there comes to light the woman's hostile bitterness against the man,
which never completely disappears in the relations between the sexes, and which is
clearly indicated in the strivings and in the literary productions of the 'emancipated'
woman"[!] (Freud, ibid., 205).

42. "Above all the earrings are *the forbidden*, since unlike other objects, they do not

wholly belong to Louise. They are hers to use but not to dispose of; otherwise she could sell them openly" (Williams, *Max Ophuls and the Cinema of Desire*, 131).

43. Louise's look may indeed be a "look" as defined by Kaja Silverman in her analysis of Lacan's distinction between the look and the gaze. Thus, it is not the "phallus" that Louise wishes to appropriate but rather her own desire. See "Fassbinder and Lacan: A Reconsideration of Gaze, Look, and Image," in *Male Subjectivity at the Margins*, 125–56.

44. In *Adultery in the Novel* (Baltimore: Johns Hopkins University Press, 1979), Tony Tanner describes the marriage contract as fundamentally oppressive to the nineteenth-century woman because she is not an autonomous subject. The contract cannot, therefore, be voluntary. See also Anne Martin-Fugier, *La Bourgeoise* (Paris: Grasset/Figures, 1983), an informative study of the life of the upper-class Parisian woman at the turn of the twentieth century. In "L'Adultère" Martin-Fugier lists the tortuous double standards of the French legal system concerning male and female adultery. Until recently, the law favored the man as both plaintiff and accused (ibid., 106–107).

45. In "The Text's Heroine: A Feminist Critic and Her Fictions," *Diacritics* 12, no. 2 (Summer 1982): 48–53, Nancy K. Miller points out that Foucault's discussion of the effacement of the author (in "What Is an Author") "authorizes the 'end of woman' without consulting her." Miller reminds us that it matters who is speaking "to women who have lost and still routinely lose their proper name in marriage, and whose signature—not merely their voice—has not been worth the paper it was written on; women for whom the signature—by virtue of its power in the world of circulation—is *not* immaterial. Only those who have it can play with not having it." Miller urges us to recall the status of women's signatures in France before the legal reforms of 1965, when married women could not own property, exercise a profession, or open a bank account without her husband's permission. (Louise de Vilmorin wrote her novella and, of course, Ophuls made the film from that novella before the law of 1965 changed the legal status of women.)

46. Doane, in "The Dialogical Text," 231.

47. Ibid.

48. The logic of this veiled name is an instance of what Lacan calls the "ostrich policy (politic)," which refers to the ostrich's (*autruche*) well-known habit of burying its head in the sand, and to the "blindness" of the Austrian empire (*L'Autriche*), as well (an issue relevant to Ophuls' De Mayerling à Sarajevo). Lacan discusses the *politique de l'autruiche* in his "Seminaire sur 'La Lettre volée'" in *Ecrits* (Paris: Editions du Seuil, 1966), 1:24. The essay was also published as the "Seminar on 'The Purloined Letter,'" trans. Jeffrey Mehlman, *Yale French Studies* 48 (1972): 39–72, and reprinted, along with numerous other texts on Poe's story, in John P. Muller and William J. Richardson, eds., *The Purloined Poe: Lacan, Derrida, and Psychoanalytic Reading* (Baltimore: Johns Hopkins University Press, 1988).

49. I have already noted that Alan Williams, Robert Chamblee and Robin Wood discuss the dichotomy between the theatrical and military worlds in Ophuls' films. Immediately grasping the dialectical nature of the opposition, Robin Wood comments, during the course of his discussion of Ophuls in "Ewig hin der liebe Glück,"

that when he deals with military men, Ophuls' "stress is always on ceremony and performance, on the army as an extension of 'theatre,' the humanity of older and more high-ranking soldiers [Madame de . . .'s husband] in danger of becoming atrophied beneath their role" (224). One thinks of the role of the uniform as "masculine display" in Murnau's *The Last Laugh* (*Der Letzte Mann*, 1924): in that film the stripping of the uniform is tantamount to a social castration. Ophuls commented that his very first acting role, in Tolstoy's "The Living Corpse," was that of a military officer, for which he wore "a magnificent sea blue uniform, generously gold braided," as well as a monocle (Roth, *Max Ophüls par Max Ophüls*, 56–57).

50. The earrings will later function (as does the *key* to Fritz's apartment in *Liebelei*, which the Baron finds *chez* the Baronne) to incriminate the woman. Both objects are, at some point in each films, illicitly smuggled into the home of the cuckolded husband.

51. See Peter Lehman, "Texas 1868/America 1956: *The Searchers*," in Lehman, ed., *Close Viewings* (Tallahassee: Florida State University Press, 1990), 411–15, for a valuable discussion of the role of money as sign and the related marginality of the tradesman and the outsider in Ford's film.

52. Kaja Silverman, "Masochism and Subjectivity," *Framework* 12 (1980): 8. See also her "Historical Trauma and Male Subjectivity," in E. Ann Kaplan, ed., *Psychoanalysis in Cinema* (New York: Routledge/American Film Institute [AFI] Reader, 1990): 110–27.

53. A nice graphic match ends this scene: as the servants reach the top landing, a cut to another staircase shows Louise and her suitors descending.

54. In "The Dialogical Text," Doane describes this scene as one of the many examples of delaying tactics employed in the film which (like repetition itself) serve to hold back the narrative by concentrating on the time between major narrative events. Doane connects the phenomenon to Freud's notion of the death drive, where repetition, postponement, and desire are ultimately linked to the biological individual's impetus toward death (metaphorized by Ophuls as the end of the story). Ophuls' films emphasize the mechanisms for postponing those deaths that almost inevitably take place at the end of his films. Doane also discusses the "uncanny" nature of these repetitions (especially the repetition of exchanges), noting that in Freud's work the uncanny represents a "return of the repressed," but she does not elaborate upon what such a return might mean in the specific context of this film, as I attempt to do below.

55. As Alan Williams points out, M. Rémy's name is very close to the French past participle for the verb *remettre*, "to put back" (*Max Ophuls and the Cinema of Desire*, 110).

56. One is reminded, in the context of the woman's role as circulator of fictions, of the role of the fiction-producing prostitute in *Le Plaisir* (Rosa, also played by Danielle Darrieux), who tells a "story" (somewhere between a lie and a fiction) on a train, as does Lisa Berndle in *Letter from an Unknown Woman*.

57. For a discussion of the narcissistic woman's "unstable" sexuality see Sarah Kofman, *The Enigma of Woman*, trans. Catherine Porter (Ithaca, N.Y.: Cornell University Press, 1985). Gayatri Spivak, in "The Politics of Displacement," discusses the always already citational quality of the woman's orgasm: "women impersonate themselves as having an orgasm even at the time of orgasm" (170). See also Luce Irigaray, "Le marché des femmes," in *Ce Sexe qui n'en est pas un* (Paris: Editions de Minuit, 1977);

"Women on the Market," in *This Sex Which Is Not One*, trans. Catherine Porter with Carolyn Burke (Ithaca: Cornell University Press, 1985).

58. Sarah Kofman, "Ça Cloche," in Philippe Lacoue-Labarthe and Jean-Luc Nancy, eds., *Les Fins de l'homme: à partir du travail de Jacques Derrida*, Colloque de Cerisy, 1980 (Paris: Galilée, 1981).

59. In my discussion of masochism later in this chapter, I refer both to Freud's theories on masochism and to Giles Deleuze's reading of Sacher-Masoch in *Masochism: An Interpretation of Coldness and Cruelty*, trans. J. McNeil (New York: Faber and Faber, 1971), as well as to Gaylyn Studlar's reading of Deleuze in *In the Realm of Pleasure*. Deleuze's volume on Sacher-Masoch also contains a complete edition of Sacher-Masoch's *Venus in Furs*.

60. In *Speculum of the Other Woman*, trans. Gillian C. Gill (Ithaca, N.Y.: Cornell University Press, 1985), Luce Irigaray describes, from an economic perspective, this "very old point of contention, whose different transformations can be followed throughout the history of philosophy"—woman as "receptacle," "matrix"; man as endowed with the seed/capital that activates her reproductive/economic potential (18).

61. The confrontation between the Jewish jeweler in *Daniel Deronda* (1876) and the beautiful young woman repeats a common nineteenth- and early twentieth-century literary topos (the oxymoronic juxtaposition of the "horrifying" Jewish pawnbroker or moneylender and a "lovely" young woman who is in his clutches) that is strongly ironized not only by Eliot's text but also by such works as Dickens's *Our Mutual Friend* (1865). In Trollope's *The Eustace Diamonds* (1873), Lizzie Eustace tries to hold on to the "family jewels" given to her by her husband just before his death. Lizzie is, in fact, a slippery character, fickle and dishonest, who ends up wedded to a "greasy Jew." See also Edith Wharton's *The House of Mirth* (1905) for a similar constellation of characters. Striking a typically bizarre note, von Sternberg's 1941 *The Shanghai Gesture* depicts the usurer as a Chinese woman who owns a gambling house, and who is the mother of the woman she destroys.

62. Donati's role in this film is not a simple one. As Alan Williams points out (*Max Ophuls and the Cinema of Desire*, 119–20), Donati is a "bad good man"—that is, "a male character who appears "good" but is covertly identified as "bad." (Williams is citing the terminology of Martha Wolfenstein and Nathan Leites, *Movies: A Psychological Study* [Glencoe, Ill.: Free Press, 1950].) This dichotomy (often deconstructed by more recent feminist film criticism) may be related to that in Laura Mulvey's "Afterthoughts on 'Visual Pleasure and Narrative Cinema,'" in which she describes two psychic configurations typifying the psychosexual investment of the female spectator. These are, more or less, active and passive polarities of love: the woman as "womanly," displaying socially approved (and therefore pleasurable, in its way) submission to male law, or the woman as playful, in alliance with a masculine outlaw, through or with whom she relives her "masculine" competitive impulses, supposedly overcome during Oedipalization, although the process is rarely "complete." This situation is recognizable in a number of Ophuls' films, including *Madame de . . . .* Donati would, of course, represent the "outlaw" pursued by the woman, as does Stefan (Louis Jordan) in *Letter from an Unknown Woman*. The woman's refusal to give up the aggressive element of her sexuality, much too narrowly lexicalized as "masculine," will have tragic consequences in both films.

63. During another scene in a train station in *Letter from an Unknown Woman*, Lisa Berndle says, "I won't be the one who disappears."

64. As Gallagher remarks ("George Eliot and *Daniel Deronda*," 48), the casino is a place of pure exchange where one person's gain is another's loss in a form of non-productive money-getting, a "grotesquely passive war of all against all . . . [where] roulette winnings are a double sign of credit and debit." In this film, as in *Daniel Deronda*, such gambling is regarded as a frenetic and whorish relationship to the multitude, spelled out in baldly monetary terms. It is also, however, a place where the woman competes freely on the "marketplace," just as in *The Bartered Bride* Marie is shown playing and winning at the wheel of fortune, whereas in most of the film she will otherwise be a passive element in the financial arena.

65. André asks the jeweler to excuse the *étourderie* (foolishness) of his wife.

66. Sigmund Freud, "'The Uncanny,'" *SE* 17:248.

67. Ibid., 235.

68. Marcel Mauss, *The Gift: Forms and Functions of Exchange in Archaic Societies*, trans. Ian Cunnison (London: Cohen and West, 1954). For a less pessimistic view of gift-giving, see Lewis Hyde, *The Gift: Imagination and the Erotic Life of Property* (New York: Random House, 1979, 1983). In *Donner le temps* 1: *Fausse monnaie* (*Given Time*, vol. 1, *Counterfeit Money*, trans. Peggy Kamuf [Chicago: University of Chicago Press, 1992]), Jacques Derrida attempts to answer the question, "Is *giving* possible?" He describes the *circularity* of the gift that is "given back" (12): "Indeed, the metaphysics of the gift have, *quite rightly and justifiably*, treated together, as a system, the gift and the debt, the gift and the cycle of restitution, the gift and the loan, the gift and credit, the gift and the countergift." Derrida attempts to "depart" from this traditional economic circle: "For there to be a gift, *it is necessary* [*il faut*] that the donee not give back, amortize, reimburse, acquit himself, enter into a contract, and that he never have contracted a debt" (13). The "traditional" circle described by Derrida is one that Ophuls' characters almost never break out of, although they almost always try to.

69. "'Notre' mensonge, alors, c'était à moi que vous le faisiez." As I have noted, Louise desperately tries to keep the earrings in the maternal camp: when Donati discovers her lie, she says at first that it was her mother who had given them to her.

70. Ora Avni, "The Semiotics of Transactions: Mauss, Lacan and *The Three Musketeers*," *MLN* 100, no. 4 (1985): 728–57. I have anticipated my discussion of Avni's article by referring to Mauss's theories of gift-giving, which is one of the main topics of Avni's piece.

71. Lacan, "Seminar on 'The Purloined Letter.'"

72. Jacques Derrida, "The Purveyor of Truth," *Yale French Studies* 52 (1975): 89. The "idealizing" tendency discerned by Derrida is Lacan's, who maintains the inviolability of the letter, that it cannot be changed but transcends the situations in which it is found.

73. Doane comments, at the end of her essay on the film (in "The Dialogical Text," 257), that "as soon as the earrings achieve a stable signification, an anchoring, an investment—the subject for whom they signify dies. In the terms set by the text, then, signification is not a holding operation, a strategy for anchoring meaning, but a matter of movement."

74. See Keenan, "The Point Is to (Ex)Change It," 169, on the ghost as "the remnant that resists incorporation" in Marx's discussion of the commodity.

75. Vilmorin, *Madame de*, 61–62 (my translation).

76. In *Between Men*, Eve Sedgwick comments that William Makepeace Thackery's *Henry Esmond* (1852) ends with the "banishment of the woman in an 'affair of honor' between men" (146). She also points out that "homosocial desire" is fulfilled, in George Eliot's *Adam Bede* (1859), when the rivals for Hetty's love grieve over her death and resolve to try to be friends again. Vilmorin's *Madame de* is, I think, less critical of this tradition than is Ophuls' film.

77. This is the reading given the film by, among others, Marcel Ophuls, cited by Alan Williams in *Max Ophuls and the Cinema of Desire*, 130. Madame de . . . is a society woman "who has lived frivolously, who has never fathomed the depths of her own emotions, and who is suddenly confronted with the seriousness of real feeling, but by the time this happens, it is too late." The quotation is from an interview with James Blue, Rice University Media Center, Houston, March 7, 1973.

78. Michael Fried, *Absorption and Theatricality: Painting and Beholder in the Age of Diderot* (Berkeley: University of California Press, 1980).

79. Diderot, "Le Paradoxe du comédien" (1773–1778), cited by Fried (*Absorption and Theatricality*, 220–21n). The "Paradoxe" emphasizes the actor's imitation of a *model*, rather than his or her reliance on inner feeling to shape the performance, as some earlier writings by Diderot had urged. The main issue is the separation of the act of beholding from that of acting, so that the beholder need not feel conscious of his or her own situation. The actor *may*, according to some permutations of the schema Diderot sets up, be aware of himself or herself, but must not show it. Diderot is describing an aesthetic imperative to efface the very existence of the beholder for the actor, something effectively accomplished by the cinema in the twentieth century.

80. This transformation is also to be read in light of my comments above on mimetic violence as Girard describes it. The woman is moving away from her association with the dangerous image.

81. We might wonder if this privatization of our situation as beholders is not merely a way to increase our pleasure in looking. Louise is finally not "really" being beheld, the film now claims, although, of course, she still is.

82. Louise does specifically refer to herself as being "d'une coquetterie effroyable," in the first ball scene of the film. It is interesting to note that Diderot spoke harshly, in the *Salon de 1767* (see Fried, *Absorption and Theatricality*, 111), of a portrait that made him look like "une vieille coquette." By this he may have meant that he appeared too self-conscious.

83. See Alan Williams, "Reading Ophuls Reading Schnitzler," 2. La Rochefoucauld: "Our virtues are only our vices in disguise."

84. In *Max Ophuls and the Cinema of Desire*, Alan Williams also notes that the earrings have a "contractual" role in the marriage relationship between André and Louise (131).

85. Deleuze's theory in *Masochism* presents a view of masochism that claims a completely different etiology for the complex than that of sadism. Deleuze in this way

opposes Freud, who describes masochism and sadism as more or less reversible. Deleuze describes the masochistic contract between the masochist and the woman who is to abuse him as a procedure by means of which the masochist wards off the encroachments of reality into the world of phantasy and symbol, which the masochist uses to defy the superego. Such a masochistic contract *creates* the law, which can then be used to defy institutions associated with the patriarchal superego (and with sadism, according to Deleuze). This disavowal of reality has a specific goal, according to Deleuze: "Disavowal challenges the superego and entrusts the mother with the power to give birth to an 'ideal ego' which is pure, autonomous and independent of the superego" (110). Further page citations appear in the text.

86. Masochism involves an aestheticism that entails suspense, the "freezing" of a particular aesthetic moment. The model for this, in Sacher-Masoch, is the "amorous apprenticeship" of the masochist by means of moonlit vigils beneath a cold marble statue of the goddess of love. Similarly, in Ophuls' cinema, a statue or other kinds of artworks may function to dominate (amorously or in the manner of a superego) the spectator. The painted image of Lola Montès wrapped in furs and riding a sleigh is a double-edged one, demonstrating both her domination of the king of Bavaria and her temporary capture by him. Vienna is often depicted under a blanket of snow in Ophuls' films. The pioneering work on Deleuzian masochism and the cinema is, of course, Gaylyn Studlar's *In the Realm of Pleasure.*

87. On the subject of the subjugation of the *woman* to an unwanted contract see Juliet Flower MacCannell's analysis—appropriate to a study of Ophuls—of Stendhal's *Le Rouge et le Noir* (1830) in "Oedipus Wrecks: Lacan, Stendhal and the Narrative Form of the Real," in Robert Con Davis, ed., *Lacan and Narration: The Psychoanalytic Difference in Narrative Theory* (Baltimore: Johns Hopkins University Press, 1984). See also Leo Bersani, *A Future for Astyanax: Character and Desire in Literature* (Boston: Little, Brown, 1976) for related remarks on the role of the (vestigial) father in Stendhal.

88. Silverman has written extensively on the psychic and political implications of masochism (see especially *Male Subjectivity at the Margins*). In "Masochism and Subjectivity," Silverman claims that because we all wish to repeat the primary state of subjection to the nurturer, masochism is the preferred subject-position for men as for women. Indeed, she claims that the sadist's point of view would only be desirable as a position from which to observe and identify with the victim-masochist. Such an emptying out of the sadist's position seems problematic.

89. In "Masochism and the Perverse Pleasures of the Cinema," *Quarterly Review of Film Studies* (Fall 1984): 272, Studlar cites Janine Chasseguet-Smirgel, "Freud and Female Sexuality: The Consideration of Some Blind Spots in the Exploration of the Dark Continent," *International Journal of Psycho-Analysis* 57 (1976): 196.

90. See Freud, "A Child Is Being Beaten," *CP* 2:184–85. The Deleuzian masochistic scenario would dictate that, in this film, André is the means by which Fabrizio sacrifices himself to the woman. According to Studlar, masochism is always connected with death because the final union with the mother, which the masochistic scenario delays but to which it leads, means oblivion and death. It is this primacy of the woman that has attracted feminist critics to Deleuze's text.

91. For further discussion of the status of the pre-Oedipal mother in masochism, see chapter 4 of this volume, and Silverman's astute critique of the Kristevan notion of the pre-Oedipal in *The Acoustic Mirror* (99–120, 123–32). Through her look at the "negative Oedipal" phase, Silverman instead proposes a means of making contact with the "originary" power of the mother, without reducing her to preverbality (155–59). Silverman places these issues historically in her analyses of current women's cinema.

92. Louise's profound sense of loss at the end of the film is illuminated by Silverman's compelling study of female melancholia in *The Acoustic Mirror* (155–59). Silverman describes how Freud, Irigaray, and others have "connected melancholia with female subjectivity" (155). She focuses on the question of the female identity-formation, during which the girl is faced with the double bind of her need to identify with a mother who is culturally devalued: "the only identification with the mother which would be available to her would be one predicated upon lack, insufficiency, and self contempt." The negative Oedipal complex, with its positive investment in the mother, would be a way of eroding pervasive female melancholia. Louise's earrings symbolize both the loss of self-value, and, at the end of the film, her attempt to regain it by reinstating the ideal mother. See also Julia Kristeva, *Black Sun: Depression and Melancholia*, trans. Leon S. Roudiez (New York: Columbia University Press, 1989). In "Masochistic Performance and Female Subjectivity in *Letter from an Unknown Woman*," *Cinema Journal* 33, no. 3 (Spring 1994): 35–57, Gaylyn Studlar argues convincingly that Deleuzian masochism can offer valuable insights into female desire. For further discussion of her essay, see chapter 4 of the present volume.

93. This "reading of the pre-Oedipal through the Oedipal" is reminiscent of Christian Metz's argument concerning the (Lacanian) imaginary and symbolic registers in the cinema: although we may surrender to the former (or, rather, it may be revived by the cinematic image), we are always apprehending the imaginary as subjects who have undergone the transition to the symbolic. See Metz, *The Imaginary Signifier*, trans. Celia Britton (Bloomington: Indiana University Press, 1982).

94. See Octave Mannoni, *Clefs pour l'Imaginaire ou l'Autre Scène* (Paris: Editions du Seuil, 1969), 9–33. This volume also contains several other essays closely related to the problem of belief in the theater and, by extension, in the cinema.

95. One might also follow Derrida's description of the true gift—one that does not enter into the circuit of exchange—and say that the saint has permitted Louise to give her a gift, to break the pattern of exchange that destroyed the young woman's life.

96. That the woman would be more able to construct or sustain the fetish-object than are the men is ironic, in light of theories claiming that women are unable to fetishize because they are unable to distance themselves from the desired object. See, for example, Mary Ann Doane, "Film and the Masquerade: Theorizing the Female Spectator" in *Femmes Fatales*, 19. Another, more flexible, model for the way women look at women is currently being forged, particularly in the work of Judith Mayne, Chris Straayer, Judith Butler, and others.

97. Alan Williams, *Max Ophuls and the Cinema of Desire*, 135.

98. Catherine Stimpson, "Ad[d] Feminam: Women, Literature, and Society," in

Edward W. Said, ed. (with a preface by Said), *Selected Papers from the English Institute, Literature and Society*, (Baltimore: Johns Hopkins University Press, 1978), 9, cited in Miller, "The Text's Heroine," 51.

99. See Christopher Faulkner, "Theory and Practice of Film Reviewing in France in the 1930s: Eyes Right (Lucien Rabatet and Action Française 1936–1939)," *French Cultural Studies* 3 (1992): 133–55; and Simon P. Sibelman, "*Le Renouvellement Juif:* French Jewry on the Eve of the Centenary of the *Affaire Dreyfus*," in ibid., 263–76.

100. Simmel, *The Philosophy of Money*, 221.

101. The film also transformed the actor Herman Bouber, "an inveterate theater performer" who plays the protagonist Brand, into a "sensitive film actor." Kathinka Dittrich van Weringh, *Achter Het Doek: Duitse Emigranten in de Nederlandse Speelfilm in de Jaren Dertig* (Hooten [Weesp]: Wereldvenster/Unieboek, 1987), trans. as *Der Niederländische Spielfilm der dreißiger Jahre und die deutsche Filmemigration* (Amsterdam: Amsterdamer Publikationen zur Sprache und Literatur, Rodolpi, 1987), vol. 69:51. See also pp. 14, 32, 51–52, 87, 115 for discussion of Ophuls' film. Many thanks to Jean Goetinck for his translations of Dutch essays and articles on this film.

102. The only actual *film* director depicted in an Ophuls film is the one in *Die verliebte Firma*, although we see a producer in *La Signora di Tutti*. Contemporaneous Dutch critics noted, both admiringly and dismissively, the resemblance between the *Spieleiter* figure in this film and in Brecht's *Threepenny Opera* (1928), filmed by Pabst in 1931.

103. Thanks to the staff at the Amsterdam Filmmuseum for their translation of the film, including this rather obscure song.

104. Marc Shell, *Money, Language, and Thought*, 7.

105. Ibid., 19.

106. For an in-depth discussion of the "reciprocity of character and milieu," the atmospherics, the detailing of French working-class life, the notorious "fatalism," and other elements characterizing this period of French cinematic history, see Sandy Flitterman-Lewis, "Epstein in Context: French Film Production in the Thirties," in *To Desire Differently*, 169–87. The misty Parisian streets, the dance-hall atmosphere, the concern with the working class, and the seemingly inevitable doom of the heroine bring *Sans Lendemain* into the fold of Poetic Realism.

107. Robert Lang, "Lucia Harper's Crime: Family Melodrama and *Film Noir* in *The Reckless Moment*," *Literature/Film Quarterly* 17, no. 4 (1989): 262. See also William Paul's useful essay, "*The Reckless Moment*," in *Film Comment* 7, no. 2 (1971), a special issue on Ophuls; and Framework Editorial Board, "*The Reckless Moment*," *Framework* 4 (Autumn 1976): 17–24.

108. Barry Salt, *Film Style and Technology*, 371.

109. Paul, "*The Reckless Moment*," 65. Actually, a number of the European films of the thirties might be called genre pieces, though the fifties films are more difficult to classify as such.

110. Lang, "Lucia Harper's Crime," 263.

111. Paul, "*The Reckless Moment*," 66.

112. Lang, "Lucia Harper's Crime," 263–64.

113. Doane, *The Desire to Desire*, 92.

114. Donnelly is so described in Columbia's publicity release for the film, in the Museum of Modern Art's Stills Archive.

115. Lang, "Lucia Harper's Crime," 264.

116. Donnelly's ability to "see himself" in Lucia, as William Paul puts it ("*The Reckless Moment*," 66), is another of the many marks of his fatal femininity. Doane notes that Donnelly both seems to intercept the letters and phone calls addressed to Tom Harper (embodied by the daughter's clichéd love letters, which Donnelly reads to Lucia), and ends up "reduced to a son, paying homage to a maternal ideal" (*The Desire to Desire*, 94). Regarding Donnelly's feminization, Lutz Bacher informs me that Ophuls deliberately chose to linger on Mason's rather than Bennett's face in a pivotal phone conversation. See Bacher's discussion of the film in *Travails/Travelings*.

117. Lang, "Lucia Harper's Crime," 262.

118. Ibid., 265.

119. Robert Lang, personal communication, February 9, 1989. Mary Ann Doane describes Sybil as "the locus of otherness and an instinctive and specifiable form of maternal knowledge, she can distinguish between those who will ultimately protect the family structure [Donnelly] and those who threaten it [Nagel]. Sybil assumes a maternal function in relation to Mrs. Harper (constantly questioning her as to whether she's had enough to eat, etc.) and hence becomes a kind of meta-mother. . . . Perceived as closer to the earth and to nature and more fully excluded from the social contract than the white woman, the black woman personifies more explicitly the situation of the mother, and her presence, on the margins of the text, is a significant component of many maternal melodramas" (*The Desire to Desire*, 80). See also Lucy Fischer, "Three-Way Mirror: *Imitation of Life*," in Fischer, ed., *Imitation of Life* (New Brunswick, N.J.: Rutgers University Press, 1991), in which she discusses the *scarcity* of live-in housekeepers during the post–World War II period. Bea's relationship to Sybil seems particularly idyllic—from the white woman's perspective—if considered in the light of the historic disappearance of this kind of living situation.

120. Lang, "Lucia Harper's Crime," 264. See also Doane, *The Desire to Desire*, 85.

Three. Directorial Protocol and the Failed Sacrifice in
De Mayerlingà Sarajevo

1. The difficult production circumstances of *Sarajevo* affected the technical quality of the film, especially the editing and the mise-en-scène of the second half of the film. Although the war prevented thorough commercial exploitation, the film was released in May 1940 to critical praise. It also had a successful run in the United States, where it was widely distributed and favorably reviewed. See Claude Beylie, *Max Ophuls*, 67–71, and Lutz Bacher, "Max Ophuls's Universal-International Films" 1:44.

2. For a theoretical and historical perspective on Ophuls' tendency to use moving long takes in his films see Lutz Bacher, *The Mobile Mise en Scène: A Critical Analysis of the Theory and Practice of Long-Take Camera in the Narrative Film* (New York: Arno Press, 1978).

3. See Barry Salt, *Film Style and Technology*, 352. These figures do not include tracks with pans, which are comparable in number.

4. Of course, von Sternberg's cinematography and mise-en-scène share many of

these characteristics, although his interest in the close-up reveals a more developed fascination with the perverse than we find in Ophuls' work, where long shots are favored.

5. Salt notes in *Film Style and Technology* (352) that *Sarajevo*'s forty-eight pans, eighteen tracking shots, nineteen tracking shots with tilts or pans, and two crane shots are about average for a *musical* of the period, although these numbers are quite high for a nonmusical film.

6. The Emperor Franz Josef, whose reign over the Austro-Hungarian Empire lasted from 1848 until 1916, was Rudolf's father and the uncle of the Archduke Franz Ferdinand. Franz Josef had the misfortune of seeing four of his prospective successors die before him, three by violence. See Vladimir Dedijer, *The Road to Sarajevo* (New York: Simon and Schuster, 1966) for more information on the personality and family history of the Archduke Franz Ferdinand.

7. Richard Roud, *Max Ophuls: An Index*, 25. According to Roud, Ophuls worked with Litvak as a dialogue director at Ufa in 1930 (8).

8. It is likely that Ophuls did not completely finish the film himself, at least as it exists in the prints in distribution today. Jean-Pierre Jeancolas, *15 ans d'années trente* (Paris: Stock Cinéma, 1983), 284, believes that playwright André-Paul Antoine (who worked on this film and two others by Ophuls, and whose play, "L'Ennemie," was adapted by Ophuls) may have contributed to the end of the film. The print of *De Mayerling à Sarajevo* that I used was obtained from the French American Cultural Service and Education Aid (at 972 Fifth Avenue, New York, N.Y. 10021). Although that organization has now lost distribution rights to the film, it may be available for research purposes only. Thanks to Tag Gallagher for the use of his print of the film.

9. Billy Wilder, a friend of Ophuls' from the early days at Ufa, pays him and *Sarajevo* a strange homage in *Sunset Boulevard* (1950) by naming the von Stroheim character (a "retired" director) "Max von Mayerling."

10. Even in those films where kingship is at issue, the woman's role in constructing alternative institutions or in defying those that exist is vital. Bacher has discovered that Ophuls in fact wanted to shift *The Exile*'s story toward the woman's perspective—to look at the king's predicament from the point of view of the woman left behind when he ascends to the throne. See "Max Ophuls's Universal-International Films," 1:95.

11. Because I refer often to *The Exile* in this chapter, it seems appropriate to summarize that film's plot and its major thematic and stylistic concerns. The film is, of course, Ophuls' first in the United States and thus the first film he completed after *Sarajevo*. In his study of *The Exile*'s production circumstances and stylistic "solutions" to the staging and editing problems put before Ophuls, Bacher details Ophuls' struggles to push for his long-take style, while conforming to the budgetary constraints and stylistic conservatism of the newly merged and completely restructured Universal-International. (Ophuls was also signed with the Fairbanks Company, which produced the film for U-I). The result was "a film of striking contrasts" in staging and editing techniques, varying from "the most fluid and longest takes in the American films—some of his most audaciously original work—to conventional, sometimes nearly pedestrian solutions" (Bacher, "Max Ophuls's Universal-International Films" 1:85).

(Also, see 33–34 for a superbly articulated discussion of the technical characteristics of Ophuls' style.)

Douglas Fairbanks Jr., who stars in this swashbuckling homage to his father's career, recruited Ophuls as director, on the recommendation of Ophuls' friend Robert Siodmak. Although Fairbanks had owned the literary rights to Cosmo Hamilton's novel, *His Majesty the King*, "for more than eight years before the production of the film began" (88), and although various writers worked on the script before Ophuls became involved, Ophuls seems to have been crucial in shaping the final script (95). This is obvious in many of the film's details, and even in its larger structure. The story is that of the exiled King Charles II, son of the king beheaded in 1648. Bon vivant Charles II is wandering in Holland—a price on his head—with his loyal followers, when Cromwell's puritanical Roundheads discover his whereabouts. Rumors of a decisive action by Cromwell incite the itinerant king to take refuge on the farm of a young Dutchwoman, where he is the ideal guest. Not only does he plow and perform other chores, he also saves the farm from takeover by Katia's (Paule Croset) brother-in-law, to whom it is mortgaged. Naturally, Katia falls in love with Charles. Comic relief appears on the scene in the form of a false pretender to the throne, a phony King Charles, who earns a living by showing a wanted poster to the sympathetic Dutch. Pretender Dick Pinner (Robert Coote), a harmless chap, stays in the inn that Katia also runs. Another visitor is an old love of Charles's, played by Maria Montez. (Montez was imposed by Universal-International. Because of her salary, Bacher notes, there were not enough funds to make the film in color. Her appearance out of nowhere, descending in lace and silk from her carriage, ordering her servants around, and calling out "We stay!" anticipates *Lola Montès* almost eerily, considering the coincidence of name.) Meanwhile, Ingrahm is closing in on Charles. A dramatic recognition scene takes place in the inn, when Charles steps forward to defend Dick from Ingrahm ("Is your sight so distorted that in this poor craven clown you see a king?"). After a sword-fight, Charles escapes to a nearby windmill, with Katia in hot pursuit. At the windmill, the final showdown with Ingrahm takes place, and he is killed at the head of a stairway. News from England arrives, conveniently announcing that "the people" are crying out for Charles's return. Katia knows her day is done, and runs away. She is summoned before Charles as he makes ready to present himself to his courtiers, gathered in Holland to greet him. As the farewells are sounded, and an enormous wig is put on Charles's newly mature head, he steps out on the stairway to assume his place in the processional. The last image echoes the first in the film—a plaque with Charles's profile inscribed, along with the date of his assumption of the throne.

The film's extensive motif of barter and exchange is an obvious connection to the rest of Ophuls' film corpus. Indeed, our first sight of the king is a tricky close-up, where he is "gallantly" kissing a woman's hand. A pull-back reveals that he is actually trading a ring for provisions. Charles also meets Katia when he attempts to purchase flowers from her with English pennies—which spurs a conversation that attracts the attention of Roundhead spies. (The exiled king is no more discreet than Dick Pinner.) Charles is a bourgeois king, one who *uses* money instead of merely having his image struck on coins. Of course, the fact that there is a reward on his head makes Charles a potential object of barter himself. The mortgaged farm, and Charles's efforts to get Katia out of hock, are obviously the culmination of this important motif. Concerning the issue of "femininity," the king's feminization (and Katia's "masculin-ization") begins with his status as object of exchange. He is explicitly compared to Katia through dialogue in which they both refer to the "farms" they must manage, and when Katia speaks of her farm as her "kingdom." Staircases, often in combina-tion with complex, long-take camera work, are omnipresent in the film. Strikingly similar to the "needle and thread" sequence in *Lola Montès*, and to that in *Madame de* . . . when the jeweler sends his son back for his hat and cane (both of which take place on staircases), the first scene features the arrival of a wounded messenger to the exiles. His words, "News from home," are carried from voice to voice as they ascend the stairway and upper floors, while complex crossings and intercrossings of charac-ters on the stairway are observed by a camera that wanders through the banisters. Symmetry is achieved by the final staircase scene when Charles assumes his kingship (another ending, with Katia assuming Charles' abandoned throne, was also shot). Theatricality and kingship—vital themes in *Sarajevo*—are literally linked in the per-son of Dick the actor, whose presence functions to allow us to divide our ambivalent feelings toward the actor-king Fairbanks between the noble and ridiculous halves of his persona. The parallel between the two wanderers is marked in a number of ways, not least of all when Charles speaks the words cited above ("is your sight so distort-ed"), referring to "this craven clown"—obviously meant to be read as Dick, but curi-ously ambiguous because it is Charles who actually says it, equivocating the referent. And of course, as at the end of *Sarajevo*, the "bourgeois king" is finally forced to play his role to the bitter end. He wants to be recognized "for what he is"; but when, dressed as his own circulated image, Charles accomplishes this, he is eternally, onto-logically frozen as image—and finally as a plaque, like Louise de . . .'s.

12. René Girard, *Violence and the Sacred*, 146–47.

13. See, for example, Kaja Silverman, *The Acoustic Mirror*, 213–18, and "Masochis-tic Ecstasy and the Ruination of Masculinity in Fassbinder's Cinema," in *Male Subjec-tivity at the Margins*, 214–96.

14. See Robert A. Kann, *The Multinational Empire: Nationalism and National Reform in the Habsburg Monarchy, 1848–1918*, 2 vols. (New York: Columbia University Press, 1950), 2:188.

15. Dedijer, *The Road to Sarajevo*, 146.

16. Karl renounced the title of archduke and all other privileges of his rank. He lived in Munich as Ferdinand Burg—what greater symbolic allegiance could he have made to the bourgeois mode of life than to adopt such a name? This incident is vir-tually reproduced in *Sarajevo*, in which Franz Ferdinand has characteristics not only of Rudolf but of his more bourgeois younger brother as well. See Dedijer, *The Road to Sarajevo*, 100.

17. Kann, *The Multinational Empire* 2:187.

18. The Duchess of Hohenberg was actually the more fervent Catholic of the two. The Archduke was also decidedly anti-Semitic, associating the Jews with what he most detested about the Hungarian Magyars, with whom Austria shared imperial power. See Arthur J. May, *The Hapsburg Monarchy, 1867–1914* (Cambridge: Harvard Univer-sity Press, 1951), 157, and Dedijer, *The Road to Sarajevo*, 104–107.

19. The film struggles, toward the end, with the double-edged character of the sacrifice of the royal personage. Dedijer remarks that the revival of the "noble tyrannicide" during this period is relevant to the case of Franz Ferdinand. The assassin of the tyrant would, according to this logic, be in the position of self-sacrifice (*The Road to Sarajevo*, 22).

20. Sidney Bolkosky, "Arthur Schnitzler and the Fate of Mothers in Vienna," *Psychoanalytic Review* 73, no. 1 (Spring 1986): 13.

21. The family romance involves the child's first rejection of the family, in the guise of a pretense that he or she actually belongs to a more wealthy, sophisticated, or even royal family and has only been adopted by the "real" parents. See Sigmund Freud, "Family Romances," *SE* 9:237.

22. So, too, is the word "vergonga" repeated in *La Signora di Tutti* (1934).

23. In *The Bartered Bride* (1932), as well, the deal for Marie's marriage is forged at a table around which Kezal runs. Alan Williams describes "a complicated above-table tracking sequence–shot of a conversation among the officers [in *Liebelei*, 1932], which will reappear with little change in *La Tendre Ennemie* (1936) at a wedding banquet" ("Reading Ophüls Reading Schnitzler," 83). Although this scene in *Sarajevo* does not involve a tracking shot, there are nevertheless strong similarities with the scenes Williams describes, and with the "board of directors" scene in *La Signora di Tutti*.

24. As in *Signora*, a phone call during this all-male meeting interrupts the action and precedes an escape: in that film it is the woman's escape; in *Sarajevo* it is that of the royal couple.

25. In *The Film Encyclopedia* (New York: Perigree, 1979), Ephraim Katz notes that Ernst Lubitsch appeared in a series of film comedies as a young man. These comedies, made around 1913, emphasized Jewish humor. Interestingly, Lubitsch's very successful character was named "Meyer" (739). The name the Archduke takes when he is fleeing his role as heir apparent may have Jewish as well as "middle-class" connotations.

26. As Mary Ann Doane observes in "Female Spectatorship and Machines of Projection," camera movements can have the status of symptoms. In this case the symptoms are hysterical ones (*The Desire to Desire*, 155).

27. Girard borrows a page from Victor Turner, noting that "the individual who is 'in passage' is regarded in the same light as a criminal or as the victim of an epidemic: his mere physical presence increases the risk of violence" (*Violence and the Sacred*, 281). See the discussion, in chapter 2 (in the section "Spectacle, Debt, and Scandal") of the present volume, of the dangers involved in the woman's loss of virginity.

28. Freud, "The Taboo of Virginity" (1918), *SE* 11:205.

29. The "honorable bourgeois in glasses," as Beylie (*Max Ophuls*, 15) puts it, tells his friends in the billiard parlor that he already envisions the sign for his store: "Oppenheim and Son." Patrilinear succession in this scene has particular resonance for Ophuls, whose father was named Oppenheimer.

30. In "Ewig hin der Liebe Glück," Robin Wood compares this reframing of the scene from Sophie's point of view to similar changes of perspective in *Letter* and elsewhere. As is the case with Lisa Berndle, the shift from inner to outer point of view

emphasizes the character's "aloneness" in the scene (*Personal Views*, 227–28; also in Wexman, ed., *Letter from an Unknown Woman*, 220–36: citations are from the latter source).

31. Isabelle in this way resembles the madam of the brothel in *Le Plaisir*, who is equally forceful but more indulgent of pleasure.

32. See Susan Hayward, *French National Cinema* (London and New York: Routledge, 1993), 121.

33. Faulkner, "Theory and Practice of Film Reviewing in France in the 1930s," 144. Further page citations appear in the text.

34. See also Helmut G. Asper, "Antifascist und Kosmopolit oder ein unpolitischer Herr?" in *Max Ophüls*, a Special Issue of *Reihe Film* 42 (Munich: Carl Hanser Verlag, 1989): 73–108.

Four. Aggressivity, Image, and Sound in Letter from an Unknown Woman

1. The expressions in quotations are from Lutz Bacher, "Max Ophuls's Universal-International Films" 2:570, 572. As in his first volume on *The Exile* (1947), Bacher here presents a convincing case for Ophuls' continual effort toward longer, more mobile takes, fewer camera setups, master shots, and reverse-shot sequences—a departure from the reigning Hollywood style. This scene happens to be one in which Ophuls' "previsualization" (as indicated in the shooting script: see note 3, below) is actually less fluid and precisely timed than is the result in the final version of the film.

Most of the time, Ophuls was forced to compromise on his vision in the interests of time, money, and commercial appeal. In her introduction to *Letter from an Unknown Woman: Max Ophuls, Director*, Virginia Wright Wexman describes this scene as opening with a "bravura crane shot," during which Lisa remarks that "nothing happens by chance. Every moment is measured; every step is counted." Wexman aptly points to the seeming conflict between Ophuls' (apparently) "wandering" camera and Lisa's sense that all her movements are measured (which, of course, they are—by Ophuls, who stands in as fate in the film's production). I return below to Wexman's invaluable analysis of fate and chance, time and history. See Wexman, "The Transfiguration of History: Ophuls, Vienna, and *Letter from an Unknown Woman*," in Wexman, ed., *Letter from an Unknown Woman*, 10.

2. Here, again, is an important Ophulsian staircase: it is a place where the woman is presented and framed, but also one from which she may express her will, be it passionate or furious. Attempted rape (in *Le Plaisir*), suicide (in *Liebelei*, *La Signora di Tutti*, and *Le Plaisir*), humiliation (in *De Mayerling à Sarajevo*), and other extreme acts take place on staircases in Ophuls' cinema. *Letter* is characterized by the intensity of feminine fantasy that is concentrated on stairway scenes, as expressed in terms of the family romance (discussed below).

3. Quotes are corrected using the continuity script published in Wexman, ed., *Letter from an Unknown Woman*. Bacher ("Max Ophuls's Universal-International Films" 2:568–69) refers to these two gentlemen as "critics," as they are termed in the shooting script.

4. Alan Williams, *Max Ophuls and the Cinema of Desire*, 54.

5. See Howard Koch, *As Time Goes By* (New York: Harcourt Brace Jovanovich, 1979) for details of his treatment by the House Un-American Activities Committee (HUAC), and his subsequent blacklisting. Koch was actually subpoenaed to appear at the congressional hearings during the last week of *Letter*'s production (Bacher, "Max Ophuls's Universal-International Films" 2:622). Most of Koch's remarks on Ophuls in this book were reprinted as "Script to Screen with Max Ophuls," in Wexman, ed., *Letter from an Unknown Woman*, 197–203.

6. Koch, *As Time Goes By*, 157.

7. Bacher observes, however, that Ophuls "knew that the continuity structure of most of his scenes did not facilitate extensive tampering," so he succeeded for the most part in achieving his vision of the film ("Max Ophuls's Universal-International Films" 2:648).

8. See Bacher, "Max Ophuls's Universal-International Films" for details of the distribution process, see ibid., 2:660–63.

9. Jacqueline Rose, "Paranoia and the Film System," *Screen* 17, no. 4 (1976–77): 92, reprinted in *Sexuality in the Field of Vision*. Page references refer to the former version, and appear in the text.

10. Miriam Hansen's "Pleasure, Ambivalence, Identification," is an especially useful interrogation of the binary model underlying Rose's remarks. An insightful essay by Glynis Kinnan, "Masochism and Subjectivity in Max Ophuls' *Letter from an Unknown Woman*," presented at the annual conference of the Society for Cinema Studies, Washington, D.C., May 1990, also emphasizes the film's "play" with dualities and its eventual undoing of them, as in its "masculinization" of Lisa, and "feminization" of Stefan.

11. Catherine Clément, *Opera, or the Undoing of Women*, xv. She continues: "Music itself is treated much like Carmen: that which is alluring and seductive about it also threatens a world of rational order and control. It can be enjoyed and even adored in private, but in the public realm it must be knocked down to the Schenkerian graph so as to show who's boss."

12. In "Multiplicity in *Letter from an Unknown Woman*," in *Narrative Comprehension and Film*, Edward Branigan examines the status of image and voice in producing the film's narration. In his close analysis of the film's narration, Branigan demonstrates "how a text may exploit what is missing and undecidable about a narration in order to raise fundamental issues about character and spectator perception" (177). Branigan lists the various conceptions of narration underlying different interpretations of the film, including a number of essays not mentioned in my work on the film. Among those conceptions are those holding that "the voice-over is independent of the images"; that "the voice-over is past and subjective, and the images we see are determined/directed by Lisa"; and that "the voice-over is present and subjective, and the images we see are determined/directed by Stefan" (179). Also useful is what Branigan terms the "moderate" view of the film's narration promoted by George Wilson in *Narration in Light*. Wilson "permits *non*-character narrations to coexist with Lisa's voice-over so that the viewer is able to clearly see what Lisa cannot see, namely that she has an imperfect understanding of herself" (181). Thus, I believe that "non-character narrations"—such as that of the "authorial" agency—"are interacting with, or

supplementing, narrations attributed to Lisa and Stefan" (180). Branigan aptly remarks that "if the spectator wishes to understand the film's complexity as a 'woman's film' within a historical context of patriarchy, one will need to give up simple answers to the problems posed by its surface narrations, and instead search for opposing, masculine discourses interwoven with feminine discourses" (190).

13. Walter Benjamin, "The Storyteller," in *Illuminations*, ed. Hannah Arendt (New York: Schocken, 1969), 94.

14. See Stanley Cavell, "Psychoanalysis and Cinema: The Melodrama of the Unknown Woman," in Joseph H. Smith and William Kerrigan, eds., *Images in Our Souls: Cavell, Psychoanalysis, and Cinema* (Baltimore: Johns Hopkins University Press, 1987), 11.

15. Cavell ("Psychoanalysis and Cinema," 13) is citing Freud's *Three Essays on the Theory of Sexuality* (*SE* 7).

16. No doubt *Letter* has long functioned as a "queer" text, giving gay spectators the opportunity of reflecting on gender roles and desire as they play themselves out between same-sex partners. The work on this aspect of the film remains to be done.

17. Cavell, "Psychoanalysis and Cinema." It will become obvious why the presence of mother and children is important to the subtext of this and other "women's" films.

18. Ibid., 18, 19.

19. In E. T. A. Hoffman's "The Sandman," the male protagonist, Nathaniel, fears that the uncanny Sandman will pluck out his eyes. Nathaniel falls in love with a lifeless automaton, Olympia, and goes mad when (among other catastrophes) her eyes are pulled out. See Freud, "The Uncanny" (1919), *S.E.* 17:219–52.

20. As a mute, John links the film more firmly to the tradition of melodrama, as described by Peter Brooks in *The Melodramatic Imagination: Balzac, James, Melodrama, and the Mode of Excess* (New Haven: Yale University Press, 1976). The prototypical melodramatic heroine is literally or figuratively mute: she cannot speak to her own defense, declare her innocence in the face of false impugnings of her virtue. Tania Modleski points out that this inability to "express themselves, to make themselves known" also characterizes hysterics, in the Freudian definition (Modleski, "Time and Desire in the Woman's Film," in Wexman, ed. *Letter from an Unknown Woman*, 250). Lisa, however, is only *apparently* hysterical, as we shall see. For an account of the valet's role as author-surrogate, see George Wilson, "Max Ophuls' *Letter from an Unknown Woman*," in *Narration in Light*, 125. The positioning of the valet as author is also considered briefly by Modleski in "Time and Desire," 252.

21. See David Bordwell and Kristin Thompson, *Film Art: An Introduction*, (Madison: University of Wisconsin Press, 1979; 3d ed., 1990), 64–67.

22. See Stefan Zweig, *Letter from an Unknown Woman* (the novella, originally published in 1922), in Wexman, ed. *Letter from an Unknown Woman*, 162. The male protagonist's status as the implied author of this tale is altered by the change in his profession from writer in the novella to pianist in the film. However, as a musician, Stefan creates music that is integrated into the soundtrack. The irony of Stefan having been given his author's name is no less emphatic than is the same situation in *Madame de . . . .* "Writing" serves many purposes in Ophuls' films: often it is linked with femininity, with treacherous engulfment, with the deferral and inevitable arrival

of death (cf. Derrida). It also figures, however, as the instrument of male desire and of the erection of monuments.

23. Zweig, *Letter from an Unknown Woman*, 175 (in Wexman).

24. Wilson, *Narration in Light*, 109.

25. Ibid. Wilson goes on to say that "the shot is from below the level of the keyboard, emphasizing the downward force of his hands." Robert Chamblee correctly observes that "the framing of most of the shots of Stefan at the piano are identical to the compositions which Ophuls used for Alexander Brailowsky in his 1936 short film, *Valse Brillante de Chopin*. . . . Franz Planer shot both films" ("Max Ophuls' Viennese Trilogy," 167). See Branigan, "Multiplicity in *Letter from an Unknown Woman*," 189–90, in which he describes this low-angle shot as the first in a *hyperdiegetic* series ("a special case of implied authorial narration"). In the scene where Lisa kneels beside a piano as Stefan plays, we have a delayed reverse shot: Lisa *looking* at the piano, depicted in a high-angle shot that matches the earlier low-angle shot of the piano and Stefan's hands. Branigan demonstrates that "no simple ascription" (189) either of objectivity or of character subjectivity accounts for the way that these two shots are related. This is also true of the two staircase scenes, when Lisa moves from observer to observed. This ambiguity is, I believe, crucial in supporting Branigan's view that "the film oscillates between portraying Lisa as a distant, unacknowledged subject who is denied a legitimate position of view and portraying her as overpowered by an intimacy wholly defined by the male subject, Stefan" (184).

26. See Gaylyn Studlar, "Masochistic Performance and Female Subjectivity in *Letter from an Unknown Woman*," *Cinema Journal* 33, No. 3 (Spring), 6, on the film's masochistic suspension of narrative progress, its emphasis on waiting, which characterizes Deleuzian masochism. Further page references appear in the text.

27. Sigmund Freud, "Some Psychical Consequences of the Anatomical Distinction Between the Sexes" (1925), *SE* 19:252. There are few passages in Freud's work that have been so thoroughly taken apart by feminist critics as has this one. The epistemological basis one might imagine to provide the groundwork for such immediacy is, to say the least, difficult to fathom. And yet we see the effects in many works of this supposedly immediate recognition of her inferiority by the woman.

28. Williams provides a very complete technical description of the various kinds of dissolves linking the frame narrative with the framed one, and linking scene to scene within the framing device. From a complex "focus-dissolve" linking the first flashback with the frame narrative, the film moves to the use of straight dissolves. "A comparable progression of structured oppositions first separates and then slowly unites past and present in the film. The first flashback introduces most of these contrasts: night (in the "frame")/bright studio "day-light" (in the flashback), few people in the image/many people, middle-age/youth, comparative lack of motion/confused and abundant motion, silence (except for the narration)/talkiness, and so on." Williams points out that all of these "oppositions" are resolved as the film progresses, until "the final transition from flashback to Stefan's apartment in 'real' time matches two shots that are almost identical, of Lisa writing at a table, Stefan reading at a table—both alone, both about to die" (*Max Ophuls and the Cinema of Desire*, 57–58).

29. See Joan Riviere, "Womanliness as a Masquerade," *Psychoanalysis and Female*

Sexuality, ed. Hendrik M. Ruitenbeek (New Haven: College and University Press Services, 1966); Mary Ann Doane, "Film and the Masquerade: Theorizing the Female Spectator" and "Masquerade Reconsidered: Further Thoughts on the Female Spectator," in *Femmes Fatales*, 17–32, and 33–43.

30. According to Bacher, the last moment of this action was filmed but was then edited from the film ("Max Ophuls's Universal-International Films" 2:438). It seems to me that Lisa's separation from the other children is nevertheless emphasized by the scene, perhaps even more so since a conscious decision was made *not* to show that she eventually joined the other children. Someone sensed (rightly, I think) that the scene was stronger without such a closure. Wilson also comments on Lisa's partnerless state in *Narration in Light*, 110.

31. The provincial town where Lisa is temporarily exiled away from her lover is not Linz but Innsbruck in Zweig's novella. It is possible that the screenwriters are making a sly reference to the backwaters of Austria, with their pompous and sluggish military mentality, as the breeding ground of fascism, in that Linz is Adolf Hitler's "hometown" (while Innsbruck is Mozart's). Although Hitler was born in another town in the province of Upper Austria, Braunau am Inn, he was living in Linz with his family in 1907 when he left for Vienna to begin his political career. Howard Koch informed me, in a 1986 interview, that it was Ophuls who chose make this interesting change from novella to script.

32. In "Kiss Me Deadly: Heterosexual Romance," in *Shot/Countershot: Film Tradition and Women's Cinema* (Princeton: Princeton University Press, 1989), Lucy Fischer also describes Lisa as Stefan's "double," 96–97.

33. Mary Ann Doane, "Theorizing the Female Spectator," 25–26.

34. Bacher makes many interesting remarks on the way the film's camera movements and settings "comment visually on [the mother and daughter's] relationship" ("Max Ophuls's Universal-International Films" 2:404). Further page numbers appear in the text.

35. See, on this topic, Nancy Chodorow, *The Reproduction of Mothering*, which maps out the female infant's movement through and away from her investment in the mother. Freud, of course, compared woman's "unheimlich" sexuality—her continued libidinal interest in the mother and the woman's body—to the ruined matriarchy (Minos) hidden under a patriarchal civilization (Greece): "We have, after all, long given up any expectation of a neat parallelism between male and female sexual development. Our insight into this early, pre-Oedipus phase in the little girl's development comes to us as a surprise, comparable in another field with the effect of the discovery of the Minoan-Mycenean civilization behind that of Greece" (Freud, "Female Sexuality" [1931], in *CP* 5:252–72).

36. See Modleski, "Time and Desire," 259, 261.

37. Freud, "A Case of Paranoia Running Counter to the Psychoanalytic Theory of the Disease," *SE* 14:263–72.

38. Although Lisa sometimes has a "privileged" view of Stefan (from the stairway landings, etc.), which she seems to lose when she is drawn into his life by sleeping with him, there is a tendency in the film to cut down on the spying activities detailed in Zweig's novella. See also Bacher, "Max Ophuls's Universal-International Films" 2:421, and Zweig, *Letter from an Unknown Woman*, 143 (in Wexman), for production details.

39. For a discussion of Michel Chion's *La voix au cinéma* (Paris: Editions de l'Etoile, 1982), in which such notions as the "sonorous envelope" and "uterine night" are advanced, see Kaja Silverman, *The Acoustic Mirror*, 72–85.

40. See Mary Ann Doane, "The Voice in the Cinema: The Articulation of Body and Space," *Yale French Studies* 60 (1980): 33–49 (reprinted in Philip Rosen, ed., *Narrative, Apparatus, Ideology: A Film Theory Reader* [New York: Columbia University Press, 1986], 335–48), and "Ideology and the Practice of Sound Editing and Mixing," in Teresa de Lauretis and Stephen Heath, eds., *The Cinematic Apparatus*, (New York: St. Martin's, 1980).

41. See Claudia Gorbman's interesting analysis of classical cinema's "inaudible" sound/music tracks in her *Unheard Melodies: Narrative Film Music* (Bloomington: University of Indiana Press, 1987).

42. See Silverman, *The Acoustic Mirror*, 107–108, and passim.

43. Carol Flinn, "Sound, Woman, and the Bomb: Dismembering the 'Great Whatsit' in *Kiss Me Deadly*," *Wide Angle* 8, nos. 3–4 (1986): 123, 125.

44. Flinn, "The 'Problem' of Femininity in Theories of Film Music," *Screen* 27, no. 6 (November–December 1986): 72.

45. Latter quote is from Silverman, *The Acoustic Mirror*, 76. For a more general look at the way voice-over works in Hollywood cinema, see Sarah Kozloff, *Invisible Storytellers: Voice-Over Narration in American Fiction Film* (Berkeley: University of California Press, 1988). Silverman sees the voice-over narration as emanating from Stefan's auditory impulse—"her voice exists only in and through Stefan's consciousness." Silverman reasons that this must be the case since Lisa is actually dead during the unfolding of the narrative (Silverman, *The Acoustic Mirror*, 58). Although this makes sense, I believe it is impossible to assign any agency as the *one* desiring/producing entity in the film.

46. Gertrud Koch, "Die masochistische Lust am Verkennen: Zur Rolle der Hörwelt in Max Ophüls' Film *Letter from an Unknown Woman* (1948)," *Frauen und Film* 39 (1985): 67–72. Further page numbers appear in the text. The essay is reprinted, with a new foreword, as "Die masochistische Lust am Verkennen: Zur feministischen Rezeption von Max Ophüls," in Helmut G. Asper, ed., *Max Ophüls: Theater, Hörspiele, Filme*, 88–100

47. Both Wilson (*Narration in Light*, 115) and Fischer (*Shot/Countershot*, 98) comment on Lisa's status as "would-be religious acolyte" or "novitiate"—with Stefan as her object of worship.

48. See Branigan, "Multiplicity in *Letter from an Unknown Woman*," 36–37, where he describes a "flagrant disregard of space" in this scene—in which Lisa seems to leap thirty feet across the room from one shot to another. This is one of the many gaps in the narration that Branigan documents. In his discussion of the film's production, Bacher relates how this jump occurred: see Bacher, "Max Ophuls's Universal-International Films" 2:482–83.

49. In her introduction to *Letter from an Unknown Woman* ("The Transfiguration of History"), Wexman notes that Lisa is "confronted with her mother's prior claim to the possession of sexual power" (8).

50. Such a juxtaposition of scenes, in which one comments on or supplies material

"censored" from the other, is analyzed in Freud's *Interpretation of Dreams* (*SE* 4 and 5).

51. Modleski, "Time and Desire," 250.

52. Cavell ("Psychoanalysis and Cinema," 13) sees the "remarriage comedy" as "an enactment of what Freud calls, in *Three Essays on the Theory of Sexuality*, the diphasic character of human sexuality." Such films, of which *Letter* is a variant, "reveal the internal affinity of the phenomenon of nostalgia with the phenomenon of film as such."

53. This is the only interruption of the mobile long take comprising the scene. Bacher notes that this shot was added in postproduction, as a means of emphasizing Lisa's decision to run away. See "Max Ophuls's Universal-International Films" 2:443.

54. Freud, "Family Romances," *SE* 9:237 (emphasis added).

55. See Wilson, *Narration in Light*, 109, for an analysis of that scene's sexual content.

56. Bacher, "Max Ophuls's Universal-International Films" 2:464.

57. Ibid., 2:451.

58. See Wilson's remarks on the theatrical nature of this scene in *Narration in Light*, 111.

59. Riviere, "Womanliness as a Masquerade," 217.

60. Lynda Zwinger, "Blood Relations: Feminist Theory Meets the Uncanny Alien Bug Mother," *Hypatia* 7, no. 2 (Spring 1992): 77. Zwinger here makes reference to Julia Kristeva's notion of "abjection"—what one might call the introjected horror of the maternal which the subject seeks to expel and objectify—from *The Powers of Horror: An Essay on Abjection*, trans. Leon S. Roudiez (New York: Columbia University Press, 1982).

61. Carol Flinn ("The 'Problem' of Femininity in Theories of Film Music," 59) cites Guy Rosolato, "Répétitions," in *Musique en Jeu* 9 (November 1972): 39–40. The translation and parenthetical comment are Flinn's.

62. Studlar has observed that in the film "the time frame of the novella is moved back (from the late 1910s or early 1920s) to the more characteristically Ophulsian fin de siècle period," 59*n*49.

63. This view of masochism (that it is a "payment in advance") is Theodor Reik's formulation, taken up by Deleuze. I am not entirely convinced that masochism can be rendered as economically balanced as this though Studlar's reading of the film is very astute. See also Kaja Silverman, "Masochism and Male Subjectivity," *Camera Obscura* 17 (May 1988): 45 (reprinted in *Male Subjectivity at the Margins*), where she analyzes the masochist's "flight forward" toward punishment as described in Reik's *Masochism in Sex and Society*, trans. Margaret H. Beigel and Gertrud M. Kurth (New York: Farrar, Straus, 1941; rpt., New York: Grove Press, 1962).

64. Madame Spitzer's boutique, as the symbol of "specularity" par excellence in *Letter*, is one of the few places in this film where we see mirrors—usually a pervasive device in Ophuls' cinema.

65. As I have already indicated, this womanliness strikes one as a disguise, since this is the phase of Lisa's most "masculine" behavior, her return to the phallic phase as it is characterized by Laura Mulvey in "Afterthoughts on 'Visual Pleasure and Narrative Cinema.'" On the contrary, one must, I think, regard Lisa as living her "femininity" actively in these scenes.

66. The fact that Lisa seeks so strenuously *not* to show herself may seem to contradict the theatrical or performative characteristics of her masochistic pleasure. How-

ever, in the larger context of the film—in which she is "showing" her life to Stefan, Lisa is exhibitionistic in the way that women in the "sacrifice film" often are. Silverman notes that masochism almost always has what Reik termed a "demonstrative feature," demanding an audience, flaunting desire for punishment, etc. ("Masochism and Male Subjectivity," 43–51). Studlar notes that the "desexualized," "spiritual ecstasy" of the masochist—i.e., Lisa's virtually religious worship of Stefan—is one of the deceptive and perverse strategies used in masochism to "'give permission' to sexual desire and hide [ ] the provocative, aggressive act of the perversion" (44).

67. The appearance of an effigy of woman with child is an anticipation of the consequences of this scene: Lisa's pregnancy. The doubleness of Lisa's character—virgin and streetwalker (the idealized and the contemptible woman)—is also evident in this scene. Lisa's peculiar motivations and modus operandi with respect to motherhood both reinforce and challenge the "traditional" conception of that contradictory social role. The mother, like the bride, is a liminal figure, disturbing in that her carnal knowledge cannot be tidily separated from her socially necessary "purity." Through the image of the Virgin Mary, and the taboos she tacitly sanctions, Catholicism seeks to "isolate insistent ambiguity, persistent anomaly, recurrent liminality—anything our cultural, aesthetic, political taxonomies find it impossible to control by separation into categorically pure divisions." Zwinger ("Blood Relations," 79) refers here to Mary Douglas's definition of the taboo in *Purity and Danger: An Analysis of Concepts of Pollution and Taboo* (London: Routledge and Kegan Paul, 1966).

68. The street singers are, according to remarks made by filmmaker Paul Glabicki, singing an air from Strauss's "War Between Men and Women." Neither Lisa nor Stefan enjoy their rendition of the tune, which haunts this, their one night together. See Branigan, "Multiplicity in *Letter from an Unknown Woman*," for a description of the "cheat cut" that occurs when Stefan begins to walk toward Lisa. "A match on action covers a large gap in space when we see Lisa in the background from over his shoulder as he draws near her" (59*n*43).

69. See Tania Modleski, *Loving with a Vengeance: Mass-Produced Fantasies for Women* (Hamden: N.J.: Archon Books, 1982), for an in-depth discussion of "the mystery of masculine motives" (39)—the woman's need to constitute the man as an object of investigation in the Gothic melodrama and in most women's popular fiction, so that she may interpret his behavior as she wishes.

70. Mary Ann Doane, "*Gilda*: Epistemology as Striptease," in *Femmes Fatales*, 102.

71. Williams cites V. F. Perkins ("*Letter from an Unknown Woman*," lecture delivered at the Summer Institute of Media Study, State University of New York at Buffalo, August 15, 1975) on this point in *Max Ophuls and the Cinema of Desire*, 47. Perkins's essay later appeared, with the same title, in *Movie* 29–30 (Summer 1982): 61–72.

72. In *Jacques Lacan and the Philosophy of Psychoanalysis* (Urbana: University of Illinois Press, 1986), Ellie Ragland-Sullivan makes a comment concerning the male (and female) hostility to the female image whose importance, which has been mentioned many times above and will be considered further below, can scarcely be exaggerated: "The long-established structure of patriarchy perversely blames woman for the loss that occurred at the father's behest. Because birth and the early care network are identified with the female gender, the painful dissolution of the nurturing bond by

castration leads to permanent ambivalence and profundity around the idea of the m(Other). . . . The primordial m(Other) at the mirror-stage, structural base of the ego becomes confused with woman; and women are consequently seen as secretly powerful. The mother within both sexes therefore implies an unseen dominance. . . . The primordial corporal-maternal effects of the mirror-stage consequently haunt males and females with an evanescent female image in the internal mirror forever" (295, 297, 299).

73. Wexman, "The Transfiguration of History," 6, cites Bakhtin's *The Dialogic Imagination*, 250.

74. Modleski, in "Time and Desire," follows Kristeva in describing this conception of time as "feminine." That the circle formed by the flashback structure of the film might be characterized as "feminine" is an intriguing idea, especially considering the relationship between femininity and the cycle of exchange often present in Ophuls' films. In "Time and Desire" Modleski asserts that women enjoy the kind of repetition to be found in melodrama, while Stefan's memory lapse with respect to Lisa is to be taken as evidence that his relationship to temporal events is flawed. Even when he finally realizes what is happening to him, he can only internalize the object as "lost" and live it as a kind of castration to be mourned. The man repeats himself unconsciously and, like the hysteric, suffers from his reminiscences, while the woman— who, contrary to stereotypes, is thus antihysterical—evokes them gladly. Modleski's position on the moral and psychological triumph of the female protagonist in this film opposes the darker view of Stephen Heath ("The Question Oshima") and, by extension, that of Teresa de Lauretis in *Alice Doesn't: Feminism, Semiotics, Cinema*, 199. In *The Desire to Desire*, Mary Ann Doane describes how, in Freud's model of female hysteria, "The woman's assumption of the position of narrator is thus constituted as therapeutic, an essential component of her cure. . . . the woman must channel all of her energy into narrativity and thus exhaust the other more aggressive or 'unpleasant' tendencies she might possess," p. 53. In *Letter* the woman's narrative also acts as the *means* of expressing the aggressive tendency.

75. Freud, "Family Romances," *SE* 9:238. Modleski discusses the film's delineation of "true" and "false" fathers—a reading that astutely picks up on the Ophulsian subtext. The false father, Stefan, who fills in for the idealized parent in the family romance, is nevertheless a "true" one. See "Time and Desire," 259.

76. As previously indicated, the signing of documents is a pervasive theme in Ophuls' films, one that is usually associated with the tying of a more or less unwilling individual to an oppressive contract.

77. See René Girard, "Triangular Desire," in *Deceit, Desire and the Novel: Self and Other in Literary Structure*, trans. Yvonne Freccero (Baltimore: Johns Hopkins University Press, 1961, 1965), 15–16.

78. This doubling by way of hats also serves to connect Lisa's romance to that between her mother and her stepfather.

79. The figure looks like Schubert. Bacher ("Max Ophuls's Universal-International Films" 2:649) notes that a scene in which Lisa was to have visited the Schubert Museum (during her "preparation for Stefan" montage) was eliminated during production.

80. In "Photo-gravure: Death, Photography, and Film Narrative," *Wide Angle* 9, no. 1 (1987), Garrett Stewart discusses the still images in *Letter from an Unknown Woman* as part of "Ophuls' cross-referencing of mortality and textuality," which prompts "a pensive meditation on the difference between the two visual media with which it is concerned" (17). Stewart refers to Barthes' notion of photography as canceling life by capture and notes that the photos in *Letter* "clarify death's role as narrative motivation for photographic phenomenology within film discourse" (14). The photograph is always, in a sense, "dead on arrival" and carries with it "almost a contagion of death" (15).

81. Ragland-Sullivan, *Jacques Lacan*, 293.

82. See Hansen, *Babel and Babylon*. As Alexander Doty puts it in *Making Things Perfectly Queer*, there seems to be "something queer here": as the "binaries" are broken down in Ophuls' (and Valentino's) films, diverse spectatorial practices become available, challenging the hegemony of the heterocentrist position. Certainly, as noted earlier, aspects of Lisa's relationship to Stefan encourage exploration of male-male and female-female desire. Doty describes Ophuls as having a "particularly meaningful place within queer cultural history." Doty, "Whose Text Is It Anyway?" *Making Things Perfectly Queer: Interpreting Mass Culture* (Minneapolis: University of Minnesota Press, 1993), 24.

83. See Molly Haskell, *From Reverence to Rape: The Treatment of Women in the Movies* (New York: Holt, 1974), as well as Gledhill, ed., *Home Is Where the Heart Is*, for a consideration of women's films as middle-class phenomena.

84. Since this passage was originally written, Gaylyn Studlar's *In the Realm of Pleasure* has powerfully demonstrated the importance of Dietrich's conflation of the maternal and the politically potent aspects of her character in von Sternberg's films. Studlar makes a convincing case, as well, for a reading of Ophuls' films according to Charles Sanders Peirce's conception of the "nonlinguistic sign system" in his non-Saussurian semiotics. Studlar suggests that Ophuls might fruitfully be regarded as an "iconic" filmmaker—that is, one who is less concerned with an "indexical" relationship to reality in his films than he is with a more self-referential aesthetics. Thus, for Ophuls as for von Sternberg, "The reality of imagination, of sign creation, is exalted over any presupposed objective reality" (92). Studlar appropriately associates this reveling in the sign as self-contained aesthetic realm with what Deleuze calls the masochist's "supersensual heterocosm," the world he creates for his own pleasure. Obviously, Studlar's more recent piece, "Masochistic Performance and Female Subjectivity," is an even greater contribution to Ophuls studies.

85. Williams, *Max Ophuls and the Cinema Desire*, 50. In "Max Ophuls' Viennese Trilogy," 201–202, Chamblee challenges some aspects of Williams's description, but his objections do not strike at the heart of the argument. This scene in *Letter* is, of course, one of a host of "voyages" made by Ophulsian lovers. Mary Ann Doane (*Femmes Fatales*, 290n2) points to the similarity between *Letter*'s imaginary railroad and *Hale's Tours and Scenes of the World*, a form of early cinema, that took the guise of moving railway cars. The show ran in the United States from about 1904 to 1906.

One of Ophuls' most striking "voyages," combining both the visual and the aural components of fantasy (in that it depicts the couple's presence at an imaginary opera), can be found in the much-maligned *Yoshiwara* (1937). While this is certainly not among Ophuls' best films—being rather like a dime-store Mizoguchi—it deserves our attention for several reasons. The film, shot by Eugen Schüfftan and adapted (according to Beylie) by Ophuls, Jacques Companeez, Arnold Lippschutz, and Wolfgang Wilhelm from Maurice Dekobra's screenplay of his own novel, is the first of two films Ophuls made starring Pierre-Richard Willm. (According to the video version of the film in my possession, the film's alternate title is *Kohana*, and J. Dapoigny assisted with the adaptation.) Willm plays Lt. Serge Polenoff, a Russian officer stationed in Japan just before the Sino-Japanese War, who falls in love with a young geisha forced to prostitute herself in the ill-famed Yoshiwara district of Tokyo. (The nightclub in the 1926 *Metropolis*, in which the "bad" Maria dances her wicked dance, is also called the "Yoshiwara.") The young woman, Kohana, played by Michiko Tanaka, is sold to the brothel to save her little brother from losing his home and family honor (figured as a large sword) after their ruined parents kill themselves. As the opening title puts it: "Often [the geishas'] presence behind these walls was nothing other than a nobly accepted sacrifice." (Once again, Haskell's breakdown of the "sacrifice" film in *From Reverence to Rape* is useful here.) The form of sacrifice, made to preserve a young boy's home, is much like that in *Sans Lendemain* (1939). Indeed, the acting style of the two films also has much in common—and is characteristic of Ophuls' films of the late 1930s. (As Thomas Elsaesser puts it, "The German directors used their French [and, one assumes, Japanese] players slightly against type, to achieve performances that were anti-psychological and anti-naturalistic" "Pathos and Leave-taking: The German Emigrés in Paris During the 1930s," *Sight and Sound* 53 [Autumn 1984]: 279.) *Yoshiwara* contains many fascinating vignettes and occasionally makes gestures toward a technical sophistication that ultimately founders. The film suffers from pasteboard japonisme, von Sternbergian orientalism, and a heavy hand with the fog machine, but several of its rather remarkable scenes are relevant to the issues at hand in *Letter from an Unknown Woman*, and certainly in other films by Ophuls.

What is most intriguing about *Yoshiwara* is the barely submerged masochistic scenario, a rather more emphatic one than is found in most of Ophuls' films. A "coolie" (played by Sessue Hayakawa), who is also a painter, falls in love with Kohana as he takes her to the brothel. He attempts to buy his "mistress" from bondage but doesn't have enough money, and soon the Russian officer Serge comes along with superior currency. The brothel keeper is happy to accept Serge's money, even if it is only to keep the shy geisha pure. She faints when being told of her duties: "One clap means bring tea. . . . Four claps means remove the geisha's kimono." When men from the newly arrived Russian ship hit the Yoshiwara district, Kohana is attacked by her first client, and she tries to kill herself with his rapier. In an unusual shot (which has a hand-held quality), the camera pans and tracks along with the ship's officer, Serge, as he rushes to rescue the beautiful woman, whom he knows only from a portrait drawn by the "coolie" who had drawn his rickshaw. The camera wavers as it tracks forward to a close-up of the male attacker (the film has more expressive close-ups than do most of Ophuls' films). Tall, blonde, and disinterested, Serge will, like Stefan in *Letter*, remain to die because of his love for a self-sacrificing woman. Kohana falls in love with her savior, and a triangle is formed in which Kohana is the exacting though

humiliated mistress, Serge the "beautiful Greek" as described by Sacher-Masoch, who
is both detested and admired by the cringing "coolie," but who is both master and
slave to the woman. An espionage subplot pits the "coolie" and the officer against
one another. Kohana accidentally ends up with a document making her a cocon-
spirator with Serge in spying on the Japanese for China. She is judged and—as in von
Sternberg's *Dishonored* (1931), minus the lipstick—put before the firing squad. Serge
dies of his wounds at the same time, falling to the floor along with the candle he lit
for Kohana, in the Russian chapel where they had performed a symbolic wedding
ceremony.

Earlier in the film, Serge and Kohana share a moment of epiphany that curiously
brings together several of the "nodal points" found in other Ophuls films. The couple stands before a full-length mirror; Kohana has put on the Western clothing Serge
gave her and is (like Sophie in *Sarajevo*) fascinated by her own virginal image—a virginity she is about to lose. To mark the occasion, Serge takes Kohana through a series
of imaginary voyages, perhaps even more intense than the imaginary train ride in *Letter*. He suggests they go to the opera. "The opera? What's that?" she replies. (Aha, a
virgin to opera, as well!) Little does she know that she is living out a version of
Madame Butterfly, another turn-of-the-century tale of West and East: "For lack of anything better to do, [Lieutenant Pinkerton] plays at marrying a very young girl, named
Butterfly, who is fifteen years old and has had to work as a geisha ever since her father,
a high official of the Nippon Empire, committed suicide on the orders of the Emper-
or" (Clément, *Opera, or the Undoing of Women*, 44). The deeply operatic structure of
Ophuls' stories of women emerges. Unlike Butterfly, Kohana is not even allowed to
die by her own hand. But no, it is not *Butterfly* being presented by Serge to Kohana,
with the magic of cinema. Rather, an air from *Fidelio*, the opera appropriately chosen
for this scene, is played as Serge teaches her to applaud—to clap without prostituting
oneself? But now Serge takes her chair and fetches a fur blanket—to be seen again in
Lola Montès—from the next room, transforming the table into a sled being pulled
through St. Petersburg as its scenery unfolds behind them. Serge points out the sites
of the city (just as Stefan in *Letter* shows the places he knows to Lisa). Finally, the humble table becomes a plank for a feast, as the camera dissolves from the bare wood to
a huge fish and caviar, with Russian sword dancers whirling around it. Opera, carriage ride, imaginary voyage, restaurant—each is an apparatus of seduction that
Ophulsian men bring forth to celebrate sexual consummation.

86. As I argue with regard to *Madame de . . .*, Studlar observes ("Masochistic Performance," 46) that the obsession with frozen vignettes and repetitions found in *Letter* is characteristic of Deleuzian masochism.

87. This is just one more of the many means of conveyance that seem to fascinate
Ophuls. The old couple's commentary on the events resembles that of Lola Montès's
maid and carriage driver.

88. This might be described as a "primal scene" in that it is the moment when the
child seems for the first time to be aware of the sexual contact between its parents.
Freud's most complete description of the function of the primal scene is found in the
"Wolf Man" case, that is, in *From the History of an Infantile Neurosis*, especially the sec-
tions entitled "The Dream and the Primal Scene" and "A Few Discussions" (*SE*

17:29–60). These passages describe the deferred effects of the Wolf Man's *Urzene,* his first sighting of the parents' copulation, a scene that is understood only *retrospectively* (*nachträglich, en après coup*), at a later age, when a second scene revives the memory traces from the first.

89. Williams, *Max Ophuls and the Cinema of Desire,* 62.

90. Ibid., 60–63.

91. Ibid., 63.

92. Ibid., 50.

93. The "fort-da" game is the one played by Freud's grandson in what Freud described as an effort to attain symbolic mastery over his mother's comings and goings. The game opened the window on what Freud was to call the repetition compulsion, ultimately propped on the virtually inaccessible "death drive." See *Beyond the Pleasurable Principle* (*SE* 18).

94. Howard Koch notes that Ophuls suggested that the all-male orchestra be changed to women musicians, who "were often employed in Viennese amusement parks" (*As Time Goes By,* 159). I assume that if it had suited his purposes, Ophuls would have retained the "conventional male orchestra" Koch initially sketched in.

95. Freud, "Family Romances," *SE* 9:239.

96. Wexman, "The Transfiguration of History," 7. Additional page numbers appear in the text.

97. Curtains appear at a number of important junctures in the film, notably, in the restaurant scene; during the imaginary train ride; at Madame Spitzer's shop; and at Stefan Jr.'s birth. The effect is often a theatrical one, with overtones of the tension between public and private spheres mentioned above, as well as of more overtly sexual implications. Stefan Jr.'s birth date is problematic, by the way: "The birth data in the script, 'BORN MARCH 12, 1901,' as Renata Lenart pointed out to this writer and to Ophuls on the set before he shot the scene, were written with obvious disregard of the human gestation period in view of the fact that Stefan Jr. was conceived in the winter" (Bacher, "Max Ophuls's Universal-International Films" 2:474).

98. Raymond Bellour comments upon these very photos, using language that recalls Cavell's formulations: "What purpose do these photographs serve? A narrative one, to be sure. In the very next sequence, we pick up on the heroine and her son in the middle of everyday life. The photos act as a hinge between the two major parts of the story; they express the passage of time. Yet, these photographs also seem to resist time. It isn't only that they symbolize it, as one might believe. They in fact open up another time: a past of the past, a second, different time. Thus they freeze for one instant the time of the film, and uprooting us from the film's unfolding, situate us in relation to it. . . . Finally the hero himself confirms the fascination of the photograph in its ability to rivet the gaze. . . . What the photos bear witness to upsets him; he is, at the very thought of what they suggest, petrified" (Bellour, "The Pensive Spectator," *Wide Angle* 9, no. 1 [1987]: 7). These remarks match my own sense that there is something petrifying for Stefan in the sight of this, his own surrogate image, captured in the photograph that also (we will learn) spells the child's death.

99. In Zweig's novella Lisa becomes a high-class prostitute at this point. Many reasons for this change are possible, including the pressures of the Production Code and

those resulting from Fontaine's marriage to William Dozier. There are also thematic concerns that might have pushed Ophuls toward this solution, as is evident in his treatment of similar situations in his other films. It is only within the context of marriage that the problems faced by the "honorable" man (Stauffer) can be examined as Ophuls wants.

100. Williams notes that Stauffer looks as though he is in fact strangling her with the necklace (*Max Ophuls and the Cinema of Desire*, 59–60).

101. Compare this with the scene in *Lola Montès* in which Lola seduces (before the second act of a play begins) the man who was to have become her stepfather.

102. Chamblee notes that "Ophuls has taken unusual dramatic license with this segment of *The Magic Flute*, rearranging the order so that Papageno sings of his desire to be married at the very time when Lisa's marriage is in peril. [The aria] falls, in fact, slightly before the opera's long finale begins." Chamblee also observes that (as mentioned) Ophuls *never shows stage performances in progress*, though he offers no interpretation of this fact. The effect, I believe, is to emphasize the "performances" of the spectators. See "Max Ophuls' Viennese Trilogy," 221.

103. Modleski, "Time and Desire," 257 (further page numbers appear in the text). Bacher strenuously objects to Modleski's use of this insert as supporting evidence for Ophuls' intended "feminization" of Stefan at this point in the film ("Max Ophuls's Universal-International Films" 2:37). Ophuls himself was actually opposed to putting such close-ups in the film: the shot was "introduced as an added scene during Ophuls' absence late in post-production"—although, as Branigan points out, all the shots in the film were directed by Ophuls (*Narrative Comprehension and Film*, 276n49). A number of fill-in shots were filmed by Ophuls *in one day* under factory-like circumstances upon his return, Bacher has observed. Ergo Stefan's vague expression and the nondescript background. These shots do stand out in contrast to the usual distance kept from the actors by Ophuls' (Planer's) camera. I believe that there is a way out of the apparent impasse indicated by Modleski's and Bacher's disagreement—a disagreement that raises important issues about authorial intention and historical documentation versus "textual analysis," as it is sometimes called. Perhaps Ophuls objected to this kind of close-up because it states the underlying tensions of the film too blatantly, just as the final recollection (visual "capture") of Lisa by Stefan was too exact, too explicit for Ophuls' taste. Ophuls' ambivalent attitude toward using the camera to capture human images would surely have made such crude Hollywoodian stylistic devices distasteful to him. And yet these close-up views of Stefan and Lisa achieve what Ophuls also expresses otherwise: the images loom forth as prey or predator, to take or to be taken, pinned up like captured butterflies and yet somehow ominous. Certainly more needs to be said about conflicts within the industry over what was expected by the anticipated audience. See also Studlar, "Masochistic Performance and Female Subjectivity," 44–45.

104. Fischer (*Shot/Countershot*, 96–97) does not believe that Stefan's "femininity" *undermines* him, as Modleski claims, but, rather, simply makes it easier for the woman to narcissistically "double" him—thus losing herself in the process.

105. There are also statues of sphinxes outside the home of M. and Mme de . . . .

106. Clément, *Opera or the Undoing of Women*, 4.

107. Williams, *Max Ophuls and the Cinema of Desire*, 55.

108. Stauffer meets his wife who left the opera early, just as the Baron in *Liebelei* almost catches *his* wife with her lover after the latter leaves the opera early to meet the Baroness.

109. Hilary Radner states that "as long as [Lisa] is content to remain unknown (and, thus, the image of her husband's wealth, and the image of the feminine as desire), stability is maintained. Once she asserts her desire and acts upon it (mimicking Stefan's actions in the initial seduction), the social fabric is torn apart. The fiction of paternity (Lisa's husband had adopted Stefan's son) and family collapse. Death and chaos ensue." Radner, "*Lola Montès* and Cindy Sherman: Women and Representation" (Paper presented at the Society for Cinema Studies Annual Conference, New Orleans, May 1986), 6.

110. Thus there is a strong similarity between this scene and that with the "aimless" old soldier as well as with the scene where the couple first meets. Bacher ("Max Ophuls's Universal-International Films" 2:594) describes how Lisa is trying to repeat that first meeting, going through each of its "stations." By this I assume he is referring to the Stations of the Cross, which are part of the Catholic ritual.

111. Bacher (ibid., 2:639–40) describes this as one of the "impressionistic" scenes shot late in production as an experiment on Ophuls' part, despite studio resistance. It is not a "typical" Ophulsian setup, but it is very effective just the same.

112. Bacher describes Ophuls, Dozier, and Houseman as engaging in a very complex series of negotiations (among themselves, with the studio, and with Production Code administrator Joseph Breen's office) concerning the ending of the film. Ophuls resisted the more complete recognition of Lisa by Stefan which the studio wished to impose in order to solidify the causality leading to the duel. He wanted, instead, to remain more faithful to Zweig's novella, in which R.'s "stirrings of memory . . . would not fuse into a picture" (Zweig, *Letter from an Unknown Woman*, 185 [in Wexman]). However, his resistance seems to have diminished during postproduction, and he, too, came around "to wanting a strong dramatic resolution of the plot and consequently was now interested in revising scenes to enhance Stefan's remembering Lisa toward that end" (Bacher, "Max Ophuls's Universal-International Films" 2:623–24, 629).

113. Jacques Derrida, *La Carte Postale: de Socrate à Freud et au-delà* (Paris: Flammarion, 1980), 127. I consulted Alan Bass's translation, *The Post Card* (Chicago: University of Chicago Press, 1987), 115, and adopted several key words from his translation of the passage. Thanks to Catherine Macksey for her advice on the translation of this paragraph.

114. Wexman, "The Transfiguration of History," 11, cites George Steiner, "Dream City," *New Yorker*, January 28, 1985: 92.

115. Wexman, ibid., 12, cites Max Ophuls, "Der Kampf," in Herbert Kline, ed., *New Theatre and Film, 1934–1937: An Anthology* (New York: Harcourt, Brace, Jovanovich, 1985), 342.

116. See Modleski, *Loving with a Vengeance*, for such translations of apparent masochism as anger, as well as "Time and Desire in the Woman's Film"; and Silverman, "Masochism and Male Subjectivity," 189–90, where she cites Reik, *Masochism in Sex and Society*, 216. One might also consider whether Silverman's discussion of the

"look" in opposition to the "gaze" (the look being less "phallic" and thus capable of expressing nonoppressive desire) in "Fassbinder and Lacan," 125–56, is relevant to reading *Letter from an Unknown Woman.*

117. Wexman, "The Transfiguration of History," 11–12.

118. Ophuls in fact continued to adore his native tongue to his last days, writing poetry in German until the end. Thanks to Lutz Bacher for his generous translations of Ophuls' poetry for me.

Five. To Hear Is to Obey: The Acoustical Imperative

1. This communication, printed on Columbia letterhead, is dated June 1, 1949, and concerns the filming of *The Reckless Moment* (1949). Thanks to Lutz Bacher for showing me this and other archival materials on that film.

2. Max Ophuls, "The Pleasure of Seeing: Thoughts on the Subject Matter of Film," in Paul Willeman, ed. *Ophuls*, 33.

3. "Il faut tuer la publicité," *Arts* 549 (January 1956), cited in Claude Beylie, *Max Ophuls*, 134 (my translation).

4. Martina Müller, "Vom Souffleurkasten über das Mikro auf die Leinwand: Max Ophüls," *Frauen und Film* 42 (August 1987): 60–71. Of interest in this context is Jeffrey Mehlman, *Walter Benjamin for Children: An Essay on His Radio Years* (Chicago: University of Chicago Press, 1993). Like Ophuls, Benjamin wrote and performed on German radio in the late 1920s and early 1930s. Both were interested in writing for children, were influenced by Brecht, and were persecuted as Jews in Germany during this period. See also Hermann Naber, "Die geheimen Neigungen des Max Ophüls: Der Filmregisseur als Hörspielmacher," in Helmut G. Asper, ed., *Max Ophüls*, 13–33.

5. Müller, "Vom Souffleurkasten," 67 (my translation). Further page references appear in the text.

6. Glynis Kinnan, "Masochism and Subjectivity in Max Ophuls' *Letter from an Unknown Woman*" (Paper presented at the Society for Cinema Studies Annual Conference, Washington, D.C., May 1990), 6.

7. See Carol Flinn, "The Most Romantic Art of All: Music in the Classical Hollywood Cinema," *Cinema Journal* 29, no. 4 (Summer 1990): 35–50. Further page numbers are cited in the text.

8. Kaja Silverman, *The Acoustic Mirror*, 2, quoted by Flinn, "The Most Romantic Art of All," 36.

9. The Italian newspaper publisher Angelo Rizzoli asked Ophuls to direct a film from the popular novel by Salvator Gotta, *La Signora di Tutti* (Milano: Rizzoli, 1942), originally published in serial form in one of Rizzoli's newspapers. A contest was held to cast the female lead, and the career of the winner, Isa Miranda, was strongly bolstered by the film's success. *La Signora di Tutti* has only recently begun to receive the critical attention it deserves.

10. Gotta's novel differs considerably from the script for the film. Among other things, Gaby ("Chicchi" in the novel) has a mother who is alive but very cold to her daughter. There is no music teacher (though it is easy to see why Ophuls added one), and certainly no frame narrative, in the novel.

11. See Andrew Sarris, "*La Signora di Tutti*," *Film Comment* 10, no. 6 (November–December 1974): 45.

12. This phrase is taken from Amy Laurence, "*Sorry, Wrong Number*: The Organizing Ear," in *Film Quarterly* 40, no. 2 (Winter 1986–87): 20–27 (further page references are cited in the text). Laurence sees the 1948 film *Sorry, Wrong Number* (adapted from a radio play) as incorporating certain aural/radiophonic challenges to the dominance of the visual in the classical cinema. She also connects this aural emphasis in the film with a specific challenge to male domination of women through the feminization of the device of the telephone (the woman "overhears" what her subject-position is to be—that of victim—and seeks to elude that victimization through the telephone).

Ophuls had a strong predilection for the radio- and telephonic media: "He chose his main actor for *Liebelei* after simply hearing his voice over the telephone. 'He spoke clearly and simply. His voice was warm, tangible and impressive. I became a member of an audience, and could see him at the other end of the telephone'" (Frieda Grafe, "Theatre, Cinema, Audience: *Liebelei* and *Lola Montès*," in Willeman, ed., *Ophuls*, 51). In "Kulturelle Vermittlung und politische Auseinandersetzung: Aspekte der Theater-Rundfunk und Filmarbeit von Max Ophüls" (Paper presented at the Ophuls Symposium in Lyon on April 26, 1986), Helmut G. Asper describes Ophuls' distinctive treatment of Goethe's disembodied authorial voice in his radiophonic adaptation of Goethe's "Novelle." See also Asper, "Das andere Ufer—Max Ophüls und das Theater," in Asper, ed., *Max Ophüls*, 101–24.

13. Gertrud Koch, "Die masochistische Lust am Verkennen," *Frauen und Film* 39 (1985): 67–72.

14. In her superb essay on the film ("The Abstraction of a Lady: *La Signora di Tutti*," in *Femmes Fatales*, 119–41), Mary Ann Doane hypothesizes that the peculiar force of the woman's passivity, her simultaneous perilousness and submission to destiny, arises from its explicit reference to the Italian institution of the *diva*, who is strongly associated with the fatality of visual fascination. "The *diva* is a woman of exceptional beauty who incites catastrophe—not by means of any conscious scheming but through her sheer presence" (125). Drawing on Walter Benjamin's sense that narrative loses its "specific relation to temporality" (the words are Doane's) through mechanical reproduction, Doane describes how modernism *restabilizes* narrative space and time, "and the figure of the *diva* demonstrates that this is partially accomplished through a projection onto woman of a certain view of history—a view of history which compensates for the growing unreliability of narrative as a process. The incapacity, inadequacy, or lack of narrative is covered over by the displacement onto the woman of historical determination (and hence . . . narrative determination) conceived as inexorable fate. . . . The *diva*, in the very predictability of the doom she incarnates, in the mechanicity of her effects, embodies a view of history and temporality which is consonant with the era of mechanical reproduction. For all her allure, her aura, her eroticism, the *diva* is a machine, a narrative machine" (137–38).

Doane goes on to note that Gaby "differs from the *diva* . . . in the impassivity of her body, the absence of the exaggerated gestures of the heroine of silent film. That excess resides instead in the hyperbolic strategies of the Ophulsian style" (128). The spatiotemporal "contours" of *Signora* are unreliable because of (among other things) the overuse of the dissolve, which blurs the boundaries of time and space. Further page references to Doane in the text are for this essay only.

15. As Flinn notes, "Doane's notion of the 'fantasmatic body' is useful in this regard [in discussing the "weakened" film body that must be "cured" by music—itself a fragmented "body"] since, as she describes it, it is shaped and upheld by Hollywood's strict use of synchronized sound-image relations." Flinn, "The Most Romantic Art of All," 45, is paraphrasing Mary Ann Doane, "The Voice in Cinema: The Articulation of Body and Space," in Philip Rosen, ed., *Narrative, Apparatus, Ideology: A Film Theory Reader*, 335–48.

16. The fetishized woman here serves only to remind the man of primordial losses, rather than functioning as a reassurance against loss. Of course, he is also the masochist who attempts "union" with the powerful woman through his death. This grasping at "presence" coincides with what Derrida has referred to as "phonocentrism": regarding the "word" as essentially *spoken* rather than written, *alive* rather than dead, *present* rather than absent. The search for the mother as origin, as voice—as the representative of being-as-presence—is carried out in *Signora* only to be "deconstructed" by the other reigning metaphor: woman-as-endebted. See Jacques Derrida, *Of Grammatology*, trans. Gayatri Chakravorty Spivak (Baltimore: Johns Hopkins University Press, 1976), 12 and passim.

17. Mary Ann Doane, *The Desire to Desire*, 74.

18. Koch, "Die masochistische Lust am Verkennen," 69.

19. It vies for this honor with such films as *Possessed* (1947), in which a catatonic Joan Crawford is injected with truth serum to incite the flashback of *her* life.

20. The surgical and the gas masks might be seen as the point of juncture between the theatrical and the medical. In a conversation about the film, Neil Hertz noted that this mask resembles a weird eye.

21. Of course, it is significant that the agent is using the medium of radio to broadcast lies about Gaby's past—while she is trying to tell the truth (the film up to this point could be seen as a flashback from both the last hours of Gaby's life and from the perspective she is taking in this scene—a very unusual ambiguity in flashback structure). The agent and the producer in this film share the complicated role of the director-figure who stands in an antagonistic and market-oriented relationship to the woman (running the enormous publicity machines that process her), while, at the same time, demonstrating in this film "personal" concern for her welfare.

22. "In a preparatory moment, displaying a kind of narcissistic self-sufficiency, the woman is taken in by her own image. It is almost as though her own desire for her image were deflected, dispersed outwards to infect the men in the film" (Doane, "The Abstraction of a Lady," 125). Gaby's fascination with her own image is in part rooted in her fascination with the image of the mother: she knows her mother only through a photograph (taken when the mother was twenty years old—that is, about Gaby's age in these scenes), as she tells Alma. Alma, interestingly, reciprocates the young woman's fascination with the "maternal image," by falling in love with Gaby's look and manner.

23. "In *Sorry, Wrong Number* we see what amounts to a network of women talking behind men's backs. . . . To some extent, the telephone empowers women, enabling

them to combine their piecemeal knowledge and find out what is going on in the men's separate world." Laurence, *"Sorry, Wrong Number,"* 24.

24. The "disembodied" repetition of emotion-laden words often occurs over the mechanical rhythm of a machine, and to the accompaniment of multiple dissolves: "shame!" over the ticking of the clock; "forget, forget," over the sound of the train's wheels as the couple attempts to escape their guilt; the producer's order that Gaby's creation as a star should "continue, continue, continue" over the sound of the printing press that cranks out Gaby's image. Gaby is caught in a relentless and impersonal star-machine, which, like painful, irrepressible thoughts, or like the death drive itself, is horrifying precisely because of its mechanical ruthlessness. (Compare this with the scene in *Liebelei* in which the young couple in love dances to a number on the jukebox—artificial music played for a "real" love—while, ironically, in the same film a dead love affair is treated with "real" music played by live musicians.)

25. Doane also notes the relation between sound, sexuality, violence, and off-screen space: "The deployment of sound in relation to space also participates in this interrogation of the image and its limits" ("The Abstraction of a Lady," 134).

26. At the end of the film, Gaby "reads" Roberto's love for her in this scar. He is, however, able to overcome this wound inflicted through his association with the woman and to live on, albeit sadly. Roberto has managed to "accept" castration (the scar) and to find a substitute for his first love.

27. After checking with a number of opera source books and with several Ophuls scholars, I have been unable to determine what opera is performed in *La Signora di Tutti.* It may be a rather obscure one, playing in Milan in the 1930s but no longer part of the modern repertory. Or, possibly, this opera is an invention by Ophuls and/or his scriptwriters (and/or by Daniel Dax, songwriter for the film, a pseudonym for composer Danièle Amfitheatrof).

28. In Gotta's novel, the first "love scene" between Leonardo and Chicchi takes place, predictably, in his car, not at the opera.

29. This is another interrupted physical contact, on the pattern of their first handshake.

30. Sarris, *"La Signora di Tutti,"* 46. Geoffrey Nowell-Smith also refers to the film's two main themes (Gaby's search for love and her creation as star) as "ambiguities" (*"La Signora di Tutti," Monthly Film Bulletin* [September 1982]: 212): Gaby both loves and competes with Alma; she is "innocent" and yet her image is a destructive force.

31. Anna's courtship of Roberto (for it must be seen as such) begins under the auspices of the maternal portrait, which is being sold at auction after Leonardo Nanni has been bankrupted and sent to prison, and after Gaby has left for France to become a film actress. Roberto is bidding on his mother's portrait when Anna approaches him (as we learn in a flashback from Roberto's point of view at the end of the film).

32. It is odd that Alma would have recognized the music ("our music," as Leonardo describes it to Gaby in the garden) since she did not attend the opera and seemed unfamiliar with its plot earlier in the film.

33. Samuel Weber, "The Debts of Deconstruction," in Joseph H. Smith and William Kerrigan, eds., *Taking Chances: Derrida, Psychoanalysis, and Literature* (Balti-

more: Johns Hopkins University Press, 1984), 47. See also Jacques Derrida, "Mes Chances [My Chances]," in Smith and Kerrigan, ibid.

34. Friedrich Nietzsche, *On the Genealogy of Morals*, trans., Walter Kaufmann and R. J. Hollingdale (New York: Vintage, 1967), 88, cited by Weber, "The Debts of Deconstruction," 48.

35. For discussions of Heidegger's *Ruf des Gewissens*, his call to conscience, metaphorized as an *Anruf* (a phone call), see Jacques Derrida, *La Carte Postale*, 25–26 (note), and Weber, "The Debts of Deconstruction," 34–36 and 58–63 (see Chapter 4, note 114, for a complete reference to *La Carte Postale*). In his discussion of the "call to conscience," Heidegger takes up and radically nuances the notion of guilt as debt. See *Being and Time*, trans. John Macquarrie and Edward Robinson, 2 vols. (New York: Harper and Row, 1962), 2:2, sec. 56–59. Heidegger's "primordial" fact of Being-guilty, upon which *Dasein* (the ground of any possible subjectivity) is based, is not chronologically but *phenomenologically* prior to the indebtedness of that subject. Even the possibility of an indebtedness that could be redeemed depends on the phenomenological priority of the guilt understood in this film as feminine guilt toward the mother. The phone call acts as the place where sound tears apart the image — and it may, in fact, be a collect call from Hegel that we must accept. In *Reading in Detail* Naomi Schor notes that "[M]usic is the locus of the emergence of the tension always present throughout the *Aesthetics* between a drive toward unity, articulation, and wholeness and an equally strong countervailing drive toward fragmentation, disjunction, and particularization" (p. 31) — that is, the calling forth of the "individual."

36. Weber cites Derrida's *La Carte Postale* in "The Debts of Deconstruction," 59–60.

37. Gayatri Chakravorty Spivak, "Displacement and the Discourse of Woman," 186.

38. Barry Salt very aptly—and wryly—observes that *Werther* is an "anti-Nazi" film: "In one scene Werther is told that Rousseau's *Contrat Social* is 'subversive literature, forbidden in the Grand Duke's territory,' but the issue is confused by having Werther's partner in radicalism suddenly become, for no reason other than sexual jealousy, an extreme conservative condemning Werther in the name of society and the family, and effectively executing him when it is clear that he intends suicide. Though I suppose there *may* be an audience these days eager to believe that Fascist monsters are created by sexual jealousy" ("Stylistic Analysis of the Films of Max Ophuls," 364). To say that sexual jealousy "creates" fascism is obviously an oversimplification. However, in addition to economic and other catalysts, sexuality and gender roles are certainly factors in the etiology of fascism. Salt's stylistic comments on the film are valuable as well. *Werther* was shot by Eugen Schüfftan, as was *Dann Schon Lieber Lebertran* (1930), *Komedie om Geld* (1936), *La Tendre Ennemie* (1936), *Yoshiwara* (1937), *Sans Lendemain* (1939), and *De Mayerling à Sarajevo* (1940). Salt observes that the scale-of-shot distribution is very similar to that in *Yoshiwara* and *Komedie om Geld*, using "conventually composed long shots," and avoiding close-ups. I agree with Salt that the rather long average shot length (twelve seconds), combined with the uninspired decor and the relatively static camera, makes *Werther* less visually interesting than the average Ophuls film. Some versions of the film, including the one I screened at the Cinémathèque Française, are tinted blue.

39. The film was shot in Alsace, on the Maginot Line, where the French and German armies were carrying out maneuvers. Ophuls remarked that the sound of cannon fire often covered their words as they were filming. This adds an interesting dimension to my analysis of the use of sound in *Werther*. See Roth, *Max Ophüls par Max Ophüls*, 197.

40. Abel Gance's 1936 *Beethoven's Great Love* (*Un Amour de Beethoven*) may have influenced Ophuls' use of sound in *Werther*. In Gance's film, Beethoven is tormented by cacaphonous sound as he goes deaf.

Six. Spectacle, Economics, and the Perils of Directorship

1. Paul Dehn, *Sunday Chronicle*, cited in Richard Roud, *Max Ophuls: An Index*, 31.

2. Rightly or wrongly, the American distributors seemed to feel that if the film were to be tailored to fit Hollywood narrative norms, the longest sketch should go last. Audiences still didn't like it.

3. See Georges Annenkov, *Max Ophüls*, 41.

4. Jean-Luc Godard's *Masculin/Féminin* (1966), filmed in a more permissive era, is partly based on "La Femme de Paul."

5. See also Pierre Cogny's introduction to Guy de Maupassant, *"La Maison Tellier," "Une Partie de Campagne" et autres contes* (Paris: Garnier-Flammarion, 1980), 22, for a brief discussion of Ophuls' cinematic "impressionism" in this film.

6. Alan Williams, *Max Ophuls and the Cinema of Desire*, 89. In his discussion of the film, Williams also notes that the version distributed in the United States is badly mutilated in that it reverses the order of the sketches, possibly in part so that the film could have a "happy" ending.

7. See Williams, ibid., 87. Williams gives a vivid account of the complex process of dubbing this film, with its multiple levels of narration, into English.

8. This dialogue is taken from the French version of the film but also occasionally makes use of phrases from the voice-over and subtitles of the English version.

9. This is Williams's translation of a part of the script of *La Ronde*, originally published in *L'Avant-scène du cinéma* 25 (April 15, 1963). See Williams, *Max Ophuls and the Cinema of Desire*, 75, and "Keeping the Circle Turning," in Andrew S. Horton and Jean Magretta, eds., *Modern European Filmmakers and the Art of Adaptation* (New York: Ungar, 1981), 41. Further page numbers from these works are cited in the text.

10. See Kaja Silverman, *The Acoustic Mirror*, 55.

11. I have not always attempted to distinguish between "director-figures," "directorial relays," "impresarios," and others involved in the manipulation of the actor, sound, and image—though important distinctions may occasionally be made (as is the case in *Caught*, discussed below).

12. In his essay, "The Ophuls Text: A Thesis," in Willeman, ed., *Ophuls*, Paul Willeman describes how the camera remains outside the walls of this bordello, "peering through windows but never cutting to the inside of the house," moving along the walls in a convoluted crane shot: "Behind its doors and windows is locked away what a rigorous social morality excludes from its legal order" (71). Although Willeman's description of the camera work is accurate, I have already objected to the "inside-outside" dichotomy as a model for Ophuls' films: the irony of *Le Plaisir*

is that what is thought of as outside the law actually regulates the functioning of the social body.

13. Williams, *Max Ophuls and the Cinema of Desire*, 103.

14. See Guy de Maupassant, "Le Modèle," in *Contes et Nouvelles* 1 (Paris: Editions de la Pléïade, 1974).

15. See Silverman, *The Acoustic Mirror*, 39–40.

16. Hilary Radner, "*Lola Montès* and Cindy Sherman," 8.

17. This is my translation from the script of *La Ronde* in *L'Avant-scène du cinéma*.

18. Robert Chamblce, "Max Ophuls' Viennese Trilogy," 313.

19. Robert Chamblee, "Max Ophuls' Viennese Trilogy," 50.

20. Of course, many have thought that Smith Ohlrig (Robert Ryan) is Ophuls' portrait of Howard Hughes, with whom Ophuls had a difficult relationship during the filming of *Vendetta*. Lutz Bacher cites Renata Lenart, Ophuls' production secretary for his American films: "By that time [when the script taken from Libbie Block's novel, *Wild Calendar*, had been finished by Ophuls and Paul Trivers in May 1948] the hero-villain, Smith Ohlrig, had been turned into a fairly merciless composite or caricature of Preston Sturges and Howard Hughes" (Lutz Bacher, "Trivers, Hughes, Berry and Breen: Their Impact on Ophuls' *Caught*" [Paper presented at the 1987 meeting of the Society for Cinema Studies], 3.) Director John Berry was called in to direct several scenes early in the film when Ophuls was unable to be on the set.

21. Mary Ann Doane, "Female Spectatorship and Machines of Projection: *Caught* and *Rebecca*," in *The Desire to Desire*, 155. Further page number citations appear in the text.

22. Doane's focus in this essay is not on sound but on the "centrality of the axis of seeing and its relationship to aggressivity" (ibid., 155).

23. Alain Silver and Elizabeth Ward, eds., *Film Noir: An Encyclopedic Reference to the American Style* (Woodstock, N.Y.: Overlook Press, 1979), 54.

24. I would love to know what the Breen office had in mind about this character: "There were continuing demands for the 'greatest care' . . . throughout with the characterization of Franzi to avoid anything objectionable." Bacher ("Trivers, Hughes, Berry and Breen," 10) cites a letter from Joseph Breen to David Hopkins, dated July 13, 1948. Breen did not want Franzi to look too much like . . . a pimp? a homosexual? a Jew?

25. And, of course, partial objects are only partially "other." Like so many other Ophuls characters, Ohlrig maintains an "umbilical" connection to his associates through the telephone. Through it his will is done. But after the projection scene, and Leonora's departure, the phone buzzes. Ohlrig answers it "Leonora," but it is, appropriately, just the projectionist. And near the end of the film, the pregnant Leonora (umbilically attached to a small Ohlrig) leaves her phone off the hook. Thus even the "imaginary" relationship made possible by various forms of visual and auditory projection is ended.

26. The Production Code Administration, already suspicious of Ophuls since *Letter from an Unknown Woman*, came down especially hard on the ending of the film, which was, in fact, censored. "The NLD [National Legion of Decency] asked MGM and Enterprise to delete 'those lines of dialogue which stated that her husband, Robert Ryan, would live. . . . Through the deletion of these lines the audience impres-

sion now was that Bel Geddes was free to marry Mason, and the assumption is that her husband, Robert Ryan, had died. While not eliminating the entire offense in the picture, nevertheless, we feel that it substantially lessened it.' It certainly added much ambiguity" (Bacher, "Trivers, Hughes, Berry and Breen," 11).

27. "Laurents was compelled to contrive story developments which only permit Leonora to react to events: she has a choice of reactions to Ohlrig's offer of a divorce on his terms (to give up or not to give up her baby) and to his heart attack (to help him survive it or not)" (Bacher, "Trivers, Hughes, Berry and Breen," 9). The confusion in Leonora's character may also partly derive from her being a composite of both Leonora and Velma, a naive young woman in Leonora's apartment building at the beginning of the film; the subplot involving Velma's pregnancy was written out of later versions of the script (ibid., 8).

28. The deceptiveness of appearances is a motif in the film, especially concerning Ohlrig and Leonora. Leonora "seems" to be a rich woman when we first see her in the mink. Smith Ohlrig does not look like a millionaire when Leonora first meets him. His "nervous reactions" look like heart attacks. Quinada takes Leonora for a society woman who has never worked, and she doesn't bother to disabuse him of this notion except indirectly. When Leonora is leaving the doctor's office after confirming her pregnancy, the nurse says, "Funny, you don't look it." "Look what?" Leonora nervously asks. "Like you stayed up all night,"replies the nurse.

29. Williams, *Max Ophuls and the Cinema of Desire*, 64–65.

Seven. *Closing the Circle:* Lola Montès, Divine, *and* La Tendre Ennemie

1. Catherine Clément, "Prima Donnas, or the Circus of Women," in *Opera, or the Undoing of Women*, 25.

2. Colette, "Backstage at the Studio," in Alain and Odette Virmaux, eds., *Colette at the Movies*, trans. Sarah W. R. Smith (New York: Ungar, 1980), 74–75.

3. In *Le cinéma français* (Paris: Flammarion, 1962), Georges Sadoul states that the industry was in a slump between 1930 and 1935. Alan Williams expresses a more complex view of the economic and aesthetic elements of the period, describing the achievements of early sound films such as *La petite Lise* (Grémillon, 1930), *La Chienne* (Renoir, 1931), and *Le Million* (Clair, 1931), as well as the works of Marcel Pagnol, Jacques Feyder, Luis Buñuel, Jean Cocteau, Jean Vigo, and others. According to Williams, Ophuls adapted to the French film industry more readily and with greater success than did the numerous other German directors who arrived in the early thirties (Billy Wilder, Curt Siodmak, Fritz Lang, G. W. Pabst, Anatole Litvak), and "unique among the anti-Nazi refugees, he returned after the war to become one of the leading exponents of the Tradition of Quality" (Williams, *Republic of Images: A History of French Filmmaking* [Cambridge: Harvard University Press, 1992], 209). For a more detailed overview of the French film industry of the period, see Colin Crisp, *The Classic French Cinema, 1930–1960* (Bloomington: Indiana University Press, 1987).

In his discussion of the director's considerable power during this era, Raymond Borde lists *La Tendre Ennemie* (1936), along with *Liebelei* (1932), *Werther* (1938), and *Sans Lendemain* (1939), as "ris[ing] above the commercial routine and the assembly-line production" of sound films between 1929 and 1939. Borde, "'The Golden Age': French Cinema of the '30s," *Rediscovering French Film* (New York: Museum of Modern Art, and Boston: Little, Brown, 1983), 78.

4. Williams refers to this film as *The Sweet Enemy* in *Republic of Images*, 211.

5. Roth, *Max Ophüls par Max Ophüls*, 183–85. Ophuls cites one critic who described *La Tendre Ennemie* as "René Clair minus the snobbery," and notes that the film was distributed in the United States as a Clair film, an error that Ophuls, out of "laziness," didn't correct. Lutz Bacher has told me that Ophuls actually sued the American distributing company and won. In *Republic of Images* Williams describes the "Brechtian" elements of Clair's *Le Million*, such as its "ironic, distanced narration" (170–71). As noted, in both style and content, Clair's film shows a good deal of similarity to the radical aspects of Ophuls' work.

6. In Roth, *Max Ophüls par Max Ophüls*, 183–89, and Beylie, *Max Ophuls*, 160–63, Ophuls and Beylie contradict one another on the order of the films of 1936. Beylie places *Komedie om Geld* before *Ennemie*, and Ophuls places it after. Beylie's precision with the release dates indicates that his is probably the more accurate account. Between *Divine* and *Komedie* (according to Beylie), Ophuls made the two shorts "Valse Brillante de Chopin" and "Ave Maria de Schubert" for a series entitled "Music and Cinema," which included works by a number of well-known directors. The shorts were photographed by Franz Planer.

7. The film is the third Ophuls shot with Schüfftan, whose work in Ophuls' films seems rather uneven—though production circumstances, Ophuls' directorial decisions, and budgetary considerations are more likely to be the reasons for this, rather than Schüfftan's lack of consistency as a cinematographer.

8. Roth, *Max Ophüls par Max Ophüls*, 185.

9. Barry Salt, "Stylistic Analysis of the Films of Max Ophuls," 363.

10. Ibid. Further page numbers appear in the text.

11. Richard Roud, *Max Ophuls: An Index*, 20.

12. Miriam Hansen, *Babel and Babylon*, 277.

13. Hansen, *Babel and Babylon*, 281.

14. Roud pans the film as "unbalanced" and declares "the whole last quarter a failure" (*Max Ophuls: An Index*, 17).

15. The film was marketed as Colette's first screenplay, which it was not. In the publicity packet for the film, Eden Productions suggested that "a display of the works of Colette in bookstores and in the theater would be an excellent propaganda tactic for *Divine*, on the condition that this display could be set up a week in advance." (The publicity packet for *Divine* was kindly provided to me by the archives of the Photothèque française. Translations from this document are my own.) A thorough history of Colette's work in the cinema, as well as a transcription of *Divine*'s dialogue (taken from the film itself, rather than a continuity or shooting script), can be found in Alain and Odette Virmaux, eds., *Colette at the Movies*. The production of this film seems typical of the "fragmented," star-generated film productions of the French cinema of the thirties, which produced some of the most brilliant films in history, partly because of the "fragmentation" from which it also suffered. See Sandy Flitterman-Lewis, *To Desire Differently*, 169–72.

16. Alain and Odette Virmaux, eds., *Colette at the Movies*, 170.

17. On the history of this period see Philippe Bernard and Henri Dubief, *The Decline of the Third Republic, 1914–1938*, trans. Anthony Forster (Cambridge and London: Cambridge University Press, 1985), 179. "On the whole, peasant incomes were badly hit after 1931. By 1935 they had probably fallen by about one-third, for the prices of farm produce had fallen. . . . Of course, small and unprofitable farms began to be squeezed out, to the advantage of medium-sized ones" (ibid., 236). Women were especially likely to go to the cities, particularly in light of the shortage of able men (a continuing result of World War I). Divine (Simone Berriau) follows a predictable trajectory in going to the city, and then in moving from a small (probably rented) to a medium-sized farm, whose proprietor has the makings of a small but substantial capitalist. Among other events, 1935—36 saw the Saar region's referendum resulting in its return to the German Reich, the advent of Léon Blum and the Popular Front, and the continuation of the economic crisis of the early thirties (never as extreme as the American Depression because of France's lesser degree of capitalization, but more long-lasting). Anti-Semitism was, of course, on the rise, and Ophuls experienced its negative effects in France, though to a lesser degree than he had in Germany. He became a French citizen after the Saar referendum (at the invitation of the French government: Williams, *Republic of Images*, 212). In 1940, when Ophuls left France, Jews had already been prohibited from working.

18. See Bernard and Dubief, *The Decline of the Third Republic*, 242–47, for an analysis of class relations in France during the first third of the twentieth century. In my discussion of the American and European middle class, I have been faced with the fact that "the term 'bourgeoisie' covers such a variety of living standards that it is hard to avoid providing a collection of vague generalisations" (244), even as I have attempted to sort out the subtleties of Ophuls' use of the class system in half a dozen countries.

19. Quoted from the publicity packet cited in note 15, above.

20. Alain and Odette Virmaux, eds., *Colette at the Movies*, 181. Further page citations are in the text.

21. Hubert's astonishing screen credits include *Napoléon*, *La Chienne*, *Fanny*, *J'Accuse*, *Les Visiteurs du soir*, *Les Enfants du Paradis*, and *Thérèse Raquin*.

22. I am referring to the character played by Marlene Dietrich in *The Blue Angel* (1930), Lola Lola, noted for her ability to dominate her spectators. Rainer Werner Fassbinder was obviously fascinated by both Lolas: in *Mother Küsters Goes to Heaven* (1975), a woman performs a song in what appears to be an homage to Dietrich's Lola Lola in a sleazy café called the "Lola Montès."

23. For a discussion of the Bakhtinian qualities of the film see Masao Yamaguchi, "For an Archaeology of *Lola Montès*," in Willeman, ed., *Ophuls*, 65.

24. As William Paul has observed: a dollar was approximately the price of a theater ticket in 1955.

25. See Maureen Turim, *Flashbacks in Film: Memory and History* (New York: Routledge, 1989), for a comprehensive listing of premises for flashbacks in cinema history.Gertrud Koch discusses the role of the Freudian "drive" in her analysis of flashbacks and the space-time continua of Ophuls' films in "Zeitsprünge," in *Max Ophuls/Reihe*

Film 42: 7–26. Thanks to Barbara Kosta for her translation of this essay.

26. See Isabel Ross, *The Uncrowned Queen* (New York: Harper and Row, 1972); and Horace Wyndham and Alan Walker, *Franz Liszt*, vol. 1, *The Virtuoso Years, 1811–1847* (London: Faber and Faber, 1983), 391–94.

27. Alan Williams, *Max Ophuls and the Cinema of Desire*, 142.

28. Williams (ibid.) refers here to George Annenkov's description of the production details in *Max Ophüls*, 84–94.

29. Judith Mayne, *The Woman at the Keyhole*, 199.

30. Salt ("Stylistic Analysis," 374) sees the use of masking in *LM* as a sign of Ophuls' inability to work effectively with CinemaScope, in that the mask recreates Academy aspect ratio. There may be some merit to this argument, but it is also true that Ophuls often used curtains and other devices to mask the screen and create a theatrical effect even in his Academy ratio films.

31. This platform is placed within another white carousel-like structure during the "tableau vivant" of Lola's wedding, which features dwarfs in white riding the outer rim, providing a scaled-down model of various incidents surrounding the wedding and Lola's life. Lola's platform spins counterclockwise while the "carousel" spins clockwise. This, in addition to the film's use of 360-degree tracking shots, creates a vertiginous circularity in shocking contrast with the congealed images within the circus.

32. This "Q & A" period is the first of the official events of the show, each of which is called out by Ustinov, sometimes in voice-over during the flashbacks.

33. Yamaguchi, "For an Archaeology of *Lola Montès*," 61.

34. For a discussion of the "arabesque" and the straight line in Ophuls' films see William Karl Guérin, *Max Ophuls*, 26–28, 64, 76, 86, 103–104, 112, 114.

35. Williams, *Max Ophuls and the Cinema of Desire*, 154.

36. Kaja Silverman, *The Acoustic Mirror*, 57.

37. Sacher-Masoch, *Venus in Furs*, 121–22. This quote from Sacher-Masoch's novel indicates some thematic continuity between the films by Ophuls and von Sternberg that have been described as at least partly influenced by the masochistic scenario. Ophuls' Lola Montès, however, succumbs to love and thereby loses some of her power, while von Sternberg's Catherine (*The Scarlet Empress*, 1934) is completely triumphant even in love. See Gaylyn Studlar's work on the latter film in *In the Realm of Pleasure*. The influence of von Sternberg upon Ophuls' cinema is discussed by Douglas Sirk in Jon Halliday's interview, *Sirk on Sirk* (New York: Viking, 1972).

38. Clément, *Opera, or the Undoing of Women*, 25.

39. See George Perle, *The Operas of Alban Berg*, vol. 2, *Lulu* (Berkeley: University of California Press, 1955). Clément also comments on the resemblance between the opera and the film, in *Opera, or the Undoing of Women*, 24.

In "For an Archaeology of *Lola Montès*," Yamaguchi comments on Wedekind's influence on Ophuls. He also notes that some of the major influences on Ophuls—Hoffman, Offenbach, Blok, Schnitzler, Wedekind, Meyerhold, Eisenstein, and Reinhardt—combine the tradition of the spectacle (emblematized by the merry-go-round and the circus) "with avant garde experimentation[,] producing a specific mode of representation straddling popular spectacle and avant garde practices" (64). In tracing the Russian and Soviet aspects of this influence, Yamaguchi points to the fact that

Ophuls had heard about Fedor Kommisarzhevsky's staging of *Lulu* in Moscow in 1918 from Georges Annenkov. Finally, Yamaguchi speculates that it was Ophuls' love of Offenbach that made him accept the "trite" *Lola Montès* script, and traces the relationship between Offenbach's *La Péricole* (featuring an Hispanic woman of the people—a "trickster" figure—involved with a nobleman), which, like Renoir's *Carosse d'Or* and Ophuls' film manqué, *Vendetta*, is derived from Mérimée's *Colomba* (67). I might add that Lola Montès is known to have had an affair with Mérimée.

40. This discussion of Lulu is drawn from Mary Ann Doane, "The Erotic Barter: *Pandora's Box*," in *Femmes Fatales*, 142–62 (quotes taken from 154 and 152). All further page citations appear in the text.

41. Doane, "The Erotic Barter," 156. Doane also observes that Alwa's fascination with Lulu is clinched *backstage*, in a strangely shot sequence involving an "Oedipal" encounter between Alwa and his father (also competing for Lulu's affection). Obviously, the backstage elements of Lulu's story would be of interest for Ophuls. In *LM* an important encounter between Lola and the fatherly king takes place in the wings of the theater.

42. This is not the case in *Pandora's Box*: "When Alwa, influenced by Schigolch, attempts to cheat, and hence to introduce a directionality and a continuity into the game, reducing the element of chance, the entire fragilely ordered (or disordered) social system of the gambling ship (which Elsaesser specifies as 'the fictional metaphor for the economic chaos of the Weimar Republic') is disrupted" (Doane, "The Erotic Barter," 157). Doane cites Thomas Elsaesser, "Lulu and the Meter Man," *Screen* 24, nos. 4–5 (October 1983): 31. The presence of a menorah in Lulu's apartment, and the stereotyped behavior of Schigolch, her "manager," indicate that the film may be referring to the role that Jews (supposedly) played in the "economic chaos of the Weimar Republic."

43. For a literary history of the tightrope walker and trapeze artist see John Stokes, "*Aux Funambules*: Acrobatics and Aesthetics," *French Cultural Studies* 3 (1992): 277–98.

44. Mayne, "Primitive Narration," in *The Woman at the Keyhole*, 157.

45. Mayne, ibid., 164, cites Tom Gunning, "The Cinema of Attraction: Early Cinema, Its Spectator, and the Avant-Garde," *Wide Angle* 8, nos. 3–4 (1986): 64, 66.

46. Anders Stephanson, "Regarding Postmodernism—A Conversation with Fredric Jameson," in Andrew Ross, ed., *Universal Abandon? The Politics of Postmodernism* (Minneapolis: University of Minnesota Press, 1988), 12 (quotation is from Jameson). Further quotations (Stephanson/Jameson) and page numbers are cited in the text.

47. It was the fate of *Middlemarch*'s Mr. Casaubon to seek this key, a *colonizing* project Eliot lets us know is doomed to fail.

48. Hal Foster, "Wild Signs: The Breakup of the Sign in Seventies' Art," in Ross, ed., *Universal Abandon?* 251.

49. Jacqueline Rose, "*The Man Who Mistook His Wife for a Hat*, or *A Wife Is Like an Umbrella*—Fantasies of the Modern and Postmodern," in Ross, ed. *Universal Abandon?* 237–38.

50. Rose, ibid., 240, cites Fredric Jameson, "Postmodernism or the Cultural Logic of Late Capitalism," *New Left Review* 146 (July–August 1984): 63.

$\mathcal{F}ilmography$

◆

1930 Germany *Nie Wieder Liebe* (*No More Love*), dir.: Anatole Litvak. Ophuls worked as German dialogue director on the film. Franz Planer was its photographer.
Germany *Dann Schon Lieber Lebertran* (*I'd Rather Take Cod Liver Oil*), dir.: Max Ophuls; prod. co.: Ufa; script: Erich Kästner (based on original story); adaptation: Emeric Pressburger and Max Ophuls; photo.: Eugen Schüfftan, Karl Puth; Sound: Walter Tjaden; sound system: Tobis-Klangfilm; Cast: Käthe Haak (Frau Augustin), Heinz Günsdorf (St. Peter), Paul Kemp (St. Michael), Hannelore Schroth (daughter Ellen), Gert Klein (son Peter). Running time: 35 min. (approx.)
1931/2 Germany *Die verliebte Firma* (*The Company in Love*), dir.: Max Ophuls; prod. co.: D. L. S. (Berlin); script: Fritz Zeckendorf, from an original story by Bruno Granichstädten and Ernst (Hubert?) Marischka, adapt. by Ophuls and Granich-städten; photo: Karl Puth; editor: Else Baum; sound: Carlo Paganini; music: Bruno Granichstädten with Grete Walter and Ernst Hauke; assistant director: Peter Willy Riethof; sound system: Tobis-Klangfilm. Cast: Gustav Frölich (Werner Loring Jr. , film director), Anny Ahlers (Peggy Barling, Star), Lien Deyers (Gretl Krummbichler), Ernst Verebes (Heinrich Pulver), Leonard Steckel (Harry Bing), Hubert von Meyerinck (Fritz Willner), Fritz Steiner (Tony Bauer), Hermann Kre-han (Karl Martini), Werner Finck (Franz Klingemüller). Running time: 65 min. Released Jan.-Feb. 1932.*
1932 Germany *Die verkaufte Braut* (*The Bartered Bride*), dir.: Max Ophuls; prod. co.: Reichsliga Film (Munich); script and adapt.: Max Ophuls, Curt Alexander and Jaroslav Kvapil, from the comic opera *Prodaná nevesta* by Bedrich [Friedrich] Smetana (score) and Karel Sabina (libretto); photo.: Reimar Kuntze, Franz Koch,

*Release dates given only for films that come close to the end or beginning of the year.

Herbert Illig, Otto Wirsching; editor: Paul Ostermayr; sound: Friedrich Wilhelm Dustmann; music: Theo Mackeben (after Friedrich Smetana); songs: Robert Vambery; choreography: Senta Born; décor and costume: Erwin Scharf; assistant dir.: Peter Willy Riethof, Walter Behr; sound system: Tobis-Klangfilm. Cast: Max Nadler (Mayor Krusinova), Jarmila Novotna (Marie, his daughter), Otto Wernicke (Kezal, marriage procurer), Hermann Kner (Micha), Maria Janowska (his wife), Paul Kemp (their son), Karl Valentin (Brummer, circus director), Liesl Karlstadt (Frau Brummer), Annemarie Sörensen (Esmeralda), Willy Domgraf-Fassbaender (Hans, the postillion), Max Schreck (Indian). Running time: 77 min. Released Dec. 1932-Jan. 1933.

1932/33 Germany *Lachende Erben* (*Happy Heirs*), dir.: Max Ophuls; prod. co.: Ufa; script: Trude Herka (original story under her pseudonym, Herrmann); adapt.: Max Ophuls, Felix Joachimson; photo.: Eduard Hoesch; editor: Herbert Fredersdor; sound: Walter Rühland; music: Clemens Schmalstich; décor: Benno von Arent; assistant dir.: Herbert Fredersdorf. Cast: Heinz Rühmann (Peter Frank), Max Adalbert (Justus Bockelmann, his uncle), Ida Wüst (Britta Bockelmann, Peter's aunt), Walter Janssen (Robert Stumm), Lien Deyers (Gina, his daughter), Lizzi Waldmüller (Liane Heller), Julius Falkenstein (Dr. Weinhöppel), Friedrich Ettel (Schlemmel, cellarmaster). Running time: 75 min. Released March 1933.

1932/33 Germany *Liebelei* (*Flirtation*), dir. Max Ophuls; prod. co.: Elite Tonfilm (Berlin); prod.: Fred Lissa; script and adapt.: Hans Wilhelm, Curt Alexander, Max Ophuls, Felix Salten, based on Arthur Schnitzler's play; photo.: Franz Planer; photo. assistant: Bruno Stephan; editor: Friedel Buckow; sound: Hans Grimm; music: Theo Mackeben, from motifs by Ludwig von Beethoven, Johannes Brahms, Wolfgang Amadeus Mozart, Josef Lanner, Johann Strauss, Carl Maria von Weber, Joseph Haydn, Charles Gounod, Richard Wagner; décor: Gabriel Pellon; assistant dir.: Walter Sternheim; still photo.: Walter Lichtenstein; sound system: Tobis-Klangfilm. Cast: Paul Hörbiger (Old Weiring, musician), Magda Schneider (Christine, his daughter), Luise Ullrich (Mizzi Schlager, shop girl), Gustaf Gründgens (Baron von Eggersdorf), Olga Tschekowa (Baronness von Eggersdorf), Willy Eichberger (Lt. Theo Kaiser), Wolfgang Liebeneiner (Lt. Fritz Lobheimer), Paul Otto (Major von Eggersdorf). Running time: 88 min. Nazi censors removed Ophuls' name from the credits.

1933 France *Une Histoire d'Amour* (French version of *Liebelei*), dir. Max Ophuls; dialogue: André Doderet; photo.: Ted Pahle; editor: Paul Salten. Cast: Abel Tarride (Old Weiring), Simone Héliard (Mizzi Schlager), Georges Rigaud (Lt. Théodore Berg). The rest of the cast remains the same, since most of the film was not re-shot.

1933–34 France *On a volé un homme* (*A Man has been Stolen*), dir. Max Ophuls; prod. co.: Fox Films Europe; prod.: Erich Pommer; script: René Pujol; adapt.: René Pujol and Hans Wilhelm; photo.: René Guissart; music: Bonislaw Kaper and Walter Jurman; assistant dir.: Ralph Baum; sound system: Western Electric; décor: Max Heilbronner. Cast: Henry Garat (Jean de Lafay), Lili Damita (Annette), Fernand Fabre (Robert), Charles Fallot (Victor), Nina Myral (old woman), Pierre Labry (man with scar), Robert Goupil (Legros), Raoul Marco (inspector). Running time: 90 min. Released Oct.-Nov. 1933. This film is lost: the story revolves around a shady young fiancier, Jean de Lafay, who has fled to Antibes after having made unsound speculations on the Stock Exchange.

1934 Italy *La Signora di Tutti* (*Everybody's Lady*), dir. Max Ophuls; prod. co. Novella Films (Milan); prod.: Angelo Rizzoli, Erich Pommer; script and adapt.: Curt Alexander, Hans Wilhelm, Max Ophuls, based on the novel by Salvator Gotta; photo: Ubaldo Arata; editor: Ferdinando M. Poggioli; sound: Giovanni Bittmann; music: Danièle Amfitheatrof; songs: Daniel Dax (pseudonym for Amfitheatrof), sung by Nelly Nelson; décor: Giuseppe Capponi; assistant dir.: Ralph Baum, sound system: RCA Photophone. Cast: Isa Miranda (Gaby Doriot), Nelly Corradi (Anna), Memo Benassi (Leonardo Nanni), Tatiana Pavlova (Alma Nanni), Federico Benfer (Roberto), Andrea Cecchi, Lamberto Picasso. Running time: 97 min. Won technical prize at 1934 Venice Biennale. Released Dec. 1934.

1935 France *Divine*, dir. Max Ophuls; prod. co.: Eden Prod. (Paris); prod.: Paul Bentata, Simone Berriau; script: Colette de Jouvenel, from her book *L'envers du music hall*; adapt.: J. G. Auriol and Max Ophuls; photo: Roger Hubert; music: Albert Wolff; songs: Roger Féral and J. G. Auriol; sound: Fred Behrens; editor: Leonide Moguy; décor: Jacques Gotko, Robert Gys; assistant dir.: Ralph Baum, Pierre de Hérrain. Cast: Simone Berriau (Ludivine Jarisse, "Divine"), Catherine Fonteney (her mother), Yvette Lebon (Roberte), Georges Rigaud (Antonin, the milkman), Philippe Hériat (Fakir Lutuf-Allah), Thérèse Dorny ("Poison"), Marcel Vallée (director of the Empyrée Theater), Gina Manès (Dora), Gabriello (Nero). Running time: 82 min.

1935/1936 France *Valse brillante de Chopin*, dir. Max Ophuls; prod. co. CGAI for Fox Films; photo.: Franz Planer; décor: Emile Vuillermoz; sound system: Western Electric. Cast: Alexandre Brailowski (pianist). Running time: 6 min. Released Dec. 1935/Jan. 1936.

France *Ave Maria de Schubert*, dir. Max Ophuls; prod. co.: CGAI for Fox Films; photo: Franz Planer; décor: Emile Vuillermoz; sound system: Western Electric. Cast: Elizabeth Schumann (singer). Running time: 5 min. Released Dec. 1935/Jan. 1936.

1936 France *La Tendre Ennemie* (*The Tender Enemy*), dir. Max Ophuls; prod. co.: Eden Productions; prod.: Simone Berriau; script: Curt Alexander, Max Ophuls, from the play, "The Enemy," by André-Paul Antoine; dialogue: André-Paul Antoine; photo: Eugen Schüfftan; camera: René Colas; music: Albert Wolff (from period music, including "Fascination"); editing: Pierre de Hérain; sound: Antoine Archimbaud; décor: Jacques Gotko; assistant dir.: Ralph Baum; sound system: RCA Photophone. Cast: Simone Berriau (Annette Dupont, the "enemy"), Georges Vitray (her husband), Jacqueline Daix (her daughter), Catherine Fonteney (her mother), Maurice Devienne (daughter's fiancé), Marc Valbel (Rodrigo, the lion tamer), Lucien Nat (sailor), Laure Diana (girl from Chez Maxim's), Germaine Reuver (Aunt Jette), Pierre Finaly (Uncle Emile), Camille Bert (Doctor Desmoulins). Running time: 69 min. Prix Lumière, 1936.

Holland *Komedie om Geld* (*Comedy about Money/The Trouble with Money*), dir. Max Ophuls; prod. co.: Cinetone Prod. , Maatschappij, Amsterdam; dir. of prod.: Willy Tuschinski; script: Walter Schlee; adapt.: Walter Schlee, Alex de Haas and Max Ophuls; cinematography: Eugen Schüfftan and Fritz Meyer; sound: I. J. Citroën; editor: Noël van Ess and Gérard Bensdorp; music: Max Tak; arrangements: Heinz Lachmann; songs: Alex de Haas; décor: Heinz Fenschel, Jan Wiegers, Theo van der Lugt; assistant dir.: Noël van Es; sound system: Tobis-Klangfilm. Cast: Herman Bouber (Brand), Rini Otte (Willy, his daughter), Matthew van Eysden (Ferdi-

nand, his brother-in-law), Cor Ruys (Director Moorman), Edwin Gubbins Dooren-
bos (Speaker); Richard Flinck (head of the construction firm), Arend Sandhouse.
Running time: 88 min.

1937 France *Yoshiwara* dir. , Max Ophuls; prod. co.: Les Films Excelsior/Milo Film;
prod.: M. Milakowski; script: Maurice Dekobra, based on his novel *Yoshiwara*;
adapt.: Arnold Lippschitz (Lipp), Wolfgang Wilhelm, J. Dapoigny, Max Ophuls,
Jacques Companeez; photo.: Eugen Schüfftan; camera: René Colas and Paul
Portier; editor: Pierre Meguérian; sound: Sauvion; décor: André and Léon
Barsacq; music: Paul Dessau; sound: Sauvion. Cast: Pierre-Richard Willm (Serge
Polenoff); Sessue Hayakawa (Ysamo, the "coolie"), Michiko Tanaka (Kohana),
Roland Toutain (Pawlik, the midshipman), Gabriello (M. Pô, the patron of the
teahouse), Lucienne Le Marchand (Namo, head geisha), Camille Bert (com-
mander of battleship), Foon Sen (Kohana's brother). Running time: 88 min.
(bathhouse scene missing)

1938 France *Werther* (*Le Roman de Werther*), dir. Max Ophuls; prod. co.: Nero Film;
script and adapt.: Hans Wilhelm, Max Ophuls, from Goethe's *The Sorrows of Young
Werther*; dialogue: Fernand Crommelnyck; assistant dir.: Henri Aisner; photo:
Eugen Schüfftan; camera: Fedote Bourgassoff, Georges Stilly; editor: Gérard
Bensdorp, Jean Sacha; costumes: Annette Sarradin; décor: Eugène Lourié, Max
Douy; music: Henri Herblay (following themes from Bach, Grétry, Mozart, Schu-
bert, and Beethoven ["Ich liebe dich"]); sound: Monnot. Cast: Pierre-Richard
Willm (Werther), Annie Vernay (Charlotte), Jean Galland (Albert Hochstätter),
Paulette Pax (Aunt Emma), Henri Guisol, Jean Périer, Georges Vitray, Henri
Herblay, Roger Legris. Running time: 85 min. Released Nov. /Dec. 1938. Some
prints tinted blue.

1939 France *Sans Lendemain* (*No Tomorrow*), dir. Max Ophuls; prod. co.: Ciné-Alliance
and Inter-artistes Films/Gray Film; prod. Gregor Rabinovitsch and Oscar Dan-
cigers; assistant dir.: Henri Aisner; script: Jean Villeme (Hans Wilhelm); adapt.
André-Paul Antoine, Jean Jacot (Hans Jacobi), Max Ophuls; dialogue: André-Paul
Antoine; photo: Eugène Schüfftan; camera: Paul Portier, Delattre, Ferrier, Henri
Alekan; editor: Bernard Séjourné, Jean Sacha; décor: Eugène Lourié, Max Douy;
music: Allan Gray; conductor: R. Goer; sound: Pierre Calvet. Cast: Edwige Feuil-
lère (Evelyne Morin), Georges Rigaud (Dr. Georges Brandon), Michel François
(Evelyne's son, Pierre), Daniel Lecourtois (Armand), Paul Azaïs (Henri, emcee at
La Sirène), Georges Lannes (Paul), Jeanne Marken (concierge at elegant apt.),
Mady Berry (concierge at cheap apt.), Pauline Carton (Ernestine, the maid).
Running time: 82 min.
Released Mar. 1940.

1939/40 France *De Mayerling à Sarajevo* (*From Mayerling to Sarajevo/ Sarajevo*), dir. Max
Ophuls; prod. co.: BUP Française; prod. Eugène Tuscherer, Ivan Foxwell; assistant dir.: Jean Faurez and Jean-Paul Dreyfus [Le Chanois]; script: Carl Zuckmay-
er; adapt.: Curt Alexander, Marcelle Maurette, Jacques Natanson, Max Ophuls;
dialogue: Jacques Natanson, André-Paul Antoine; photo: Curt Courant, Otto
Heller, Eugen Schüfftan; camera: Jacques Mercanton, Robert Lefebvre, Viguier,
Natteau; editor: Myriam and Jean Oser; décor: Jean d'Eaubonne; costumes: B.
Balinsky; music: Oscar Straus; orchestra conductor: Marcel Cariven; sound: Girar-
don and Yvonnet. Cast: Edwige Feuillère (Countess Sophie Chotek), John Lodge

(Archduke Franz-Ferdinand), Aimé Clariond (Prince Montenuovo), Jean Worms (Emperor Franz Josef, Gabrielle Dorziat (Archduchess Maria Theresa), Aimos (Janachek, Archduke's valet), Jean-Paul Dreyfus (Prinzip, the assassin), Marcel André (Archduke Frederick), Colette Régis (Archduchess Isabelle), Jean Debucourt (Minister of Foreign Affairs). Running time: 89 min. Shooting began July, 1939, was interrupted in Oct. , recommenced in Dec. , finished in Jan. 1940. Released May 1, 1940.

1940 Switzerland *L'Ecole des femmes* (unfinished), dir. Max Ophuls, adapted from Molière's play; photo: Michel Kelber; décor and costume: Christian Bérard. Cast: Louis Jouvet, Madeleine Ozeray, the Louis Jouvet Co. (Athénée Co.).

1946 U. S. *Vendetta*, dir. Max Ophuls, Preston Sturges, Stuart Heisler, Howard Hughes, Mel Ferrer (whose name appears in the credits); prod. co.: RKO-Radio; prod. Howard Hughes; script: W. R. Burnett and Preston Sturges, from Prosper Merimée's *Columba*; photo: Frank (Franz) Planer, Al Gilks; editing: Stuart Gilmore. Cast: Faith Domergue, Nigel Bruce.

1947 U. S. *The Exile*, dir. Max Ophuls; prod co. , Universal-International, in assoc. with the Fairbanks Co. ; prod. Douglas Fairbanks, Jr. ; script and adapt.: Douglas Fairbanks, Jr. , Max Ophuls, Clemence Dane, from Cosmos Hamilton's novel, *His Majesty, the King*; asst. dir.: Ben Chapman, George Lollier; photo: Frank (Franz) Planer; editing: Ted J. Kent; décor: Russell A. Gausman, Ted Offenbecker; prod. design: Howard Bay, David Sharpe (action sequences); special effects: David S. Horsley; costumes: Dwight Franklin and Laure Lourié; music: Frank Skinner; sound: Leslie I. Carey, William Hedgcock. Cast: Douglas Fairbanks, Jr. (Charles Stuart), Paule Croset (Katie), Maria Montes (Countess), Henry Daniell (Col. Ingrahm), Nigel Bruce (Sir Edward Hyde), Robert Coote (Pinner), Otto Waldis (Jan), Eldon Gorst (Seymour), Milton A. Owen (Wilcox), Colin Keith-Johnson (Capt. Bristol). Running time: 92 min. Some prints in Sepiatone.

1948 U. S. *Letter from an Unknown Woman*, dir. Max Ophuls; prod. co.: Universal-International/Rampart Prod. ; prod. John Houseman; assistant dir.: John F. Sherwood; script and adapt.: Howard Koch, Max Ophuls, based on the novella by Stephan Zweig; photo: Frank (Franz) Planer; editor: Ted J. Kent; décor: Alexander Golitzen, Russell A. Gausman, Ruby R. Levitt, with the collaboration of Charles Baker; costumes: Travis Banton; music: Danièle Amfitheatrof; sound Leslie I. Carey, Glenn E. Anderson; prod. co-ordinator: John Hambleton. Cast: Joan Fontaine (Lisa Berndle), Louis Jourdan (Stefan Brand), Mady Christians (Frau Berndle), Marcel Journet (Johann Stauffer), Art Smith (John, Stefan's valet), Howard Freeman (Herr Kästner), John Good (Lt. Leopold von Kaltnegger), Leo P. Pessin (Stefan, Jr.), Otto Waldis (concierge), Erskine Sanford (porter), Sonia Bryden (Frau Spitzer). Running time: 90 min. (cut to 87 min.)

1949 U. S. *Caught*, dir. Max Ophuls; prod. co.: Wolfgang Reinhardt Enterprise for MGM; asst. dir.: John Berry; script and adapt.: Arthur Laurents, from Libbie Block's novel, *Wild Calendar*; photo: Lee Garmes; sound: Max Hutchinson; editor: Robert Parrish; music: Frederik Hollender; artistic dir.: Frank Sylos. Cast: Barbara Bel Geddes (Leonora Ames), Robert Ryan (Smith Ohlrig), James Mason (Dr. Larry Quinada), Frank Ferguson (Dr. Hoffmann), Curt Bois (Franzi), Ruth Brady (Maxime), Natalie Schaefer (Dorothy Dale), Art Smith (Ohlrig's psychiatrist), Barbara Billingsly (woman shopping for mink). 88 min.

U. S. *The Reckless Moment*, dir. Max Ophuls; prod. co.: Columbia/Walter Wanger Production; prod.: Walter Wanger; script: Henry Garson, R. W. Soderburg; adapt.: Mel Dinelli, Robert E. Kent, from a "Ladies Home Journal" serialized novel, *The Blank Wall*, by Elizabeth Saxnay Holding; assistant dir.: Earl Bellamy; photo: Burnett Guffey; editor: Gene Havlick; décor: Cary Odell, Frank Tuttle; costumes: Jean Louis; music: Hans Salter; musical dir.: Morris Stoloff; sound: Russell Malmgren. Cast: James Mason (Martin Donnelly), Joan Bennett (Lucia Harper), Geraldine Brooks (Beatrice Harper), Henry O'Neill (Mr. Harper, Lucia's father-in-law), David Blair (David Harper), Roy Roberts (Nagel), Frances Williams (Sybil, the cook and housekeeper), Shepperd Strudwick (Ted Darby), Roy Roberts (Nagel). Running time: 82 min.

1950 France *La Ronde*, dir. Max Ophuls; prod.: Sacha Gordine; dir. of production: Ralph Baum; assistant dir.: Paul Feyder, Tony Aboyantz; script and adapt.: Jacques Natanson, Max Ophuls, based on Arthur Schnitzler's play *Der Reigen*; dialogue: Jacques Natanson; photo: Christian Matras; camera: Alain Douarinou, Ernest Bourreaud; music: Oscar Straus (orchestrated by Joë Hajos), songs by Louis Ducreux; editor: Léonide Azar, S. Rondeau; décor: Jean d'Eaubonne, Marpaux, M. Frédérix; costumes: Georges Annenkov; orchestra conductor: Poussig; sound: Pierre Calvet. Cast: Anton (Adolf) Walbrook (narrator/*meneur de jeu*), Simone Signoret (prostitute, Léocadie), Serge Reggiani (young soldier Franz), Simone Simon (chambermaid, Marie), Daniel Gélin (young man, Alfred), Dannielle Darrieux (married woman, Emma Breitkopf), Fernand Gravey (Charles, her husband), Odette Joyeux (grisette), Jean-Louis Barrault (poet, Robert Kühlenkampf), Isa Miranda (Charlotte, the actress), Gérard Philippe (lieutenant-Count), Robert Vattier (Professor Schüller), Jean Clarieux (officer on bench). Running time: 97 min.

1951 France *Le Plaisir*, dir. Max Ophuls; prod. co.: C. C. F. C. /Stera Films, François Harispuru, Ben Barkay;; dir. of prod.: Ralph Baum; assistant dir.: Jean Valère, Tony Aboyantz; script: Jacques Natanson and Max Ophuls, based on Guy de Maupassant's stories "Le Masque," "La Maison Tellier," and "Le Modèle"; photo: Christian Matras ("Le Masque" and "Maison Tellier"), Philippe Agostini ("Le Modèle"); camera: Alain Douarinou (I and II), Walter Wottitz (III), Jean Lalier, Rolland Paillas, Changlesy; editor: Léonide Azar; décor: Jean d'Eaubonne, Jacques Guth; costumes: Georges Annenkov; music: Joë Hajos, Maurice Yvain (themes from Offenbach and song by Béranger); sound: Jean Rieul, Pierre Calvet. Cast: "Le Masque": Claude Dauphin (doctor), Janine Viénot (his date) Jean Galland (M. Ambroise, the "mask"), Gaby Morlay (Denise, his wife), Gaby Bruyère (dancer); "La Maison Tellier": Madeleine Renaud (Mme Tellier), Danielle Darrieux (Rosa), Ginette Leclerc (Flora), Mila Parély (Raphaële), Pauline Dubost (Fernande), Mathilde Casadesus (Louise), Jean Gabin (Joseph Rivet), Hélèna Manson (Mme Rivet), Joëlle Jany (their daughter, Constance, the communion girl), Pierre Brasseur (pedlar); "Le Modèle": Daniel Gélin (the painter, Jean), Simone Simon (Joséphine), Michel Vadet (journalist on the beach), Jean Servais ("Maupassants"'s voice). Running time: 95 min. Released Feb. 1952.

1953 France *Madame de. . . (The Earrings of Madame de. . .)*, dir. Max Ophuls; prod. co.: Franco-London-Films (Paris), Indusfilms, Rizzoli (Rome); dir. of production: Henri Baum; assistant dir.: Willy Picard, Marc Maurette, Tony Aboyantz; script and adapt.: Marcel Achard, Annette Wademant, Max Ophuls (from the novella by Louise de Vilmorin); photo: Christian Matras; camera: Alain Douarinou; sound: Albert Petitjean; décor: Jean d'Eaubonne; costumes: Georges Annenkov and Rosine Delamare; editor: Boris Lewyn; music: Georges van Parys (Oscar Straus theme), and "Les Huguenots" by Meyerbeer. Cast: Danielle Darrieux (Madame Louise de. . .), Charles Boyer (her husband, General André de. . .), Vittorio de Sica (Baron Fabrizio Donati), Mireille Perrey (Nanny), Jean Debucourt (M. Rémy, the jeweller), Serge Lecointe (Jérôme, his son), Jean Galland (M. de Bernac), Hubert Noël (Henri de Maleville, suitor of Mme de. . .), Madeleine Barbulée (friend of Mme de. . .), Jean Degrave (debtor of General de. . .), Georges Vitray (journalist), Beauvais (majordomo), Léon Walther (theater manager), Guy Favières (Julien, M. de. . . 's servant), Jean Toulout (ambassador), Robert Moor (diplomat), Claire Duhamel (niece of M. de. . .), Germaine Stainval (ambassador's wife), Colette Régis (candle seller), Paul Azaïs, Albert-Michel (coachmen), Georges Paulais, Michel Salina (witnesses at the duel). Running time: 100 min.

1955 France *Lola Montès*, dir. Max Ophuls, CinemaScope/Eastmancolor; prod. co. Gamma-Films/Florida Films (Paris), Unionfilms (Munich); prod.: Albert Caraco; dir. of prod.: Ralph Baum; assistant dir.: Willy Picard, Tony Aboyantz, Claude Pinoteau, Marcel Wall Ophuls, Schlissleder (German version); script and adapt.: Jacques Natanson, Annette Wademant, Max Ophuls, Franz Geiger (German version), based upon the (unpublished) novel by Cécil Saint-Laurent, *The Extraordinary Life of Lola Montès*; dialogue: Jacques Natanson; photo: Christian Matras; camera: Alain Douarinou, Ernest Bourreaud, Henri Champion, Luc Miro; sound: Antoine Petitjean; décor: Jean d'Eaubonne, Jacques Guth, William Schatz (German version); costumes: Georges Annenkov, Madeleine Rabusson, Jean Zay, Monique Plotin, Marcel Escoffier (Martine Carol's dresses); editor: Madeleine Gug, Etiennette Muze (the latter cut the film down against Ophuls' wishes). Cast: Martine Carol (Maria Dolorës Porriz y Montez, Countess of Lansfeld, Lola Montès), Peter Ustinov (ringmaster), Anton Walbrook (King Louis I of Bavaria), Ivan Desny (Lieutenant James, Lola's first husband); Lise Delamare (Mrs. Craigie), Henri Guisol (Maurice, Lola's coachman), Paulette Dubost (his wife, Joséphine, Lola's maid), Oscar Werner (student), Will Quadflieg (Franz Liszt), Jacques Fayet (steward), Daniel Mendaille (captain), Jean Galland (the baron's secretary), Claude Pinoteau (Claudio Pirotto), Willy Eichberger (Carl Esmond, the doctor at the circus), Werner Finck (painter), Hélèna Manson (James's sister), Gustav Waldau (ear doctor), Friedrich Domin (circus director). Running time: 140 min. , cut down to 110 min. for distribution. Released Dec. 1955.

Index

✦

Vision, 136–41, 144–49, 159–61, 165,
169, 175–79, 182–84, 187–88. *See also*
Image
Voice, 15–17, 148–49, 197–98, 202, 235,
291; in *Letter from an Unknown
Woman*, 148–49, 152, 163, 183,
187–89, 262, 281; male, 148, 235
von Sternberg, Josef, 34, 90, 169, 288,
296–97, 327(n61), 333(n4),
347(n84), 362(n22), 363(n37)
von Stroheim, Erich, 71, 173–74

Wall, Hilde, 9
Wanger, Walter, 10, 96, 239
Weber, Samuel, 215–16
Wedekind, Frank, 298–99, 363(n39)
Welles, Orson, 197, 241, 244
Werther, 9, 44, 198, 219–22, 294,
357(n38), 358(n39), 360(n3)
Wexman, Virginia Wright, 161, 178,
190, 193, 338(n1), 343(n49)
Wharton, Edith, 327(n61)
Wilder, Billy, 334(n9)
Willeman, Paul, 315(n37), 358(n12)
Williams, Alan, 87, 240–41, 256, 317(nn
43, 45), 337(n23), 360(n3), 361(nn
4, 5); and *Letter from an Unknown
Woman*, 132, 169–70, 172–74, 184,
306(n11), 341(n28), 351(n100); and
Lola Montès, 280–81, 293; and
Madame de . . . , 59, 61, 95, 322(n18),
323(nn 27, 34, 35), 324(n40),
326(n55), 327(n62), 329(n84); and
Le Plaisir, 228, 233, 358(n6)
Willm, Pierre-Richard, 348
Wilson, George, 12, 14, 139, 311(n39),
339(n12), 341(n25), 342(n30),
343(n47)
Woman, 24, 74, 87, 114, 137–38; as
authors, 63, 64, 66, 69; and body,
148, 238, 243; as castrated, 76–77,
140–41. *See also* Castration; as commodity, 58, 201; and debt, 53–54, 81;
and deception, 60–61, 92–93; and
director-figure, 66, 125–26; and eco-

nomic production, 63, 64, 75, 77,
327(n60); as exchange object, 31, 33,
41, 54, 58, 64, 75, 321(n6); "fallen,"
5–6, 50, 307(n13); as fetish, 34, 58,
143, 331(n96); films for. *See* Women's
films; in freeze-frames, 33–37,
315(n32); and image, 121, 201, 203,
221–23, 242–43, 265, 345(n72); individuation of, 14, 113, 318(n50),
331(n92); in masquerade, 141–44;
and money, 43, 96; and movement,
35–37, 40–41; objectification of, 16,
31; in Ophuls cinema, 4–5, 16, 18–19,
113, 118–19, 205–7, 263–64, 266, 274,
288. *See also individual films*, woman
in; representations of, 6–8, 13, 16, 31,
117, 227, 301, 303–4; as scapegoat,
31, 33, 38, 50; and sexuality. *See* Sexuality; and sound, 148–49, 197–98,
202–3, 222–23, 235, 243; as spectacle,
28, 66–68, 235, 243, 261; as spectator,
34, 48–49, 67, 87, 89, 261–62, 264,
327(n62); voice of, 15–17, 197, 235.
See also Voice
Women's films, 4, 152, 160, 168–69,
172–73, 191, 242–43, 306(n9)
Wood, Robin, 4, 320(n67), 325(n49),
337(n30)
Writing, 340(n22), 346(n76)

Yamaguchi, 299, 363(n39)
Yoshiwara, 9, 13, 37, 315(n27),
348–49(n85), 357(n38)

Zauberflöte, Die. See Magic Flute, The
Zweig, Stefan, 56, 133, 139, 180,
340(n22), 342(nn 31, 38), 344(n62),
350(n99), 352(n112)
Zwinger, Lynda, 157, 344(n60)

Designer:	Teresa Bonner
Text:	Baskerville MT
Compositor:	Columbia University Press
Printer:	Edwards Brothers
Binder:	Edwards Brothers